Snapshots

Bill & Irma,

As you spend time each
day with the Lord may He show you His
Perfect will for your lives!

-In His Service Always

S N

·14/2010

Snapshots

A spiritual look at daily life

Craig Clouston

TATE PUBLISHING & Enterprises

Published by Tate Publishing & Enterprises, LLC
127 E. Trade Center Terrace | Mustang, Oklahoma 73064 USA

1.888.361.9473|www.tatepublishing.com

Tate Publishing is committed to excellence in the publishing industry. The company reflects the philosophy established by the founders, based on Psalm 68:11, *"The Lord gave the word and great was the company of those who published it."*

Book design copyright © 2009 by Tate Publishing, LLC. All rights reserved.
Cover design by Amber Gulilat
Interior design by Jeff Fisher

Published in the United States of America
ISBN: 978-1-61566-651-5
Religion, Christian Life, Devotional
09.12.30

Dedication

This book is dedicated to you, the reader. By purchasing this book, you have fulfilled a dream God placed in my heart. May you be as blessed in the reading of this book as I was in the writing.

Acknowledgments

God, my Father: May You receive all the joy and praise this book inspires!

Jesus, my Savior and Redeemer: Thank You for Your precious blood that covers all my sin! I write for You alone!

Holy Spirit: That You choose to live inside a vessel like me takes my breath away! You are the true inspiration of every word on every page!

My wife, Nancy: Very few know the warrior you are or the battles you have fought. You are God's gift to me as a true help-mate. You make me want to be a better man. Without your support, this would have been work; you made it a labor of love. Your assistance in listening to, reading, editing, and cowriting stories in this book was a blessing. Thank you for sharing your life with me.

My children, Eric and Lindsay and my other son, Lindsay's husband, Corey: I love each of you; you are a tremendous inspiration! Sharing life with each of you has brought laughter and tears, especially to this compilation. Your work on the manuscript was invaluable.

Dad and Mom: Thank you for introducing me to Jesus and raising me in the faith. You gave me the foundation from which I write. Thanks for always being there. Your consistent love and encouragement have given strength to my writing. As you know, several stories were drawn from my childhood. I dedicate June 17 to your wedding anniversary, as this story was about you in the early years of your ministry. I love you!

T.J. and Irene: To be your son-in-law has been my privilege. You are my second parents. History will show how loving and compassionate your spirits are. Both of you have been a tremendous influence in my life. I love you!

My extended family, too numerous to mention by name: You have witnessed a chrysalis effect take place in my life. You have been part of both worlds. Your influence in my life has helped me grow. Thank you for your longsuffering.

John Cleland: Your inspiration has been a great motivator, your friendship priceless. Thanks for all the time you spent reading and encouraging. May God bless your writing as well.

Larry and Beulah Grindle: Your guidance and influence in my life has been immeasurable. Only God knows the depth you've helped lift me from and the heights you've boosted me to.

Roger Tickle: You have walked as a brother with me through difficult times. There are no words for what you mean to me.

Mike Brue: You helped unlock my mind to possibilities. Your friendship and involvement in my life are truly God's gift.

Tate Publishing: Dr. Richard Tate, you saw a diamond in the rough and took a chance that it would shine! To all those who worked on this project: Editing, Design, Print, Marketing, and Distribution Departments: thank you for tirelessly answering all my questions and allowing me freedom in creativity.

Special thanks to Vince Conn for guiding me through the polishing stages of the manuscript.

*The following stories were written and contributed by Nancy Clouston: "Splendor of the Son," January 19; and "Snow," February 11.

*"Blocks," written for May 16, was adapted from the story, "The Block Box" by John Cleland.

*"Precious Insults," January 9, was adapted from *Safely Home* by Randy Alcorn and appears with Randy's permission: www.epm.org and www.randy-alcorn.blogspot.com.

*"I Am the Greatest," written for May 6, was inspired by the song of the same name. Artist: Kenny Rogers. Permission to print was granted by Mr. Rogers's manager. It is with sincere thanks and deep appreciation that this story appears in my book.

*"It's a Short Trip Back," written for December 16, is adapted from *Escape to God*, written by Jim Hohnberger and is included with his permission.

Jim Hohnberger, Empowered Living Ministries; www.EmpoweredLivingMinistries.org 406–387–4333

Mortality statistics in "Age Doesn't Matter," written for November 4, are from Section 13: What About Those "Without the Gospel?" Copyright Michael Bronson 1997, 1999, and 2000 BibleHelp.org and are used with Michael's permission.

January

The Spotlight

January 1

You are the God who performs miracles; you display your power among the peoples.

Psalm 77:14

The officer listened as the radio dispatch reported a westbound motorist in the eastbound lanes of the interstate he was patrolling. The driver was traveling in the wrong direction at a high rate of speed, heading toward his position. Entering the westbound lanes, he turned on his spotlight, hoping to alert eastbound drivers to the danger while systematically looking for the wrong-way vehicle. Radio reports told him that he was ahead of the vehicle, so he slowed down.

Scanning back in the direction the vehicle was coming from, he spotted the car's headlights, a stark contrast among the taillights in that lane. He could see motorists taking evasive action to avoid the oncoming car.

As the vehicle approached, he matched its speed, shining his spotlight on the driver-side window in hopes of getting the driver's attention. Finally, the driver responded and pulled over. As two other cruisers pulled up, he turned off the spotlight.

Just as the light winked out, he remembered the repair order he'd issued on this car two weeks before for a broken spotlight. Trying the spotlight once again, it failed to work. Exiting the cruiser, he used his flashlight to illuminate the spotlight. He noticed the same broken bulb from two weeks ago lying at the bottom of the lens. The repairs had not been completed!

✝

There are those who question whether God still performs miracles. Some feel the need to explain how things happen.

Whether you believe this story or not will be determined by Who you perceive God to be. By explaining how things happen, we maintain a false sense of control over them. If we are unable to explain the how of events, we are then required to believe by faith.

God continually displayed His power among the nation of Israel during the exodus, yet they continued to rebel because miracles themselves do not ensure belief.

The story above is true. Events are related exactly as they happened. God *is* big enough to make a broken spotlight work. He leaves the belief part up to us.

Prayer

"Teach us to have faith, Lord. And forgive us
for our doubt. It's not always so easy to believe
without seeing. In Jesus' Name, amen."

Mourn Just a While

January 2

Blessed are those who mourn, for they will be comforted.

Matthew 5:4

In a daze at the graveside, the young parents were thinking about that moment three days ago when the switch to the respirator had been turned off. Their infant son, Michael, had been born with no brain function. Prenatal ultrasounds and sonograms had been business as usual. There had been no cause for alarm, no telltale signs, until Michael was born.

A void so vast with a sense of unending pain gripped them as they laid their son to rest. They were to begin grief counseling with their pastor tomorrow. An older couple from church had called last night to offer words of comfort and hope. Right now, comfort was elusive and didn't feel like an attainable goal. They felt the pain of a loss so unspeakable that it tore at their hearts with relentless realization. Their son was gone! They didn't know if they would ever recover. Quite honestly, today, they didn't much care about the future. In time, they would learn that grief is a process. Comfort would come. But today they mourned.

The older couple had reached out in experience. They had lost twin daughters several years before in a car crash. They knew firsthand the pain that gripped this young couple, and they wanted them to know that God could heal their pain. It would not go away immediately, but with love and support, they would weather this storm.

✝

The loss of a child seems so unfair. Death has a way of seeming final. And comfort is so elusive in a child's unexpected passing.

Mourning is a process; it teaches us to respect and appreciate the sanctity of life. The process of mourning grows us in ways nothing else can; it causes an urgency of purpose, and focusing on that purpose is where the healing begins.

Death is not the end; it is the promise of a new beginning. Mourning may last for the night, but joy comes in the morning.

Prayer

"Abba! We cry out in our pain. Bring comfort and peace
to those who know this pain. Bring direction to their lives
this day. Show them how to bring this pain to You so they
might be healed and find peace. In Jesus' Name, amen."

Don't Let Me Go

January 3

If your Presence does not go with us, do not send us from here.

Exodus 33:15

Don and Candy had a decision to make. Their attorney had called, telling them they had been given Candy's childhood home, a Brownstone duplex in Ohio, in an estate settlement. Her aunt, who had lived in the upstairs apartment, had recently passed away, leaving Candy the property with a clear deed.

But, having worked in their church's youth ministry for over twenty years, they felt a strong call to stay here in California and minister to the kids of their neighborhood. They were unsure of whether their time here was to come to an end at this time.

Lying in bed that night they discussed their options and prayed, asking God to show them what *He* wanted them to do. During the night both dreamt the same dream. In the dream they were driving away from the duplex, waving goodbye to a stranger standing on the porch. Upon awakening, they shared their dream with each other and came to the conclusion God was telling them to rent out the duplex and stay in California for now.

✝

We all have difficult choices in which we would like to know that our final decision was inspired by God. And God will not always be as conspicuous in His answers as He was with Don and Candy. Yet, learning to listen for His response to our prayers and petitions can be achieved. Hearing God is not rocket science, but it does require active listening on our part.

By reading and studying God's Word each day, we learn to draw on Spirit-inspired insight and wisdom hidden for us within the pages of Scripture. There are tremendous benefits to submitting everything to God and asking for His guidance.

As in Moses' case, we should cry, "If You're not where I'm going, don't let me go!" Through active listening can we develop the ability to hear God's response to our requests.

Prayer

"Please let me know Your will for the days and events
of my life, Lord. Teach me to listen and hear what
Your Spirit reveals to me and then act accordingly
with courage and peace. In Jesus' Name, amen."

The Sunday Paper

January 4

Cast all your anxiety on him, for he cares for you.

1 Peter 5:7

One minute Stevie was laboring through snowdrifts, the next he was flat on his back.

A rural paperboy, Stevie was held captive under the weight of two hundred Sunday edition papers jammed into the bags crisscrossing his shoulders. It was 3:15 a.m., and there was no one he could call on for help.

Slight of build, it was all he could do to hoist the bags in place before leaving the house on his early morning trek. His route usually took him an hour and a half to deliver. The deep snow would increase that by fifty percent. But right now it stood to be several hours! He realized he had to extricate himself if he didn't want to spend several hours waiting for someone to miss him and come looking.

Spurred on by the thought of freezing to death at the tender age of eleven, he managed to dig himself out from under the bags. Free of his predicament, he left one bag lying there, returning for it in a circuitous route after emptying the first bag.

Stevie learned two valuable lessons that morning: never carry more than you can handle, and fear is a great motivator!

✝

God never intends us to carry the burdens of life alone. We make that choice ourselves. Today's headline speaks of sharing the load. Too often we try to extricate ourselves from the burdens of life. We struggle under intense, self-inflicted weight, not understanding that God is right beside us, waiting for us to ask for help. As with Stevie, we sometimes try to carry more than we are meant to. Succeeding on our own in the beginning, we come to believe that it is God's plan for us to do it ourselves. If we do that enough times successfully, we end up like Stevie—with the weight of the world on our shoulders.

As we learn to become God sufficient instead of self-sufficient, we find that our burdens decrease as our dependency on God increases.

Prayer

"Teach me to share, Lord. Sometimes I'm not so good
at it. I've been told to be self-sufficient in order to be
strong. Show me the benefits of giving You the heavy
weight of daily living. In Jesus' Name, amen."

Against All Reason
January 5

The flames will not set you ablaze.

Isaiah 43:2

Ten-year-old Nancy and her older sister, Rachel, jumped off the school bus and ran into the house. It was a frigid winter afternoon. The house was cold!

"The furnace is out," Nancy said, her disappointment evident. "Your turn," Rachel responded. With Mom working all day for a church-affiliated conference center, the girls were responsible for restoking the furnace.

Nancy headed to the basement. Tossing some kindling on top of the few remaining coals, she opened the damper a bit to get a draft going, adding larger pieces of coal and wood on top of the kindling.

Twenty minutes later, she checked on the fire; it still hadn't caught. So, opening the damper completely, she watched until the wood began to burn. "Finally!" she said, closing the furnace door and heading back upstairs.

Fifteen minutes later, it hit her. *I forgot to shut the damper!* Running to the basement, she saw the furnace glowing red hot! *I've got to cool the fire down somehow!*

Grabbing the garden hose, she opened the furnace door with gloves, stood back, and sprayed. *Foohm!* The fire's reaction was immediate; Nancy's reaction was instinct-driven. Her eyes slammed shut, just as hot ash, soot, and flames shot out the furnace door!

Having heard the roar from upstairs, Rachel ran to the basement. There stood Nancy—covered in soot from head to toe, except for her eyes, which she'd managed to open again—miraculously unharmed. Rachel broke into hysterical laughter.

✝

It was a miracle the furnace hadn't exploded the instant the water hit it. It defied the laws of physics. Flames and hot embers had been ejected from the furnace and had landed on her, and though blackened, even her clothes had not been singed. Nancy had not received a single burn.

Through the hand of God, Nancy was spared tremendous pain and injury, horrible disfigurement, and possible death. The realization of what could have happened has been spoken of fondly during the ensuing forty years. The picture of that little ten-year-old girl, assaulted by fire yet unharmed, speaks of God's protection as loudly today as it did back then.

Prayer

"You, God, are the God of promises and
miracles, and we give You praise. Amen."

Our Daily Bread

January 6

Give us today our daily bread.

Matthew 6:11

The Ryersons were in for the evening. So upon hearing the doorbell, Christian asked his daughters if one of them was expecting a caller. "No, Dad," they answered in unison.

Rising from his chair, he answered the door, surprised to find three young children pressed against a diminutive woman, trying to hide within the folds of her skirt. They peeked at him with shy smiles. "Excuse me, sir," the woman began. "I saw the light in your windows. My car has broken down, and I would like to use your phone if I could to call for assistance." She appeared to struggle with her own shyness but remained resolute about getting this matter resolved.

"Come in, please," Christian said, waving his hand for them to enter. "There's a fire in the hearth if the kids would like to warm themselves," he added, winking at the children, who looked hopefully up at their mother.

"Yes. Go ahead," she responded. "But behave yourselves, do you understand?"

"Okay, Mommy!" they hollered over their shoulders, running for the warmth emanating from the den.

Christian ventured, "Perhaps I can take a look at your car while you and the children remain here? I might just be able to repair it."

"Oh, I wouldn't want to put you out," said the woman quickly.

"It's no problem." He assured her, grabbing his coat. "Which way down the lane and how far is it?"

✝

God sends our daily bread as we need it in myriad forms.

Are we ready, like Christian, to be used to meet a need at an unexpected, and possibly at an inconvenient time in the name of kindness and compassion? Or more aptly defined, in the name of the Lord?

The Lord's Prayer is not an empty petition to be recited by memory with no thought of its depth or meaning. How better to show the love of the Father than by the giving of ourselves rather than our possessions?

It's far easier to offer our phone than our services. And being used as a blessing is not a requirement. But if this were your wife and children, would you not pray they find their daily bread?

Prayer

"May You find me willing to be used as someone's
daily bread today, Lord. Amen."

The Devil We Know

January 7

In my anguish I cried to the LORD, and he answered by setting me free.

Psalm 118:5

Doug and Cheryl had never been in this part of town. They ran a homeless shelter on the north side but had felt led to the east side tonight. It was an especially cold evening, and they'd come here to pass out blankets and coats.

Passing among the men and women huddled around fire barrels, they shared words of encouragement, speaking of God's love and how He wanted to make a difference in their lives.

"Lady," one man responded in anger, "if God loves everybody so much, then why are there so many homeless people? God doesn't give a rip about us!" He turned his back on Cheryl and walked away.

"Please, sir," she pleaded. "He does care. He sent us here to help you."

He turned back momentarily, and in a trembling voice and with bitterness in his eyes, he said, "Lady, I don't want your charity! And I don't want God's either!"

Doug tried to follow, hoping to reason with the man, but was cut off by one of the man's friends. "He's been here a long time, mister," the man said. "He's bitter about the past. You mean well, and we appreciate your kindness, but his memories outweigh your gift."

Taking a blanket for himself, he said, "Give him time to see how others respond. Maybe someday he'll figure out that God didn't put him here."

✝

Sometimes we prefer the devil we know to the deliverance we don't understand. Fear of the unknown can keep us from investigating our inner selves and keep us from finding out there is strength within that would fight to see ourselves set free.

One of the hardest lessons regarding free will is that God is no more to blame for our poor choices than He is responsible for the decisions we get right. He can only suggest. Then we are free to do as we please.

There is no forcing hope on someone who resents his or her circumstances yet refuses to change. Only when we give God permission to care can we overcome the devil we know.

Prayer

"Lord, sometimes I feel untrusting and alone. Help me see these chains of bondage for what they are: lies to keep me bound. Deliver me from Satan's lies. In Jesus' Name, amen."

Pay Attention

January 8

If only you had paid attention to my commands.

Isaiah 48:18

As Wendy put her foot on the ice, Bridgette cautioned her, "I wouldn't go out on the ice yet, Wendy. It hasn't been cold long enough to be safe."

"Oh, you're just a wuss!" Wendy said and stepped completely onto the pond.

"There's no ice in the center of the pond, Wendy!" Bridgette stressed. "It's not as thick as you think! Don't be foolish, please!" she begged.

"Aw, come on, it's safe enough right here!" she chided and jumped up and down to make her point.

In the next instant, they heard a loud crack. Fear and panic replaced Wendy's bravado as she disappeared through the ice! She came up flailing and screaming, "Help!"

As Wendy floundered, Bridgette ran to the farmhouse. She was met by her father who'd heard her screams and come to investigate. Bridgette's explanation came spilling out in a terror-filled voice. Grasping the situation, he turned and ran to the barn, grabbed a rope and sprinted for the pond. Hollering to Wendy to keep treading water, he hurriedly tied the rope to the dock, secured it to his waist, and crawled out onto the ice. As he neared his frantic daughter, the ice gave way. Swimming the remaining distance, he grabbed Wendy, then using the rope, slowly pulled them back to solid ground. Once she was safe, he verbalized his displeasure, "Now you know why I told you to stay off the ice until I said it was okay. Next time, pay attention."

✝

It is my belief that God would like us to pay attention. But being the self-sufficient people we are, we set out on our own when His instructions don't lead in the direction we're headed. We foolishly tell ourselves, "It won't happen to me, I'll be fine!" only to find out too late that it happens to us all at one time or another.

God is not a domineering Father who doesn't want us to enjoy life. On the contrary, His commands have a purpose meant to protect us from ourselves and others. But free will being what it is, keeps God from enforcing our obedience.

Prayer

"Lord, Help me understand that Your commands
are meant for my own good and not the demands
of a high-handed Father. Amen."

Precious Insults*

January 9

> Blessed are you when people insult you, persecute you … because of
> me. Rejoice and be glad, because great is your reward in heaven.
>
> Matthew 5:11–12

The prisoner lay in a huddled ball in the corner of the damp, dark cell. It smelled of urine and vomit from not being cleaned in weeks, if not months. They had just thrown him head first into the cell. Unable to brace himself because of the beating he'd just received, he landed on his face, reinjuring the broken nose he'd suffered two weeks ago in another similar beating.

Le Chen whispered, "Yesu, you are stronger than Mogui[1] and all who torment Le Chen. I thank you that you think Le Chen is worthy of suffering for Your name." Chen had been a prisoner for three months now. He'd been charged with subverting Chinese law by worshiping in his home and possessing part of Shengjing[2]. It was unlawful to worship outside the Chinese government's 'Three-Self Church' in Honshu Province, or anywhere in China, for that matter, or to possess a Bible in part or whole.

Being tormented for their faith was nothing new to Chen or his family. The Le family counted it a blessing to suffer for the cause of Christ.

✝

Many Christians will never suffer the pain and persecution portrayed in today's scenario. Many, however, do or will.

If given the circumstances of Chen, how would we fair? Would we count it a blessing to suffer for the cause of Christ, or would we complain about the conditions?

The secret is in how we relate our lives to the suffering of Christ. Have we died unto ourselves in Christ? Or is that just a fashionable statement?

Jesus wants us to relate to him in such a way that our desire is to look just like him in every way.

Eternal perspective is about bringing the kingdom of Christ to the here and now so it can be seen by those in need. It's about understanding that our suffering is not to be considered a high cost in light of eternity.

Prayer

"Yesu, I ask for strength and courage to stand up in your name.
Tell me when and where to speak, for I am not ashamed of
the Gospel of Jesus Christ. It's in Your Name I pray, amen."

[1] Chinese for Satan
[2] Chinese for Bible
* See Acknowledgements

Garbage Tampering

January 10

This day I call heaven and earth as witnesses against you that I have set before you life and death, blessings and curses. Now choose life, so that you and your children may live.

Deuteronomy 30:19–20

He carried the garbage to the curb as he had for the last two years, leaving the bags the prescribed three feet from the road. It seemed innocent enough, yet today it felt deceitful. You see, he'd been putting his trash out with the neighbor's, allowing her garbage man to pick it up.

It hadn't seemed like such a big deal. After all, he gave his neighbor money once in a while to help her out and ease his conscience. But today, as he carried the bags to the curb, he was overcome with a startling conviction that this was wrong.

Admitting his actions had been a form of stealing, he carried the bags back to his trash bin, went into the house, and called the refuse company to admit his deception, asking forgiveness and offering to pay restitution if they required it.

✝

We spend our days making choices that affect our lives not just for the immediate future, but by setting patterns. When we set wrong patterns, we hinder God's ability to bless us. We dismiss these little issues without much thought because we've ingrained these patterns in our lives to the extent that we categorize our sins—a form of desensitization. "Nope, can't do that; that one will bring lots of grief!" "That's not so bad as long as no one finds out; it won't really matter."

Today's text reveals that God sees everything we do, knows every thought we embrace, and we alone are subject to His blessings or curses. We live our lives asking for and expecting God's blessings but are frustrated and can't understand why life is an uphill battle most days. Could it be because we don't recognize or admit that the little things we're hiding stand in His way? It is *God's desire* to bless us.

Prayer

"Father God, giver of blessings and curses, help me to live a life worthy of blessing. I don't do well on my own. Reveal to me anything that would bring death. Help me remove them from my life and draw nearer to you. In Jesus' Name, amen."

Little Arrows

January 11

Like arrows in the hands of a warrior are sons born in one's youth.
Blessed is the man whose quiver is full of them.

Psalm 127:4–5

Having received three calls in the last two hours, the police chief was compelled to respond to the clinic's complaints and asked the protestors to move an additional fifty feet from the clinic.

Suddenly, everyone's attention went to the young couple exiting the building. They were smiling and holding hands. Still in college, they had not planned for children this early in the marriage. Unsure of how they would meet the medical bills or find the needed finances to raise the child, they had considered abortion.

They stopped and shared their decision to keep the child with the group outside the clinic. Elated by the news, several protestors donated money to help with immediate expenses. They gave them names and phone numbers of people willing to provide assistance, from aftercare to babysitting.

One protestor, an OB/GYN, gave them her business card and asked them to call her office for an appointment; she offered them free prenatal care.

✝

We are mistaken when we believe that the choices we make don't influence others. Abortion is a procedure that ends life. The child is persecuted to death; they have no say in the matter, and the miracle of life is snuffed out in an act so wrong that there are no words to define how a holy God feels about it.

Roe v. Wade provides the legal right to end life in the womb; it does not justify it before God. It neither has the ability to stop the truth of how precious life is nor when it is conceived.

God alone is judge and jury; as His servants, we are to champion the unborn, love the unlovable, and be a guiding influence in difficult circumstances, reaching out when each opportunity presents itself. God can change lives when we make ourselves available.

Prayer

"Father of all Creation, forgive us for a selfishness and arrogance
that allows us to end life in the name of personal choice. There
are no excuses we can bring you. Reveal to the world Your
heart regarding the sanctity of life. In Jesus' Name, amen."

Plans of Hope

January 12

For I know the plans I have for you, declares the LORD, "plans to prosper you and not to harm you, plans to give you hope and a future…You will seek me and find me when you seek me with all your heart.

Jeremiah 29:11, 13

Work was coming slower due to the housing crunch, and Gary was stressed. The bills were mounting; there was unspoken strain between he and his wife, and he didn't know what to do. He'd been trusting God for as long as he could remember, yet this was different; there seemed to be a silence on God's part right now. He felt they were being tested to see if they really believed what they professed, that God *would* meet all their needs.

A friend suggested they allow their prayer time to become a time of listening rather than petitioning. So over the next two weeks, Gary and Beth spent their mornings together, asking only for God's wisdom to deal with each day and what it brought, looking to Him for guidance and strength.

Job contracts remained flat lined; it seemed as if nothing was happening, yet during those two weeks, they had felt God's peace. This morning, they'd received a card in the mail containing well wishes and fifty dollars from an anonymous donor. Two days later a friend dropped by with a bag of potatoes and a sack of onions. Over the next several weeks, they watched as God provided in ways they never would have imagined.

✝

When we're stressed out and fretting over unmet needs, we can get emotionally bogged down. God's voice can become white noise in our lives, and we can lose hope.

The art of listening is something we develop. It requires intentional thought. In a chaotic society that vies for every thought, we must force ourselves to slow down, spend time alone with God, and listen. By listening for His voice instead of immediately trying to resolve problems on our own, we become aware of God's leading. It is then we learn to walk beside God and not run ahead into hopeless frustration.

Prayer

"God of hope, we ask to hear Your voice so that we
may know You are near. Help us trust You and Your
plan for our future. In Jesus' Name, amen."

When God Says Hello

January 13

What is man that you are mindful of him?

Psalm 8:4

When Chuck found out the church of his childhood was being sold, he and his wife drove up for a visit. Thirty-five years of his absence melted away as they walked the halls of the old building. Chuck had given his life to Christ in this church; his father had entered the ministry here.

Near the end of their visit, they entered the fireside room, noticing a card table in the center of the room. On it were two pictorial directories, two pieces of construction paper, and several old bulletins, all of which sat on an old, heavily bound church ledger. After a cursory inspection of the ledger, Chuck opened the directories to find they held significance; the first was the year his father entered the ministry; the second was the year they had moved away. Turning his focus to the construction paper, Chuck noticed that on each page were two photographs. Upon closer inspection, he discovered that staring back at him from two of the photos, one on each paper, was ten-year-old Chuckie in VBS class! Now, even if the pastor had known who he was, which he didn't, he couldn't have dug up these items before their arrival! This was from God for Chuck. He was saying hello in such a personal way that it was almost audible! Tears filled Chuck's eyes as he felt God's embrace.

✝

Sometimes we get the idea that a God big enough to help us during our greatest needs is too busy to be watching us with affection. Or even more astonishingly, that He would spend time sorting through our memories to prove it!

God wants us to understand that it doesn't dim the lights of heaven when He acts on our behalf. Nor does it remove His focus from others when He bends low enough that we feel His breath on our face. He is Almighty God, the God of all Creation who had each of us in mind before the foundations of time!

Prayer

"Papa, I am in awe to know how much You care for
me. Thank You for being a personal God, able to bend
down to my level when I need You. May I always
sense Your affection. In Jesus' Name, amen."

Finish Well!

January 14

Forgetting what is behind...I press on toward the goal to win the prize for which God has called me heavenward in Christ Jesus.

Philippians 3:13, 14

The young man was pleased with the progress he had made. The model of his latest architectural masterpiece was taking shape! It wouldn't be long before he could present the project to the marketing department. He thought back to the break he'd been given three years ago.

He had landed the job with this firm, had his own office, and even had an expense account. He had become dependable, earning their trust and thanks by producing exceptional buildings with beautiful renderings and visual stimulation. His designs were second to none; his talents were much sought after in the construction industry.

But what many people were unaware of was that Jason had been in prison. There had been a time in his life that he had broken the law. He had paid his debt and now worked hard to build a better life for himself and his family.

✝

We are sometimes judged, justly or unjustly, by our mistakes. What matters more than the mistakes of our past is how we finish. We are unable to personally atone for the past; only the blood of Christ has that power. But by making changes and right choices in the pattern of our lives, things can change for the better.

People tend to judge with historical data, not affording grace to those who have made mistakes. In Jason's case, they knew of his criminal record and still chose to extend him an opportunity. Like that firm, God sees our full potential and withholds judgment until we finish.

Throughout biblical history, we see evidence of esteemed men and women making mistakes yet finishing well: Abraham, Isaac, David, Rahab, and the Samaritan woman, even Mary Magdalene. All of them broke God's law, yet each changed and finished well. We have the ability to do the same. By forgetting the past and pressing forward in Christ Jesus, we too can finish well.

Prayer

"Judge of the universe, thank You for calling me in
Your direction. I get so bogged down when I focus on
my past failures. Help me focus on the right course in
life and keep my eyes pointed in the right direction
with my head lifted up. In Jesus' Name, amen."

On Sale, Forgiveness!
January 15

When we are cursed, we bless; when we are persecuted, we endure it; when we are slandered, we answer kindly.

1 Corinthians 4:12, 13

Carol silently prayed for peace as she headed for her car. She hadn't spoken what was on her mind when the sales manager had belittled her in front of everyone in the store. Knowing she had done the right thing by not making a scene didn't alleviate her frustration. And to top it off, her manager was wrong! Carol wasn't the one who had placed the incorrect sales price on the shirt rack. She knew who was responsible, but chose to remain silent.

This past week's Bible study had been about forgiveness. She knew it was the right thing to do, but the last thing she wanted to do right now was forgive that man! Forgiving the manager wasn't about him; it was about her. If she chose to remain angry, she would open the door to resentment and bitterness. Experience had taught her how miserable that would be. "Give me the desire to forgive Connor, Lord. I don't want to right now, but you know what really happened. Help me be content in knowing that." It wasn't immediate, but peace would come.

✝

When we are injured by others, we have two choices: allow it to harden our heart or turn it over to God. In choosing the former, we reap anger and resentment; bitterness takes over our emotional mindset. Left unresolved, it will turn us inside out, and we lose any chance we might have at peace. Though we may have a right to our anger, we must understand that by hanging on to that right, we become ill—emotionally and physically.

But by giving up our right to our anger and by turning things over to God and allowing Him to bring resolution in our heart, God can handle the problem, and we benefit from His peace.

It's our choice; we can receive peace or reap illness of the soul. Only by giving up our rights can we overcome and answer kindly when wronged.

Prayer

"Lord, I don't have the ability to forgive without Your help. I'm guilty of offending You and others, and I want to be forgiven. So please give me the desire to forgive. In Jesus' Name, amen."

Praise and Cursing

January 16

Out of the same mouth come praise and cursing. My brothers, this should not be.

James 3:10

Brian vigorously shook his hand, cursing, as if by doing so it would alleviate the pain in his thumb, the one he'd just smashed with that blasted hammer.

"Sorry, Lord," he said sheepishly. "It just slipped." Nowadays, he didn't slip as often as he used to. Nevertheless, his vulgar language was something he needed to work on. He hadn't realized how *trashy* his language had become until three years ago when his four-year-old son had sworn in public, using God's name in vain, along with some other embarrassing language. Unfortunately, it had been said in front of Brian's aunt who was visiting the family.

The epitome of a lady, his aunt had attempted to alleviate everyone's embarrassment by saying, "Oh, the things kids learn in school these days."

But Brian had to admit that Bruce had picked up the language at home. After all, he wasn't even in school yet!

✝

Brian attended church on a regular basis, and he truly believed he was living a godly life. But when we use our own moral compass to guide ourselves, we will end up off course.

God knows our weaknesses and loves us in spite of them. We are to be the best representative of Christ we can. And that requires conscious effort.

James wrote much about our tongues and how they can create serious issues. Our words will either lead others toward Christ or away from Him. We need to be conscious of the way we speak and the words we use.

Swearing does not bring glory to God. Consistency is important, not only when in public, but especially when we are by ourselves. It requires spiritual discipline to be a good example. There are no occasions in which we are totally alone; God always hears what we say. Being consistent begins with being conscious of Whose we are.

Prayer

"Loving Father, I need Your strength. I try to deny that it's a big deal when I swear. Help me understand the effect my words have on others. Show me the truth of my actions. Help me to be a better representation of Your Son. In Jesus' Name, amen."

Let's Go Fishin'!

January 17

But I tell you, Do not resist an evil person. If someone strikes you on the right cheek, turn to him the other also.

Matthew 5:39

Billy stood by as Cindy pounded mercilessly on Ryan. She had Ryan's arms pinned to the ground with her knees, taunting him, "So how's it feel now, tough guy?"

Cindy, sixteen, beautiful, and a tomboy, had come around the corner of the house to find Ryan punching Billy in the face, and Billy's nose bleeding. Hollering, "Get off my brother!" she dove, tackling Ryan and rolling on top of him. Ryan wanted to hit back, but he'd been raised to never hit a girl and to turn the other cheek. Right now, he didn't think much of his parent's teaching—this hurt!

He covered up the best he could, but Cindy still managed to land a few. *So much for her ever being my girlfriend!* he thought. *Besides, Billy and I fight like this all the time. What's the big deal?!* When Cindy finally let him up, Ryan's arms ached from defending himself.

But true to how ten-year-olds view such matters, less than five minutes later, he and Billy grabbed their fishing poles and headed for the creek, recent events forgotten.

✝

Kids are able to take things in stride without placing blame or harboring resentment. Ryan would never forget that beating. With fondness, laughter, and exaggerated animation, Ryan told and retold the story to his children as a way of leading by example, holding with the philosophy that "Boys do not hit girls; little or big ones."

Violence breeds violence; it never solves problems. Though turning the other cheek is not an easy thing to do, Christ managed to do it. He lovingly endured horrible beatings for me and you. With Jesus as our example, how then, shall we live?

Prayer

"Lord Jesus, it doesn't feel natural to back down when confronted. I get embarrassed and want to strike back! Help me do what You did when they beat You; help me understand the true meaning of turning the other cheek. Amen."

The Right of Succession

January 18

Children, obey your parents in the Lord, for this is right. Honor your father and mother—which is the first commandment with a promise—that it may go well with you and you may enjoy long life on the earth.

Ephesians 6:1–3

The right of succession is a powerful thing. It tells little boys and girls that freedom is just around the corner. Here is but one example.

The three boys had built a tree house for the ages. But they had gone against their parents' admonition to build it low for safety, on the first or second limb, which was sissy stuff as far as they were concerned.

Instead, they built the tree house as high as they could. Besides, this gave them a better vantage point from which to watch the neighborhood!

The floor was made of two-by-fours and plywood leftover from recent construction on a nearby house. The sidewalls were made of interwoven twine with no gaps big enough to fall through.

Young boys become bored quickly. And seeking a challenge, they began climbing in from above, over the walls. Unexpectedly, one of the neighbor boys fell, breaking his arm.

Their disobedience had caused serious injury. It also brought about the dismantling of the tree house.

✝

Disobedience has consequences. And most little boys don't think much about their impulses. That's why God created the fifth commandment: "Listen to Dad and Mom. They're not out to ruin your day; they're just trying to keep you from killing yourselves!" (Slightly paraphrased).

Quite honestly, disobedience isn't limited to youth. Society tells us, "Grab the gusto in life!" "Get what you can when you can get it!" and "Take care of *numero uno!*" Grown-ups, as well as children, tend to think they know what's best and, in disobedience to God, reap death and destruction.

Paul in Ephesians reiterates God's promise that if we are obedient: God will bless us. Not necessarily with millions of dollars and perfect health, but we will reap something more desirable: peace, love, and a clear conscience.

Prayer

"Lord, speak to me about each choice and decision
in my life. Help me be obedient to You out of love.
Teach me to not give in to the excitement and
allure of this world. In Jesus' Name, amen."

Splendor of the Son*

January 19

Come to me, all you who are weary and burdened, and I will give you rest.

Matthew 11:28–30

The rain sounded so relaxing with a cadence that lulled you into restful slumber. It fell all through the night. In the early morning hours, when the temperature was at its most frigid point, layer upon layer of ice formed, causing tree branches to bow down, almost touching the ground. As the sun rose over the horizon, the boughs glistened with dazzling beauty. And although the rays of sunshine continued to dance on the frozen limbs, the temperature remained at the freezing point.

Some branches that had been shielded from the full cascade of rain began to gently ease upward as droplets of water fell from their grasp. Some remained bent and looked as though they longed for relief.

Unfortunately, the early morning sun hadn't reached many of the heavier, ice-laden branches, and they snapped, broken and lifeless—branches that had glistened in the splendor of the sun, branches that wished to grow, but could no longer bear the strain of the weight.

†

What a tremendous waste that so many trees would be destroyed because they weren't strong enough to bear the additional load. And so it is with us as the wounds and disappointments accumulate, causing unbearable strain because, due to embarrassment and pride, we cut ourselves off from the critical help we need. We pridefully believe that no one else could ever understand. And so the wounds continue to build, weighing heavily on us, our emotional and spiritual stability ready to break at any moment. If we refuse to share our pain, it will eventually consume us.

Jesus never meant for us to carry such burdens alone, and we should never allow them to cling to us until they gradually overwhelm us. Unlike the tree, we need not be broken. We can be wonderfully wholehearted, overcoming the seemingly insurmountable pressures of life if we turn to Jesus. Jesus wants to carry our burdens so that through His efforts we will reflect the splendor of the Son.

Prayer

"Jesus, thank you for giving me rest. Help me learn how to give you all my burdens, both great and small, so the things of this world don't overtake me. Amen."

* See Acknowledgements

The In Between

January 20

I urge you to live a life worthy of the calling you have received.

Ephesians 4:1

There were tears mixed with laughter at the dinner. There must have been three hundred people in attendance. All of them had come to share precious memories of the man they had laid to rest that morning.

He had not been a pillar of the community, nor was he well known outside this circle of friends. Yet his life had a profound effect on the people he touched.

A philanthropist of sorts, Byron had given over seventy percent of his meager earnings to others in need. He'd held on loosely to what he had; it was his way of giving to the Lord. He never made it public and would have denied any connection to the prosperity others enjoyed due to his generosity. He lived a simple life in a simple home.

His wife had preceded him in death. He'd kept her memory alive by spending time doing things they'd done together: walking in the morning dawn, watching the sunrise, or watching the eagles soar over the river bottoms, so majestic and awe inspiring. Simple. Yes, that was how he'd seen himself.

But these people knew him for who he really was. He'd shared selflessly with each one of them somewhere between the day of his birth and today. They each had a personal story of his eager generosity. And together they represented his in between.

✝

Gravestones are purchased to memorialize the life of loved ones. On them we place a date of birth and a date of death. But what happens between those two dates is how we will be remembered.

In verse four of today's text, Paul spoke of "one hope": the hope we have in Jesus through His Holy Spirit. It is His Spirit at work in us, the Spirit of God Who teaches us how to live. Our response to His urgings can make a difference in the lives of untold numbers of those in need if we respond accordingly.

How will we be remembered for our in between?

Prayer

"Spirit of God, lead me. Help me make a difference in
the lives of those who need a special touch. And help me
remain obscure whenever my pride screams for recognition.
Help me be a vessel of hope. In Jesus' Name, amen."

Relentless Pursuit

January 21

No one comes to me unless the Father who sent me draws him.

John 6:44

With a smile of satisfaction, the hunter listened as the beagle made his turn, bringing the rabbit back around for the second time. With a chuckle, he thought back several years to when he'd begun training the pup to track. Chief had been relentless in his pursuit of rabbits, but he unknowingly steered them in a straight line, away from the hunter. Being wise, the hunter had used a more seasoned dog to train the youngster, allowing the more mature female, named Brownie, to teach the passionate young male that being good on the trail wasn't the only goal in his pursuit. He must learn to guide the rabbit in the preferred direction by making a wider circle than the rabbit, resulting in the rabbit turning back toward the hunter. In essence, the rabbit was given his own free will while being pursued. It was up to the dog to guide that free will.

✝

Like the young beagle, we sometimes strike out on the wrong track in life, seeking freedom and unattained goals. Without guidance, these efforts can lead us into misery and bondage. But God, in His wisdom, circles a little wider, pursuing us, yet allowing our free will to remain intact. He leaves the twists and turns up to us, all the while speaking to us through circumstances, others around us, and directly to our spirit. He whispers about the freedom that is available through His Son, Jesus. His goal is for us to accept His sacrifice, repent of our sin, turning in the right direction by submitting our free will in trade for true freedom. His pursuit is relentless. He will never leave us nor forsake us. But the choices are ours. Unlike the rabbit, when we turn back to Him, we choose life.

Prayer

"Father God, I sense Your pursuit. Thank You that
You never leave me totally alone. When I get off track,
please bring me back around where it's safe. Draw
me closer to Jesus. Help me understand that there is
true freedom in Christ. In Jesus' Name, amen."

Dignified

January 22

The King will reply, 'I tell you the truth, whatever you did for one of
the least of these brothers of mine, you did for me.

Matthew 25:40

As a hospice nurse, Mandy had been tending Harlan's needs for several weeks.
Early on she'd learned about his love for Jesus and the old hymns. An integral
part of her life growing up in the church, hymns spoke to Mandy's heart as
well. So as she tenderly wiped his brow with a soft, cool cloth, or massaged his
atrophied muscles to aid in blood circulation, she sang hymns. It didn't matter
that Harlan never responded to her efforts because of his deteriorating condition; she sang as if he could. Yet deep inside she wondered if Harlan heard the
words he held so dear?

Today, as she finished singing *At The Cross,* Harlan opened his eyes, turned
his head toward her, and smiled, as tears of gratitude slipped from the corners
of his eyes. His whole countenance was transformed in that moment; and so
was Mandy's! For with that smile came the understanding that he had heard!
No longer did she wonder if her service was witnessed by the Father only. It
was as if God were saying, "Thank you for treating Harlan with dignity. He has
served me faithfully, as you are doing now. Well done!"

Then, as quickly as the moment had come, it passed. Harlan closed his
eyes, turned his head back to center, and slipped away into the arms of Jesus.

Having lived his life unto the Lord, this humble servant was now with
his Redeemer. His last breath on earth was followed immediately by his first
breath in heaven! Harlan was now face-to-face with Jesus!

✝

The dignity shown to Harlan, by a woman having limited knowledge of his life
and how he'd lived, was grounded in the understanding that all life is precious
to God.

Young or old, healthy or infirm, we are directed to be considerate of others,
showing them respect and dignity. For when we dignify them, we dignify Jesus.

Prayer

"Lord Jesus, please make me sensitive to those who need a touch
of Your love so that I might serve You by serving them. Amen."

Love Your Neighbor

January 23

Therefore, as God's chosen people and dearly loved, clothe yourselves with compassion, kindness, humility, gentleness and patience.

Colossians 3:12

It was raining hard when they drove by the man walking along the side of the road. Soaking wet, he blended into the darkness. They'd seen him before and knew he was headed for the bridge up ahead. He would spend the night under the bridge above the river.

Continuing across the bridge, Kenny dropped Betty off at home and quickly gathered a few items. Returning across the bridge, he found the man just reaching the point where he usually dropped off into the underworld he preferred. Rolling down the window, Kenny asked if there was anything he could do. The man shyly declined and began to step over the guardrail. The urgency in Kenny's voice stopped him, and the rain-soaked man turned, saying, "I could use a little bit to eat if you've got something." Asking him to get in, Kenny headed home where he and Betty shared conversation and a meal with the man. Finished eating, he declined lodging. He was given dry clothes, a backpack, and an umbrella. Eagerly accepting the items and excusing himself, he left the house, opening the umbrella as he walked down the hill toward the bridge.

Neither Kenny nor Betty would ever forget the broken-toothed grin that was shyly given in response to the love they had shared with this child of God as he walked out of their lives.

✝

Blessings beyond our wildest imagination are both given and received when we step outside our comfort zone in an effort to treat others with respect. We are given opportunities to minister in difficult circumstances. It is God's desire that we take the time to let our hearts express the kindness and compassion He inherently gave us. We don't know what this act of kindness did for that man on that rainy night, but we rest in the knowledge that God never leaves seeds unwatered.

Prayer

"Father, please make me an instrument of Your love.
Teach me to give of my time as well as my finances. Help
me recognize the opportunities for what they really are,
Your test of my love for You. In Jesus' Name, amen."

Open Waters

January 24

Fear not, for I have redeemed you…When you pass through the waters, I will be with you; and when you pass through the rivers, they will not sweep over you.

Isaiah 43:1, 2

He had never known real fear. He hadn't realized this kind of fear even existed before today. Sure, he'd been scared, but never anything like this. Surfacing after jumping off the pier, Phil was facing open waters; he had an unobstructed view of Lake Erie through his diving mask. All he could see was the vast expanse of water, and he was instantly paralyzed; he couldn't breathe! To say he was afraid would have been a tremendous understatement. Then his training and experience kicked in; survival mode took over. Perplexed and still unable to draw a breath, he turned, and in a state he would later describe as controlled panic, swam back to the dock and climbed up the ladder. Finally able to draw a breath, he emerged from what had felt like a death trap.

✝

With an understanding that God has redeemed us by our act of repentance and turning to Jesus, the promise from Isaiah applies to each of us. As with literal open waters, spiritual waters hold danger. Phil was an experienced swimmer and lifeguard, yet he wasn't ready for the shock he received when the only thing his eyes could see was open water. Left completely unprepared, it could have meant death. His training had been enough to save his life. It is imperative that we understand the dangers we face ahead of time; there are predators in those spiritual waters seeking our spiritual death. We may not know in what form they will come, but by preparing ourselves with biblical wisdom, the training needed for survival, we will be better able to recognize and fend off the attacks when they do come.

Prayer

"Holy Spirit, please show me where I lack wisdom. Teach me Your ways as I open the Word so that I might be able to stand against the enemy when he comes. Train me so that I may also help others stand against the enemy. Thank You for Your presence when I pass through the waters of life. Amen."

The Chair and Tuesdays

January 25

I will lie down and sleep in peace, for you alone, O LORD, make me dwell in safety.

Psalm 4:8

I had noticed the chair but hadn't asked about it. It sat just to the right of the headboard of her bed, close enough that she could reach out and touch it. The story she shared was from her soul. "That chair's been sitting right there since 1984. That's the year Bill died. I put it there so I could talk to him. I sure do miss him. I never really got over losing him, you know. I was angry at God for a while, especially about Tuesdays. It was a Tuesday when Bill died. The following Tuesday, Bill's best friend died. The week after that, my dog died, and the week after that, Mom had a stroke and died fourteen months later on a Tuesday. I hate Tuesdays!"

She shared her pain with me that day, and I understood; we all have things we get angry at God about. Even the most God-fearing people get angry at God from time to time. She finished by saying, "I'm not angry at God anymore, but I still hate Tuesdays! Now the chair is there so me, Bill, and God can all spend time together; then they don't feel so far away. I sure miss Bill."

✝

We have a God who knows our pain, every wound of our heart. He knows every thought, too. So He's not surprised when we finally admit that we're mad at Him for one reason or another. He has enough love and patience to hear us out, walk beside us, or carry us when that's necessary. He knows all our faults and waits us out, hoping our rebellion will end so He can lead us into deeper understanding.

God's desire is that we bring Him the burdens we weren't meant to carry. He always meets us where we are and accepts any advancement in His direction.

Prayer

"Abba, forgive me for my unrepentant anger. Help
me want to give it all to You. I struggle with forgiving
others. I feel it's my right to hang on to the pain. Help
me understand what Jesus meant when he taught the
disciples, 'And forgive us our trespasses as we forgive
those who trespass against us.' In Jesus' Name, amen."

Pop Bottles
January 26

Give, and it will be given to you. A good measure, pressed down, shaken together and running over, will be poured into your lap. For with the measure you use, it will be measured to you.

Luke 6:38

It was a hot Saturday afternoon, and the boys of Scout Troop 429 were on a pop-bottle drive. They needed new pup tents. The torn and leaky World War II leftovers just weren't cutting it anymore, so they were in search of anyone who would donate to their cause. Coming to a place that appeared to need of a lot of yard work, the boys noticed several bottles lying by the back door. It looked as if they'd been discarded where they'd been finished. Knocking, they were greeted by a gruff-voiced old man leaning on a cane. They explained why they were there and proposed that they be allowed to keep the bottles in exchange for mowing his lawn, saving him the trouble of cleanup. The old man thought a moment, rubbed his bald head, then smiled, saying, "Tell you what. If it's okay with your parents, and you younguns would like to help me out a mite by cleaning things up and such around here, I'll just buy each of you a tent myself, and you can have all the bottles you find." Wow, what an offer! With their father's permission and the details ironed out, the boys spent the rest of that day cleaning off the porch and with a mower retrieved from the backyard shed, mowed the lawn, restoring the Jenkins place to its former charm. Per their agreement, they would tackle the windows and garage next week.

✝

What the boys hadn't known before striking their bargain with Mr. Jenkins was that his garage was stacked full of old soda bottles he'd never gotten around to redeeming—over two thousand bottles at three cents apiece! What a deal indeed! Willing to help Mr. Jenkins for the promise of only a few bottles, they were rewarded beyond their wildest dreams.

Prayer

"Lord, we ask for your guidance. Teach us to care about
others, not for personal reward, but because it's the right thing
to do. Lead us to those who are unable to help themselves
and use us to meet their needs. In Jesus' Name, amen."

Anchors Away

January 27

Do not wear yourself out to get rich; have the wisdom to show restraint.

Proverbs 23:4

They had a swimming pool in the backyard, a five-bedroom, thirty-two-hundred-square-foot home on seventy well-groomed acres, a cabin in the mountains, and stress that wouldn't be assuaged! Brad and Beth worked nonstop, six days a week, and never seemed to have enough time to relax and enjoy the things they'd worked so hard to obtain. Brad could still hear his father assert, "Be the best at what you do, Brad." He'd taken it to heart. He was the CEO at Corporate HQ and Beth was a successful civil attorney. Top in their individual fields, they had gone on numerous business vacations over the years for business personnel only. Their kids were being raised by a nanny and seldom saw their parents during daylight hours. It had all seemed so grand in the beginning; now it seemed as if they worked too hard and missed too much just to pay the bills.

†

Having material possessions is not wrong in and of itself. However, how we make use of those possessions and our time does matter. Brad's father had died young, leaving Brad as the man of the house at an early age. What Brad had thought of as sound advice had driven him to his version of success. He had achieved the top of the hill. But since Sundays were their only day off, they spent them maintaining their property, including spring cleaning and fall closure of the cabin, which was mostly rented out to people they would never meet. They hardly ever had time for family outings, rarely used the pool, and never made it to church. All the things they held precious had turned out to be anchors around their necks. Brad remembered how in Sunday school his father had told the class, "We should live our lives as pleasing unto the Lord." Somehow in his youth Brad hadn't made the distinction between working like a dog and working for the Lord. It was time to make some changes.

Prayer

"Father, please give me the wisdom to know when
I'm working for me instead of You. Help me to know
when enough is enough. In Jesus' Name, amen."

Granddad's Treasure Chest

January 28

For where your treasure is, there your heart will be also.

Matthew 6:19

As Tom brushed dirt from the miniature treasure chest, he was transported fifteen years back through time to the day he and his Grandad had buried it in the backyard of the family farm. Grandad had said, "Tom, there are only a few things really important in life: the love of family, the feel of a good book in your hands, and most of all, the love and faithfulness of God. Without the latter, the others don't have any significance." Throwing dirt over the chest, he had said, "Let's dig it up on your twentieth birthday and weigh the importance of the things we're burying today." As Tom opened the chest, he couldn't suppress a sob; he wished Grandad were here to do this with him. The first item he uncovered was the medal Grandad had received for service to his country. Next was an old pair of Grandad's eyeglasses; Tom had always liked them and thought he might need them in the future. There was an old report card, a few old coins, and a pack of baseball cards. The last item Tom pulled from the chest was a pocket-sized Bible. It had been the first item Grandad had placed in the chest.

✝

Tom remembered what his Grandad had said when he'd placed that little Bible in the chest. "Son, everything we have placed in here will have a price placed on it when you dig it up, all except this one; this little Bible is priceless. The words of this book will sustain you when all these other things are gone. Never place a higher value on the things of this world than you do the Word of God. If you trust in God, you'll never be alone, never be poor, and never be lost." Tom smiled. He had adhered to his Grandad's faith.

Prayer

"Lord Jesus, I want my heart to be in heaven. Help me live
for You here so that I can live with You there. Amen."

Proper Timing

January 29

Whoever obeys his commands will come to no harm, and the wise heart will know the proper time and procedure.

Ecclesiastes 8:5

He stood silently by and watched as I swung the sledge against the wedge, attempting to fell the tree. It was a big, old tree, seventy feet tall and spreading out some forty feet. It would make a lot of firewood. I began to hear a chuckle every now and again.

After ten minutes of pounding, I was tiring quickly and sweating profusely. I'd made no progress, and he was openly laughing. In my wounded pride, I said, "If you think you can do it better, have at it." He stepped over, re-placed the wedge, and in three, well-timed swings, dropped the tree right were he wanted.

Exasperated, all I could do was shake my head, smile, and ask, "So what's the secret?" My father-in-law winked, pointed at the sky, and said, "You have to look up when you're wedging a tree. You wait until the tree sways against the wedge, then, as it begins to sway the other way, you drive the wedge deeper and wait, driving it deeper with each swing. It's all in the timing. To get the timing right, you have to look up."

✝

Often, we struggle against unseen pressures, forgoing the council of those wiser than ourselves. Instead of seeking their experience in regard to the pressure we're facing, we forge ahead, making our own way. Our self-sufficient mind-set doesn't leave much room for admitting we could benefit from someone else's wisdom, and our efforts are diminished when we navigate life on our own. Like wedging a tree, we need wisdom concerning our actions in overcoming the pressures we face. God, if we will allow Him, can move people and sway things to work in our favor, moving them in such a way that it increases our strength, not deplete it. "A cord of three strands is not easily broken." That's God, us, and others.

Prayer

"Lord, I tend to have tunnel vision at times. Please
whisper for me to look up to You. Help me change
from my self-sufficient ways in an effort to become God
sufficient. I admit I cannot do this on my own. Amen."

Unequally Yoked
January 30

Do not be yoked together with unbelievers.

2 Corinthians 6:14

The farmer led the oxen into the stall preparing to put them under yoke for plowing. He laid the wooden crossbeam over their necks. Next, taking the yoke itself, he sent the stave end up through the hole on one side of the beam while his son held the other end in place; he then spun on the wooden nut. At that moment, the low-side ox was stung by a bee. Jerking his head and causing the loosely tied cinch reigns to come undone, the ox stepped out of the yoke, causing the full weight of it to fall on the off ox, who twisted its head sideways under the strain. The farmer quickly grabbed the yoke, lifting it and relieving the unwanted pressure. His son grabbed the trailing reigns, coaxed the ox back into the yoke, and tightly tied the reigns to the stable cinch. Back under the yoke, the oxen shared the weight of the load.

✝

When we choose to disobey God's directive not to become unequally yoked with unbelievers, we expose ourselves to unnecessary problems and heartache. Unbelievers don't respond the same as believers to trials or difficulties. Unbelievers do not adhere to God's directives, nor do they care that we do. And when problems arise, a believer can be left with the full weight of responsibility, thereby twisting his neck out of joint, causing emotional turmoil. This diametric opposition can cause broken relationships.

Some of us enter relationships thinking, *I can help them believe,* and so we go about implementing change in an effort to mold the person into the image we desire them to be. In the end, we only cause or reveal insurmountable barriers.

Only God can affect that kind of change. And His desire is that we leave it to Him and not enter into those relationships unless the person changes. It's our responsibility to refrain from relationships with anyone who does not follow God's instruction.

Prayer

"All Knowing Father, help us to steer clear of relationships
that are not founded on You. Help us to deal rightly
with human desire. Please show us grace when we
fail to listen to Your decrees and gently bring us back
under Your instruction. In Jesus' Name, amen."

The Breath of Life
January 31

The LORD God formed the man from the dust of the ground and breathed into his nostrils the breath of life, and the man became a living thing.

Genesis 2:7

The car came out of nowhere, slamming into the driver's side door of her SUV. The side airbags deployed immediately, preventing her serious injury. But the man in the oncoming car had been ejected through his windshield, coming to rest on the hood of her car. Regaining her senses, she climbed over the console and exited the passenger side door, coming around the front of the car to check on the man. Holding her fingers to his neck, she discovered he had no pulse. Climbing up beside the man, she began first aid. Looking for blockage in his airway and finding none, she pinched his nose and began respirations, then pumped on the man's chest. She continued CPR, and after five repetitions, the man responded, yet remained unconscious. He was transported to a nearby trauma unit where he eventually recovered from his injuries. The very person he hit had saved his life by providing the precious breath necessary to sustain his life.

✝

It has been said we breathe some of the very air Jesus himself breathed two thousand years ago. Science says that all oxygen is recycled, stating that .00037 percent of all air molecules have been co-breathed by everyone who has ever existed. Regardless of the validity of that statement, we have all been given the gift of life. When God "breathed into his nostrils," He created life and an oxygen-rich environment capable of sustaining that life. We should never mistake the truth of the statement made in this passage. He didn't just bring Adam to life; He created an atmosphere that would sustain us forever, giving us an opportunity to understand the awesome power of God.

Prayer

"Breath of Life, we thank You for life-giving oxygen. Without it, we could not survive. Help us to understand the power You possess and Your desire that we become vessels of that same power through the gift of the Holy Spirit. May we become fresh breath in a stagnant world. In Jesus' Name, amen."

February

His Strong Right Hand
February 1

Though I walk in the midst of trouble, you preserve my life … with your right hand you save me.

Psalm 138:7

Steve and Rita traversed the snow-covered rocks to the floor of the gorge. Virtually unknown to the general public, Ice Rocks is hidden less than three miles off the main highway and just yards off the beaten path. Yet without knowledge of the rock formation, you would never suspect its presence.

A beautiful waterfall any time of the year, it is striking in mid- to late winter. A crescent-shaped gorge with a waterfall in its center, it boasts stalagmite and stalactite icicles as large as semi trailers. The gorge is sixty feet deep with a forty-foot mound of rock in the center. The falls becomes a frozen chute in winter, solid on three sides, water continuously pounding the creek bottom. Steve had Rita stand at the base of the falls to give the photo a sense of proportion. Hearing a loud crack, they moved quickly away from the immediate area. As they rounded the mountain of rock, putting distance between them and the ice, they heard a thunderous crash. Something had let go! Returning, they found a forty-foot piece of ice lying at the base of the falls, right where Rita had been standing. Had they not been warned by the *crack*, Rita might have been killed!

✝

Steve and Rita had experienced God's protection many times in their lives. They recognized His intervention on this day, moving them out of harm's way with a warning crack. Although God is at work in all His children's lives, we sometimes chalk His supernatural protection up to coincidence, good luck, or what some call fate. Regardless of what we read or see in movies, we are not two ships passing in the night. Nor are we feathers just floating about on the wind, guided by every breeze that comes along. Our Father has a strong right hand. With it, He preserves our lives. As His children, our choices will always be His concern. He protects us when we heed His warning. His desire is that we choose wisely, making some of the rescues unnecessary.

Prayer

"Thank You, Papa, for Your loving protection. Help us recognize Your right hand at work in our lives so we might give You praise. In Jesus' Name, amen."

When Fear Becomes Trust

February 2

But blessed is the man who trusts in the LORD, whose confidence is in him. He will be like a tree planted by the water that sends out its roots by the stream. It does not fear when heat comes...and never fails to bear fruit.

Jeremiah 17:7, 8

The gentleman sitting across from him was six feet and four inches tall, three hundred fifty pounds, and barrel-chested. He'd always been intimidated sharing his faith with big men. Today's circumstances changed all that. He felt God urging him to pray with this man. He'd just been told that the medical equipment the man needed to survive had been denied as he had no means to pay for the machine or the care involved. Stuffing his fear, he asked the man, "Would it be all right if we pray about this?" The man answered, "Sure, I guess." He prayed a short but direct prayer that God would have His way, removing any obstacles between the man and the care he needed. Finished, they completed the interview, and the man left.

Fifteen minutes later, the phone rang. Picking up the receiver, he heard sobbing on the other end of the line. Through sobs, the big man explained that upon his return home, he had listened to his voice mail. The lone message had been the medical provider. The message said, "It's against our policy, but we're bringing the equipment you need, and we'll worry about payment later."

✝

When we answer God's call, He works in ways we cannot imagine. He moves the hearts of people that know and follow Him, and He works on the hearts of those who don't.

When God gets us in the classroom, He intends that we learn these lessons for future reference. The man behind the desk learned that he could share his faith with anyone as long as God was in control. The big man had learned to trust God for his very existence. Stepping out in faith pays exponential dividends.

Prayer

"Almighty Father, teach me to trust You in every part of my life. Help me to step out in faith and give the fear of my life to You so I can be better used by You. In Jesus' Name, amen."

Useful Hands
February 3

He who has been stealing must steal no longer, but must work, doing something useful with his hands.

Ephesians 4:28

He had come to the hardware store to buy a new ball glove. As he walked by the fishing equipment, he was mesmerized by the brightly colored assortment of lures. There were shysters, rapallas, spoons, and jitterbugs. But one lure caught his eye more than the others. It was a chartreuse popper! For no reason he could understand, the boy looked around to see if anyone was watching, reached around the counter, and took the lure, pocketing it.

He left the store without even looking at ball gloves. He couldn't seem to get away fast enough! On his way home, he pulled the box from his pocket and removed the lure. He couldn't wait to try it out! Then, as unexplainable as his first urge, he knew he must return it and apologize for stealing.

The storeowner listened to the boy's story and proposed the boy work for him until he had paid restitution. It took the boy two weeks of hard work to pay his debt. He never forgot that lesson or the storeowner.

†

The owner of the hardware had been a wise man, understanding that the deed could not go unpunished or the boy may repeat his offense. Contacting the boy's parents and using work as a way of teaching the boy the value of putting his hands to good use, he was able to help the young boy with not only his guilt but also caused him to be able to appreciate what he could accomplish through honest labor.

Left unchecked, who knew what this young boy would do. The owner understood that little thieves are easier to rehabilitate and always worth the effort. He gave of himself for the future of the boy, understanding that, "But for the grace of God, there go I."

Prayer

"Lord, only You know the evil that inhabits the hearts of men. Please lead me in such a way that I will not judge others, nor fall under judgment myself. Cause me to have useful hands. In Jesus' Name, amen."

Brokenhearted Prisoners

February 4

He has sent me to bind up the brokenhearted, to proclaim freedom for the captives and release from darkness for the prisoners.

Isaiah 61:1

She spilled some of the precious liquid as muscle spasms caused a twitch. Cooking the smack was getting harder. It was just before 11:00 a.m., and her stash was gone. She'd care in about two hours, just not right now. Firing the load, she fell back on the couch, the rush driving every thought from her mind. That's what she was after, numbness. She wanted the pain to go away.

For a sixteen-year-old, childhood seemed so long ago. Two hours later, she came to in restraints in the psych ward of a hospital where she underwent detox. She wasn't sure when the young woman had begun visiting. She'd started out just sitting with her. By the end of the first week, she was helping her dress and eat. Then one day the young woman didn't come. In her place was a book with a note paper clipped to it. The note read, "The rest is up to you. This saved my life; it can save yours too." With tears running down her cheeks, she opened it at the bookmark. There was a verse highlighted with a name superimposed over two words; it read, "For God so loved Janet that he gave his one and only Son," (John 3:16). Tears flowed unabated as she sobbed. She didn't know what her next move was; she just knew she couldn't live like a prisoner anymore.

✝

Addiction takes many forms, stealing the soul of millions of God's Creation, leaving them destitute and alone. Many die, still searching for that elusive "first high," not understanding their motives, and never having known or experienced the love of Christ.

Those who have been rescued from addiction know it's impossible to attain true victory on your own. In Christ alone can we find the strength to live. He will bind up the brokenhearted and set the captives free!

Prayer

"Saving Lord, we petition for the souls of those lost in addiction. Draw them near, tear down the veil the enemy keeps in place, and set the captives free. In Jesus' Name, amen."

Soiled Parts

February 5

This then is how we know that we belong to the truth, and how we set our hearts at rest in his presence whenever our hearts condemn us. For God is greater than our hearts, and he knows everything.

1 John 3:19, 20

The walls were soiled and stained; the wallpaper was curling at the edges and hanging loose in places. The furniture was run-down, sagging cushions and gouges in the wood. The curtains were torn but still not much light penetrated them, and the dust took on the appearance of silt. It was dirty and repulsive here. That was all right; the more silt covered, the better.

She came here so seldom she couldn't remember the last time she'd been here. Pausing, she looked amidst the rubble. It was then she noticed Him standing there, just inside the door. She'd almost forgotten; she'd invited Him. He was waiting for her to acknowledge His presence, but what was there to say? It was all here for Him to see, those things in her life she was ashamed of and not sure how to deal with. Time seemed to drag on forever, but He never moved. She knew He was waiting for her to speak. "I can't seem to get rid of these things," she said. "I try and try." He spoke softly, "Will you let me help?" She awakened with a start. What a dream! Jesus had just seen the darkest part of her heart and still loved her!

✝

Omniscience doesn't mean knowing some things; it means knowing everything. God's desire is that we come into a relationship with Him where meaningful conversations about the issues of our heart bring healing.

His hope is that our hearts will bend in such a way that we give Him those silt-covered parts for cleansing. He wants us to know the truth: belonging to Him removes condemnation from the heart.

Prayer

"Lord, there are things that I wish You didn't know about me, but You do. That You could still love me is hard to grasp, so sometimes I act like You don't. Help me be open and honest with myself so we can talk about the soiled parts of my heart. In Jesus' Name, amen."

A Matter of Perspective
February 6

For my thoughts are not your thoughts, neither are your ways My ways, declares the LORD. As the heavens are higher than the earth, so are my ways higher than your ways and my thoughts than your thoughts.

Isaiah 55:8–9

Through a clear and cloudless sky, the jet banked hard left, preparing for final approach. Looking out the window, the businessman saw the hand and heard the voice of God. There, below him, was a single, fluffy, white cloud. Centered on the cloud was a perfect, vibrantly colored rainbow—not an arch as we see from the ground, but a perfect circle. And in the center of it all was the shadow of his plane cast by the noonday sun.

In that moment God whispered, "This is My promise. There is no place that exists outside my love; no valley is below this circle; no mountain rises above it. There is no east; there is no west; there is only my love. This is My promise."

There wasn't time to snap a picture before the plane leveled out, but that didn't matter; he would never forget the image. A sense of peace replaced his harried and stress-filled mind.

✝

Following the flood, God promised Noah to never again destroy the earth with water. His covenant was the first recorded rainbow. "I have set my bow in the cloud." Never having witnessed one before, Noah must have been awestruck!

In the fourth chapter of Revelation, John describes how God remembers that promise: "A rainbow resembling an emerald, encircling the Throne of God," not arching above it, but encircling the throne, all encompassing and never ending, just like God's promises.

The image and the whisper through the window of that plane let the businessman know that God was aware of his life and the problems he faced. From God's perspective, the things we deal with and witness each day are usually not what they appear to be; there is a purpose. God asks that we trust Him to work in our lives for that purpose.

Prayer

"Lord, I don't look at things the way You do. Help me to
see what You see as I look at the issues of my life. Help
me to trust in Your promise. In Jesus' Name, amen."

The Good Fight

February 7

> Let us not become weary in doing good, for at the proper time we will reap a harvest if we do not give up.

> Galatians 6:9

She'd left the house in a huff—the typical Sunday morning routine lately. Kids in tow, arguing, "If Dad doesn't have to go to church, why do we?" She pressed on, angry and feeling defeated. This was a battle she no longer felt like fighting; she was ready to give up. "Are You watching, God? Do You care about my family? I hate fighting with Rick." He'd been wounded at church years ago and refused to allow it to happen again. "Why did You let that happen, Lord? Don't You care that he was wounded?"

As she pulled into the parking lot, she glanced toward the digital marquee in front of the church. Doing a double take, she looked back. Today's message read, "I know sometimes it doesn't feel like it, but I am watching. God." Staring at the marquee as the message scrolled by once more, she sensed God's presence and peace. "Give me strength, Lord." she whispered.

✝

We are never alone. Occasionally, when it seems He is nowhere near our galaxy, the God Who set the stars in the sky and calls them by name, kneels down and speaks ours.

Singlehandedly rearing children in the Lord was never God's design. Many deal with spouses who would rather play nine holes, sleep in, or just relax and read the Sunday paper than attend church.

If you are one who is fighting this battle, remember that God is at work while you are being faithful for both of you. He wants you to know this is a battle for your children's future and spiritual direction, as well as your spouse's. When you choose to fight the good fight, you follow the exhortation in Galatians. Those who walk away from God must come back on their own. It's called free will. But God says, "Do not become weary, for at the proper time you will reap the harvest."

Prayer

"Lord, give me strength to continue this fight. Heal my heart and the wounds of those I love. Bring resolution to painful memories and restore us to complete spiritual health. In Jesus' Name, amen."

Do This

February 8

Do this in remembrance of me.

1 Corinthians 11:24

He donned a hygienic mask, latex gloves, and sterilized the communion kit. Then he prepared the elements. He was bringing the Lord's Supper to a recovering cancer patient. She had been isolated from the public for the past twelve weeks due to an insufficient white cell count as a result of chemotherapy.

He thought about God's healing power as he broke the matzo into the tiny tray. As he poured the juice, the blood of the Holy Lamb of God, he reflected on last night's phone call. "Hi, Dana. It's Pastor Chuck. I was wondering if it would be all right to bring communion to you and Paul tomorrow morning."

"That would be wonderful!" she replied. "I just hung up from talking to a friend. He mentioned that he was getting ready to take communion to a shut-in. As I hung up I said, 'Oh, Paul, I wished our church did that.'"

Chuck was never surprised when he found that God's urging was in response to prayer.

✝

Divine appointments are opportunities to do the work of the kingdom for God, to be His instrument of blessing. In our busyness, we sometimes view these as inconveniences. Yet if we listen closely, stop rushing, and respond to His urging, we discover God's eager desire to bring blessings. When Chuck brought the Lord's Supper to Paul and Dana, he brought God's love and healing power. When we obey, God sends His power through us to encourage others. It always amazed Chuck that he was the recipient of a large portion of that blessing.

As our relationship with God deepens, He asks us to carry His love further into His kingdom. Fear from the enemy wishes to stop that from happening. God wants us to know His strength is sufficient to meet that fear head-on and walk right through it. Our obedience will determine if someone receives a blessing.

Prayer

"Father of inspiration, right now we give ourselves over to
You to be used in bringing a blessing to those in need of
one. Touch our hearts and minds so that we can respond as
Your instruments of love. Blessed be Your Name, amen."

The Look

February 9

Immediately a rooster crowed.

Matthew 26:74

This wasn't the first time Jeff had played the part of Peter in the passion play. He'd even felt a small portion of Peter's anguish in past performances. But tonight something shocking had happened. As he turned from the fire barrel, having denied Christ a third time, he was looking into the eyes of Jesus. Not the actor playing the part, but Christ himself! He folded to the floor and wept uncontrollably, great sobs racking his body. To the audience, it appeared to be a tremendous performance. To Jeff, it was as if he *were* Peter! He had received a large measure of the agony the apostle must have felt that night. He couldn't stem the flow of tears as he pried himself from the floor.

Jeff didn't share his experience immediately. When he finally did, the tears came again, unabated. Yet this time there wasn't shame and conviction. In their place were love and restoration. Jeff understood that Jesus had done for him what He had done for Peter.

✝

Romans 5:10 says, "That while we were still God's enemies…Christ died for us." The look Jeff saw in Jesus' eyes wasn't one of condemnation but of sorrow— a sorrow born of the knowledge that there is within each of us a weakness that places flesh ahead of spirit.

Jeff received a gift, a revelation. Jesus showed him the depths of His love. Christ freely came knowing we would kill Him. First as an infant—in an infant there is no fault. This baby was pure enough to meet the demands of Justice. He grew into a warrior with the strength to lead us through the murkiest waters and lift us from the pits of hell; so fierce is His love that He left His throne to live in our world! Finally, as a Savior willing to stand in our place and be defiled because He could not stand that we would spend eternity without Him! The look says, "I love you!"

Prayer

"Jesus, we come humbly in response to that look into
our soul. Though we have denied You in the past,
forgive us today as we ask to understand and surrender
to You. Lead us into reconciliation. Amen."

He Exceeds Expectations!

February 10

Now to Him who is able to do immeasurably more than all we ask or imagine … be glory …"

Ephesians 3:20, 21

Having lost a kidney to cancer years ago, Donna's remaining kidney was failing for the same reason. On dialysis five days a week and needing a kidney transplant, there was less than a one in four hundred thousand chance of a match.

The elders anointed her as the church body gathered around. They prayed for a match to be found, prayed for God's peace, and for God to sustain her. What happened wasn't on the list.

At her next doctor's appointment, an MRI was ordered to check on the progress of the tumor. As he entered the exam room, the doctor had a dismayed look on his face. Holding the film to the light, he said, "I believe you have another tumor where your first kidney was removed." The negative revealed a small growth resembling a lima bean. Donna felt a rush of hope. "I know what that is! It's a new kidney, not cancer!" The doctor tried to reason with her that *kidneys do not replace themselves, especially after so many years.* But to his surprise, over the next two weeks, this lima bean grew to become a viable, working kidney. Donna has not needed dialysis to this day. And by the way, the diseased kidney was also healed.

✝

We are amazed and somewhat surprised when God steps onto the scene in *power.* We pray in faith and yet are stunned when God chooses to answer in a way that eclipses what we pray for.

Miracles and healings did not pass away with the apostles. It is for God's glory that they occur. He is sovereign and will bestow or withhold healing as He sees fit. We should always pray in unshakable faith, believing for miracles and healing, leaving room only for God's decision as to how He will answer our petitions. With boldness, in prayer and thanksgiving, we are to approach the throne of our Creator.

Prayer

"Sovereign God, we are humbled when You recreate
what You first created. Teach us to come boldly
before Your throne, with faith that produces hope!
We yield to You in all we do and continue to believe
for healing when it serves Your purpose. Amen."

*Snow**

February 11

Come now, let us reason together," says the LORD. "Though your sins are like scarlet, they shall be as white as snow; though they are red as crimson, they shall be like wool.

Isaiah 1:18

The air was cold and crisp as she sat in her car, awaiting her husband. The snow had started out light and then quickly became heavy. The flakes were nickel-sized wafers, floating gently down, touching everything within her view. A hush fell with it, covering everything.

As she watched, it began to cover trees, bushes, grass, parked cars, the street, even the wires strung overhead, blanketing everything in a layer of pure white. It was as if God was speaking to her through the beauty of this moment.

It was so white! The world looked so clean! No dirt! Not a single track from a car.

When she'd arrived an hour earlier, there had been visible clutter and dirt. There were things people had discarded and left behind, such as gum, candy wrappers, and cans. Things that had been splattered by passing motorists, leaving a layer of grime on everything in its wake, were now unseen, even the layers of thick dirt between the bricks that paved the street. It was as if God were saying, "I make all things white as snow. I can wash away all the dirt, all the wrong."

✝

As we walk down life's path, making choices that cause us to become dirty, God wants us to know we are still redeemable. When we are willing and obedient, choosing to follow Him, Jesus promises to cleanse us and make us white as snow. Unlike the things covered by the snow, God's cleansing touch completely removes the dirt in our lives. Psalm 103 says, "As far as the east is from the west, so far has he removed our transgressions from us."

When we repent, turn from our sin, and submit to His will, we can be assured we are covered with the righteousness of Christ; we are made pure as the driven snow.

Prayer

"Lord Jesus, thank You for being our spiritual healer.
As we come surrendering our lives to Your will, please
cleanse us and cloak us in Your righteousness. Amen."

* See Acknowledgements

Boundaries

February 12

Where there is no revelation, the people cast off restraint; but blessed is he who keeps the law.

Proverbs 29:18

Paula looked in her rearview mirror to see red and blue flashing lights; the siren wailed as the cruiser gained on her. Pulling over and rolling down the window, she waited on the officer. He shined his flashlight on her as he bent over and asked for her license and registration, asking, "Do you know how fast you were going, ma'am?" Paula explained, "The dash lights just went out as I came over the hill back there, so I'm not really sure. Somewhere around twenty-five miles per hour, officer." She wasn't lying; her dash lights really had failed. It was almost 5:00 a.m., and she was on her way to work. Figuring she'd get away with a warning, she was angry when the officer came back with a ticket. "I can't believe you'd write me a ticket when my dash lights failed on me at 5:00 a.m.!"

To which he replied, "You were doing thirty-five miles per hour in a twenty-five mile-per-hour zone, ma'am. And this happens to be the time of day I work."

✝

Boundaries are limits placed upon mankind to avoid anarchy and assure everyone's safety. Boundaries are guidelines that teach us how we are to act and treat each other. They are as old as the foundations of the earth. The universe is full of them, both physical *and* spiritual.

Satan is also limited by boundaries. He tries to cross them and gain entrance into our lives, sometimes subtly, sometimes in frontal attacks. We, as believers in the power of God, must exercise our authority in Christ to maintain those boundaries. We enforce Satan's boundaries by resisting temptation and speaking truth from the Word, by standing firm in the knowledge of God. It's up to us to contend for our freedom from the enemy by entering the battle. By seeking God's will for our lives, we're halfway there.

Prayer

"Help me stay within the boundaries You set for my life, Lord. I understand that when the enemy comes in temptation, I must put up barriers to keep him from leading me into destructive behaviors. Speak to me through Your Word, circumstances, and others. In Jesus' Name, amen."

The Chimneys of Life

February 13

But whenever anyone turns to the Lord, the veil is taken away ... and where the Spirit of the Lord is, there is freedom.

2 Corinthians 3:16, 17

Dave knew what the thump from the basement was. So getting out of his chair, he grabbed his gloves from the coat rack and headed downstairs. An old brick chimney rose from the cellar up through the middle of the house, allowing the gas furnace to be vented.

During the coldest months, birds would swoop into the chimney, warming themselves in the updraft. Occasionally one ventured too far, and unable to fly out, it would drop into the furnace where it could become trapped and die. The fortunate ones made it through the vent pipe into the basement, escaping an immediate death sentence, but remaining trapped.

Trapped by means of deception, they would fly against the basement window, believing it to be a way of escape. The very thing that appeared to bring gratification brought entrapment and sometimes death. Dave, knowing they would die without his intervention, would go into the basement and catch them, cradling them in his hands until he set them free outdoors. To not do so would impose a death sentence.

✝

Starved for love and security, we swoop into the chimneys of life, seeking life-giving warmth and protection, never realizing that to venture too far traps us, and we are unable to find our way out alone. We are deceived! Without intervention, we may die in these traps.

But God, in His infinite mercy and grace, reaches into the chimney, offering to set us free. He desires to remove the veil Satan has placed over our spiritual eyes and heart, keeping us captive. God urges us to turn to Him. He wants to cradle us in His hands, bringing us out of captivity and setting us free in the Spirit. God speaks to our hearts, saying, "See the chimney for what it is; take hold of My hand. I want to exchange the death sentence for eternal life."

Prayer

"I sometimes end up in places I'm not supposed
to be, Lord. Psalm 139 says no matter where I go,
You will hold me fast. Hold me, Lord. Don't let
me go. Set me free. In Jesus' Name, amen."

Guard Their Hearts

February 14

Above all else, guard your heart, for it is the wellspring of life.

Proverbs 4:23

As she crossed the threshold, her senses came alive. It took a moment for the scent of apples and cinnamon to register. Then came the aroma of garlic, lemon pepper, and onions. She was smiling as she set her purse on the stand by the door.

Her husband appeared and took her jacket. "What are you up to?" she asked with a question in her eyes. "Your table is ready, madam," he teased with a mischievous wink and escorted her into the dining room. He'd used their best china in a table setting for two. Long stemmed roses woven into a twisting candelabra created a beautiful centerpiece. The plates were adorned with linen napkins arranged in the shape of hearts. The lights were low with a dozen candles burning here and there and rose petals scattered on the table. He had gone to great lengths to let her know how special she was. Aware that he had spent the better part of the afternoon in preparation, the sensation of being loved and adored flooded her heart.

✝

Proverbs instructs us to guard our hearts, for from it we live! If not well provided for, it loses the capacity to engage. Our hearts must be healthy and whole to relate to the world the way we're supposed to.

We were created for relationships. In them, we learn how to treat one another. In marriage, we learn what it means to give of ourselves, to become selfless, and to display our love for each other. We are given charge to guard not only our heart, but the hearts of those we love. Their hearts, and therefore their ability to love and live in covenant, is given over to us to care for and nurture. When we place their needs ahead of our own, showing them we intend to guard their hearts, we are filled with wonder and completeness.

Prayer

"Help us understand that Your mandate to "guard our hearts" does not give us license to care only for our own. Lord, teach us to love in a way that others may benefit from our actions. In Jesus' Name, amen."

The Call

February 15

Then I heard the voice of the Lord saying, "Whom shall I send?
And who will go for us?" And I said, "Here I am. Send me!"

Isaiah 6:8

He was fourteen when God called him the first time. It was through a wonderful woman he'd known for years. Although deaf, she served God faithfully. She asked if she could share something she felt God wanted him to know. "I guess so," the boy tentatively answered. Holding his face in her hands, looking directly into his eyes, she said, "God told me that you would be a great minister for Him some day!" Not really understanding, he answered, "Okay." And that, as they say, was the end of that.

Over the years, the call was replaced by other desires, yet a sense of longing plagued him. Still, he continued to resist. He knew what the *call* was—God's invitation to be in relationship with Him in a way that would make him wholehearted. He couldn't tell you why, but he was afraid of the *call*. But as a patient Father does, God waited. The man finally answered the *call* and in that answer found a joy and contentment that fulfilled the longing in his heart.

✝

Isaiah's relationship with God was so close that he overheard God asking for someone to go. In those close relationships, we are conscious of God's voice. We overhear Him speaking in our presence, asking us to go for Him. We can be so uncertain and fearful that we want God to call us by name, saying, "John, please do this for me." God rarely calls us that way. His hope is that we would be in a close enough relationship with Him that when we hear Him say, "Whom shall I send?" we answer, "Here I am, send me."

Everyone's call is different; for one it's a helping hand to someone in need, to another it's giving someone a ride to the store. It is not to be feared, but embraced. All are *called*. Sadly, few answer.

Prayer

"I get afraid when I hear You speak, Lord. I don't know why;
I just do. Help me walk through the fear. Help me understand
that by serving others I serve You. In Jesus' Name, amen."

Honesty or Salary?

February 16

Do not use dishonest standards when measuring length, weight, or quantity. Use honest scales, and honest weights.

Leviticus 19:35, 36

Three months on the job and he'd just had his salary doubled! It was the most exciting position Mike had ever had. But he was in a quandary because he felt the company was using questionable business practices known as job shopping.

Though widely accepted in the industry, Mike considered the practice dishonest. Once the company was awarded the bid on a job Mike had submitted, they would ask him to call all the suppliers they had used to compile the bid and ask them to give him a lower price on the materials or they would find someone else to provide the product they needed at a lower price, hence, maximizing the company's profit. Mike, in an act many viewed as bordering on lunacy, told his boss that unless the company stopped the practice, he would no longer be able to work for them.

✝

God set a standard to live by. He expects us to act accordingly. When we compromise principals or ethics in any way, we sacrifice part of our integrity. Done frequently enough, we become desensitized to what we are doing. "It's not really so bad," we tell ourselves to alleviate guilt and conviction. If left unchecked, it spills over into every part of our lives.

Mike knew he would someday stand before God and give an account of his actions. He knew there was no answer that could excuse being dishonest to justify a large salary. We want others to treat us fairly. We teach others about who we are by our adherence to our integrity. In Mike's case, the company refused to change business practices, and so he chose to leave. We may never be faced with a decision as big as Mike's, but when we are faced with unethical issues, we must make a choice. Honesty or deceit? Which will it be?

Prayer

"I am tempted to look the other way sometimes,
Lord. Help me witness truth when I am confronted
with unethical issues. Help others to see the affect
You have on my life. In Jesus' Name, amen."

The Wind and the Waves

February 17

He replied, "You of little faith, why are you so afraid?" Then he ... rebuked the winds and the waves, and it was completely calm.

Matthew 8:26

The sky was pregnant with rain. In the next instant, it pounded on the metal roof of the ground floor room of the lighthouse. He was uneasy. Watching as the waves buffeted the side of the building, he sensed this was going to be a bad storm.

The salt spray beat against the windows as the wind whipped the waves into whitecaps. Though he was on dry land in a lighthouse that had stood the test of time, he was afraid.

It was then he noticed the smallish captain of a sixty-foot fishing vessel preparing to leave port. He ventured, "Aren't those waves too big for your ship? I mean, isn't it too dangerous to leave just now?!"

The captain took a sip of his coffee and said in the calmest of voices, "Son, those swells aren't much. By the time we pass the break wall, they'll be thirty footers." There was a gleam in his eyes that made the man wonder if he'd taken leave of his senses. "I've faced much rougher weather at sea; we'll be just fine." The perfect picture of peace with a calmness about him, the captain finished his coffee, nodded at the man, and headed for his ship.

✝

Jesus was sleeping right up until the disciples, in fear for their lives, awakened him. He rebuked the winds and the waves, and then he rebuked them. "Why are you so afraid?" Can you hear them? "What? Are you crazy? Look at the situation we're in!" Seasoned fishermen are used to rough weather. So this was one bad storm.

In an instant, the storm subsides. Awestruck, they asked, "Who is this man that even the wind and waves obey him?" They were to discover that peace is not dependant upon circumstances, but upon Whom our faith rests. Like the captain in today's story, they knew the One who calms the storm in each of us and tells the wind and the waves, "Be still."

Prayer

"Please still the storm in my soul, Lord. Help me weather this battle; help me trust that You will never allow me to drown under the burdens of life. In Jesus' Name, amen."

Perfectly Unique Imperfections
February 18

But when perfection comes, the imperfect disappears.

1 Corinthians 3:10

As the master glassblower puffed gently, a small bulb appeared at the end of the forging tube. Working with quick, decisive motions, she rolled the six-foot tube along a lintel while her apprentice held thick, wet newspaper under the glass, creating a more slender tube. A more forceful puff of air and a larger bulb was created at the end of the tube. The apprentice now used a cup-shaped, cast-steel ladle to shape the vase as the forging tube continued to spin.

Working in unison—one blowing and spinning the tube, the other handling the glass with different tools—they achieved the desired effect. Frequently, the entire work of art was placed back into the furnace for reheating.

When asked why the glass was continually placed in the furnace, she answered, "The glass has many imperfections. As we re-fire the glass, we remove many, but not all, of them. The remaining imperfections are what make each creation unique; it gives the piece more value."

✝

Until the day Jesus comes back for the church, we will be imperfect. This does not translate into *useless*. In the same way the vase has great value even though it is flawed, we too are of great value to God.

The trials of life refine us. God uses the Holy Spirit to influence our lives in one way while He reveals truth to us in another. He places us into the forging fires to remove our imperfections. What is left is a less-flawed vessel.

As we walk through the fire, we become a purer version of the person God means us to be. The Holy Spirit urges us while God directs us. Our refining yields the desired effect. As the forgings cool, we reflect a clearer image of the One Who is perfect in every way.

Prayer

"Please use me, Lord. I need to feel valuable. I want to make
a difference in this life. Guide me through the refining
fires so I reflect a better representation of Your image to
those I meet along life's path. In Jesus' Name, amen."

Out of the Blinding Darkness

February 19

I will lead the blind by ways they have not known, along unfamiliar paths I will guide them; I will turn the darkness into light.

Isaiah 42:16

Craig had been lost for hours when he saw the light in the distance. "Finally!" he uttered in relief. A wildlife photographer, he had set out that snowy morning following fresh elk tracks, hoping to get some good photos. The animal had entered the dark timber where the snow wasn't as deep.

In dark timber, things are a lot closer, trees are only feet apart, and landmarks appear the same in every direction. Taking a new compass reading, he set out. As he continued trailing the bull, he encountered other tracks. It became harder to distinguish the original trail. He decided to take another compass reading before continuing on. That's when he realized his compass was gone! Somewhere in the heavy brush, it had been torn from his pack!

With fading daylight, the elk was forgotten; finding his way out took precedence. He walked for forty minutes as his anxiety mounted. Then he saw a light in the distance. Heading toward it, he found a hunting cabin. After a short explanation, the cabin owner said he knew exactly where Craig was parked. Thirty minutes later, he deposited a weary and grateful Craig at his vehicle.

†

Craig had been four miles off course. Had the man in the cabin not lighted the lantern, Craig would have had to rely on his wilderness skills for survival. During daylight, he might have been able to backtrack. But in the dark, with failing light, he would have been forced to spend the night where he was, so he didn't stray even further off course.

We can lose our way spiritually and get caught up in things that appear innocent and harmless. In the midst of our hunt, we can become lost. It's only a step or two farther into the dark timber. Without a spiritual compass, we can die. Thankfully, God gave us the Holy Spirit as our compass. But it's our responsibility to take frequent readings to assure ourselves we are on the right path.

Prayer

"Help me see Your guiding light when I stray,
Lord. Please point me in the right direction when
I get off track. In Jesus' Name, amen."

Faith, Hope, and Love

February 20

> Now these three remain: faith, hope and love. But the greatest of
> these is love.
>
> 1 Corinthians 13:13

Looking across the room, his gaze fell upon the two candleholders sitting on
the table. They'd been a gift to him and his wife on their twenty-fifth anniversary. Four inches square, the relief cuts on the sides held significance to faith
and love. A lighthouse illuminating the world was the symbol of faith while
a large, flourishing heart, surrounded by stars defined love. It struck him that
there wasn't one for hope. And right now *hope* was what he needed because
hopelessness was threatening to beat him into submission. He knew God was
at work. He just wasn't sure how or where.

Having just been turned down for full-time employment in a job he'd been
doing part-time and way behind on the bills, he wondered what God was up to.
There seemed to be no resolution. Yet his faith in God's abiding love, and that
of his wife of thirty years, gave him hope. These two constants could never be
taken away. God was not taken unawares. He would work things out.

✝

When things don't go our way, we can become disillusioned, perhaps even broken. Unless we have a solid foundation built on the knowledge that our lives
are anchored in God's love, we can lose hope. Paul told the Romans at the end
of chapter eight there was nowhere they could go that God's love could not
find them. Nothing they could do would separate them from the depth of that
love. "Neither height nor depth, nor anything else in all creation, will be able to
separate us from the love of God that is in Christ Jesus" (verse 39).

The events in our lives can bring us low. Whether we stay there is up to
us. God wants to encourage us in our trials. We do well to remember we have
the greatest love of all at our disposal. That love builds faith and hope. God's
embrace is two moves away—just turn and reach up.

Prayer

"Thank You for the hope we have in You, Abba.
Draw me close to You as I reach up and give you
my heart for mending. In Jesus' Name, amen."

Time Is Running Out
February 21

Just as man is destined to die once, and after that to face judgment.

Hebrews 9:27

Joe had invited several friends over to watch game four of the NBA finals: Cleveland versus San Antonio. The Cavs had made it to the finals for the first time in franchise history; the Spurs were last season's league champs.

The score was tied at ninety-eight, and the Alamo Dome was alive with anticipation. It was Cavs ball with thirty-seven seconds left in the fourth quarter and two timeouts. Spurs were up three games to none in the best of seven series; it was win or go home for the Cavs. Inbounding the ball, they moved up into the frontcourt. With eight seconds left, James drove the lane. The screen went blue! "Nooooo!" everybody screamed. "Not now!" Joe was livid. He tried to find the game on another channel, but all one hundred fifty-eight channels were lost; he dropped into his recliner in disbelief. By the time the picture was restored the game was over.

✝

In the same way, the clock is counting down on our lives. Time is running out on each of us, and the game will end without warning. From the moment of our birth we are headed toward the day of our death. There is no guarantee of our next breath. Yet some of us live in denial of that truth.

As suddenly as the satellite signal was lost in the basketball game, our lives will end. We will find ourselves before the One Who offered to set us free. If Jesus Christ is Lord of our lives, we should live in such a way that makes those who don't know Him curious about where we get our strength.

We are spiritual beings in a physical body. Our spirit will live for eternity, either in heaven or hell. Both are real, only one is inhabited by God. In the other will be realization that any chance of being near your Creator has been missed forever. Don't allow the world to feed you lies that imply you have all the time you need. The clock is ticking.

Prayer

"Father of all Creation, speak the truth of this message to every heart that reads it. Please draw them into a relationship with You, now. In Jesus' Name, amen."

Obedience

February 22

But Samuel replied: "Does the LORD delight in burnt offerings and sacrifices as much as in obeying the voice of the LORD? To obey is better than sacrifice."

1 Samuel 15:22

She had come to the hospital because of God's urging. She was here to minister in prayer. She found the family surrounding her friend's bed. Each face said they knew their mother wouldn't last the night. The doctor had said as much. She looked at them and simply said, "God asked me to come here tonight and pray for your mother." With that, she left the room and crouched down in the hallway.

All through the night she prayed, knowing this friend's adult children did not know God. All through the night she asked Him to bring glory to His Name and draw these men and women unto Himself. Frequently, one of them would come out to see if she was still there and thank her for what she was doing. Her presence seemed to bring them comfort. When morning dawned, there was marked improvement. Several days later, this mother of seven walked out of the hospital under her own power.

✝

Our obedience allows God to work through us in ways we can't imagine. When God is involved, the impact of our witness is immeasurable. This prayer warrior was an instrument of God. He had urged her during prayer that evening to come to the hospital and pray. She never hesitated. Her presence had opened a door for those who witnessed her obedience to God.

They didn't know this woman very well before this night, but they knew their mother did. Because of her obedience, they were comfortable enough to ask questions about the One who had healed their mother.

We can show others the door to salvation with one act of obedience. God wants us to know when we respond, He moves.

Prayer

"Healer of our souls, we give You glory. Speak to us in such a way that we recognize Your urging. We want to be instruments that lead others to salvation. Give us courage to do what You ask when You ask without question. In Jesus' Name, amen."

Timeless Hope

February 23

Plans to give you hope and a future.

Jeremiah 29:11

"Okay! Okay! I've got it!" Leslie said emphatically to her older brother. "Let's make Mom a quilt out of all the scrap material from the last ten years, and we'll use the rest to make Dad a pair of slippers!" she expressed with excitement.

"Sweeeet!" Kellen answered. "That's perfect! We'll use the camo pattern for Dad's slippers!"

Leslie said, "This one may take us several nights! We'll need to get started early."

Christmas was two months gone, and they were already planning next year's presents. It had become their timeless tradition when they were very young to lock themselves in their bedroom on Christmas Eve and make this final Christmas gift out of love for their parents.

Each year their imagination and creativity were put to the test to come up with the perfect gift. And as each year passed, it became more of a challenge. Yet each year they elicited huge smiles from Mom and Dad in recognition of their labor of love.

✝

Love from the bottom of a heart is priceless. It speaks a timeless language all its own.

Leslie and Kellen were not making presents for the sake of tradition; they did it because they were part of a loving family. The love they poured into their gifts was immeasurable. They were already looking to the future, anticipating the time they would spend together creating a gift of love for their parents.

Loving God with this depth of devotion requires spending intimate time with Him.

Because of the loving relationship with their parents, Leslie and Kellen eagerly anticipated working together to create something of lasting value for them.

As God's children, we can do the same; we can build hope for the future!

As co-laborers with Jesus, we can help create timeless relationships between the lost of this world and our Father. We can help give them timeless hope and bring them to the Father Who holds their future.

Prayer

"God of hope, we thank you for the hope we find in Jesus.
Help us to excitedly prepare to help create lasting and
timeless relationships for You. In Jesus' Name, amen."

Poor by Choice
February 24

Blessed are the poor in spirit, for theirs is the kingdom of heaven.

Matthew 5:3

This soon-to-be mother made up her mind and walked into the hospital. *This is the right choice,* she told herself. She'd recently been downsized out of a job and her medical benefits. Thinking only of the baby, she stepped to the registration counter and said, "I'm in labor. I'm not due for another two weeks, but my water broke about an hour ago. I have no insurance and cannot promise you when, but I will pay for this somehow."

The receptionist called for the doctor on call and had a nurse assist the young woman to an exam room. "Have you had any prenatal care, hon?" the nurse asked. "Oh, yes," she answered with a shy smile. "You see, I only lost my job six weeks ago, and the coverage just ran out. I couldn't afford to pay the ongoing premiums." With a smile that said she understood, the receptionist chuckled and said, "We'll worry about the bill later, hon. For now, let's concentrate on bringing your child into the world. We have programs that will help, so don't you worry about that right now. Have you picked out names for the little one yet?"

✝

The self-sacrifice of motherhood wasn't lost on the receptionist. She'd raised four of her own. This young girl was putting the needs of her unborn child ahead of her pride. She instinctively understood that self-sacrifice is the cry of a mother's heart, an ingrained willingness to put her children ahead of herself.

Being poor in spirit is not about financial destitution; it's about making the choice to go without for the sake of another. We are constantly faced with this choice during the course of our lives. We can choose to allow pride and fear to tell us, "Take care of *numero uno!*" or we can ask for kingdom eyes to see the true needs around us, to look at others with spiritual discernment and concern, to be poor in spirit for the sake of another.

Prayer

"Father, help me fight the selfish desire to meet my needs ahead of those less fortunate. Help me to see where I might be able to make a difference in someone else's life today. In Jesus Name, amen."

The Right Time

February 25

At just the right time, when we were still powerless.

Romans 5:6

"Stop worrying, Loran. He'll be here like he promised," Gail said to her son.

"You think so?" asked the apprehensive twelve year-old. "I sure hope he doesn't forget. He never called to remind me, you know."

"Honey, Uncle Bob knows how much this game means to you. He knows you'll be ready to go. You're worrying for no reason. You'll see. He'll be here at 6:30 like he said," she reassured him.

At 6:25, Bob's truck pulled in the driveway. He jumped out with a smile on his face and waved at Loran, who had jumped off the porch and was running to meet him. "You goin' somewhere, Loran?" he asked teasingly.

"Aw, Uncle Bob. Stop teasin'!" he said as he threw a punch at his uncle's stomach. "You know darn well where we're goin'."

Bob eluded the punch and rubbed Loran's head. "We're gonna have a great time tonight, buddy! Fifth game, tied at two apiece. Our guys are gonna do it this year. I can feel it!" Bob's excitement transferred to Loran.

"If we don't get goin', we're gonna be late!" Loran scolded.

Jumping back in the truck, Bob looked at his sister and winked. "Guess he's right. We don't wanna be late for the game. I'll have 'im back kinda late, sis. Don't wait up."

✝

Paul spoke to the Romans about God's timing. How God's *appointed* time, or *kairos* time, a specific moment when God shows up, is always the right time.

This verse in Scripture tells us that God's timing is impeccable. He's never early, never late. Yet we fret and invite stress into our lives because we doubt He's remembered His promises. Like Loran, we think because we haven't heard from Him lately that we've fallen off His radar.

Waiting stretches and tests our faith. During a time of God's silence, we can lose hope and sight of the truth. In the silence is where Satan whispers, "God doesn't care." But that's a lie. If we immerse ourselves in His word while we wait, we will find the assurance that He will show up at just the right time!

Prayer

"Sometimes I doubt that You'll show up when I need
You, Father. Help me wait in faith. Amen."

Little Buddy

February 26

Love does not delight in evil but rejoices with the truth. It always protects.

1 Corinthians 13:6, 7

He ran onto the field, dragging the portable water fountain behind him. As each player took his turn drinking, he'd smile at Pete and rub his head.

Pete was team manager and waterboy. Standing four feet tall at age twelve, he was affectionately known among these athletic young men as their little buddy. Nobody bullied Pete, whether at a game or in school. If the players got wind of someone giving him a hard time, they paid him a visit and convinced him to rethink his actions.

Pete had had growth issues. And despite his short stature, instead of making fun of this little sixth-grader, the team adopted him in brotherly love as a full-fledged member. And, as a member of their team, he was afforded their protection. And protect Pete they did. As Pete grew older and taller, the bond remained. These young men would always feel a special connection to Pete, one born in love. Eventually, out of college and settled in his career, Pete hosted the football team's Web site. It was his way of paying forward the bonds built in those early years.

✝

There are almost an identical number of references in Scripture admonishing us to refrain from oppression and harm as there is instructing us to encourage and protect. We are to not only abstain from ridiculing others but also stand with them against oppression.

Psalm 83 instructs us to, "Defend the cause of the weak…maintain the rights of the poor and oppressed." The members of Pete's high school football team chose to support rather than devalue his life.

We are all given opportunities to come alongside others, to become their encouragers. Many times these opportunities are ripe with confrontation, and we may feel uncertain and uncomfortable. But wrong actions must not go uncontested. If left unchecked, they foster growth. We are called to take a stand against the fear mongers of the world.

Prayer

"I get uncomfortable in the midst of controversy, Lord. Help me do the right thing, to stand in love against those who would defile and beat down those who are weak or those who are tired. I am a soldier of Christ. Help me act like one. In Jesus' Name, amen."

Rebuilding Hope

February 27

Be joyful in hope, patient in affliction, faithful in prayer. Share with God's people who are in need.

Romans 12:12, 13

As they boarded the plane to return home, there were mixed feelings of fulfillment and abandonment. The destruction seen on TV was incomprehensible prior to having witnessed it firsthand. Walking among the ruined buildings, seeing the empty lots where nothing remained and where lives had been lost, had been sobering. They had come here to give of themselves, to try to help make a difference in someone else's life, to share God's love with those who weren't able to pick themselves up on their own.

The number of homes that had been swept away by Katrina was mindboggling. They had spent a week working out of a church that had been converted into a workstation/sleeping quarters/diner/clinic, and yes, still a church on Sunday and Wednesday. They had been the tenth crew to have worked on this specific house and were privileged to have completed all the necessary repairs and construction. It was time for the family, who was currently staying in Ohio, to come home.

✝

Paul exhorted the Roman church to be encouragers not only in word, but also in deed. They were to share their resources with those in need. Because there are still those in need around the world, those same words apply to us.

Jesus said, "You will always have the poor among you." His hope was that we wouldn't leave them in their need. He asks and expects us to take an active part in rehabilitating those who can't make it on their own.

Does it matter to you why your children have needs? Or do you help meet those needs because you love them or because they may not be able make it on their own?

As children of God, we are to look for, not away from, opportunities to restore hope and help for those less fortunate around the world and in our own neighborhood.

Prayer

"I know it's as important to pray as it is to go, Lord. Help me know how to share with those in need around the world and in my backyard. Tell me if I am to go. In Jesus' Name, amen."

There Are No Soft Rocks

February 28

And do not give the devil a foothold.

Ephesians 4:27

The driver slammed on his brakes! The bush the kid was hiding behind wasn't nearly big enough to keep him from eventual discovery. Panic gripped his heart! Why had he thrown those limestone pebbles in the first place? He was paralyzed by fear! Even though everything in him screamed *run,* his body wouldn't respond.

Time stood still; then a flashlight with an angry voice attached emerged and started probing for him. "Who threw those rocks? Where are you?" He sure was mad! As he was about to bolt, the beam of light found him.

Oh no! He jumped up and turned to run, but the man had anticipated his move and intercepted him, grabbing his sweatshirt by the collar, pulling him up short. "What do you think you're doing, kid? You could've killed us!" At that moment, he heard the little girl crying in the car.

"I'm sorry, mister!" he offered, scared to death. "I didn't think it was such a big deal. I thought it would be fun," he blurted out, realizing this wasn't fun at all. It was about to get a lot worse when Dad found out!

✝

Rarely as children do we contemplate how our actions affect others. Uninformed choices usually lead to consequence rather than reward. Unrestrained, pranks can, and often do, graduate to more daring exploits in order to elicit excitement. Childhood traits are patterns that become footholds for the enemy. Left unchecked, they become strongholds. It requires substantial effort to unlearn bad behaviors, so it is critical that we help our children learn good behaviors that breed character and integrity. Well-informed children stand a much better chance of making right choices more consistently. This requires investment of ourselves and our time in our children in order to raise up caretakers for their generation.

If we fail to do this, our children will reap the harvest of their own experiences. We will be leaving them open for innumerable enemy footholds.

Prayer

"I love the children You have entrusted to me,
Lord. Help me invest in their character and future.
Help me nurture them instead of allowing the
world to raise them. In Jesus' Name, amen."

On Eagle's Wings
February 29

> But those who hope in the LORD will renew their strength. They will soar on wings like eagles.
>
> Isaiah 40:31

It was clear and cold as she stepped out the back door, heading for town. The sun had risen into a brilliantly blue winter sky. The snow on the ground made it almost blinding. She spotted two cardinals sitting in the walnut tree at the back of the property. There were few birds around this time of year.

Just as she reached the car, she heard a *screeeech*. Looking in the direction it had come from, she spotted the eagle! He was just hanging there, circling as if weightless. These were her birds! Well, God's birds really. But she felt He had given them to her. They had been His witnesses to her in rough times. God had always brought them on just the right day at just the right time, letting her know He was watching.

These majestic birds had migrated to this river bottom some twenty years ago. They had made tremendous advancement; there were now some ten nesting pairs in a twenty-square-mile area. Each time she witnessed the awesome grace and beauty of the huge birds, she gave God thanks.

✝

We are witness to God's creative power and imagination. Eagles are but one example of His love of beauty in majesty. They are also the model He chose in Scripture to convey power, strength, and safety.

Isaiah pronounces God's promise of renewed strength and the ability to overcome, rising above the cares of the world if we trust and hope in the Lord. God wants us to understand that our daily strength should come from Him alone.

By putting our trust in Him, we will never grow weary. He doesn't promise life will be easy. But if we allow Him to draw us apart from our labor, He will replace our weakness with His strength. The text suggests that we do this expectantly, trusting Him to produce in us a work we are incapable of.

Prayer

"Lord, we thank You that You send us signs of Your strength
to encourage us. Help us come to an understanding that we
can exchange our limited strength for Your unlimited power.
Teach us as we come in faith. In Jesus' Name, amen."

March

Hopelessly Lost
March 1

I am the way, the truth, and the life. No one comes to the Father except through me.

John 14:6

They had been lost in the mountains of western Colorado for two days and were at the end of their rations. They had filled their canteens that afternoon beside a beautiful waterfall, the beauty secondary to their mounting concern, and continued on downstream, hoping to intersect a trailhead. It had only led them deeper into the wilderness. It had begun when they had taken a footpath not marked on their topo map. It had looked like a well-used trail. Two miles farther along and several hundred feet lower in elevation, it had played out, becoming a dimly discernable animal trail. Not wishing to double back, creating extra climbing, they had followed the side hill direction the trail had been taking, sure they would find a way out.

Night found them camped beside a small creek just above a deep gorge. Matters were compounded by the fact that they had no compass; each had thought the other had brought one. They had also failed to complete a prehike checklist. Three days later, haggard and hungry, their S.O.S. was spotted by search and rescue eight miles from any trail that would have led to civilization.

✝

Not taking a compass into the wilderness is a sure way of getting lost. Even novice outdoorsmen know it's one of the first laws of hiking. To break that rule is to invite unnecessary exposure to the elements and possible death.

As Christians, we should carry our compasses wherever we go. In it, Jesus reveals the way home. Without it, we can become hopelessly lost, unsure of where to go and what to do. Not knowing the Way, we will die a spiritual death. It's up to us to explore between the covers of the Bible, reading God's instructions for the situations we find ourselves in. With the help of other, more seasoned students of Scripture, we can gain hope and knowledge that will keep us on the right path.

Prayer

"Creator of the universe, thank You for providing the map I need to navigate rough terrain. Please guide me through Your kingdom. Keep me from unnecessary exposure to the evil elements in this world. In Jesus' Name, amen."

Not Crushed, Not Abandoned

March 2

We are hard pressed on every side, but not crushed; perplexed, but not in despair; persecuted, but not abandoned.

2 Corinthians 4:8, 9

Unable to find the restaurant they were seeking, they settled on this steakhouse. Their waitress was very personable and pleasant. She was a Hurricane Katrina transplant, now living thirty miles inland. She hoped to get home to the coast in the next couple months.

They asked her about how life had changed. She was quick to share how her former employer had provided a fifteen-thousand-dollar debit card to help with temporary relocation.

She spoke about how normal things had seemed the day the storm hit and how much her life had changed since. She and her sister had gone to Florida to ride it out. They had taken nothing with them, expecting to return home in the morning. They returned to the neighborhood ten days later to find the house gone. There was nothing left but the cement slab with the ceramic tile still in place. Yet she quickly downplayed their loss, citing how others had lost their lives.

When she finished, the group asked if they could pray with her. As they held hands and prayed, tears fell. The waitress felt God's embrace that night; she felt loved.

✝

Eighteen months after the storm, it was the first time anyone had offered to pray for her. One act of love can bring the beginning of healing. They had reached out to the waitress in sensitivity and obedience. God uses us when we are available and obedient. If we are willing to step out for the cause of Christ, He will teach us great and wonderful things. This small act of compassion produced several testimonies for the future. When we follow the Holy Spirit's leading, we discover the outcome is God's goal, not our comfort. Mostly, we find that others are hungry for spiritual nourishment. Taking time to ask your waiter or waitress if he or she has a prayer need may be the first step to healing. God whispers in our ear, "Tell them I care."

Prayer

"Show me the opportunities where a prayer can make a difference in someone's life, Lord. Then give me the courage and strength to pray with them. In Jesus' Name, amen."

Not on Our Own

March 3

This righteousness from God comes through faith in Jesus Christ to all who believe.

Romans 3:22

As they reached the trendy restaurant, the couple noticed the scruffy-looking teenager soliciting passersby on the corner. Panhandlers were a city staple. "Got a couple bucks, mister?" came his routine greeting. "What are you doing out here, young man? And where are your parents?" the woman asked, the mother inside her rising up.

"Whadda ya care, lady?" came his defensive response. "I got no parents. I take care a' myself. You got any cash or not?"

"Have you eaten, son?" spoke the man, kindly. "We would be honored if you would join us for dinner."

Unsure why, he accepted their offer.

Having settled the matter, they headed into the restaurant with the young man in tow. When the maitre d' saw them, a quick, disapproving manner assumed his countenance. It was his way of trying to discourage them from bringing street trash into his establishment. This was an establishment they frequented. So letting the maitre d' know that the young man *would* be joining them, they were grudgingly seated at their usual table. The young man couldn't believe what he'd just witnessed, someone taking a stand for him in the presence of resistance.

†

There are those who frown on persons who are unable to pull themselves out of the mire under their own power.

Where would we be if God had left us to pull ourselves out of our own sin? Without Jesus going to the cross, we would be damned for eternity. We could not, regardless of the length of time given, manage to do something we are incapable of.

Sometimes people need help. Salvation seeks out the surrendered, those who are aware of their inability to defend themselves before a righteous God. The maitre d' has as much right to it as the orphan. If we assign salvation to those who look worthy, we will miss opportunities to show others the door to salvation in Jesus Christ.

Prayer

"I really don't know whose heart You're working on at
any given moment, Lord. Help me understand that
none are worthy, but all may come. Lead me to someone
in need of Your love. In Jesus' Name, amen."

Comfort Zone

March 4

Fear of man will prove to be a snare, but whoever trusts in the LORD will be kept safe.

Proverbs 29:25

David received a call from a friend who was offering free tickets to the political event of the year. His first impression was negative; he disliked political socials.

After a moment of discussion with his wife, they accepted the generous offer. David and Gwen were determined to see what God would lead them into at this event.

In black tie and evening gown, they walked into the ballroom. Finding a table amidst the hundreds of people was uncomfortable for David. Surveying the room, they found a relatively vacant table occupied only by a retired pastor and his wife. The couple introduced themselves and was seated.

They were joined at the table by a county commissioner and his wife, as well as one of the wealthiest men in town. As the evening progressed, David and Gwen spoke openly with everyone at the table but had extended conversations with the wealthy businessman. David exchanged business cards with the man as the evening ended, expecting this might be his last contact with the man. David was surprised and delighted to receive a phone call from him the next day. Over time, God built a strong relationship between these men, allowing one to share his faith and the other to share his wisdom.

✝

God will never ask us to go somewhere and do something He's not willing to equip us for. Had this couple decided to yield to the negative inclination of the initial contact, they would have missed out on a relationship that enriched their lives. They were not looking for what this rich man's wealth could do for them. They were looking to see where God could use them to deepen this man's relationship with God.

Fear of power and even money can keep us from experiencing unique relationships with some of God's most creative individuals. When we open up to possibilities and expand our horizons mentally, God will expand them literally.

Prayer

"I'm uncomfortable in some situations, Lord. Help me
put that fear to rest. Teach me to bring my fear to You,
where it belongs, in Your hands. In Jesus' Name, amen."

Bullied

March 5

Rescue me, O LORD, from evil men of violence … they make their tongues as sharp as a serpent's.

Psalm 140:1, 2

Carl wet his pants in the third grade. The teacher wouldn't let him out of class. Her rule was, "You go before or after, not during classes." Seated right behind Carl that day was the class bully. Bully's harassment of Carl began that day. He never let up, always calling him derogatory names.

After years of Bully's abuse, Carl became aware of two things: he was afraid to stand up for himself, and nobody else was going to do it for him. He lived in constant fear of his next encounter with Bully.

Carl never forgot those years and became an angry man because of those unresolved wounds, venting his anger in ways that caused additional pain for himself and those he loved. He developed a quick temper and frequently spoke in clipped sentences to let people know they were an annoyance.

God tried to help Carl, but Carl was angry at God for allowing Bully to do the things he had done. For all intents and purposes, Carl appeared to be an upstanding, confident man. In silence, Carl's private wound continued to ache; he refused to talk about it.

✝

Carl isn't alone. Many of us walk around with deep, secret wounds inflicted by the bullies of the world, hoping no one will ever find out. Satan wants us, like Carl, to remain silent, for in the silence there is no healing.

God wants those who have known bullies to come to Him for healing. He alone can take away the pain. *He alone can speak His truth into the wounds of our heart.* God is heartbroken over the bullies of the world because they abuse free will.

Free will means that God could not stop Bully from doing what he did anymore than He would stop us from committing the sin in our lives. To do so would mean we had no free will. But God is there in our pain, asking us to let Him heal our wounds. Free will is ours in this matter also.

Prayer

"Come and set me free from this pain, Lord. Speak Your truth to my heart. Bring healing to my soul. In Jesus' Name, amen."

Posers

March 6

I sought the LORD and he answered me. He delivered me from all my fears.

Psalm 34:4

Jake was known for motivating the less confident to greatness. Standing behind the lectern, he exuded confidence. He had this crowd of thousands laughing. They were listening intently, hanging on his every word. His delivery received frequent applause, energizing him to bring it home for them.

As he began his closing comments, Jake began to stutter. You could see real fear grip him as his words began to pile up on one another. The more he stammered, the worse it got. In a span of sixty seconds, Jake went from well-known motivational speaker to a stumbling, broken man.

He never finished his speech; he couldn't get off the platform fast enough. His past had surfaced, he was found out, and the façade he had lived out over the last decade had failed him. Jake would eventually recover from his humiliation. God led him to a good Christian counselor who would eventually guide him through his embarrassment to a place of understanding and healing.

It was two years before Jake returned to the speaking circuit. When he did, he possessed a newfound confidence. His foundation had changed. Gaining this level of confidence had required Jake to admit he had been posing for many years. In his shame, Jake had learned to compensate for something he saw as repulsive; he pretended to be someone he wasn't. He locked the "little loser" away. Through counseling, Jake came to discover the truth; he wasn't a loser. A traumatic event had occurred in his childhood, resulting in his inability to articulate his thoughts.

†

Learning the truth set Jake free. Unresolved, his stuttering had held him captive. Satan wants nothing less than to hold us captive.

Posing is a widespread epidemic. Some don't recognize they are posing; some know and don't want others to find out. God wants us to learn to be ourselves, the wonderful child He created. He wants to deliver us from the lies of the enemy and tell us who we really are.

Prayer

"I need healing and closure to these unpleasant, even horrible events in my life, Lord. Deliver me from the fear that grips my heart! Please answer my prayer, Papa. In Jesus' Name, amen."

Fearless Integrity
March 7

The man of integrity walks securely, but he who takes crooked paths will be found out.

Proverbs 10:9

The roadside billboard asked, "Are you a person of integrity? God." Harold was troubled by the question. He had just left a business meeting and had to admit he had hedged his bets. He hadn't exactly lied, but he had not shared some important information that could have benefited the committee. He believed he might be able to benefit by withholding this information.

The next two hundred miles were spent seeking God's resolution to the issue. Returning to his office, he called the committee via teleconference and advised them of the information. He went on to explain he would understand if they backed out on the deal due to his deceit. To his surprise, the group knew of the information themselves and had to admit to their own duplicity in the matter. Asking forgiveness, they committed to complete disclosure in the future. Their openness marked the beginning of tremendous growth for each of them, spiritually and in their business.

✝

God wants us to reflect His Son's attributes. Deceit is inconsistent with integrity. The handing over of integrity began in the garden, and the process continues today. Satan still whispers in our ear, "What they don't know won't hurt them. You deserve an edge. Keep quiet." His attempt to persuade us to listen to his lies reveals that his character never changes. He only wants to steal and kill and destroy us.

God's character never changes either. Holiness won't allow Him to lie or hedge his bets. Only His kids have that ability. It remains *our* choice whether we seek an edge in the world or choose to bring all temptation, and therefore the outcome of our lives, to God's care.

He commanded us to be honest and forthright. Whether we've been dishonest in the past or not, He asks us to become men and women of fearless integrity.

Prayer

"You see everything we do, Lord. But because others don't, it's easy to be less than honest in our dealings. Help us desire to be men and women of integrity. In Jesus' Name, amen."

I Want to Fight Back!

March 8

Blessed are the meek, for they will inherit the earth.

Matthew 5:5

He'd been defenseless against the school bully and hadn't stood a chance. As Tim, in frustration and shame, finally got to his feet, the crowd was dispersing. They jeered him and branded him a coward. They couldn't believe he had allowed the other boy to pound him mercilessly without retaliating.

Tim had learned earlier than most that he would experience pain in his life. He had also learned to rise above a sense of helplessness. He knew from experience that fighting would never solve his problems. But this time he had wanted to lash out at his adversary. He felt like the coward they kept calling him.

As he brushed himself off, the crowd walked away. He noticed one girl still standing nearby.

She stepped closer. "Are you okay?" she asked. Then, looking toward the bully, she added, "He's such a jerk." Not getting a response from Tim, she offered, "I know you're not a coward. So why didn't you fight back?"

"Because fighting for the wrong reason never solves the problem," came his answer.

†

We are born with an instinct for survival. Allowing something or someone to threaten or harm us is beyond human logic. But when Jesus was beaten, he didn't offer resistance. Why choose to be beaten to the point of death when you have the power to resist or stop it altogether?

We sometimes confuse meekness with cowardice and fail to understand that it's our right to refuse to inflict harm on another. Christ submitted because to do otherwise would thwart his ultimate purpose. Meekness does not say, "I will not fight." It says, "I refuse to respond in kind."

When we let God deal with our adversary, we choose to yield to His wisdom rather than to react out of emotion. "What will they think of me?"

Would you beat mercilessly on one of your children because he struck you in the anger of his youth? Neither should we beat unmercifully on those who strike out in ignorance or pain.

Prayer

"Lord, I struggle with confrontation. Help me lay down my rights if it is what You desire. In Jesus' Name, amen."

Heirs of Faith
March 9

By faith in the name of Jesus, this man whom you see and know was made strong. It is Jesus' name and the faith that comes through him that has given this complete healing to him, as you can all see.

Acts 3:16

Roger was a strong if not large man. He had a deep chest, strong back, and bulging biceps from knowing the business end of a shovel and sledgehammer most of his life. There wasn't much he feared when it came to brute strength. He had entered and won arm-wrestling contests across three states. His powerful shoulders had always given him an advantage over his opponent.

But right now Roger was on his knees before God. He was facing cancer, and his physical strength could do nothing; he needed Someone else's strength.

Roger was a God-fearing man. It wasn't his strength he was relying on today. He was petitioning the One Who had what he needed. He had seen God heal before and believed that the same power that had raised Jesus from the dead lived in him and had the power to bring healing when doctors said it was impossible.

✝

Roger's faith revealed Who he looked to when his own strength was insufficient. He was giving God his undivided attention. Peter had shared the Holy Spirit's power with the lame man in today's text. God healed the man to display His mighty power left behind following Jesus' ascension.

Peter, a man reaffirmed by this same Jesus, knew Whose power he called upon. Roger also knew the Power Source and took his problem to Him immediately.

The lame man was healed because it brought glory to God and revealed the presence of the Holy Spirit in the Son of Man. As rightful heirs, we have the ability to call on that power anytime, anywhere. God is sovereign, and we don't always get the answer we are looking for. But we can, by faith, come asking and trusting that God will always do what is best for us. Because of that, we can come to the throne in confidence.

Prayer

"Power of God, we come seeking healing today for our lives and the lives of those we love. May we sense Your presence and power in our life today! In Jesus' Name, amen."

Oh My Gosh!

March 10

For out of the overflow of the heart the mouth speaks.

Matthew 12:34

I watched as Mark reeled in the huge fish. We were fishing for northern pike on Lake Michigan—Green Bay, to be specific—and Mark had hooked a monster! As he continued to drag the fish toward the boat, all he could say was, "Oh my gosh! Oh my gosh! Holy smokes! This thing is huge!" After ten minutes of line hauling, rod pumping action, he managed to net the thirty-eight pound northern.

One of the world's greatest game fish, the northern pike is a trophy; a thirty-eight pounder is the fish of a lifetime!

I remember thinking, *In the heat of battle, the heart speaks the truth of who we are.* Mark had not uttered one unsavory word while landing what for him was the largest northern he had ever caught. I was profoundly affected by the purity of his language in an emotionally charged moment. I have witnessed many fishermen who, when given the same set of circumstances, had sworn a blue steak.

✝

"Oh my gosh" and "holy smokes" may sound childish to some, especially to those who use foul language offhandedly without much thought of how it sounds or affects those around them. But to God, "oh my gosh" is pleasing.

Instead of holding up a standard, we have lowered the bar with each generation.

I remember when primetime TV used to be language free, a time when the whole family could come together and watch TV, knowing their children would not be subjected to profanity or sexual innuendoes. Nowadays, no matter what time you tune in, you can't watch thirty minutes of programming without profanity and sex invading your living room. It has permeated every aspect of society.

Caught swearing, a student told his guidance counselor, "It just slipped out." To which the guidance counselor replied, "If you don't practice it so much, it won't slip as often."

We may not go to hell for using profanity, but when using it, we aren't leading anyone to heaven.

Prayer

"Teach me to know the power of my words, Lord.
Remind me that besides You, someone is always
listening to what I say. Help me to not store up wrong
things in my heart. In Jesus' Name, amen."

Someone Is Starving

March 11

Blessed are those who hunger and thirst for righteousness, for they will be filled.

Matthew 5:6

The chef watched as the people filled their plates, choosing entrees and side dishes. Taste and preference made for diversity in cuisine, something this restaurant prided itself on. It seemed there was no end to what you could find on the menu. It never ceased to amaze the chef how people sought to satisfy their hunger with so many different delicacies—choice cuts of meat with garlic potatoes and sautéed carrots—while others ate lightly of poached fish with lemon sauce and a side of cottage cheese with fruit. There were as many salads as there were customers, and the people eagerly loaded plates with exotic lettuces and all the trimmings, anticipating the wonderful flavor. And for refreshment they served flavored lemonades and iced teas with seven distinctive blends of coffee—so many choices even the most disparaging customer was satisfied. The chef was proud of his ability to meet the culinary desires of each individual. He had never received a single complaint.

✝

The wedding feast for the bride of Christ will be the greatest banquet ever attended. Not because of the food, but because we will be feasting with the Groom! We have nothing with which to compare the delight and pleasure we will be afforded on that day. And our presence there will be owed to the righteousness of Christ.

In *this* world, we will never be satisfied or full. However, the Spirit wants to stir a hunger and thirst within those who want even more!

Like the chef in today's story, Jesus loves providing for our every need.

Yet, at times, we take our nourishment from the wrong food source. Free will allows us to eat as much of whatever we want. The cliché "You are what you eat" has never had truer meaning.

Prayer

"Jesus, we look longingly to the day when we will feast with you
in eternity. Use us to lead others to your banquet table. Amen."

We Cry Out
March 12

In my distress I called to the LORD; I cried to my God for help. From his temple he heard my voice.

Psalm 18:6

Standing in church with his hands raised to heaven, Mitch was thinking of the day God had gotten all there was of him to get. He'd been disking along the fencerow of a plowed field. As he always did, Mitch was ducking under the overhanging branches, lifting them out of the way as he circled the outer edges of the field. This time, however, he miscalculated the size and strength of one limb in particular. Trying to duck under while lifting it, the branch wouldn't give. In the blink of an eye, he was dragged out of his seat and over the back of the tractor, landing on top of the ten-foot disk. As the churning disks grabbed at his clothes, Mitch cried out, "Help me, Lord!" The tractor stopped! Amazed, he rose up to discover the limb had broken as it knocked him from his seat. It had caught in the fan belt of the engine, stalling it and stopping the forward motion of both tractor and disk. Looking up, Mitch whispered, "Thank You, Lord."

†

Helpless before God, we catch a glimpse of how deep and fathomless His love for us is. This God, the One Who loves us so much that He sent His Son to cancel a debt we owed, watches over us. That payment purchased our ability to relate with God in such a way that we can cry out and be heard! No longer must we offer blood sacrifices to be absolved from our sin. Today we can come boldly before the throne of God with an assurance of being heard. We should, however, come with reverence and the sacrifice of praise, declaring His wonderful love and mighty power. Most of the time, God's work goes unnoticed. But when we cry out in distress, be assured He will respond.

Prayer

"I am awed by Your provision, Abba. You protect me from
the enemy and myself. You rescue me from my mistakes
and warn me of impending trouble through Your Holy
Spirit. Thank You, Jesus, for the sacrifice of love that
allows me to come directly to the throne room. Amen."

The Web

March 13

No temptation has seized you except what is common to man. And God is faithful; he will not allow you to be tempted beyond what you can bear. But when you are tempted, he will also provide a way out so that you can stand up under it.

2 Corinthians 10:13

I watched as the wasp struggled to free itself from the web. The more he struggled, the more entangled he became. It began when the wasp spotted a fly stuck in the web, wings buzzing, frantically trying to escape. It seemed like such an easy meal. All the wasp had to do was kill a helpless fly. The moment he attacked, stinging the fly, the spider emerged from the funnel in the center of its web.

With the wasp's attention focused on the fly, the spider quickly attached a slender thread of silk to the wasp's leg. Trying to break free, the wasp's movements actually managed to get him more entangled. As the wasp weakened, the spider returned from the funnel and spun a cocoon of silk around its helpless prey.

✝

Like the spider in the story, Satan sets out to deceive his prey. The way he tempts us is always seductive. Although he cannot read our thoughts, he has seen enough of our poor choices to know how to tempt us. The truth is most sin feels good. But there are always consequences.

As in the wasp's case, what Satan tempts us with will initially appear beneficial. He focuses our attention away from the things that ensnare us, hoping we will take the bait. The wasp saw nourishment and was lured into the web.

We must be on guard and remember that one poor choice can trap us in a revolving door scenario that appears to have no exit. Unlike the wasp's confinement, our bonds can be broken.

As today's text shows, there is always a way of escape. But we must choose to take it. When we enter in to a relationship with Jesus Christ, He will lead us to the way out.

Prayer

"Lord, please give me strength to resist temptation
today. Help me relate to You in such a way today that
I can see any temptation for what it is. Amen."

He's My Son!

March 14

For God so loved the world that he gave his one and only Son.

John 3:16

Bob and Shari were concerned as they watched their eighteen-month-old son being wheeled toward the operating room. Knowing that he was in God's hands the danger of open-heart surgery was still real, making the next three hours difficult to endure.

When the surgeon announced the procedure had been a complete success, Bob and Shari wept openly and unashamedly.

Their elation was short lived, however, replaced by the news that another child, whom they had come to know during their stay had died in surgery. They had grown close to the family, and this was an awful blow.

They sought out the parents and not knowing what to say, just hugged them and wept. Bob prayed for words that might ease their pain somewhat. In that moment, he felt God say, "I know how they feel. My Son also died when He didn't deserve to. But because of My Son's death, their son is with me! Tell them I love their son with the same love that sent my Son to the cross of Calvary."

Through sobs, they listened to God's message of love. Though nothing could truly ease their pain right now, Bob's words brought the hope of a grand reunion in eternity.

✝

One child lives, another dies. It's unexplainable, unfair, and feels so wrong that we can't put words to the pain. Too many parents have felt the sting of the premature death of a child.

Infant death is so hard and so premature that it can't possibly be right. God says, "I know what you are feeling, child. Mourn, but allow My promise of an eternal reunion to fill your spirit. My Son has overcome the grave; because of that, you will live forever and will never again feel separation anxiety!"

Death brings a crisis of faith; do we believe in eternal life? If so, we have this hope that if we believe in His Son we have eternal life! The Father says, "Believe in Jesus; He's My Son!"

Prayer

"Thank You for Your love that is so much deeper than
ours. Thank You that You know how our hearts ache in
times of loss. Thank You for Your only Son! Amen."

Suit Up for Battle
March 15

Therefore put on the full armor of God.

Ephesians 6:13

Butch pulled the draw straps tighter on his shoulder pads, and then relaced his cleats. He'd gotten shoved around a little in the first half. It wasn't going to happen again if he could help it.

Butch was a lineman in the NFL. His job? Engage the enemy! Butch was a warrior; he loved the battle! Experience had taught him that his equipment was crucial to his ability to stand and fight. It had to fit perfectly to allow him movement, yet protect him from those who would try to do him harm. The opposing team intended to force their will on Butch and his teammates. This was a contest of strength and will.

This was also the playoffs! You didn't get here by giving your second best. If you were here, you'd given your all—devotion and hard work, continually doing the right thing over and over and over again, preparing for the battle. This included never taking the field without the proper equipment.

✝

We have a very real enemy. He means to take us out of the fighting. We are in a battle for souls, and we must engage the enemy if we are to help ourselves and help save those who are perishing. The victory has been secured, yet there are those who would be eternally imprisoned if we fail to help liberate them. We have been asked to stand and fight. And just as Butch, we must be prepared for each encounter.

Paul tells us to "put on the full armor of God—and pray in the Spirit." With preparation and guidance from God, we suit up for battle. To go into combat unprepared, without our armor or weapons, is to invite premature death. God has armor for each individual warrior. But it will do no good if it's hanging in heaven's locker room.

Prayer

"Today, I put on Your armor, Lord—the belt of truth; the breastplate of righteousness; the shoes of the readiness of the gospel of peace; the helmet of salvation. I take up the shield of faith and the sword of the Spirit, the Word of God! And I wield these weapons against the evil one. In Your Power and Name, amen."

Stewards of Our Wounds
March 16

So that we can comfort those in any trouble with the comfort we ourselves have received from God.

2 Corinthians 1:4

Wayne shared with the group about the heartache of losing his wife, Janice, to cancer four years ago. He spoke about her unfailing love for Jesus Christ and how that had translated into their marriage. He spoke of how God had held them both while they walked out that long, difficult journey and how God had comforted him since her death.

Janice never missed an opportunity in her many hospital stays to reveal the love of God to anyone who would listen. She spoke of His faithfulness and promises. Nurses and doctors alike came to know the Source of this little woman's strength and how she leaned on that Source alone for her answers. She trusted God to do what was best for her and her family as they worked out the details of life with a faith that would not be shaken.

As Wayne closed, he could sense healing taking place in the room. God was using his wounds to minister to others. They were experiencing what he and Janice had gone through. He could feel the Holy Spirit's approval.

✝

Each of us has a story to tell. Each of us has something to offer because we have all been wounded to the point of great grief. Some are in the midst of the pain; others have weathered the storm and are beginning to rise above the heartache; still others have determined to be good stewards of their wound for kingdom purposes. They have learned that by sharing their experience, others receive peace and healing.

The Holy Spirit compels us to comfort our brothers and sisters, not only believers but also anyone in need. In that moment, we have a choice: to reach out and share the healing of our wound in order to bring understanding and healing to those in pain or to hoard the gift so freely given. Today's text says that God comforted us for a reason.

Prayer

"God of peace and healing, help me help others who are going through what You have given me victory over. Give me opportunities and courage to let the Spirit move in my life. In Jesus' Name, amen."

More Than Acquaintances

March 17

For where two or three come together in my name, there am I with them.

Matthew 18:20

Greg had met Fred on a mission trip to the Gulf Coast. They had become quick friends in the week they had spent together bringing Jesus' love to a hurting community. Determined to keep the friendship alive, they constantly stayed in touch through e-mails and extended phone calls. Fred and his family were always part of Greg's prayers.

Funny how God builds relationships in the kingdom, Greg mused following this morning's prayer and devotions. Finished with his devotional time, Greg decided to listen to some Christian music on satellite radio. Turning on the TV, he saw it was tuned to a hunting channel he frequently watched. A commercial was advertising a website for trout fishing enthusiasts. Knowing how much Fred loved trout fishing and how he was always dragging his preacher, Tink, to all the local trout streams, he decided to e-mail him the information. Nothing special, just part of the bond God had cultivated between these two men.

They had been sent out separately as individual disciples to bring the love of Christ to those in need. God had taken that time to create a lasting bond between the two. As he sent the e-mail, Greg thanked God for his long-distance brother in Christ.

✝

There is no such thing as a casual relationship in the Lord. We read throughout the gospel accounts of the apostles being sent out two by two. And the Epistles show us that the apostles surrounded themselves with like-minded believers: Paul and Barnabus, John and Polycarp, Peter and John Mark. Even in the Old Testament, pairings were evident: Esther and Mordecai, Naomi and Ruth, David and Jonathan, Samuel and Eli. In each of these relationships was one constant adhesive: God.

As we reflect on the relationships God created in the past, let us revere His ability to bring us together for the kingdom in this day and age. He will bring us together in Jesus' Name and in His power for work yet to be done.

Prayer

"You are the Creator of relationships, Abba, and we give You thanks for the friends You have given us. Grow our relationships into kingdom-changing commissions. In Jesus' Name, amen."

The Wounds of a Friend
March 18

Faithful are the wounds of a friend; but the kisses of an enemy are deceitful.

Proverbs 27:6

As Kevin sat at the bar kindling a conversation with the girl beside him, he noticed Nathan come through the front door. *Just great,* he thought through his alcohol-tainted brain. *Now I get to listen to Nathan's fidelity sermon.*

Nathan moved up beside Kevin and spoke just loud enough for Kevin and the girl to hear. "Hey, Kev. Missy was kinda wonderin' what time you'd be home for dinner. She and the kids were hopin' you'd take them to the movies later."

Kevin watched his chance for a late-night rendezvous end as the girl got up and left. "What the hell do you think you're doin', Nate?" Kevin said heatedly, shoving Nathan against the bar.

"Kev, you'll regret doin' somethin' stupid when you sober up. Come on. You know an affair won't solve anything. Missy deserves better than this from you. All you're gonna get from this kinda thing is trouble and heartache. The worst is that Missy and the kids'll pay the heaviest price." Nathan led Kevin to his car and drove him home, thankful that Kevin had not argued. It wasn't the first time he'd opposed Kevin's loose lifestyle. He hoped and prayed it would be the last.

✝

True friends don't sit idly by and allow us to throw our lives away. When we care enough to be involved in someone's life, we have a responsibility to him. If we see him making mistakes that could harm him or others, we have a responsibility to intervene in love.

Nathan's strength and wisdom had spoken truth through the alcohol's hazy temptation. Only the faithfulness of a true friend had prevented Kevin from making a huge mistake. Out of all the men in the bar that night, many whom Kevin considered friends, only one had proven worthy of the definition. All, save one, thought his actions were acceptable.

True friends tell us the truth. Confronting a friend in love can be uncomfortable. But *that* discomfort is only temporary.

Prayer

"Lord, give me strength to be a true friend. Help me to never look the other way when a friend's life is at stake. May You bless me with a friend as faithful as Jesus. Amen."

Precious Time

March 19

Do not merely listen to the word, and so deceive yourselves. Do what it says.

James 1:22

"Read the directions, Mikey!" Bruce hollered. "I can't teach you everything. Some things you just have to figure out on your own!"

Mikey was a question-a-minute kid, and Bruce didn't feel up to it right now. It had been a rough day, and all he wanted was to finish reading his devotions before dinner.

"Dad?" persisted Mikey.

"For God's sake, Mikey! Stop asking me questions! I told you read the directions! Can't you see I'm reading my Bible?"

Mikey saw. But what he heard was, "I don't have time for you. What I'm doing is more important."

Mere seconds after Bruce's outburst, God spoke to his heart; "*My* Son is worth your time, so is *yours.*"

Bruce found Mikey sitting on the basement steps, rejection written all over his little face. In his hand was a broken piece of the model he'd been working on. "I'm so sorry, Mikey," Bruce spoke softly. "I will always have time for you," he said as he wrapped his arm around his son's shoulders. "Can you forgive me for the hurtful things I said?"

Mikey's bright smile and exuberant nod told Bruce this had been the right thing to do. The next few minutes invested in his son would be priceless!

✝

Many times we allow our emotional and physical condition to reign over our spiritual lives. None of us are innocent. Thank God children are so resilient! But we can, and do, make the same mistakes with others we encounter on a daily basis.

The chance to touch hurting people as they pass through our lives is incalculable. If slighted, they may not be as forgiving, and the moment may be lost. God asks us to live out the gospel, to give of ourselves—meaning time and possibly comfort—in an effort to raise others to a place they have never been, confident that Someone else has their best interest at heart.

Our actions speak what our words cannot. Whether listening to a wounded heart or assisting in a physical need, this scripture is a call to action.

Prayer

"In the beginning was the Word. Father, may the Word be found active and alive in me. In Jesus' Name, amen."

Wise Men Seek Help

March 20

The purposes of a man's heart are deep waters, but a man of understanding draws them out.

Proverbs 20:5

Mitch was considering a career change. He'd been collaborating with Drake, seeking help instead of trying to figure it out all by himself. They had been brought together by divine appointment and both felt God leading them to pioneer new territory.

Mitch had an unquenchable desire to discover a deeper knowledge of how he could affect the kingdom of God. That was where Drake came in. Drake was a career consultant/counselor, a godly man with tremendous wisdom. He was gifted with the ability to help unlock other people's spiritual potential.

After several weeks of meeting together, God revealed what He intended Mitch's ministry to be. Mitch decided to share his intimate knowledge of the depth of God's grace with the world through writing. With a sordid past, Mitch was able to explain God's grace with profound understanding because he had needed it so desperately.

Eighteen months later, with a newly published book, speaking engagements across the country had been scheduled; they would generate enough income to allow for future writing.

†

The assertion "Wise men still seek Him" still holds true. Yet few choose to live the life required to grasp and understand the deep mysteries of God. Those mysteries are hidden for us, not from us.

God is a rewarder of those who hunger for His truth. We must recognize that short of supernatural intervention, we need help unlocking those mysteries. His intention in revealing them is that we would learn from our discoveries.

Mitch knew he was being called to something deeper; Drake understood how to discover what that was.

Pride and self-sufficiency has chained many a productive heart. God asks us to come humbly seeking His will for our lives while enlisting the help of others so the work we are called to might be accomplished.

Prayer

"Holy Spirit, set us free from the bondage of self. Help us to
not get caught up in our own version of wisdom. Teach us the
better way of joining with likeminded believers in an effort
to get at the marrow of Your nature. In Jesus' Name, amen."

Anchored in God's Love

March 21

For if, when we were God's enemies, we were reconciled to him through the death of his Son, how much more … shall we be saved through his life!

Romans 5:10

Rebecca and Brook shared a unique bond. People found it ironic. They knew it was anchored in God's love. Rebecca's son had been killed two years ago in a traffic accident. He'd been T-boned by a car eluding police in a high-speed chase.

Rebecca prayed for the young man who had taken her son's life, asking God to help her forgive him. She prayed for him to have a revelation of God's grace and healing power. When he was sentenced to prison, she began visiting, even bringing him a Bible. With each visit, Rebecca shared stories of her son's life and how he had loved Jesus and served Him faithfully. During one of their visits, the young man gave his life to Christ. He shared how his mother had also come to know Jesus through someone's selfless act of love, someone she had never met. He went on to tell Rebecca how, two years before, his mother had been the recipient of a heart transplant. It had changed her life. Before he finished, Rebecca knew—her son had been the donor, this young man's mother the recipient. Shortly thereafter, Rebecca met Brook for the first time. They hugged silently in a tearful embrace. One weeping tears of grace, the other tears of gratitude.

✝

Not bound by a heart of unforgiveness, Rebecca was able to show the love of Jesus Christ to someone in desperate need of it. Being secure in the knowledge that her son was safe in his Savior's arms, she was able to show grace and unmerited favor to someone the world would call her enemy.

Through the events that took her son's life, Rebecca was able to see God's hand at work instead of becoming bitter at the loss of her child.

It can be difficult to ask God to help us do something so unnatural. We cannot forgive this kind of wound in and of ourselves. We need divine assistance. Had God waited until He felt like forgiving us, we would be damned for eternity.

Prayer

"What shall we say, Lord, except thank You for Your mercy and grace, Your unmerited forgiveness and favor! Amen."

Good Stuff Spirituality
March 22

Consider it pure joy, my brothers, whenever you face trials of many kinds, because you know that the testing of your faith develops perseverance.

James 1:2–3

Sarah gave cake and soda to her imaginary friends. Immediately following the cake came candy; following the candy was punch and cookies. Two hours later, Sarah, complaining of severe stomach cramps, was suffering from her sugar-loaded free for all. Mom, unaware of what had taken place at the party, drove Sarah to the local emergency room. An hour later, with test results in hand, the physician asked, "Does Sarah have a history of diabetes? Her glucose level is pretty high." Answering in the negative, Mom turned to Sarah and asked if she'd eaten anything following breakfast.

"Just good stuff, Mommy." She spoke in a low groan. "What good stuff, Sarah?" she asked. "Cookies, candy, cake, and pop stuff, Mommy."

"Oh, Sarah! What were you thinking?" The anxiety was evident in Mom's voice. The doctor assured her that Sarah would be fine. But she needed to restrict Sarah's diet to nourishing, healthy food for a few days.

✝

Early in our spiritual maturation, we lack understanding. We want the good stuff all the time. But seeking only God's blessing is unhealthy. In His wisdom, he knows better than to pander to our desires. He knows that trials and sorrow will come. Without the tempering that struggles bring, we would be unable to face the hard stuff that will come our way.

A baby chick must struggle against the shell while hatching in order to gain the strength necessary to survive. If the chick is freed from its shell without struggling, it will die. As a loving Father, God allows us just enough struggles to build spiritual strength. Spiritual maturity comes from dealing with life. The Christian walk is hard stuff; we build muscle by resistance. God would not deprive us of the deepest relationship possible, and He will not leave us alone in the battle.

Learning to lean on Jesus builds good stuff spirituality.

Prayer

"God of wisdom. We ask that You hold us as we meet the
hard stuff head on. Teach us to persevere. We want more than
a good stuff relationship with You. In Jesus' Name, amen."

Living the Memories
March 23

For what I received I passed on to you as of first importance: that Christ died for our sins according to the Scriptures, that he was buried, that he was raised on the third day.

1 Corinthians 15:3, 4

It was as if he had found a great treasure. As he lifted the lid on the trunk, he was taken by a boyish excitement. He had no idea what he would find. Pulling away the sheet covering the items in the trunk, he gently began lifting each one reverently from its resting place. Greg felt his pulse quicken, and he couldn't wait to learn what secrets would emerge. A waffle iron Gramma had used still shined as though it were brand-new.

Memories of visiting Gramma's apartment down the block came flooding back; he'd been but a child. Gramma would fix him waffles and tea for breakfast. Tea was a staple of every meal, especially at 4:00 p.m. since Gramma had been born in Great Britain.

As Greg lifted each item from the trunk, a new and special memory came with it. After several hours of reminiscing, he replaced each item to its resting place and closed the lid. How precious are the memories of living. Though the items would perish, the memories would last forever.

✝

Memories are passed in many ways, all of which are meant to impart something of value. As Greg spent those hours in fond remembrance of his grandmother, he could vividly recall the events as they had unfolded because he was actually there for many of them. As it stirs our heart to read about Greg's joy in reliving the events that shaped his life, we get a better understanding that we have the privilege of reliving much of Jesus' life and death through Scripture. We have been given eyewitness testimony from those who were there! These are not bedtime stories—although it is a good time to read them to our children—but true-life events in our Savior's life. He invites us to read ourselves into the storyline.

Prayer

"We thank you for the written record of Your life,
Lord. Enlighten our hearts as we open the Word
so that we may feel some of what the disciples felt
so we may feel alive in the memories. Amen."

Wounded in Battle

March 24

Bear with each other and forgive whatever grievances you may have against one another. Forgive as the Lord forgave you.

Colossians 3:13

Kim knew Toby was furious, so she kept silent for the moment. "That really ticks me off!" he proclaimed as he climbed in the car. "I've half a mind to go back there and …" He let his words trail off.

Toby was responding like most of us have when we've been wounded by a brother or sister in Christ; he'd smiled on the outside, saying it's no big deal while a fire smoldered inside, kindling resentment and threatening to choke out all reason.

His countenance was anything but spiritual. But the farther he got from the moment, the clearer he heard God's voice. "Do you think I missed what happened? I know how much what Tim did hurt you." Then he felt God ask, "Who would benefit from you responding in anger? Your battle is not against Tim." He knew this was true, but the wound was so fresh that he didn't want to accept it. "You can refuse to follow Satan's plan," God said. "Have you never been guilty of doing what was done to you?" God asked. *Ouch, that hurts,* Toby thought silently.

Toby looked at Kim and said, "It's so much easier to be forgiven than it is to extend forgiveness."

✝

All of us, without exception, will be wounded *in* or *by* the church. It's impossible to put that many people together and not have casualties.

In the moments immediately following the wounding, we are faced with choices: to strike out in pain and anger, to simmer in bitterness until it interrupts communication between us and God. We can spread vicious rumors, slandering the one who hurt us or act self-righteous as though nothing happened, allowing ourselves to carry the wound into the future where it will affect everything we do.

Or we can take it to God, asking Him to help us do what we cannot do on our own: forgive them as God, through Jesus, forgave us.

Prayer

"God of mercy and grace, You have forgiven us so much.
Show us how to forgive when it's so hard. Be close right now
because we can't do this alone. In Jesus' Name, amen."

God's Long Arm and the Blind Man

March 25

Later Jesus found him at the temple and said to him, "See, you are well again. Stop sinning or something worse may happen to you."

John 5:14

There was a blind man who walked into an American pastor's church in Ukraine a few years ago. He came forward that night to receive Jesus Christ as his Lord and Savior. When the pastor prayed for his salvation, he was instantly saved and healed of his blindness! But, as it sometimes goes, temptation was too great for him, and he once again found himself living a life of sin.

As in the story with the cripple Jesus healed at the pool of Bethesda, the man was confronted with his return to a life of sin and told he might suffer something worse if he continued. Realizing the truth of the statement, he returned to this church, where he repented once again, this time with new understanding, and began a new walk with the Lord. God's righteous right hand had sought him out. Thank God!

†

We have a tendency to believe that once we are saved, we should be through with sin. Yes, we have a desire to stop sinning; no, it isn't automatic. It is a process by which the Holy Spirit guides us into righteousness, which translates to *right living*, not perfection.

Once we have accepted Jesus' sacrifice, we *are* clothed in His righteousness and are *seen* by the Father *through* Christ. It does not, however, remove our free will by which we make choices. The longer and deeper we walk with God, the closer we get and the less sin-filled life appeals to us. But, as with the blind man, we are still capable of sinning. The danger at this point is that we have already been forgiven our sins. By blatantly disregarding this, we open ourselves up to a more extreme onslaught by the enemy, hence Jesus' warning to the man at Bethesda.

"God's arm is not too short that it cannot save." But sinning is not supposed to be an option, despite the inevitable forgiveness we will receive from our Creator.

Prayer

"Abba, almost all sin feels good for a while. Please lead me into the truth of where that life leads and how it separates me from You. In Jesus' Name, amen."

The Black-Eyed Gospel
March 26

For God did not give us a spirit of timidity, but a spirit of power, of love and of self-discipline.

2 Timothy 1:7

One of the elders of an inner-city church showed up sporting a black eye. When asked how he got it, he stated, "I did not *get* it; I *earned* it!" and went on to relate his story.

As he was on his way home the prior night, two young men jumped him meaning to rob him. When they knocked him down, he could tell they were amateurs. Moved by the power of the Holy Spirit, he began to chide them for doing such a bungling job of it. He railed them, saying, "When I was in this business, we didn't just knock people down and make demands of them; we knocked them out and took what we wanted!" Seeing he had their attention, he began to share with them the Jesus who had changed his life. By the time he was done, they had heard the good news of the gospel. Although they couldn't have said why, both young men thanked him for sharing, returned his cell phone, apologized, and left.

✝

I am not encouraging you to risk your life unless guided by the Holy Spirit! I am encouraging you to take a stand against the wiles of the devil. Though not everyone has a story like the elder in today's scenario, we all have the ability to refuse to be bullied by Satan.

Paul admonished Timothy not to bend to the enemy's attack just because he growls loud or brings something sensuous our way. We are not namby-pamby, spineless children of a powerless god. We were bought at a price we cannot comprehend. And the Father asks us to remember that when opposition comes our way. He has invested great power in us and asks us to discipline ourselves in love. We shall be battered and bruised in *this* life. Wouldn't it be good if our suffering were attributed to the cause of Christ?

Prayer

"This world holds fears and temptation for us, Lord.
We need Your power to rise up in us when we face
opposition. Be near, O Lord, and show us how to stand
as children of the King! In Jesus' Name, amen."

Spiritual Grit

March 27

Blessed are you who hunger now, for you will be satisfied. Blessed are you who weep now, for you will laugh.

Luke 6:21

Jenny had given her life to Jesus two years ago in a prison cell and had learned to trust Him for almost everything—almost. She'd been out three months now and was still unemployed. She was living out of a homeless shelter, spending most of each day walking or taking the bus to area employers, seeking work. Her prison record kept her from getting a decent job, and she didn't know what to do next. Temporary jobs provided just enough to survive. But she was tired of just surviving.

On her knees in prayer tonight, she was asking God to direct her to where she needed to be. She was still learning this praying and listening thing. Jenny had never cared much about life before knowing Jesus. She'd always gotten what she'd needed by hustling tricks. This honest living stuff was difficult.

At that moment, she felt God speak to her heart. "You let Me embrace you in prison, Jenny. Will you embrace Me now?" She crawled into bed, thanking God that tomorrow would bring her another day closer to Him. She felt peace descend just as sleep overtook her.

✝

There is a misconception that the Christian life should be easy, a life devoid of misery and pain. But it's not—and for good reason. If it were, the whole world would become followers of Jesus. Christianity would be a wholesale religion; it would have no power or meaning.

God is a rewarder of those who show spiritual grit. He honors those commitments because He knows what following His Son has cost each of us. Falling down does not make us failures, nor is it fatal. Get up! The bumps we acquire over our spiritual journey will be put to use for the kingdom. There is nothing that rivals the satisfaction of a clear conscience and the knowledge we are following the King. No pain is so great that it can shadow the truth.

Prayer

"Lord, when we weep, catch our tears. When we laugh, hear our joy; when we fall, take our hand; as we grow, show us more. In Jesus' Name, amen."

T.J.'s Windmill

March 28

Listen, my sons, to a father's instruction; pay attention and gain understanding.

Proverbs 4:1

T.J. was a Massey-Ferguson man himself. But he didn't seem to mind his new six-foot windmill being John Deere green and yellow. The colors were a good contrast as it stood beside the American flag he displayed every day.

When his grandson erected the windmill, placing it where T.J. could catch sight of it from his recliner in the living room, no one had any idea of the effect it would have on people's lives.

T.J.'s house was situated in the bottom of a river valley running east to west, allowing the predominant westerly winds unbidden access to the windmill. Windy days were an event; not because watching the windmill itself was so interesting, but because something about that spinning windmill stirred T.J.'s memories, causing him to talk about the past. His ninety plus years spanned countless changes in our nation's history. You never knew if you were going cotton picking in Mississippi, drilling oil wells in the hills of Ohio, or crossing Germany and France as a medical battalion aide during World War II. As a matter of fact, you could never be sure of what you were in for when the wind blew. But if you listened closely, there was wisdom, experience, and instruction to be gained.

Listening is an art form. Listening to the elderly is priceless. Unfortunately, many of our elderly are discarded as senile and troublesome, despite the fact that their very presence proclaims they have yet to complete their final earthly purpose.

There is an untapped wealth of knowledge and experience stored within the memories of our elder statesmen and women.

Solomon instructs us to gain wisdom at our fathers' knees, not view them as spent and of little use.

By refusing to listen to them, we forfeit invaluable assistance and understanding. We label them of no value. This is foolish at best and at worst is complete arrogance.

They are not meant to merely mark off each day until they die. We should avail ourselves of such knowledge before it fades.

Prayer

"Teach us to respect our elders, Lord. Help us recognize
the value of their memories and appreciate their minds.
Show us how to treat them with the reverence they deserve
and the respect You decree. In Jesus' Name, amen."

A Moment Away

March 29

> Meanwhile, Saul was still breathing murderous threats against the Lord's disciples.
>
> Acts 9:1

Ben had lived a rough life. As a matter of fact, he was still living a rough life.

Six feet two inches tall, two hundred forty pounds of solid muscle, Ben was an oil-field roustabout, making his living wrestling thirty-foot joints of steel pipe and pumping oil wells in the dead middle of winter. He was strong and seasoned. He was also opinionated as far as things related to the God of the Bible. Quick witted, he always made a derogatory comment when anyone mentioned God or Jesus, saying things like, "God is an excuse for weak people who can't make it on their own!"

A friend once asked Ben what he thought he might say to God when he found himself standing before him on the day of his death. He contemptuously answered, "Why, I'm gonna ask Him, 'Where's the best fishin' hole?'" Continuing to pray, this friend never gave up on Ben. He constantly spoke to Ben about God's love, praying God would draw him into a saving relationship, perhaps on his own road to Damascus, like Saul. And after thirty years of witnessing, and interceding on Ben's behalf, on a warm summer's morning Ben invited Jesus into his heart!

✝

At times we may be tempted to give up on those who seem to have too rough an exterior toward the things of God. Tired of their rhetoric, we're tempted to distance ourselves from their unseemly actions.

Saul's story gives us hope. One moment he was cursing the kingdom, the next he was serving the King. Not everyone who rails against God, breathing murderous threats against the Lord's disciples, will be changed. But we are not to give up on them. They might be a moment away from nearing their Damascus.

Do you know someone like Ben? If so, ask God for another measure of the grace you were saved by and then extend it to the Ben God placed in your life.

Prayer

"God of grace, give us strength. Show us what the hard cases of life look like to You. Grant us wisdom to know what to say and then give us the courage to speak in love. In Jesus' Name, amen."

He Knows My Name!
March 30

The Lord knows those who are his...

2 Timothy 2:19

Ricky was on his way to his in-laws to pick up his wife. It was a warm spring day so he drove with the car windows down. As he passed by his Amish neighbor's farm he was surprised to hear one of the boys holler, "Hi Ricky!" *I had no idea any of these kids knew my name!* He waved and hollered, "Hi Guys!" to the passel of kids, and thought back to a day almost two months ago, when he and his wife had stopped by to introduce themselves to their new neighbors.

Ricky had to admit he was a bit chagrined that he couldn't remember the name of the boy who'd just called his; it was kind of disconcerting...and humbling. Yet there was another sensation, one deeper and more meaningful, which surfaced and remained: *It felt wonderfully validating for someone to know and call him by name!* It was as if the young boy had pronounced a blessing over him by speaking his name in the presence of his brothers and sisters. He was saying, "I know you, Ricky Miller. You matter enough to me to have remembered your name from that first day you stopped at my house." It was then Ricky remembered the boy had been standing beside his father when he'd introduced himself. *Abe! That's his name!* Ricky made a mental note to return the blessing...as well as learn the names of all ten of Abe's siblings.

✝

To be hailed in this manner is akin to being handed a glass of ice-water on a hot summer's day when you've been working all day in the hot sun. Its welcomed coolness penetrates every part of your being, bringing pleasant relief; and this from a mere acquaintance.

Jesus is more than *'acquainted'* with us. He knows us intimately! His death and resurrection purchased our salvation! He says, "I know you! You matter so much to me that I have known your name from before your birth! You are Mine!" See Revelation 2:17

Prayer

"There is a thrill that runs through me, that permeates
my entire being at this knowledge, Lord Jesus! I am
blessed because You know my name! Amen."

Left at the IGA
March 31

> Suppose one of you has a hundred sheep and loses one of them. Does he not leave the ninety-nine … and go after the lost sheep until he finds it?
>
> Luke 15:4

They were headed for the nursing home to visit Gramma. Sally, one of five girls, was asleep in the back seat when Momma stopped at the IGA. Living twenty-plus miles from the grocery store meant taking the opportunity to shop when it presented itself.

Awakening, Sally found the car empty. Getting out of the car, Sally entered the store undetected. Drawn to the shiny aluminum strip along the display cases in the cold-food section, Sally momentarily forgot her objective. The cool, variegated silver bar (at just the right level for a four-year-old) called to her, inviting her to run her fingernails against its irregular surface. Sally giggled as she ran to the meat case at the back of the store. From one end of the store to the other she went, fingernails gliding over the shiny, diamond-plated surface. It tickled her fingers!

As she turned to make her next pass, she could see up the long aisle and out the doors at the front of the store. She froze! Momma's car was moving! She was being left behind! She ran for the front of the store screaming, "Momma!" As she reached the doors, she was gently scooped off her little feet by a kindly woman. Comforting Sally and holding her close, she tenderly whispered, "Momma will be back, hon. Don't you worry." She knew the young mother would return. And sure enough, ten minutes later, through bullet-sized tears, Sally saw her Momma jump from her car, running, arms extended toward her.

✝

Everything changed when Momma realized her child was nowhere to be found. Her purpose shifted from a visit to Gramma to a mission of finding her lost child.

Jesus feels the same way about those who have strayed from the flock. He will not rest until they are safe in the fold. Like Sally, we can become sidetracked by the things of this world. And like the kindly woman, Jesus will send one of His own to comfort and embrace the lost child until, through the tears, he sees Him coming.

Prayer

"Thank You, Jesus, for always looking
for us when we're lost. Amen."

April

Stick Close Now

April 1

There is a friend who sticks closer than a brother.

Proverbs 18:24

Mason and his men scanned the jungle with practiced eyes. His platoon had come under heavy fire west of Dalat, South Vietnam. They were just twenty clicks north of Ho Chi Minh City. Everyone's safety depended on trusting your life to the man on either side of you. Looking at Sgt. Bowman, Mason gave him a one arm up, hand in front of the face, two fingers pointing to his eyes, then extending them toward the jungle in a flat, arching motion, ending with a closed fist. They would hold here until the scout returned. Bowman moved closer to Mason. "Whaddya think, L.T.? Seems too quiet." Bowman barely heard the lieutenant's reply. "We hold tight for now. Majors'll be back soon. Stick close now. I want everybody close enough for visuals. No matter what you see or hear—nobody moves until I give the order. Pass it on."

Majors returned two hours later. The VC had pulled out. There'd been seven of them, and he'd found indentations from the bipods of two fifty-caliber machine guns. Mason signaled the men to gather. "Okay, small fires for coffee and beans. Put 'em out and get some rest. Mitchell and Byrnes, you have first watch."

✝

There is a bond of trust in the military that transcends almost all others. To share your life with family brings closeness; to have shared the fight for life and for the freedom of others brings inseparable devotion. As close as those bonds are, there is one closer: an intimate relationship with Jesus Christ. And the reason it is the closest bond of all is due to His unyielding faithfulness to us. Our undying love will, at times, fail us and others. We are well-meaning people, yet fallible. Jesus, however, will never fail us. His love is unconditional; His mercy freely given; His grace goes as deep as necessary. He is constantly seeking to bring us under His protection. And in Him, we truly find a friend Who does stick closer than a brother.

Prayer

"I am weak, Lord Jesus. And so thankful that You are
not. Draw me into the deepest part of Your love and
protection. Stick close to me now, Lord. Amen."

We Can Expect a Complete Recovery
April 2

I will take refuge in the shadow of your wings until the disaster has passed.

Psalm 57:1

A sickening *snap* could be heard above the noise in the crowded gymnasium. Amy grabbed her leg, severe pain evident on her face. The conspicuous bulge below her right knee gave mute testimony that the leg was badly broken. While teammates and coach watched from a few feet away, team trainers tended to the injured girl. Mom and Dad had been courtside and now hurried to Amy's side. EMTs took her vitals, stabilized the leg in a temporary air splint, and loaded Amy into a waiting ambulance to the crowd's empathetic applause.

Amy was transported to the local hospital where surgery was required to mend the break. After removing tiny bone splinters, they reset the break by realigning the jagged edges and placing surgical screws through the bone. They finished by placing the leg in a cast. There had been no complications; the break would heal just fine. Amy would be on crutches for eight weeks and then placed in a walking cast. They could expect a complete recovery.

✝

We would never leave a broken leg unattended. Yet there are those who, for one reason or another, fail or refuse to admit to their broken spirit. It is God's desire that we bring Him our brokenness.

When *spiritual* breakage occurs, it leaves jagged edges that rub together, causing scar tissue to form. Left unattended, our spirits cannot heal correctly. We live in turmoil, never finding the joy or peace promised us and possibly never realizing our full spiritual potential.

We live from our hearts; they must be safeguarded! When David was hurting, he took refuge in the shadow of God's wing, allowing the threat to pass.

In the same way Amy's broken bone was realigned, our broken spirit must also be brought into a position that will promote healing. We must seek refuge in Jesus Christ. The wound must be stabilized and given time to heal so it can bear weight again. Jesus says if we come to Him, we can expect a complete recovery.

Prayer

"I don't admit to this kind of pain easily, Lord. I don't want people to know I am wounded. Help me put aside my foolish pride and begin the healing. In Jesus' Name, amen."

In the Fury of the Storm
April 3

I would hurry to my place of shelter, far from the tempest and storm.

Psalm 55:8

Clarence watched in horror as the funnel cloud dropped from the sky. He turned and shouted to his wife, "Michelle, grab Christy and Tim and head for the basement. *Now!*" He took one more look before turning to join his family.

The twister was bouncing from point to point as if it were choosing specific geographical locations. Every time it touched down, debris was lifted skyward. The closer it came, the darker the funnel got. Clarence stood, paralyzed by the awesome display of destruction.

"Clarence? What are you doing?" came Michelle's anxious cry.

Snapped to his senses, Clarence descended through the basement door, pulling it closed as the updraft threatened to rip it from his grasp. Descending the stairs two at time, he forced a measure of calm to his voice and said, "Over to the corner. Take this blanket and cover up under the workbench." As they huddled beneath the meager protection, Clarence began reciting the Twenty-third Psalm. "Even though I walk through the valley of the shadow of death, I will fear no evil, for you are with me . . ." As the family joined him, the storm raged above. They could feel the house shake and hear windows breaking. Through it all, they would remember the peace that surrounded them in the fury of the storm.

✝

God's promise to us is a place of shelter away from the storms of life. He does not promise we won't experience trouble, only that in the midst of the storms we can find peace and comfort beyond what the world has to offer.

Our response in times of crisis determines whether we will continue to be tormented or receive strength from above. Just as Clarence was mesmerized by the power of the tornado, we too can be held in a dangerous place longer than we intend. And like Michelle's cry, David urges us to take shelter from the storm. He's telling us to hurry and not delay in fleeing from our pursuers.

Prayer

"Storms come upon me so quickly, Lord. Help me see the clouds before the tempest is upon me. Rescue me from my enemies, for I am in need of Your strength. In Jesus' Name, amen."

Made for Laughter

April 4

A cheerful heart is good medicine.

Proverbs 17:22

Nancy and Craig constantly looked for little ways to make each other laugh and enrich their marriage. This particular morning found Nancy headed out the door for the day as Craig was finishing breakfast. They never parted company without a what-if kiss: *What if something terrible happens and we do not see each other again?* So, getting up from the table, Craig joined his beloved at their favorite spot: the doorway between the dining room and kitchen. Nancy stood on the step above the threshold, Craig on the kitchen floor, several inches below her. This offset their height difference, making for the *perfect fit.*

As they embraced and kissed, a mischievous thought came unbidden to Craig. Not given time to brush his teeth prior to Nancy's heading out the door, he realized, with increasing amusement, here was a moment given by God! Leaning back while still holding her around the waist, he looked into Nancy's eyes and said, "I guess this makes me a cereal kisser!" Spontaneous laughter with a twinkle in their eyes gave testimony to the love they shared. These precious moments given of God deepened their relationship with each other and God.

✝

We were created with an expressive nature, and it testifies to what's going on in our heart.

Many of us suffer from heavily burdened hearts, rarely displaying any sign of joy or happiness. God Himself desires to bring complete joy to our lives that we might recognize His nature and learn to emulate it.

It is my belief that we bring a smile to our Creator's face when we laugh with abandon. One of my favorite paintings is of a head-thrown-back, all-teeth-showing, belly-laughing Jesus.

We weren't created to walk around with a downcast countenance, showing everyone how miserable we are. We will find what we look for; joy is optional. Yes, there will be sorrow, but if we look for a light heart, we just might find one filled with laughter.

Prayer

"Help us look to create those seemingly insignificant moments in life, Lord. Teach us to laugh as You intended, to love each other passionately with fervor and great joy! In Jesus' Name, amen."

Yours Free—At a Price...

April 5

> But these are written that you may believe that Jesus is the
> Christ...and that by believing you may have life in his name.
>
> John 20:31

Art was skeptical. He'd seen mail order offers before: "This is your big chance, Art Minot!" "You could win millions!" Then, in smaller print, "Or..." and they listed several "alternate" prizes ranging from plasma TVs to a keychain. He'd always won the keychain.

But this offer was different. This was an offer for free dental care. The local dentists were dedicating one day to give back to the community by providing free dental work, regardless of economic standing. All you had to do was contact the offices between 10:00 a.m. and 5:00 p.m. on the prearranged date and schedule an appointment.

So on that day, Art began calling at 10:00 a.m. promptly, finally getting through around 10:40 a.m. Two weeks later, Art underwent a double tooth extraction he'd been in desperate need of.

He later learned that these two dentists had performed over ten thousand dollars worth of free work for the community that day. The dental work had been free. All Art had to do was hit re-dial until he got through to the receptionist—a small price for such a large reward.

✝

Not all offers or promises are genuine and valid. Nor is everything we read in print true. Many times, unsuspecting participants lose their life savings in elaborate schemes. People believe what they read simply because it was printed on decorative paper.

Most fraudulent offers rely on a desperate desire to find relief from a difficult life. The sad truth is that they offer big promises with little or no reward. There is, however, one promise we can count on no matter what it's written on. It is free to those who would receive it.

John was an eyewitness to the price that was paid to give us *life in His name.* Our cost is faith, faith that what we read in Scripture is true. This is the sweepstakes we were born to win. The price was great; our free reward is huge! Will you believe, let Jesus pay the price, and enjoy the reward?

Prayer

"Thank you for Your written Word, Lord. Send Your Holy
Spirit to testify to the truth in Scripture. In Jesus' Name, amen."

No Grading Curve
April 6

But if we judged ourselves, we would not come under judgment. When we are judged by the Lord, we are being disciplined so that we will not be condemned with the world.

1 Corinthians 11:31, 32

She stared at the red ink at the top of the paper and silently began to formulate an argument for her professor. She waited until the last student was gone and then walked to Mr. Ambrose's desk.

"Samantha?" he asked, seeing her agitation.

"How could you do this to me?" she all but screamed. "This paper deserved a better grade!"

Calmly, and with appreciation for the moment, he responded, "In looking at the basic thought behind your analysis, I found your work absent of genuine depth. As I read, I felt you had no personal connection with the facts you presented. Your words were mechanical, devoid of emotion. I know you are capable of better work, Samantha. I do not grade on a curve, as I believe it sends the wrong message. Students cannot be rightly motivated if they know they can get by simply because of a curve that allows sub-par effort. You received a grade commensurate to the level at which you performed, a level well below what you are capable of.

Knowing the truth of his statement, she was convicted of the casual effort she had dedicated to her work.

✝

Being left to grade ourselves is a dangerous assignment. Most of us do not possess the ability to assess ourselves objectively; we tend to think highly of our efforts and expect results accordingly.

As in the grading curve mentioned in today's story, we can be deceived into believing we can bypass Jesus' sacrifice. Many are under the impression that if they live a good life, they will somehow be deserving of heaven. That just isn't true. If it were so, Christ died for no good reason, and God is a liar. It requires our receiving and acknowledging the blood sacrifice of Calvary. Only by placing Jesus on the throne of our lives are we rightly motivated. We cannot enter heaven by means of a grading curve.

Prayer

"Lord Jesus, reign in my life and lead me into all truth. I put my trust in You, not in the world's flexible gospel. Amen."

Extending Grace

April 7

But by the grace of God I am what I am, and his grace to me was not without effect.

1 Corinthians 15:10

As Jim looked across his desk at Levi, he silently asked God for the wisdom to handle this situation. He'd received several calls from customers that recent orders had been missing multiple items.

Myron from Harvest Equipment had called a few minutes earlier to let Jim know that five different parts had been missing from his order. Jim humbly responded, "I'm sorry for the inconvenience, Myron. Tell me what parts were missing, and I'll ship them to you overnight, no freight."

Jim had discovered that Levi had been sent home two days ago, midshift, for drinking on the job. Seventeen orders he had sent out had been shipped incomplete. Jim was deciding what to do. He had every right to fire Levi on the spot. But he'd been twenty-one once and remembered an opportunity he'd been given to make good on a poor choice. He talked to Levi about good character and how hard it is to restore once people witness one too many of our poor choices. Jim decided to give Levi another chance and extended God's grace to someone in desperate need of it.

✝

Jim was not hasty in dealing with Levi. He had never forgotten how God had extended His precious grace at a crucial time of rebellion in his own life. Without that grace, Jim might never have recognized how dangerous the road was he had started down.

Paul never forgot God's grace either. He spoke openly and often about his past in a plea for people to stop judging harshly. His instruction to the church at Corinth was to reveal to them how God's grace not only saves, but also how it can bring about tremendous change in a person's heart. We have all been necessary recipients of that grace. How can we, in light of that knowledge, refuse to extend it to those who are perishing?

Prayer

"God of mercy, we ask Your forgiveness for the times we have
been stubborn and possessive with something so powerful
as Your grace. Teach us to be humble; show us how to walk
in grace so that we might extend it to others. Amen."

Free Yourself!

April 8

Free yourself from the chains on your neck, O captive Daughter of Zion.

Isaiah 52:2

Britton watched as the wild mustang walked right up to where the fence had been, and stopped, refusing to take another step. This was the result of an extended conditioning experiment to see if he could teach the horse to respect imaginary boundaries.

First, Britton strung a heavy page fence around the small pasture; its woven-wire a strong barrier against the mustang's efforts to escape. Once the mustang grew weary of straining against the fence, Britton strung double strands of electric fence just inside the perimeter of the page fence, and removed the higher, stronger fence.

The mustang, noticing the enclosure looked different, edged cautiously up to the thin strands of wire. Seeing less of a barrier, he sniffed, and then placed his nose against the top strand … *wham!* The charge of electricity hit his nose, causing him to lunge away! He returned and tested it again receiving the same unpleasant jolt of electricity. Twice more he tested the fence before keeping his distance.

Britton then removed the top strand, and waited to see what the mustang would do. Seeing the wild horse had no inclination to approach the final barrier, he removed the fence altogether. For all intents and purposes the mustang could run free if he so desired. But due to the fear of impending pain, he did not move past the imaginary boundary.

✝

Pain, regardless of its form, is a powerful deterrent. It can render the strong powerless. Jolted by life's pain-filled circumstances, some of us refuse to risk freedom from captivity for fear of the pain.

God wants us to know He will remove each bar from the cage until there are none left. Yet, even with all His help, at some point *we* must take a step toward freedom. For even God cannot make us submit ourselves to our greatest fears in order to trade imaginary pain for true freedom.

Jesus came to redeem us, to set us free from oppression, real or imagined. But He will only come so far. We must decide to be free.

Prayer

"I come today, Lord Jesus, trusting that You will lead me
to safety. Set me free as I take this first step. Amen."

Blue Collar Apostles
April 9

We worked night and day in order not to be a burden to anyone while we preached the gospel of God to you.

1 Thessalonians 2:9

Roger had just come off a ten-hour shift at the plant he'd worked at for the past twenty-seven years. His friend Marcus was quizzing him on how he managed to work full-time and pastor a church of some ninety parishioners.

Roger continued, "Paul did it. This is God's call, not mine. When Paul, Silas, and Timothy were in Thessalonica, Paul realized that he and the disciples' presence could be a burden on the resources of this young church. Rather than strain them and cause reason for grumbling, they paid their own way, attempting to teach the Thessalonians that hard work was something to be embraced, not shunned, as they were in the habit of doing; they would rather employ slaves than do manual labor themselves." Then Roger added, "In the same way, Grace Community can't afford to pay me a full-time salary right now."

Marcus persisted. "So how long are you willing to do this? I mean, do you actually think this is God's plan for your life—working yourself weary?"

Roger smiled and replied, "God's desire is that our little church would flourish and grow doing the work of the kingdom. Until they can afford a full-time salary, I intend to ease the burden as much as possible."

✝

In his first Epistle to the Thessalonians, Paul reminded them of how hard they had worked among them in order to have an opportunity to preach the gospel. He wasn't complaining about the work; he was teaching them that God calls us to be laborers with Christ.

Many, today, believe that God will provide everything they need on the basis of belief in Jesus Christ. And although God loves His children, He wants them to understand that hard work is synonymous to kingdom work. We cannot say, "God will take care of me" and do nothing to assist Him.

Prayer

"Teach us to embrace co-laboring with You, Jesus. May we never allow ourselves to become a burden that would cause grumbling. Move us from our perspective of entitlement to a right-minded understanding that we must labor in Your employ. Amen."

Labor Together
April 10

We proclaim him … teaching everyone with all wisdom. To this end I labor, struggling with all his energy, which so powerfully works in me.

Colossians 1:28, 29

Cora had stood by Jake's side through thirty-one years of marriage and ministry—sometimes silently, sometimes not so silently. As Jake sat in his study, he raised a heartfelt 'thank you' to heaven. As he reflected back over the years, he began to smile. Through every trial, every difficult situation, in every moment of joy and occasion of celebration, there were two constants—God and Cora. God had been Jake's strength; Cora had been his balance. God had provided a strong work mate to help Jake walk out what He had placed in Jake's heart; He had placed an unconditional love that would forever support Jake in Cora's heart.

Jake had been wise enough to understand that had it not been for Cora, he would not be the man he was today. He thought of some of the more difficult decisions they had made over the years. Cora had never tried to force her perspective or opinions on Jake. Her spirit was not offensive; she was endowed with wisdom. God had used Cora to help Jake appreciate what it meant to labor together for God.

✝

The definition of labor is to exert physical or mental effort; work; toil. Laboring is strenuous, not to be undertaken lightly or with little regard. None of us is capable of meeting every need we encounter by ourselves. We all need help when the world relentlessly pounds on our door. Jake was the recipient of a wife who possessed strong character and influence, a worthy help mate. Yet even as a couple they were incapable of meeting the needs that Jake's ministry presented. Knowing this, they relied on the power and direction of the Holy Spirit.

Paul spoke about the power of the Holy Spirit as a tangible and mighty force. As we wisely surrender our own strength, as Jake did by admitting he benefited from Cora's help, we begin to learn how to possess our inheritance—a life lived in the Spirit.

Prayer

"Father, we thank You for the power of the Holy Spirit. Teach us to lay hold of this power by means of surrender. In Jesus' Name, amen."

Do You Know My Jesus?

April 11

As the Father has sent me, I am sending you.

John 20:21

Wilson was a big man with a gentle heart. He spoke with an impediment, yet was undaunted by people asking him to repeat himself from time to time. He was uneducated, yet in spite of that, was not ignorant. Wilson was a godly man. He loved Jesus.

When Wilson's eyes were open, he had one thing on his mind: to introduce everyone he could to his Jesus. With a humble spirit and a smile that lit the room, he would look you straight in the eye and ask, "Do you know my Jesus?"

Wilson understood the spiritual death sentence that hangs over every nonbeliever. He couldn't bear the thought of allowing anyone to suffer eternal separation from the One Who could save them from their sins.

God took him home not so long ago. At his funeral, there were tears of sorrow. But you could hear people say with profound sincerity and a catch in their throat, "Well, he's with his Jesus now! You know, he asked me if I knew his Jesus! That's why I'm here."

✝

The man this gentle giant spoke of isn't a fictional character in a fairy tale, as some would believe. He is a Savior and the door to salvation to those who are perishing. In John's gospel, we can almost see Jesus imparting the Holy Spirit and all His power to the disciples in anticipation of Pentecost. He commissioned them to tell everyone they met about His gospel of grace. Wilson heard Jesus' commission. He responded with the faith and conviction of someone who knew his Commissioner firsthand.

Jesus has issued the same offer to all who believe, the offer to look someone in the eye and ask, "Do you know my Jesus?" With an eternal death sentence hanging over those who have never claimed the Name of Jesus, can we refuse the commission and look in the mirror?

Prayer

"Cause us to be weak in our own power and to stand
strong in Yours, Lord Jesus. When we are afraid,
when we would be embarrassed, help us remember
that unless we ask them, 'Do you know my Jesus', they
may spend eternity alone without You. Amen."

Ransomed

April 12

> For there is one God and one mediator between God and men, the man Christ Jesus, who gave himself a ransom for all men.
>
> 1 Timothy 2:5

The voicemail sounded like a line out of a Hollywood movie. "Bring five hundred thousand dollars to the mall parking lot tomorrow at two-thirty or your kid dies! Small bills, none in sequence, nothing larger than a twenty or smaller than a five. Drive to the southwest corner of the lot. Pull in beside the dark blue van with tinted windows. You'll see a NY Yankee's pennant on the antenna. Even trade: your daughter for the money. Don't do anything stupid. Tell anyone and she dies!" There was a muffled "Mommy!" cut off as the caller hung up.

Terrifying thoughts threatened to overwhelm Jennifer. She fought for focus. How were they supposed to come up with that kind of money? Who did these people think they were? Five hundred thousand dollars was impossible! How did they get Beth? She speed-dialed Peter's cell and franticly told him about the message and ransom demand. Peter immediately called his father, a city police officer, and explained the situation.

At two-thirty the following day, the SWAT team converged on the van just moments after the switch was made. Beth was safe! The kidnappers were on their way to jail.

✝

There are two states of existence: captive or ransomed. We experience one or the other. Every day, Satan takes hostages. Jesus waits for their cry to be set free. Many of us live in fear of Satan's authority, believing his power can keep us in bondage. But Jesus didn't die for us to remain ignorant of the enemy's limitations. We have authority to break the chains of oppression.

Satan is running a bluff! Jesus' authority over sin is superior to Satan's hold on our lives. But we have to ask for the deliverance. Jesus paid the price for our freedom. Satan is counting on you not understanding that when Jesus gave Himself as a ransom for all men, *He did it for you!*

Prayer

"We cry out for freedom, Lord. Come break the chains that bind us, Holy Spirit. The enemy says we can never get victory. Show us the way to walk into Your power. In Jesus' Name, amen."

Into Satan's Domain

April 13

On those living in the land of the shadow of death a light has dawned. For unto us a child is born.

Isaiah 9:2, 6

There had been no end to the frustration and struggles Rena had endured. It seemed like the deck had been stacked against her from birth. Born two months premature to a drug-addicted mother who couldn't support her, she'd been in and out of foster care until the age of twelve and had finally found a permanent home with the Donaldsons.

Rena, who suffered with subdued mental acuity, had struggled in the school's special needs class. She couldn't seem to make the pieces of the puzzle fit. The Donaldsons prayed that before the next school year something would break in their daughter's favor.

When next year arrived, Mom led Rena into her new classroom. They were greeted by bright colors and life-size animated figures pasted on every wall in the room. On the chalkboard was a pastel rainbow arching over the words, "Welcome to Miss Jenny's Classroom!" Rena pulled Mom down to her level and exclaimed, "I like this place, Mommy! Can we stay awhile?"

Miss Jenny greeted them with a bright smile, knelt down, and said, "I've been so excited and just couldn't wait to meet you, Rena. Welcome to my classroom! We're going to have so much fun!"

†

In one brief moment, Rena's struggles changed. Instead of it being Rena against the world, it became Miss Jenny and Rena in a partnership that could see possibilities for the future. Miss Jenny loved to turn on the lights for those who struggled to understand. She was gifted in discerning a child's needs and developing a curriculum to meet those needs.

When Jesus entered Satan's domain over seven hundred years after Isaiah's prophecy, it was a light-switch event. In one brief moment, Israel had a new teacher; One Who cared about their welfare and future.

Jesus showed them a brighter path that led out of the darkness into His marvelous light. You can hear Him say, "I've been so excited and just couldn't wait to meet you!"

Prayer

"Father of the bright and morning Star, we give thanks for Your precious gift of light and love. Teach us to faithfully follow Jesus' path through this dark world. Amen."

When He Calls

April 14

And this is love; that we walk in obedience to his commands.

2 John 6

Clay sensed God calling him to assume a more prominent role in Dennis's life, so he took Dennis up on his job offer. Currently in the midst of a writing project, he felt he could handle both. Three months into his new position, he was experiencing writer's block. He couldn't seem to silence the marketing voices at the end of the workday and recover the writer once again. Unable to formulate even a single sentence, his writing had come to a standstill. The sales position wasn't providing enough income to justify staying on, yet this wasn't about the money; this was about Dennis. Since the writing project had also been commissioned by God, Clay struggled over what to do.

After praying for revelation, Clay realized that God wanted him in close proximity to Dennis for now, mentoring and nurturing him. So, out of obedience, he would stay on with Dennis, and the book could wait. Clay had learned through experience to trust God. He knew that if and when God wanted the book completed, He would fan the flames of literary creativity. His task right now was to be God's voice in Dennis' life.

✝

Spiritual flexibility is one mark of spiritual maturity.

There will be times when God will ask us to drop what we're doing just to see if we'll obey. This can be a frustrating experience for someone who is rigid in their faith, especially if there are no open lines of spiritual communication.

Knowing what God wants at any given moment requires talking with Him. Trusting Him enough to let ourselves be moved from one assignment to another requires faith and an even temperament. These are virtues gained through experience.

As our children grow, they are given opportunities to learn the benefits of obedience. Some lessons come hard-learned. We can almost hear God whisper, "But don't you love it when they respond immediately when you call?"

Prayer

"Lord, sometimes I don't do spontaneous very well.
Help me submit my will and life to Yours. Show me
what today's right thing is. In Jesus' Name, amen."

Me-ism

April 15

Do nothing out of selfish ambition or vain conceit, but in humility consider others better than yourself.

Philippians 2:3

Gretchen slowed her vehicle as she approached the construction area. With no flagmen to direct traffic, and even though the road crew was working in the opposite lane, vehicle after vehicle continued to ignore Gretchen's legal right-of-way by pulling out from behind the crew and into her lane, hurrying toward their destination.

As car after car repeatedly disregarded traffic laws and safety, Gretchen fought for composure, resisting the urge to lay on her horn and shake her fist out the window in protest.

Finally, after some twenty additional vehicles played follow-the-leader, one vehicle stopped, deferring to Gretchen's lane of traffic. As she eased forward, Gretchen observed the driver giving her a shoulder-shrug, with hands raised in the *I have no idea why people do what they do?* gesture. It was his way of letting her know he'd noticed her predicament and that he appreciated the way she'd handled the long line of impatient drivers.

Someone had been watching! Gretchen smiled, returned the gesture, and was extremely thankful she'd fought the urge to retaliate. *"What kind of witness would it have been if I had gone off on one of them, Lord? Thank You for helping me act as one of Your children should,"* she prayed silently.

✝

Many, if not all of us, have experienced me-ism. It's blindingly apparent in other people; but how often do *we* barge ahead, failing to consider others and whether what we are doing will have an adverse affect on them?

Paul urged the Philippians to act like Christ instead of the world. For in doing so they would provide a good witness and find opportunity to share the gospel. How many times have we regretted our actions *after the fact,* wishing we had it all to do over again? Someone is always watching. And when we bull our way through life because of a sense of entitlement, the selfishness of me-ism speaks loud and clear. On the other hand, if we imitate Christ, we, and those who need to see Him, won't rob God of the opportunity to be seen.

Prayer

"Help me put my selfish ambition and me-ism
to death, Lord. Teach me to consider others
ahead of myself. In Jesus' Name, amen."

What Will Your Harvest Look Like?

April 16

Therefore, as we have opportunity, let us do good to all people.

Galatians 6:10

Before she lifted dinner, Nancy had one last errand to run. "I'm taking a plate to Dorothy. I'll be right back; then we'll eat!" she hollered from the kitchen and headed out the back door, across the yard to her next-door neighbor's.

As she came through the door, Dorothy said, "Oh, hon, you didn't have to do this. But it sure does smell wonderful! You're just too good to me." Tears filled her eyes.

Nancy loved to give of herself to her seventy-something neighbor. "I just figured you might be tired after doing yard work all day, and I didn't want you to have to spend time making yourself something for dinner, too. Besides, it blesses me to see the smile on your face!" she teased as she brought the food to the table, placing it in front of Dorothy. "I'll come back later to get the plate, so don't fuss about it," she spoke over her shoulder as she headed back out the door.

✝

God *could* meet every need for everyone, so why doesn't He?

Because He has chosen to exhort *us* to do good to all people. In essence, He's saying, "If something is going to get done, I'd like you to do it."

Servanthood 101 is a lesson in crop production. This classroom gives us ample opportunities to learn how to sow seed from the heart. When Paul advised the church in Galatia to do good, he was challenging them to sow *good* seed. He challenged them to prove a point: what goes around comes around. It's a spiritual harvest law. As we move the focus off our self-centered nature to one of compassion, off of our me-first attitude to a this-matters-more-than-my-personal-comfort mind-set, we see this law in action.

God challenges us to do random acts of kindness on His behalf, not looking for something in return, but to bring His blessing with the understanding that He rewards His servants.

Prayer

"Help me look for and see opportunities to serve others, Lord. Stretch me for Your purposes and teach me to have a servant's heart. In Jesus' Name, amen."

Where Do Goldfish Go?

April 17

In that day the Root of Jesse will stand as a banner for the peoples.

Isaiah 11:10

It was a somber occasion. Goldie the goldfish was being laid to rest in the backyard beneath the big maple tree. Six-year-old Lynn and ten-year-old Pete had tears in their eyes as Daddy shoveled dirt over the little box they'd helped him construct. "Will we see Goldie when we get to heaven, Mommy?" came Lynn's wonder-filled question.

Death is like that, Dad thought as he finished the burial. *It brings out those difficult-to-answer questions.*

Mom thought for a moment and then said, "Well, honey, the Bible says when we die, if we love Jesus, we will live with Him forever. I don't know if Goldie will be there when we get there, but it won't be so important since you'll be with your best friend, Jesus."

Daddy added, "The Bible also says that there will be animals in heaven and that little children will lead them. So since other animals will be in heaven, maybe Goldie will be there too. We'll just have to wait and see."

Satisfied with these answers, the kids prayed that they would get to see Goldie when they got to heaven and then somberly went off to play.

✝

Scripture is explicit in its revelation of animals in heaven. The eleventh chapter of Isaiah leaves no doubt as to their presence. It does not, however, tell us whether our pets will be there. But just as the mother in today's story revealed to her children, our priorities will change the moment we are in the King's presence. We will no longer grieve the loss of our pets, nor will our hearts ache with that emptiness created by their passing. We will stand in awe of the Son of God and experience unparalleled joy under His banner of love.

To a young child, the hope of seeing their pet is enough. As we mature in Christ, the hope of seeing Him fills any void the death of an earthly pet might leave.

Prayer

"Death seems so permanent, Lord. Please be close and comfort
us while we wait to be with You in our permanent home.
And if Goldie is there, please tell her we said hello! Amen."

You Can't Take Them Back

April 18

Reckless words pierce like a sword, but the tongue of the wise brings healing.

Proverbs 12:18

"Get out of my house! *Now!*" Logan shouted at his sister, pointing toward the door. The muscles in his neck bulged with the fierceness of his attitude; his face was contorted in rage. In one single moment, Logan had lost control of his actions, and his tongue had become a weapon. Emotion overrode intelligence and restraint. He regretted his words the moment he heard them out loud, but he couldn't take them back now—his pride wouldn't let him. *Doggone her anyway!* he thought. *I didn't ask for her opinion!*

Stunned beyond understanding, Sarah turned and ran from the house; the wound was immediate. Jumping in her car, she slammed the door, started the car, ripped the shifter into reverse, and backed out of the driveway. In her confused state, Sarah backed right into the path of a dump truck carrying a load of gravel to a nearby construction site. Rushing out the door, Logan saw events unfolding; he was too late to help. He watched in horror as the power of his words affected his sister's life. Sarah would spend three weeks hospitalized in traction, and would need to learn to walk again.

✝

One of our greatest struggles is controlling our tongue. James wrote a whole chapter about it. Solomon speaks to the recklessness of our words, the lack of consideration we give to how our speech affects others. Logan would have given anything to take back the venomous arrows he lodged in Sarah's heart. But once they're out, they can't be recovered.

None of us is exempt in this matter.

We know how much it hurts to be wounded by someone's speech, so why is that so hard to remember when we find ourselves in moments of critical decision? Preparation and the lack of it. It's a wise man that thinks ahead. He understands the consequences of his words and acts accordingly. Kind words bring healing and favor. Harsh words pierce and destroy. Once past our lips, we can't take them back.

Prayer

"Help me bring favor in times of crisis, Lord. And forgive me for the times my tongue wounds. Teach me to think ahead. In Jesus' Name, amen."

My Dad's Taller Than You!

April 19

This day the LORD will hand you over to me.

1 Samuel 17:46

David was a spirited six-year-old. One day, a friend of his dad's came by for a visit. The moment David saw him, he climbed out of the pool and walked right up to the man and defiantly proclaimed, "My dad is taller than you!" Initially taken aback, the man smiled and quickly formulated a response. Not wanting to belittle the boy's spirit, yet wanting to have some fun, he replied, "Maybe if I'm lying down." Looking over David's head at his at dad, the friend went on to say, "But you know something, David, that's a good attitude to have. You should have confidence in your dad. He's the one who watches over you and takes care of you. We need to know our dad has the ability to handle every problem we experience." Kneeling, he added, "But would you mind if I gave you a piece of advice? You'd be more convincing if you took off the swim mask and snorkel!" He rubbed David's head and winked at his friend.

✝

David's attitude may have been a bit aggressive for a six-year-old, but his paternal perspective is a lesson we could learn from. We get our first picture of our heavenly Father through the actions of our earthly fathers. David's father must have made quite an impression on him in the first six years of his life.

We need more fathers who instill David's passion and allegiance, fathers whose children know, without having to ask, that they will always be there in times of trouble. We need the model that says, "I'll handle every problem you have. Just bring it to me." David's initial assessment of his dad's friend was one of a warrior. He wanted the enemy to know he wasn't afraid; his dad could, and would, handle him if he had come for trouble. We need to see our heavenly Father through David's eyes. And on that subject, let me ask: Who was taller, David or Goliath?

It depends on when you measured: before David's Dad had His say or after!

Prayer

"Father God, I thank You that You are taller
than any problem I will ever face. Amen!"

The Messenger
April 20

And no messenger is greater than the one who sent him.

John 13:16

Having gone over her notes for the umpteenth time, Gail looked out the window of the plane, focusing on nothing in particular. She was replaying Stephanie's earlier words of encouragement, "Look, Gail. I know you can handle organizing the final stages of the event. There's not that much left to do. It's not life and death...well...okay, maybe spiritually, but you can't do anything that will cause anyone coming to the conference to accept or reject Jesus; you're just the messenger. You do your part—God will do the rest."

The Women of Faith Conference was a week away, and Gail didn't want to make any mistakes. "Lord, I need Your help. I would never want to cause anyone to miss her chance to meet You. Please guide my actions and help me bring glory to You."

God's response was almost immediate. The woman in the seat next to her happened to see Gail's to-do list on her legal pad and asked, "I couldn't help but see your notes. Is that conference open to anyone? I'll be in town, and I'd love to come and see what it's all about."

The subsequent conversation found this stranger accepting Jesus as her Savior. As Gail deplaned, she was filled with the wonder of God. "He always knows how to reach me."

✝

Jesus' disclosure to the apostles was, and is today, revelatory in nature. We are His messengers, ambassadors of the gospel of Jesus Christ. It was, and always will be, His message unto salvation reaching for the lost. He alone is the power of the message. That should give us tremendous confidence and comfort knowing we are not held liable for someone's response, only for taking every opportunity to share the message when it comes. When those moments arise, just remember Who sent you and tell them about Jesus. All of heaven stands in awe of the privilege given to the messenger.

Prayer

"Show me who needs to hear Your gospel of love today,
Jesus. Give me confidence to look for them instead of
waiting for them to come to me. May I always remember
the day I fell in love with You myself. Amen."

It's Just Not Fair!

April 21

I am the LORD your God, who teaches you what is best for you.

Isaiah 48:17

"It's just not fair! It's not a school night. It's only eight o'clock; it's too early for bedtime!" Jeffrey argued.

"I know it doesn't seem fair, buddy, but it's your bedtime," his father said.

"But, Dad!" Jeffrey whined. "I can't sleep with you guys out there laughing and having fun! Please, Daddy? I am eight, you know," came his pitiful plea.

"Sorry, buddy. The answer is no. Now, climb in bed, and we'll say our prayers."

Three minutes after Dad left the room, Jeffrey had his door cracked just enough to listen. *I can't believe they're torturing me like this!* he thought. The temptation to eavesdrop was more than he could handle. Deciding to risk his father's wrath, he snuck out the door and down the hallway. As he peeked around the corner, he was spotted by one of his mom's friends. She smiled at him and winked. *Oh no! I'm gonna get it now!* he thought, sprinting for his room as quietly as he could. He silently closed the door, jumped into bed, and pulled the covers up over his head, pretending to be asleep. "It's just not fair!" he muttered, hoping that strange woman wouldn't tell on him.

✝

The prospect of missing something that holds the promise of fun and excitement can be overwhelming. Like Jeffrey's father, God gave His children sensible instruction. But Israel was stubborn and did not pay attention.

Sometimes God's instructions make no sense to us. In His infinite wisdom, God knows what's best for us. He hopes we will listen and obey even though we may not completely understand. As in Isaiah's forty-eighth chapter, God tries to spare us suffering. But we, like the Israelites, sometimes stomp our feet and complain when things don't suit us. We pout and rebel, defiantly proclaiming, "It's just not fair!"

As we mature, we discover that our parents were protecting us from ourselves. God wants to do the same. But here's the catch: it requires faith, faith that what He told Isaiah is true.

Prayer

"Forgive my petulant attitude, Lord. Help me learn
to trust You more. Teach me to lean on You instead of
always pulling on Your hand. In Jesus' Name, amen."

The Power of the Anointing

April 22

How I long for the months gone by, for the days when God watched over me.

Job 29:1

The crowd pressed in, as if leaning forward in their seats would get them closer to heaven. They were hungry for every word! This no-name evangelist was bringing a message full of indictment, yet it was so true that it could not be denied, and no one attempted to do so. He was calling them to repentance through a message about God's anointing.

The evangelist was speaking about Job and how in the midst of his greatest trials, Job was remembering how blessed his life had been during the fullness of God's anointing.

His words carried power and truth, conviction and challenge. People began to weep and fall to their knees in repentance. God's Word was alive with the glory of the Lord, and people were responding to God's presence.

The pastor could sense a supernatural shift in the atmosphere; it was as if a direct portal from heaven had opened and God Himself were pouring out His anointing oil on those who were bold enough to believe what the Scriptures said was true.

✝

They had come hungry for God, not just for His healing or deliverance, but also for God Himself. And in response to such hunger, God had showed up in power! He wanted them to *know* the truth imbedded in the message: Job had been blessed with God's anointing because he had rescued the poor and the fatherless; he had assisted the dying at the time of their death; he had lifted the spirit of the widow and was righteous and just. Such a clear message: "My anointing is on those who work in the trenches. They will experience power to complete this work."

God still anoints those who are hungry to love the lost and help the less fortunate.

Prayer

"Lord, bring forth rivers of oil from Your Rock, and pour them upon me so I can go forth and minister in Your power. I want to work in power for You. In Jesus' Name, amen."

What Goes Around

April 23

Give, and it will be given to you… For with the measure you use, it will be measured to you.

Luke 6:38

Luke smiled as he hung up the phone. God had a sense of humor. Luke had just been given a new-to-him used car, no charge. It had been a gift from someone at his church to replace his lately deceased Honda Accord. His smile was wonder filled, and this was where God's sense of humor applied, because now the shoe was on the other foot—on the other foot because in the past, Luke and his wife, Connie, had given away several vehicles. It had been such a blessing to see the appreciation in the beneficiary's eyes, hence God's ironic economy: "Give and it will be given to you."

Luke and Connie had both been raised in homes where helping others was a way of life. Never well off financially, they learned to love blessing people for the Lord.

This situation gave them a unique perspective. They went from blesser to blessee. Being on the receiving end was certainly different—humbling. They knew what their benefactor would feel each time he saw them driving this car and that made it easier to accept his generosity.

They blessed God for the gift and asked His blessing on their benefactor, who had been so generous in *their* time of need.

✝

This couple hadn't given away vehicles in the hopes that someone would return the favor someday. They had done it out of a spirit of love and giving, with a heart that heard the voice of the God whispering, "Someone needs My blessing. Will you be My instrument?"

This incident does, however, point out the truth of today's text: if you are a giver, it will not guarantee God's immediate blessing; it does, nevertheless, promise God will give to you in the same way you give to others.

Prayer

"Lord, because of Your great love and mercy, I give all
I have freely to You to do what You want. How could
I do anything else? It's all Yours anyway. Amen."

Love Deeply
April 24

Love ... always protects, always trusts, always hopes, always perseveres.

1 Corinthians 13:7

Adrian and Jennifer devised a unique wedding gift for their young friends. Instead of something traditional, they decided to pass along one of their favorite books. Hidden within its pages were three restaurant gift certificates and a handwritten note encouraging them to love deeply. The book, written by a Christian author, gave practical ways in which to enrich our relationships and fend off complacency in marriage.

There was a catch though; this couple might not read the book immediately and may not find the certificates for years. In truth, that was exactly how they envisioned their plan working out. Hopefully, when in times of struggle, they would remember the book, pull it off the shelf to gain some inspiration, and there find wisdom, the note, and the gift certificates.

In the note was a simple message: "When it feels like love is ebbing, press on! Remember the hope you shared in courtship. Use one of the gift certificates today. Learn to listen to each other; never give in; always persevere, dare to love deeply!"

Thirty years of marriage had provided Adrian and Jennifer with a measure of wisdom.

✝

God has provided this same wedding gift for us, His bride. Not that we would only open His Word in times of trouble, but that especially during those times we would press on and seek to find the wisdom He has buried deep within the pages of Scripture.

Wisdom comes through experience. Seldom do we learn lessons by hearing about them. Most of the time, events must first happen to us before they have any meaning in our lives. In those times, we can benefit from the experience of others, but only if we ask for help. God loves us so deeply that He has hidden timeless and pertinent treasures in His Word. Just for us, just for now.

Prayer

"In those times when we need a boost, Lord, lead us to
the correct passage in Your Word. And please send us a
messenger of love who has been where we are now. Give
us courage to love deeply. In Jesus' Name, amen."

Hypocrite? Not Me!

April 25th

God, thank you that I am not like other men.

Luke 18:11

Set free from the ravages of drug addiction, Jamaal had been out of prison for two years. He had re-surrendered his life to Christ, and his rebellion was over. He'd made a complete turnaround, his life becoming a positive influence on those around him. But recently his wife had observed another tempter enter her husband's life: the spirit of judgment!

He seemed able, and willing, to spot every small offense in others. It was as if Jamaal noticed things at the seed stage, and felt compelled to *'set things straight'*, as he put it, *'before they got out of control'*. No one could offend God without Jamal becoming aware of it.

For six months, Jamaal intervened for the Lord, keeping score of every transgression, remarking to his wife about other's shortcomings. One day his wife felt led to call him on his *righteous* behavior, saying, "When did you become the Holy Spirit, Jamaal?"

It took a few days for it to sink in, but Jamaal realized his actions were judgmental at best…hypocritical at worst. Repentant for his hypocritical spirit, Jamaal asked God to remove his eyes of judgment, and replace them with eyes of love.

✝

Quoting Oswald Chambers, "The average Christian is the most penetratingly critical individual." As Christians we can quickly qualify as Spiritual Supreme Court Justices if our hearts aren't constantly surrendered to the One True Judge. It's so easy to watch others make mistake after mistake, thinking that we, like the Pharisee in today's text, are above such things.

The world loves to call us hypocrites. And sadly, many times they're right. We don't do as we say or should. Hypocrisy is not only saying one thing while doing another; it can also be veiled behind self-righteous arrogance, unde-tectable to the one being hypocritical. Chambers also said, "…in the spiritual domain nothing is accomplished by criticism."

What we look for we will find. Hopefully, we are looking for Jesus in those around us.

Prayer

"Forgive me when I get off track, Lord. I sometimes don't even recognize when it's happening. Help me always look for the good in others. In Jesus' Name, amen."

Stop Getting Saved
April 26

For I have the desire to do what is good, but I cannot carry it out.

Romans 7:18b

Evan sensed movement and looked up to see Kenny, his twelve-year-old son, heading for the altar. Concluding a powerful message, the pastor had given an altar call. "If you need Jesus, then I want you to get up out of your chair and come stand at the altar and ask Him to be your Lord and Savior. Come right now while we wait." That's what Kenny was doing—for the third time this month.

Following the service, Evan asked him, "Why'd you go to the altar today, buddy?"

Kenny timidly answered, "I called a girl a bad name at school the other day and needed Jesus to save me again." Evan sought the right words to reach his son's tender heart. He opened his Bible and read Romans 7:14–25 to Kenny. He read it in its entirety, then reread each verse, explaining, "Kenny, Paul, a *mighty* man of God, struggled with sin all his life. It did not make him *unsaved* each time he sinned."

He finished by explaining that when we sin, it does not negate our salvation; it means we made a mistake we need to repent of and then do our best not to repeat it.

✝

Kenny is not alone in his Christian walk. Many Christians walk around without a true understanding of sin versus salvation, thinking that God is this mean bully keeping track of each offense in order that He might hold them against us.

God knows what is in the heart of man, yet chose to forgive us. He does not expect Jesus to be crucified over and over again, nor does He need to be.

When we truly give our lives and hearts to Jesus, our salvation is complete at that moment; no one can take it away.

Understanding that we *will* sin and *when* we do, it's not resaving we need, but a heart of repentance. This is a picture of reshaping and renewing *our mind, not our salvation.*

Prayer

"Lord, help me understand that once I'm Yours,
I only need to turn away from the sin and not
be saved again. In Jesus' Name, amen."

Stocking the Shelves

April 27

Bring the whole tithe into the storehouse, that there may be food in my house.

Malachi 3:10

Grace didn't understand this "tithing thing," as she put it. Yesterday's sermon had been titled, "Stocking God's Shelves." The pastor had spoken about giving God the first fruits of our labor as an act of love and obedience. He spoke of God's instruction to the Israelites on this matter, referencing Old and New Testament Scripture. He said, "In reality, everything we have is God's. But because He loves us so much, He doesn't force us to tithe." He spoke about reciprocity and how we can't outgive God, reading from Malachi where God says, "Test me in this."

Grace and her husband, Reggie, were new Christians. All this stuff was foreign to them, but they wanted to do the right thing. So, out of obedience, Reggie and Grace began giving fifteen percent of their income—ten percent for tithe, five percent of offering—to help stock God's shelves. It was difficult at first, sitting down each payday and writing that first check to God. But they did it. And within the first two months, things began to happen. Reggie received a pre-evaluation raise, and Grace received an insurance settlement she knew nothing about. God was responding to their obedience to keep His storehouses full.

✝

The subject of tithing makes many people uncomfortable, and many get offended every time the collection plate is passed.

Taking into consideration that there are those in ministry who pollute what God has ordained, Scripture is clear on our financial responsibility to God's church. Building the kingdom requires finances. Whether we make a contribution or not is up to us.

When Jesus said, "The love of money is the root of all kinds of evil," He was saying that we either trust in Him for what we need or we trust in ourselves.

When we hoard our money, we are stealing our own blessings because God cannot and will not bless those who do not sow into His kingdom. "Bring" is a command with both a choice and a promise attached.

Prayer

"Lord, teach me to trust You and believe. Help money
to become a tool for the kingdom and not a vice
that seduces my heart. In Jesus' Name, amen."

His Wonderful Light

April 28

…A people belonging to God…who called you out of darkness into his wonderful light.

1 Peter 2:9

As they gathered around Jerry's hospital bed, what happened next could only be described as something otherworldly. Jerry had been battling cancer for two years, and the doctors had called the family together, sure he would not live through the night.

As they prayed, a smile appeared on Jerry's face, and he began to chuckle. His countenance changed from one of unrest to serene peace. Jerry's chuckling grew into joy-filled laughter, his smile a tooth-exposing grin. In the span of thirty seconds, the laughter became so contagious that everyone in the room was affected. Tears appeared at the corner of Jerry's eyes, and as suddenly as the laughter began, it subsided. His body became still, his smile transfixed. His eyes snapped open. It was evident to everyone in the room Jerry was looking directly at something or Someone. His vision narrowed momentarily, then recognition crossed his face. Tears flowed like rivers down both cheeks; they fell past his ears and onto his pillow. Two words escaped his lips in the briefest of whispers: "My Jesus!" Jerry closed his eyes, took two more breaths, and was still. His spirit had departed, yet the smile remained.

✝

Dying is when time ceases to exist and eternity is met face to face.

Many people testify to loved ones speaking the name of Jesus or seeing a bright light at the moment of their death.

The hope we have in Jesus transcends this world. It is the promise that we will spend eternity with our heavenly Father. In Him there is no darkness.

The antithesis of that promise is an eternity void of our Creator, and with that void comes a knowledge of our need for salvation due to our sin, yet never receiving it. Faced with the understanding that we will not escape this world alive, the choice we make today will determine where we spend all our tomorrows.

For those who believe and call on the name of Jesus, death is when you close your eyes and walk into His wonderful light.

Prayer

"Lord of light, send your Spirit to testify to the truth of eternity. Work in the hearts of men and women, boys and girls, unto salvation. In Jesus' Name, amen."

The Extra Step
April 29

Bring a gift in proportion to the way the LORD your God has blessed you.

Deuteronomy 16:17

"*La Biblia!*" the people whispered in reverence. Their heartfelt gratitude was apparent to those passing out Bibles.

Despite the fact that these were supposed illegal immigrants, this group felt that God was leading them to introduce them to the gospel of Jesus Christ.

Midway through their mission, the group began to realize they had not thought this through completely. These Bibles were printed in English, and unless these refugees not only spoke but also read English, this act of love and generosity was simply that. It showed they cared, but the gift was virtually useless.

Realizing their mistake, one woman wryly asked, "Does anyone here speak English?" From behind her came a shy, yet clear voice. "I do," said a young girl.

Turning, the woman ruefully spoke. "I apologize for our oversight. We didn't think about the language barrier before we set out today. We only thought to bring Bibles, not Spanish Bibles."

In awe, the young girl spoke, "*La Biblia* in any language is precious. And there are enough of us who can read English that we can read to those who do not. Your gift is received in the spirit it was intended. God bless you for bringing us His life-giving Word."

✝

Although it is a wonderful beginning, caring, in itself, is not enough when we are reaching out in the name of Jesus. We must speak the other's language, if not in voice, then in consideration. Good intention is only part of reaching out in the name of Jesus.

As this story reveals, we must think deeper than our own tribe or nation, including our customs, when we bring any gift so it may be better utilized. We must take that extra step.

We see and interpret through the lens of our own experience. If we do not expand our attention to include those things we do not encounter on a daily basis, we are only reaching out superficially, not wrong, but not complete in our ability to reach others for Christ.

Prayer

"Lord of every nationality, help my gift to be considerate
of other's true needs. Help it say, 'I care' in a way
that is thoughtful. In Jesus' Name, amen."

Commitment

April 30

For the eyes of the Lord range throughout the earth to strengthen the hearts of those whose hearts are fully committed to him.

2 Chronicles 16:9

Sherry began setting up her keyboard as André assembled the rest of the sound system. André was pastoring a small church on the campus of a local college in a sleepy little community. He and Sherry felt a deep sense of commitment to this body of believers. This was a unique congregation in that it was mostly made up of transient college students with just a few people from the surrounding countryside thrown in for good measure.

Three times in the past two years there had been evictions threatened by the school, trying to stop them from meeting on campus. Two times the church had appealed and been given a stay of execution. Today, however, would be their last Sunday in Horn Hall. Last Friday's board meeting had ended in what appeared to be a victory for the school.

As they completed setting up for the morning service, André and Sherry thanked God for the time they had been given in this building, winning young lives for Christ.

Having found a new place on campus to meet, they would continue ministering to the students. But this had been where they had begun their ministry for the Lord, and it would always cling to a corner of their hearts.

✝

Jesus' commitment to us, our salvation and sanctification, is almost impossible to comprehend. He allowed Himself to be led to a day where it appeared He had lost all hope of reigning as King. Only by His great act of love do we have hope of true life. In Him we have the perfect example of how to strengthen the body of Christ.

As we live for Someone else, serving those around us that they might know Christ, we discover where our strength comes from. Only through Christ's sacrifice and the power of the Holy Spirit do our hearts receive what's needed to walk out a life committed to Christ.

Prayer

"Thank You, Jesus, for teaching me about walking in grace. When I want to run, hem me in. When I falter, hold me up. When I fall, pick me up. When I have no strength, give me Yours. Amen."

May

Created to Be Dangerous

May 1

The LORD is a warrior; the LORD is his name.

Exodus 15:3

During his personal morning worship, Jacob began praising Jesus for the work of the cross, thanking Him for the suffering he endured on his behalf and for subjecting Himself to the scorn of those who would kill Him.

At one point, Jacob's thoughts turned to what felt like blasphemy; he actually had a vision of himself trading places with Jesus on the cross, not dying for the sin of the world, but wanting to relieve Christ of His burden. He felt a momentary sense of shame for even entertaining the possibility that he could take Jesus' place.

Yet, in that moment, the Spirit of God whispered, "Do not be ashamed of such thoughts. I created you to do great and mighty things. I placed in you the desire to rise to the occasion, to save the day, to be someone's hero; I created you to be dangerous. You have been made in My image. Am I not a warrior? Do we not have a foe that comes to steal, kill, and destroy? You also are a warrior created for battle! I expect you to have such thoughts. The work of the cross is not for the weak and frightened. You must be dangerous; a formidable opponent."

†

Ladies, your husbands, sons, fathers, and brothers were created to be dangerous. And for good reason; this world we live in is not safe.

C.S. Lewis said of Aslan (a character representing Christ) in the *Chronicles of Narnia*, "He is not a Safe Lion, but he is good."

Men, we were created to be dangerous, to stand against the injustice in *this world* and *the one just outside our vision*. If we are to care for those who cannot care for themselves, those who were not created to stand against the enemy in the heat of battle, then we must be dangerous! We must take our place on the watchman's wall (Ezekiel 33:7–9), not as bullies, but as protectors, warriors who would stand between those we hold dear and the enemies of heaven.

Prayer

"Lord Almighty, teach me to stand against an enemy
who wants me dead and powerless. Help me stand
as Your image bearer. In Jesus' Name, amen."

Deliberate Investments

May 2

Be Shepherds of God's flock...

1Peter 5:2

Hardy moved quietly, trying not to awaken anyone but his eight year-old son, Griff, "Hey Buddy," he whispered while softly shaking Griff's shoulder, wanting to awaken, but not startle his son.

Griff was groggy at first. Then, in that first moment of awareness where we lay hold of understanding, Griff sat upright, *they were going fishing!* "Is it time?!" he asked excitedly.

"Yep!" Hardy could barely restrain his laughter at his son's immediate transition from a dead sleep to wide awake, *Funny how the mind works its way through the fog of unconsciousness into stark clarity so quickly when it's something fun!* he thought.

Twenty minutes later, with breakfast consumed, fishing gear loaded, and the boat hitched to the truck, they set out for the lake and a day of adventure.

Griff was a live-wire, shooting rapid-fire questions, hardly allowing Hardy time to answer before the next one burst from his lips, "Where we goin' first?! Can I drive the boat?! Do we have 'nough worms?! Didja get the bigfatjuicyones?!"

"Whoa, Buddy! Don't wear yourself out before we get there!" Hardy smiled, remembering mornings like this when his Dad had looked at him in amusement, while shaking his head and patiently answering each question.

This was going to be a great day, full of possibilities; a day of memories waiting to be made and experienced!

✝

Hardy loved to fish because his father had taken the time to introduce him to the sport. The man had deliberately invested in his son; depositing knowledge, wisdom, and time, so that Hardy had the best chance at becoming a man of character, and one who looked out for others. Hardy, likewise, wanted Griff to be a man of character; someone willing to invest in others. In short, he understood a father's charge: *shepherd your flock.*

Our sons and daughters will exhibit only the characteristics we take the time to model for them. If we deliberately invest in them they will not disappoint us, or society.

The truth about time is that it is fleeting. We should endeavor to not miss a chance to plant good seeds into each moment provided.

Prayer

"Help me plant good seeds, Lord. Show me when and what to deposit into my flock's lives, Father. In Jesus' Name, Amen. "

What I Need

May 3

Your Father knows what you need.

Matthew 6:8

"I don't enjoy the new house church as much as our old group," Ray said. "It's not that I don't benefit from this one—I just really miss our old friends. I wish we were still together."

It was the third time in as many months that Ray had made this comment. He, Brett, and their wives had been part of the old group made up of six couples. They'd been together for over five years. They had shared struggles, and in doing so, had become very close.

The old crowd had split up, each couple leading their own group. Ray was missing the closeness tonight.

Brett smiled. "God knows how much we miss the old fellowship, Ray. He just loves us too much to leave us together too long. He wants us to develop new relationships. As God stretches us, we discover things about ourselves we would never have known otherwise. Trust Him a little longer, Ray. God knows what we need. He may even choose to bring us back together."

✝

Ray's desire to go back to the more comfortable and seemingly more nourishing group is not uncommon. Unfamiliar things can be awkward in the beginning. Ray wasn't remembering that it had taken him two years to loosen up in the old group. He just remembered the benefits he'd reaped.

We tend to resist change. But we can't grow if we remain anchored in the familiar. We can unknowingly get to where we worship the atmosphere created in close-knit groups and not the Creator of the atmosphere. It can and does happen without our recognizing it. Trusting God in the uncomfortable is where we grow the most. We gain invaluable experience when we let Him move us into the center of His will instead of demanding that He submit to ours. It's not always easy or comfortable at first, but the dividends we receive from being stretched spiritually are priceless.

The next time you encounter change, embrace it in expectation. God knows what you need.

Prayer

"I don't do change too well, Lord, and I need Your help seeing the benefit of new things. Give me a heart to trust You when I step out believing You know what's best for me. In Jesus' Name, amen."

Septic or Sanctified

May 4

But you were washed, you were sanctified.

1 Corinthians 6:11

Warren listened as the group discussed sanctification. There were varying perspectives; but, the main assumption was they were saved and that was enough. He smiled as he recalled the vision God had given him a few years before at a time when he had felt the same.

"Think of it this way, Warren," God began. "You're struggling through life, doing the best you can. But then you realize you're standing up to your chin in a septic tank. In your revelation, you determine that you cannot get out of the tank on your own, yet you come to believe that Someone else has the power to lift you out of the stench and onto solid ground, i.e., salvation.

"Let's say you accept His offer to be removed from your helpless situation, and He lifts you out of the mire and stench. In that moment, you are saved—but you still stink! You are still covered in contaminants that must be removed so you can be free of the vile things in your life. That is the process of sanctification. Unless you allow Me to wash away the dirt a little at a time, you will continue to smell like the world." Warren smiled as he shared with them God's desire that we be washed in the water of sanctification.

✝

For many Christians, there is a sense of complete relief when they receive salvation, and that's as far as they care to venture. Their lives are filled with things they would need to give up if they intended to come into a deeper relationship with Jesus Christ. They don't care that they still stink like the world; saved is good enough.

Others don't know there is more. So they continue on in blissful ignorance, smelling, not knowing something can be done to 'purify them.'

Some come to the knowledge that God wants more for us, and they set out to be washed in the waters of sanctification only to become uncomfortable, stopping part way through the process. God's desire is that we make a life-long commitment to sanctification, and in doing so, find unknown depths of cleansing!

Prayer

"I still have an offensive aroma, Lord. Continue to
wash me until I am completely clean. Amen."

R-I-S-K

May 5

As you go ...

Matthew 10:7

To Jonathan, it wasn't a risk. He'd learned to trust God for the results and not worry about how he looked. He had such a hunger to learn more about the nature of his Creator. He was convinced that miracles had not passed away. His reasoning? Christ is still building His church! The miracles seen in Jesus' era served a specific purpose; they pointed to a greater truth: God.

Jonathan believed that if God is still building the church, he was supposed to continue to ask the Holy Spirit to show up in power.

Sadly, many in his church felt that Jonathan was stepping over reasonable boundaries. Their lack of understanding didn't stop him. "Lord, only You are capable of strengthening Martha's weak muscles. Only You have the power to rid her body of this torment. Satan, loose your grip on this woman in Jesus' name. Jehovah Repheka*, cause power to come into her limbs and strength to her body. Raise her from this bed of infirmity, Holy Spirit. May it bring God glory and honor to work among us today. Amen."

God had been stretching Jonathan; the results of Jonathan's obedience had been awesome! Of the sixty-some people God had led Jonathan to pray for over the last few months, ten had been completely healed of terminal illness.

†

Many of Jonathan's critics were quick to point out that fifty-some people did not receive healing. Had Jonathan allowed their powerless approach to the gospel to influence his actions, ten people would have died. He chose to believe the inerrant Word of God—that God is doing today what He did in the New Testament church: "Healing the sick, raising the dead, cleansing those who have leprosy, driving out demons." This is *still* the church age. God has not yet sent Christ to get His bride.

Your belief does not change the truth: God is the God of the supernatural. We are His children, heirs to His power and authority. His desire is that we claim and use our inheritance now, when it will have the greatest affect on the kingdom.

What would you risk for the King?

Prayer

"Father, move on Your people to quicken them to
believe. Send Your power through us today. Amen."

* Jehova Repheka means the 'Lord who heals you' as in Exodus 15:26

I Am the Greatest*

May 6

Suffering produces perseverance; perseverance, character; and character, hope.

Romans 5:3–4

"C'mon, James!" Lester pleaded. "Just throw me a few pitches, pleeeeease? I won't ever ask again—I promise!"

"I can't, buddy. I gotta get to work. Just toss it up and hit it like I showed you."

Disappointed, Lester headed out behind the barn to do as James suggested. "Maaaaan." The word dragged out. "How am I ever gonna be the greatest?"

But Lester, being who he was, made the best of things.

Imagining the hayfield was Yankee Stadium, he tossed the ball into the air; it hit the top of its arc and began its descent. Lester hauled his bat back and swung, missing the ball completely. "Strike one!" he declared. Undeterred, he picked up the ball and repeated the process, this time tossing the ball a little higher, giving himself more time to prepare. The ball came down; Lester swung and missed again. "Strike two!" his mother heard him cry.

Taking a break from hanging out laundry, she peeked around the corner of the barn in time to see her youngest son retrieve the ball and launch it skyward once more. The toss was perfect! She watched the ball drop as Lester timed his swing. He swung for the fence and missed a third time. "Strike three!" he hollered. "You're out!" What she heard next made her giggle. "I *am* the greatest; that is a fact. But even I didn't know I could pitch like that!"

✝

Lester's hope-filled character is a lesson for us all; Lester's spirit prevailed. In his mind, he succeeded in spite of his apparent failure. He chose to view things from a lofty perspective. He saw himself as a victor no matter what it looked like in the natural.

In each of our disappointments, God includes a lesson for our benefit. These are character-building moments. If we lose hope and allow disappointing results to influence us negatively, we miss an opportunity to learn and grow. If we seek to learn the lesson God provides, we gain understanding.

Are you the greatest? The choice is up to you.

Prayer

"Sometimes it seems as if I fail, Lord. Teach me
to see with eyes of hope instead of a heart of
discouragement. In Jesus' Name, amen."

* See Acknowledgements

The Curb

May 7

And this is love: that we walk in obedience …

2 John 1:6

Winnie stared at the curb, wondering why Daddy had warned her that it was *out of bounds.* In her four-year-old mind, she couldn't understand how a curb could be a boundary; it looked to be quite safe. She didn't understand boundaries. But Daddy had spanked her once when he'd caught her sitting on the curb, so it must be more dangerous than it appeared.

She didn't remember feeling scared while sitting on it. But Daddy had been so upset that he had actually shouted at her, and Daddy never shouted.

Winnie walked closer to the curb, staring at it as if it were about to tell her the secret danger it presented. But nothing happened. "Oh well. Maybe Daddy is wrong."

As Winnie started to turn away, she looked across the street. Mattie, Winnie's cat, came out from behind the neighbor's house. She'd been rummaging through the neighborhood. Seeing Winnie, Mattie began bounding in her direction. As Winnie watched, Mattie ran into the road at the same time the next-door neighbor arrived home from work. Amid the squeal of tires, accompanied by an accelerated heart rate for the driver and Winnie, Mattie managed to leap out of harm's way! In that moment, Winnie received new understanding in regard to the curb. She scooped Mattie into her arms and scolded her, "I warned you to stay away from the curb! It's dangerous! Do you hear me?"

✝

Crossing the curb represented disobedience and a total disregard for authority. Like Winnie, we may not see any immediate danger and think, "Maybe God didn't say…" In disobedience, we push on; the lines become blurred, and God's commands and authority become mute.

We know we shouldn't be there; yet each time we cross the line, we lose a little more sense of the impending danger, and we lose a little more respect for the One in authority. If we persist in disobedience, we eventually find ourselves standing on the wrong side of a chasm we cannot cross on our own. It's in that moment we recall the Holy Spirit's warning, "Please, stay away from the curb."

Prayer

"Forgive me for my disobedience, Father. Help me to accept without question the limits You place in my life. Amen."

Know Mercy

May 8

And what does the LORD require of you? To act justly and to love mercy and to walk humbly with your God.

Micah 6:8

The board was terminating his teaching contract. It didn't matter that the charges against him were false and that lies had been perpetrated against him. The fact that he had been voted teacher of the year the past two years by this very board, and that he was loved by his students and peers alike, had been blatantly disregarded.

His integrity, character, and teaching performance caused anyone who knew him to doubt the allegations, and there was overwhelming support within the community.

Yet a course had been set; fear was a strong motivator.

ACLU attorneys had brought a lawsuit on behalf of the family who'd lodged the false complaint; so the board, acting in fear, proceeded with his termination. They had thrown him under the bus, no pun intended.

Everything within him cried, "But I didn't do this!"

He'd been told years ago, "Expect no mercy, yet never cease to give it."

He silently prayed. *Lord, You have extended mercy to me when justice would have brought eternal punishment. Help me remember that my actions dictate who I am in You. Help me extend that same mercy to those who speak against me. In Jesus' Name, amen.*

✝

In line with his character, this man was asking for the grace by which he and his family could walk so they might be an example of God's mercy to a group of people who didn't understand God's meaning of justice or mercy.

We are not naturally humble. Humility is a character trait that must be cultivated. When we are wronged, our first *human* response is to get even; we want justice! And quite honestly, we may deserve it. Yet Christians know that our eternal existence is based on mercy. Were we to receive our just punishment—justice—we would be damned to hell for eternity. When Christ died, it was to teach us to love in spite of difficult situations. Do you want justice or mercy from God?

Prayer

"When I get wounded I tend to lash out, Lord. Teach me to love justice and be merciful and to walk humbly. Amen."

From Deep Inside

May 9

They will sparkle ... like jewels in a crown.

Zechariah 9:16

As he studied the stone through his magnifying monocle, the jeweler could see that this last facet needed only a bit more polishing to make it perfect. Placing the stone jig against the polishing wheel and adding just the right pressure, he proceeded to remove the final flaw from the gem.

"There, that is enough!" he whispered breathlessly. Raising the stone so he could examine it once more, he found it exquisite. "The king deserves only the best!"

If the jeweler found it acceptable, the king would be thrilled! And so he should be, for the jeweler had spent many hours cutting this diamond. He had chosen just the right stone for clarity and color. "This stone's brilliance shall be unmatched."

The master jeweler took great pride in producing only the highest quality gemstones for those who could afford his services. He knew that not all diamonds were clear or white. Many were imbued with translucent, clear-as-glass colors, making them even more precious than white diamonds. This stone, chosen from one of the king's own mines, was a deep blue, its worth beyond measure. There wasn't another stone like this anywhere. "Perfect! It shines from its depths!"

✝

Gemstones are formed under great pressure. Many centuries of compression are necessary to turn coal and other porous rock into hardened, gem-quality diamonds, rubies, or emeralds.

The same is true of our Christian walk. We are subjected to the extreme pressures of temptation, trials, and the demands of daily living.

As the jeweler labored over the precious stone, his expertise and love for his trade brought forth a masterpiece. He knew that a stone's brilliance comes from inside, revealed by the skill and experience of the jeweler.

God labors over us with the skill of the Master, desiring to bring out the best in each of us. He knows exactly how much pressure is required to produce a gem-quality masterpiece. When we have been hardened correctly, He sets to work cutting and polishing our facets so that we might shine, reflecting the light inside.

Prayer

"Help me bear up under the pressure and polishing, Lord.
Make me a perfect jewel! In Jesus' Name, amen."

Ill Conceived

May 10

After desire has conceived, it gives birth to sin; and sin, when it is full-grown, gives birth to death.

James 1:15

He wasn't thinking logically. As a matter of fact, Mason hadn't had a rational thought in three days. "If I can just get a couple thousand more, I can turn this thing around." He'd maxed out three credit cards, taken out a signature loan yesterday, and now there was no money in his children's college accounts.

Driving to the nearest check exchange, Mason wrote a predated check, knowing he could never hope to cover it, and took the five hundred dollars cash the teller handed him. After repeating this process at three other check cashing establishments, he headed back to the casino. He returned to the same table, believing his luck had to change.

Two hours later, Mason watched the dealer drag away the last of his chips and stack them on the house tray.

"Oh, God. What have I done?" he said just above a whisper. "It wasn't supposed to turn out like this! I was supposed to win." Looking at the dealer he asked, "What do I do now? I've lost everything."

"I'm sorry, sir," the dealer replied. "Sometimes you get the beast, and sometimes the beast gets you."

✝

When we allow ourselves to be led into ill-conceived plans without counting the cost of our consequences ahead of time, we usually find ourselves sitting among the ruins of our lives and the lives of those who depend on us. The beast doesn't care.

Sin is like that; it comes wrapped in the appearance of something wonderful, promising us everything we desire. Without spiritual discipline, we *will* be led astray. The initial thought comes; it looks so easy. If we give the thought room, sin has been conceived. If not dealt with immediately, it has the potential to lead us away from rational thinking into a full-blown craving that leads to death.

Paul said, "'Everything is permissible'—but not everything is beneficial" (1 Corinthians 10:23).

To those who know the beast firsthand, there *is* help. Whether it's gambling, alcohol, drugs, pornography, lying, cheating, or stealing, tell someone; reach out. When you do, you'll find that Jesus has been reaching out for you.

Prayer

"Help me, Lord. Help me do what's right. Amen. "

Voice Recognition
May 11

And his sheep follow him because they know his voice.

John 10:4

"Hello?" Marvin greeted as he answered the phone.

"Hey, Marv! Been a while, man! How you doin'?" came the voice from the other end of the line.

"I'm doing fine; how about you?" Marvin responded, his mind trying to link the voice to an identity. Whoever this was, he expected Marvin to know him without introduction, even though it had been a long time since they'd spoken.

Marvin knew he should know who this was; the man's voice was so familiar. He knew he'd heard it many times. Yet, try as he might, recognition wasn't coming.

As the conversation progressed, Marvin tried to steer it in such a way that the caller would reveal something that would give away his identity.

Then, as in answer to his silent prayer, the caller said, "You remember when Buster and I had to carry you home after you stepped on the limb of that thorn tree? Man, that thorn musta been three inches long and half of it stickin' through your sneaker and into your heel! I still remember you tryin' not to cry. Lord, how that must have hurt!"

Instant recognition! It was Danny!

Without hesitation, Marvin responded, "I was cutting a way through that mess when you pushed me into it, Danny! You shoulda carried me back by yourself!" They both broke into laughter, Marvin thankful his childhood friend hadn't seemed to notice his lack of voice recognition.

✟

For us to recognize someone's voice, we must have some history, a bond that connects our lives. In recalling one memorable event, Danny brought immediate recognition of who he was.

In the same way, once Jesus becomes our Savior, His Spirit makes a connection that relates to our spirit. Early in our relationship when He calls to us, the Holy Spirit reminds us of the day we became God's child.

As we grow into a deeper relationship, we learn to recognize His voice a little sooner.

Today's text speaks of a time when we will *know* the Shepherd's voice. The more we share our lives with Jesus, the easier it becomes to recognize His voice.

Prayer

"Lead me into a deeper, voice-recognizing relationship, Lord. In Your Name I pray, amen."

Lies

May 12

You belong to your father, the devil...for he is a liar and the father
of lies.

John 8:44, 45

Larissa stood on the edge of the diving platform, asking herself, "Why did I
lie?"

She had boasted to several girls at her new school that she could perform
a one-and-one-half somersault off the ten-meter platform, the highest in the
school's aquatic center. Larissa had no idea that two of the girls in the group
were on the school's diving team. To her surprise—and horror—they had asked
for a demonstration. They thought it was great that the new girl was a proficient diver!

Well, she had boasted, and now it was either admit to the lie in shame or
jump off the platform, revealing her inability to deliver on her claim.

Larissa decided she would rather jump and fail than admit she had lied.
So, knees shaking violently, she threw herself off the platform, plunging to the
water below. She managed to complete the first rotation of the somersault, but
did not enter the water head first, as intended. Instead, Larissa landed on her
stomach in what was commonly known as a *belly flop*. Shaken, Larissa climbed
from the pool to hear one of the girls declare, "I kinda figured you were lying;
I can't believe you went through with it."

Ashamed, Larissa said, "I'm sorry I lied. I just wanted you to like me."

✝

In every case, lying is wrong and will only cause negative consequences. Once
begun, another lie is usually perpetrated to prop up the first. Soon we find
ourselves forgetting what we told to whom. So we continue to lie, building a
precarious tower of lies, living in constant fear of being found out. And eventually all the props come crashing down.

As in Larissa's case, Satan *always* fathers the *first* lie. He told Larissa that
she would be rejected unless she lied about herself. Larissa desperate desire to
be accepted by her new classmates became the vessel by which Satan tempted
her. And by giving in to the temptation, Larissa painted herself into a corner
and was caught in her lie.

Jesus says that when we lie, we belong to the devil. So the question is, "Do
I care who I'm being used by?"

Prayer

"Lord, You are the truth. Lead my heart, my mind,
and my mouth to always speak the truth. Amen."

Finders Keepers?

May 13

Your enemy the devil prowls around like a roaring lion looking for someone to devour.

1 Peter 5:8

As he exited the parking garage, Leon noticed a moneybag lying on the sidewalk. It was from the bank up the block. Looking inside, he couldn't believe his eyes. "There must be ten thousand dollars in here!" Looking around, Leon closed the bag and stood there, contemplating his circumstances. He knew the right thing to do was return it to the bank. Yet there came a quiet whisper. "Just take it back to your car. Stick it in the trunk. Nobody will ever know; finders keepers, right?"

Leon didn't know so many thoughts could occupy his mind at the same time.

Then, one thought surfaced to quiet all the others. "It's not yours."

He started toward the bank. "To keep it would be stealing. Even if I didn't get caught, I'd have to cover this up for the rest of my life. Nothing is worth that."

Leon noticed the TV news crew as he entered the bank. There stood a cameraman, tape rolling, while the reporter walked toward him, microphone in her hand, "Excuse me, sir. We're doing a special on honesty. We planted that bag on the sidewalk to see how people respond to finding the money. Would it be all right if I asked you some questions?" At that moment, Leon was never so glad to be a man of integrity.

†

Satan is no respecter of men. His only desire is to devour as many people as he can. He consistently leads people into a life of moral and spiritual debauchery because his lies are so cunning.

Have you ever watched a cat sneak up on a mouse? It does not announce its intentions. The mouse never knows it was being stalked until it's too late.

In the same way, Satan counts on our not recognizing the package until we've opened it and it's too late. He's banking on our inability to see past the wrapping paper.

Life is full of difficult choices. We will draw our conclusions from the well in which we hold our beliefs. We should examine those beliefs prior to the attack.

Prayer

"Show me when the devil is about to attack, Lord. Don't
let me fall for his schemes. In Jesus' Name, amen."

The Greatest Treasure of All
May 14

When a man found it, he hid it again...and sold all he had and
bought that field.

Matthew 13:44

Chris turned off the trail and struck out in a more direct line toward home.
He'd never been through this part of the forest, but he was tired and wanted to
get home. As he ventured on, he recalled stories from childhood his father had
told about people getting lost in this part of the woods.

Pressing on, Chris came upon an old stone foundation. It appeared to have
been a large structure in its day. His weariness momentarily forgotten, Chris
decided to investigate.

Walking the foundation's perimeter, Chris discovered the entrance to an
old cellar. It appeared to have been covered by dirt and weeds until recently
when the rotting wood had given way, sagging into the stairway and revealing
the cellar's existence.

Pulling a flashlight from his pack, he carefully descended the rickety steps.

Chris stood in shocked awe. The beam illuminated shelves lining all four
walls. On those shelves were crates of paintings, firearms, stacks of Confederate
money, and silver tea sets.

"Someone's Civil War plunder!" he said in hushed amazement.

Determining to keep this a secret, Chris gently placed the old door back
in place and sifted dirt over it. He would find out who owned this property and
do whatever was necessary to purchase it!

✝

Like the man in today's parable, Chris had to sell everything he owned to
purchase his hidden treasure; his investment was but a fraction of the return.

Chris was quite fortunate; he hadn't set out looking for treasure, only a
quicker way home. He could have continued on in his haste; instead he chose
to investigate. The cellar door could have remained covered, or the cellar could
have been empty. But they weren't, and a great treasure was discovered!

God's Word reveals the greatest treasure of all: salvation with eternal life!

God's desire is that we would stop along life's journey, investigate the treasure's value, and then decide for ourselves if the return is worth the investment.

Prayer

"Lord, lead me into my inheritance. Reveal its
value to my heart that I would seek nothing
more and settle for nothing less. Amen."

Who Says?
May 15

For when you eat of it you will surely die.

Genesis 2:17

The boys had been friends since Carp's family had moved in beside Benny's. Growing up together in a small-town subdivision, they shared troubles and triumphs, bumps and bruises. For six years they'd been exploring life together; today they were in the woods that bordered their backyards.

"If you eat that thing, you're gonna get sick," Carp said.

"Who says? It's only a stupid mushroom, Carp," Benny fearlessly replied as he popped the pinkish-looking mushroom in his mouth and began chewing. "See, I told you. Harmless. Here, try one," he dared.

"No way! My dad said to leave the pink-colored mushrooms alone. He said they'd make me really sick, maybe even kill me." No sooner had Carp made his declaration than Benny got a funny look on his face and started choking.

"My lips and tongue are getting numb. Help me, Carp. I'm gonna die!" he blurted out in fear.

"Spit it out! Spit it out! C'mon, we gotta get you home quick!" Carp said, grabbing his friend's arm and slinging it over his shoulder.

Fifteen minutes and two shots later, a scared and remorseful Benny was loaded onto a stretcher, an IV in his small arm to offset the anaphylactic shock he was experiencing.

†

Carp and Benny represent two general mindsets within society. One believes what they are told and follows the rules set before them; the other must figure it out for themselves. Many of us fall into the latter, causing ourselves and those we love a multitude of problems.

There is within us an incessant need to discover, lay claim to, and control the issues of life. God created us to go forth; but in some areas, such as today's example and text, we are forbidden to proceed. One step across the line can result in death, physically and/or spiritually. Who says? God says!

We are given free will. His Spirit tells our spirit which things are off limits. Even in our mistakes, His grace will chase us to the ends of the earth. He leaves it up to us to respond.

Prayer

"My independent mind-set leads me to places I shouldn't go, Lord. Please help me rein in that insatiable desire to explore places that are off limits. Amen."

Blocks*

May 16

You also, like living stones, are being built into a spiritual house.

1 Peter 2:5

John's mind was filled with questions. He'd received a call from his mother saying she had something to give to him. He, his wife, Marilyn, and their granddaughter were on their way there now.

As John walked into the foyer of the old farmhouse he grew up in, he spotted a long-forgotten metal ammunition case painted with tan porch enamel sitting on the side table. A deep chuckle escaped him as the distant past came rushing into the present.

Opening the lid, John pulled out a wooden building block. He was transported sixty years into the past when he'd last held these building blocks; back to the days spent on the sewing room floor building some of the most world-changing architecture. The older he got, the more intricate the structures became. What began as three blocks stacked upon each other had evolved into foundations for shopping centers, skyscrapers, and train stations.

Tinker toys, Lincoln Logs, and of course, these beloved wooden blocks had occupied much of his time during the long winter months. A sense of nostalgia, accompanied with emotion, surprised John. He thought of how he'd learned about building a life by playing with these simple blocks. "You had to lay a good foundation in order to raise a strong structure." He smiled as he turned and handed the block to his granddaughter, letting her get the feel of it.

†

It is impossible to build anything of substance without a solid foundation. John remembered the lessons from his childhood well; how he'd always made sure the bottom row of blocks were set just right before building higher. This had become true of his spiritual life. And his foundation remained solid.

If we are to grow and become the person God intends to use in His kingdom, we must first build our lives on the chief cornerstone...Jesus.

Peter emphasized the need to crave spiritual milk that we might *grow up*. And grow up we will. Our stability will be determined by the nutrition we ingest and the foundation upon which we stand. It is imperative to be nourished correctly, and only on Christ will we stand against the storms of life.

Prayer

"On Christ, the solid Rock, I stand! Amen."

* See Acknowledgements

Quiet Words

May 17

The quiet words of the wise are more to be heeded than the shouts of a ruler of fools.

Ecclesiastes 9:17

Janet liked Reed. He was one of the most intelligent and engaging people she knew. However, because of his intellect, Reed sometimes engaged in the wrong thing at the wrong time. Reed had the potential to rub you the wrong way because he tended not to recognize or care when he was stepping on toes.

This evening's event was becoming one such occasion…"No, Sir, you are wrong!" Reed adamantly asserted.

Janet, hearing the annoyance in Reed's voice, hurried over, grabbed him by the arm, and politely excused them. Once clear of the room, she asked, "What do you think you're going to accomplish arguing with the senator?"

"I want him to admit the truth about partial-birth abortion!" he said in defense of his actions. "He spun his stand on mass murder of the unborn, sighting errant statistics slanted to meet his liberal agenda!" Reed said malignantly. "I was setting him straight!"

Janet measured her response. "Look, Reed. We agree abortion is wrong; and partial-birth is especially vile. But this event is neither the time nor the place to confront the senator. If you want to debate the issue, call his office and set an appointment." Janet felt for Reed. His stand was one she shared. But he lacked the wisdom to temper his words. Hoping he would hear the wisdom in her words, she added, "Demeaning him in public won't change his heart, Reed."

"Perhaps," Reed conceded. "But wrong is wrong…no matter how you spin it."

✝

Reed may have meant well but his actions were misdirected and inappropriate.

Colossians 4:5–6 says we should be wise and full of grace when dealing with unbelievers. The wise seek instruction from God, through His Holy Spirit, before debating matters of importance; be it abortion, or otherwise.

Being sensitive to the Holy Spirit allows God the opportunity to temper our words with grace, and opens our heart to His leading so our words plant seeds of truth, not enmity.

Prayer

"Teach me wisdom, Lord. Help me to know and present Your truth quietly in love. Amen."

Violets

May 18

And hope does not disappoint us, because God has poured out his love into our hearts by the Holy Spirit, whom he has given us.

Romans 5:5

They each held a fist full of violets as they rode the thirty minutes to see Gramma in the nursing home. They were so proud of picking them—one or two at a time—from the blanket of little flowers covering the plush grass under the grape arbor.

The sisters had picked until they had what amounted to two brilliant bouquets of blue, purple, and white love! With smiles that matched the joy in their heart and climbing on stools to be seen, they held them at arms length and announced, "Here!" Gramma, who'd had a stroke recently, managed a smile. Delighted Gramma had liked their present, the little girls jumped from their stools and ran from the room, heading for their next encounter with life.

Shaking their heads and smiling, Mom and Dad watched as the girls flew out the door. They continued to sit at Gramma's bedside, marveling at the vitality of life. In two, it was increasing; in one, it declined, and through it all, the love remained alive, attentive, and selfless. As a tear slipped from Mom's cheek to the collar of her dress, she thanked God for creating flowers so little girls could use them to say, "I love you!"

✝

The cycle of life retains a hope for the future. In each little kindness, we reflect the love of God that His Spirit produces in us. As we grow older, we become more sensitive to His leading and to the gifts He gives us along life's journey.

As flowers bloom in season, we too develop into something beautiful as we draw nearer to God. We are blessed with special moments and memories that construct the substance of life. In those memories lies hope for the future.

Prayer

"Father of love, thank You for giving me relationships that cause my heart to soar and tumble with the events of life. May hope be seen in my life as I do my best to reflect the presence of Your Holy Spirit. Forgive me when it doesn't and help me adjust my attitude. In Jesus' Name, amen."

The Tenement

May 19

Take care of my sheep.

John 21:16

Jim and Char sold their Colorado ranch and used the money to purchase a rundown Colorado Springs tenement. They immediately began renovation, believing God had led them to this decision.

Over the next seven months they experienced times when they wondered how things would work out, but they never questioned that it would. Several times the project seemed doomed to delay, only to see miraculous things bring them back on schedule. Eight months to the day they'd sold their ranch, they opened the homeless shelter.

Char hired workers and interviewed volunteers between cooking and cleaning. Jim spent his days calling and visiting local businesses and churches asking for donations. His evenings were spent doing structural maintenance and whatever else needed done.

By the end of the first month, they were feeding and housing twenty-seven men and women. Both Jim and Char fell into bed exhausted at the end of each day. Feeding cattle and horses on the ranch had been rough work that had yielded a sense of accomplishment. Yet, it couldn't touch meeting the needs of God's flock!

✝

God isn't going to ask most of us to sell our homes and take on such a daunting task. But we are all capable of feeding God's sheep, and He expects us to do our part. Learning what our responsibility is requires thought and effort.

Not all of God's sheep are starving from a lack of physical nourishment or a lack of housing. Many need nourishment of another kind. Some of our elderly need rides to the store and help with their shopping. Broken families need a compassionate ear and wisdom in how to handle specific situations; their children need a mentor that may no longer be in the home.

Most of us fit in the category of going to work every day to provide the service we were hired for. A smile from behind the counter can do more for the person who needs to see it than all the money in the world.

Nourishment comes in a variety of packages. Discovering what someone needs requires us to be discerning, looking for signs.

Prayer

"Give me discernment, Lord. Show me who needs
my help today. In Jesus' Name, amen."

The Kid and the Camaro

May 20

Feed my sheep.

John 21:17

"No way! You serious?" Benjy asked.

Kyle, his older brother, had just handed him the keys to his 1968 Z28 Camaro.

Kyle looked him straight in the eye and said, "It was always gonna be yours, kid. Just 'cause you made a mistake didn't mean I wasn't gonna follow through on my promise. Just don't do anything stupid, okay?"

Kyle was referring to a night six months ago when he was still in Afghanistan. Benjy had snuck the Camaro out for a joyride and had gotten stopped for speeding. His dad had made him write Kyle a letter explaining the incident. Benjy figured Kyle would be so angry that he wouldn't follow through on his promise to give him the car when he turned eighteen.

But Kyle understood. He'd made mistakes. Looking at the excitement on his little brother's face, Kyle had to smile. All the times he and Benjy had shared working on the car before he'd shipped out on this last tour of duty had provided precious memories while he was away. Benjy had spent more hours washing and waxing the Z than Kyle had!

He pulled Benjy's letter from his pocket and handed it to him. "Don't forget, but don't let it define your future." A look of sorrow replaced the excitement on Benjy's face momentarily; true remorse showed he was sorry for his impulsive action.

✝

Has Jesus ever reinstated you? Has He taken you back to something or someplace you have abused and given it back?

Restoring is what Jesus does. He isn't looking to break our will, just bend it in the right direction.

Peter's heart was right. He'd just demonstrated a streak of impetuousness that needed eradicated.

We've all done things that we shouldn't have—some of them pretty serious, some of them harmful. But that's what is so amazing about the grace of God. It cannot be outrun! It's always there, waiting for us to fulfill our mission, waiting to restore us to a place of healing, where our impulsiveness is turned into kingdom purpose.

As in Peter's case, he'd made mistakes. But Jesus didn't allow it to define his future.

Prayer

"Thank You for that grace that never stops pursuing
me, Lord. Help me redefine my future. Amen."

May 21

Let us fix our eyes on Jesus … so that you will not grow weary.

Hebrews 12:2,3

It was the state track and field championships, and James was confident. He'd cruised to victory in his qualifier and didn't expect any serious competition in this event.

He'd trained hard for the one-hundred-meter hurdles, spending several hours each day perfecting his technique. He could soar over all ten hurdles, clearing them by no more than an inch. It was all in the snap and lean.

"Take your mark, set …" *Pow!* The starter's pistol sounded.

James got a good start and quickly took the lead. *Snap the leg, stretch for the next hurdle, stride,* he repeated to himself.

As he approached the final hurdle, James' lead had increased to ten meters over his nearest competitor. Glancing left and right to see where everyone else was, James's focus was momentarily distracted—just long enough for him to mistime the last hurdle.

Striking the top of the hurdle with his lead foot, James stumbled and fell headlong onto the track.

What had appeared to be a state title turned into devastating disappointment.

As he lay there regaining his senses, James realized he'd struck the hurdle because he'd waited too long to look back. That split second of distraction had caused him to misjudge the distance; it had cost him the race.

✝

It only takes one brief moment to become distracted. The pride of self-sufficiency can take our eyes off our intended target. In doing so, even for a moment, we can miss the mark, become disoriented, and possibly lose the race.

Distraction is one of Satan's most frequently used weapons. "Hey, over here," he whispers. And we unwisely give credit to a defeated enemy, looking away from Jesus for a glimpse at the world.

It's hard to remain constantly focused on Christ, not giving rent to the devil.

That's why the author of Hebrews was so adamant about *fixing* our eyes on Jesus, not just casually glancing His way once in a while.

There will always be hurdles in life, and we must have single-minded purpose if we are to clear them safely.

Prayer

"I tend to lose sight of You from time to time, Lord.
Help me fix my sight on You alone. Amen."

I Didn't Tell You to Do That

May 22

Then you will be able to test and approve what God's will is—his good, pleasing, and perfect will.

Romans 12:2b

Austin knew God was speaking directly to him as the pastor said, "Sometimes we cry out to God and ask, 'What's going on, Lord? Things are so screwed up. I don't understand it. What happened?' To which God replies, 'You weren't listening. I didn't tell you to do that.'"

Austin silently said, "You didn't say no when I asked, Lord."

God's response was immediate. "I didn't say no. But I didn't say yes either. I didn't tell you to do what you did." Then he felt God say, "What you did wasn't sin; it just wasn't what I told you to do. I gave you specific instructions. You chose to do something else. Your actions delayed My plan but did not stop it."

And in that moment, Austin's frustration over a recent situation became clear. He hadn't been able to figure out why God wasn't providing in the way he thought He should. Now he knew why.

Austin silently repented of his action and committed to doing what God had instructed him to do before. He was still learning to listen to God. It seemed like listening would forever be an ongoing lesson.

✝

Austin hadn't heard the *audible* voice of God, but it was as close as it got! He knew the Holy Spirit was relating God's thoughts to him. Austin had spent time learning to interpret God's voice by spending time with God. He'd speak (pray), then listen for God's response (meditate).

God speaks to us through His Word; prayer; His Spirit; His people, and our circumstances. Each is specific, and each requires time learning to interpret. But Paul says we can figure it out.

Listening for God to speak is a discipline that requires our attention and silence. We can't hear God's answer if we're doing all the talking.

Start at the beginning. Pick up His Word and prayerfully read it a little at a time.

Once we learn to speak the language, we will make better-informed decisions with less of a chance of hearing, "I didn't tell you to do that."

Prayer

"Help me listen for Your voice, Lord. Then
help me follow in faith. Amen."

The Fleece

May 23

If there is dew on the fleece … then I will know.

Judges 6:37

What they were doing looked like foolishness to those who didn't understand spiritual matters. Yet that hadn't stopped their work. And they were ninety-nine percent sure that God wanted them to continue their ministry. But wanting to be completely sure, they decided to put out a fleece. It had worked for Gideon. "Okay, Lord. You've led us this far. You even revealed the person we are to pray about. We haven't seen him in months. If You want us to continue what we're doing, cause this man to come back into our lives by the end of the week." With that, they went back to the work of their ministry.

The fleece had been laid out on Monday. It was now Saturday morning. To this point, the man was a no-show. Time was running short, yet they continued to watch in faith.

As it happened, there was an annual festival being held that day in their small town, just a few vendors selling their wares, a country band for entertainment, and a small car show. They enjoyed the beautiful day, holding hands as they walked and talked with friends and family. Just as they were about to leave, a man appeared from the crowd; he waved and walked toward them. The man in their fleece!

God had provided unmistakable evidence that He intended them to continue in what they were doing. God had responded, and it had settled the matter for them.

†

Not all our petitions receive this obvious an answer. Most of the time, we must interpret God's response through His Word, circumstances, continual prayer, and the leading of the Holy Spirit. Yet sometimes God removes all doubt.

God is not too big to be asked the difficult questions, nor too small to deliver an appropriate answer. What He wants more than anything is for us to ask. God wasn't put off by Gideon's fleece, not even the second time he asked. It was God's opportunity to reveal His nature to Gideon. He wants to do the same with us.

Prayer

"Help me step outside the natural into a supernatural spiritual life, Lord. Cause me to disregard the distractions and remain focused on You. Amen."

Who's to Blame?

May 24

Bear with each other and forgive whatever grievances you may have against one another.

Colossians 3:13

He set the VCR on record and went back to reading. He knew she hadn't seen this episode. They could watch it together when she got home.

Returning home, his wife noticed the VCR on record and asked in apprehension, "What tape are you using?" Instantly he knew what he'd done! The look on his face said what he couldn't voice. "Nooooo!" she cried in anguish.

They'd been watching home videos of their children that morning—precious times and events they had cherished for over twenty years—and now they were gone.

Recorded over them was a meaningless TV show, and there was nothing either of them could do about it.

For the next few hours they lived under the weight of his mistake, silently blaming themselves and each other for the destruction of the tape—she feeling anger and frustration because she'd told him not to worry about recording this show; he because she left the tape in the VCR after they had finished watching it; both because they should have removed the tab present on all VHS tapes to prevent this very thing from happening. Both were responsible, each could place blame, but both chose to forgive.

✝

If we look to place blame, we will find opportunity. Each of us has at one time or another displayed glaring shortcomings.

What happens following gut-wrenching disappointment at the hands of another is determined by whether we choose to place blame or forgive. Each time we face difficulties such as this, we are given a choice: do we ask God to give us the grace to overcome the temptation to blame or allow our irritation to foster bitterness?

There will always be someone to blame. Yet, who's to blame is not as important as who loses when we blame. The act of blaming sets us up as judge and jury. The act of forgiveness sets us free of the heaviness and sorrow. We reap what we sow. Which would you rather experience? Blame or forgiveness?

Prayer

"Set me free of blame, Lord. I know I've made
mistakes and been forgiven. Help me extend that
same grace to others. In Jesus' Name, amen."

I Want Mercy!

May 25

Blessed are the merciful, for they will be shown mercy.

Matthew 5:7

"I'll never forgive them!" Jim screamed as he flew out of the pastor's office. His anger left no room for reasonable thought.

He had begun having nightmares since being mugged three weeks ago and couldn't seem to get a grip on his emotions. He'd tried sleeping pills, even tried drinking himself to sleep once; neither had the desired effect. Strained to the point of emotional bankruptcy, Jim decided to speak with his pastor and try discussing his problems.

But that had been a joke! The pastor had listened and then told Jim he should try to forgive these men. He had told Jim that forgiving them would set him free from the memories of that night. He hadn't said one word about them asking Jim for forgiveness. Jim was indignant. *How dare he tell me I need to forgive them!*

His wife continued to pray, but Jim just became increasingly bitter. Eventually it consumed his life; he became morose and died from heart complications several years later.

✝

Forgiving those who have hurt us is not about giving up revenge and getting even; it is about setting ourselves free from the burden of resentment and bitterness. It is about mercy and unmerited favor; it is about grace.

What others do is between them and God.

When Christ hung on Calvary's cross, it was an act of mercy and unmerited favor for us. He didn't have to go. He chose to out of a love so deep that he would rather be humiliated, tortured, and die a pain-filled death rather than live without us in eternity!

We can choose to hang on to the burden of acts committed against us. But at what cost do we give up our rights and give it to Jesus? If we want mercy but struggle to give it ourselves, God can't provide it. That is a spiritual law. Remember, we reap what we sow. "Vengeance is mine, I will repay, says the Lord Almighty." He meant it, so leave it up to Him.

Prayer

"Merciful Father, forgive me for my pride and arrogance. Touch my heart with a desire to forgive. Show me how to forgive others who have hurt me. In Jesus' Name, amen."

The Picture On The Box
May 26

For I know the plans I have for you, declares the LORD…

Jeremiah 29:11

Brad and Sharon loved jigsaw puzzles. However, this one was going to be a challenge. Brad had purchased what he thought was a wonderful acquisition. He'd picked up a five-thousand piece puzzle at a yard sale. The $1 dollar catch was that there was no box; only the puzzle in a cellophane bag.

He smiled as he handed his wife the puzzle. Seeing the bag, Sharon asked, "Where's the box?" The look on Brad's face told her all she needed to know. "I can't believe you bought a puzzle without the box! You know how crucial the picture is to figuring out which piece goes where. How do you propose we assemble this puzzle without it?"

Brad, having prepared for her reaction on the way home, argued, "I've already got that all figured out," he said proudly. "We'll lay the pieces out, face up, set the border by the straight edges, then assemble pieces with the same colors, and so on; we'll figure it out. C'mon. It'll be fun!"

Shaking her head in mock annoyance, Sharon answered with a disclaimer, "Only if you promise me you won't buy any more puzzles without the box."

✝

In the natural, we view our lives in terms of a jigsaw puzzle; we see innumerable events that have no apparent connection, and the sum of all the parts is still undefined. Yet, we hope that someday it will portray a beautiful and complete picture.

And as in today's story, we sometimes blindly proceed, doing the best we can in view of what we have to work with, sorting through the pieces, trying to find the ones that fit. Sometimes they fall easily into place; other times, due to a lack of spiritual perspective, we jam mismatched pieces together in our attempt to *make* them fit.

Don't become discouraged. Instead, relax in the knowledge that God sees us with Spiritual eyes. He knows what the picture on the box is supposed to look like.

If we yield the pieces of our lives to His care, He can, and promises to take each one and make them interlock perfectly.

Prayer

"Take the pieces of my life, Lord, and make
them into something beautiful. Amen."

Bitter Rivals

May 27

A brother offended is more unyielding than a fortified city, and disputes are like the bared gates of a citadel.

Proverbs 18:19

Bruce and Mitch were always trying to outdo each other. In childhood the twins had competed with and against each other in everything. But their high school years saw an unhealthy change take place. Each competition became more intense. Their motives shifted noticeably. They became driven by a passion to not only be the best, but to inflict emotional injury, making the other look bad in the process.

Mitch and Kara had been dating for several months, becoming high school sweethearts. Then Bruce stole her away. He dated her for less than a week and dumped her. It was evident he'd only done it to see if he could; it didn't matter that Mitch was devastated and Kara was humiliated.

Mitch never forgot. He vowed he would never finish second to Bruce again. As the years passed, their sibling rivalry turned into a *'king of the hill'* showdown; any semblance of decency was thrown out the window. Each set out to purposely sabotage anything the other became involved in. Eventually nobody wanted anything to do with either of them—in business or personally. In the end, they lived sheltered lives behind gated homes, rarely venturing out so as not to give the other a target.

✝

Competition is meant to teach us to excel in life. It is part of our training in learning how to humbly win and graciously lose. Winning teaches us to succeed; losing teaches us to be compassionate—both teach us to be tolerant with wisdom that is more understanding.

Once we learn how to properly do both, we are meant to put this knowledge to use in beneficial ways. Sibling rivalry is supposed to be where we safely learn to navigate both.

Unfortunately, there are those whose only goal in life is to rise to the top with a total disregard for others.

God gives us certain strengths so that we might assist others in their struggles, and it doesn't matter if it's a simple backyard ball game or a position with the biggest firm in the country.

Prayer

"Help me put competition in the right perspective, Lord. Teach
me to be humble in victory and gracious in defeat. Amen."

The Chrysalis
May 28

Behold, I make all things new.

Revelation 21:5 (KJV)

Sitting alone in the woods, contemplating her life, Bryanna wondered how she could have slipped so far from the life she'd envisioned for herself as a child. Only now did she understand the destruction she'd caused and realize her inability to atone for her mistakes. "Lord, if You're really here, now would be a good time to show Yourself," she said aloud, thinking there was about a one in a billion chance of Him showing up.

But to her utter amazement, He *appeared* in the next moment. As she surveyed her surroundings, Bryanna noticed something hanging from the small limb of a nearby bush. Moving closer, she realized with wonder that she was looking at a chrysalis. A caterpillar had woven its cocoon recently, and had begun the metamorphosis to its current state. Now, a butterfly was fighting to emerge from its protection to begin a new life.

She knelt and watched as the struggle culminated with the butterfly's emergence. It hung from its transitory dwelling, drying its wings in the brilliant sunlight. Then it flew away. As she watched it light on flower after flower, she heard God whisper, "You too can begin a new life, Bryanna. It will require a bit of struggle, but the change can be as dramatic as this insect's you just witnessed. Would you trust Me to make things new?"

✝

How sweet is the knowledge that God makes things new each time we bring our pitfalls to His throne, laying them before Him, asking forgiveness! And how many times have we, like Bryanna, made a mess of things, only to seek God's intervention? It is beyond human comprehension how God can forgive the vile things we have done and then forget them. But He does, and He will. And the life we are able to live following repentance is a life unmarred by *past sin*.

Today's text speaks of God's loving mercy. It is powerful enough to recreate our lives, making us brand new. But only if we accept His Son as our Savior and come asking forgiveness. If we do this, He promises we will be changed!

Prayer

"Lord, change me from who I am today. Transform my life and make me new. In Jesus' Name, amen."

Being Busy For Jesus!

May 29

and the fire will test the quality of each man's work.

1Corinthians 3:13

Tom and Galinda were exhausted. Misguidedly, they believed that laboring for the Lord was meant to be that way. "After all," Tom was fond of saying, "the Bible says, *'each will be rewarded according to his labor'* so the more we labor, the bigger the reward!" And with that mindset they went about *being busy for Jesus!* They had a plan and disciplined themselves to stick to it. Their satisfaction at the end of each day began to wane but they pushed on, knowing things would get better if they just stuck to their plan. After all, Jesus expected them to stay busy…didn't He?

After ten years of non-stop *being busy for Jesus,* they felt more like under-appreciated and underpaid employees than servants of the King. Serving had gone from a labor of love to hard labor. They couldn't remember the last time they'd actually enjoyed what they were doing. To the best of their recollection it had been years. And weren't they supposed to be compensated for their labor? Hadn't God promise them an exciting life of service with reward? This certainly wasn't rewarding! They had even forgone having children so they could commit more time to God's work!

Disgruntled and disillusioned, they resigned as committee heads of every group they were involved in, and left the church.

✝

God's people are designed to serve Him with zeal and passion. Yet sadly, many equate busyness to quality of service. Spurred on by this mentality they set to work, not understanding that what they're doing is not what God wants.

Failing to ask God what's important to Him will lead to spiritual frustration and a sense of overwhelming disappointment. Many Christians live in perpetual turmoil, never understanding they are laboring in vain, and their works will be consumed by fire. They themselves will be saved, but their work will be consumed.

Being busy for Jesus isn't God's idea of service. If we make time each morning to ask for instruction we will remove a lot of stress from our lives, and our works will stand the fiery test.

Prayer

"Good morning, Lord. I want to do what You want me
to do today. What would You have me do? Amen."

Marshmallows

May 30

…while we wait…

Titus 2:13

The Sunday school teacher placed one marshmallow in front of each of her ten students. "Please wait to eat your marshmallow until I say it's all right. Once I give you permission, you are free to eat it. I must leave the room. If you wait to eat your marshmallow until I return, I will give you a second marshmallow. If you choose to eat it before I return, you will not receive a second one." With that, she left the room.

Six of the children immediately grabbed and ate their marshmallow.

Three children sat patiently, hands in their laps, watching their peers enjoy the tasty treat.

As time passed, the wait showed on one little boy. Just as he grabbed his marshmallow, the teacher opened the door! The boy slowly placed it back on the table.

The teacher acknowledged the four children's restraint. "You didn't give in to a desire to eat your marshmallow." Placing a second marshmallow in front of them, she continued, "Here is your reward for waiting."

She then announced, "I must leave again. If both marshmallows are uneaten when I return, I will give you two more." The kids who had eaten their marshmallow were visibly disappointed. "For those who ate their marshmallow, if you will remain seated and silent until I return, I will give you one more marshmallow." With consequences versus reward fresh in their minds, the six remained quietly in their seats.

✝

The temptation to eat our marshmallows is great. Without hesitation, many of us devour them without a second thought. The hope within the promise isn't tangible enough to discipline our desires. But once we witness the reward of self-discipline, we gain new perspective, one that gives us hope.

"While we wait" is not a passive proclamation. It is an action-filled opportunity to bring ourselves under the control of Someone else in the hope of being rewarded with a life more like Christ's, full of love, joy, and peace.

Watching someone else do it gives us hope. Our struggle gets easier as we experience the reward.

Prayer

"The temptation is great, Lord. I can't do this
on my own, I need Your help. Teach me to wait
on Your reward. In Jesus' Name, amen."

Spiritually Fit
May 31

Train yourselves to be godly.

1 Timothy 4:7

"C'mon, B.J., let's go!" Max's less-than-enthusiastic wife was lagging a bit this morning. Just being awake at 6:00 a.m. was a sacrifice in her book! "I know it's rough getting up so early, but it's the only opportunity we have. Now, c'mon."

They headed out into the cool morning air, stretched, and then jogged the mile to the health club. Once there, they stretched again, loosening up tight muscles from their run, and then began their respective workouts.

Fifteen minutes later, B.J. looked toward her husband and said with a sly smile, "You know, Max, I love how I feel when we get home; I just hate the work. I don't so much mind the workout once I get started; I just don't look forward to it."

"I know," Max responded. "But the reward has been huge. Look at you. You look great! And I've increased my bench press to 270 pounds in just three months. I feel stronger now than I did when I was twenty!"

They completed their workouts, jogged home, showered, and then headed for work.

✝

Physical training can be unpleasant. Yet the rewards are tremendous. Exercising our body gives us strength we can draw upon each day.

Just as work in the gym may not be fondly anticipated, our daily mental preparation can be a challenge. Knowing what to do in response to the problems that arise requires educating ourselves ahead of time. Gaining additional wisdom should always be our goal.

Even more crucial is our spiritual fitness! It must be determinedly attended to; otherwise, we have little or no effect in the kingdom. Paul said he worked harder than everyone else so that he, by God's grace, might do the work Christ called him to (1 Corinthians 15:10). His instruction in his first letter to Timothy was straightforward: it requires training to be godly! Paul's words were also penned for us.

We are chosen and appointed to do good works (John 15:16). Only as a result of constant spiritual training can we expect to have the strength to perform the work as opportunities present themselves.

Prayer

"Lord, help me stay well established in Your Word. On days when I am lax, remind me of the training required to do good works. Pump me up spiritually! Amen."

June

I Saw Jesus

June 1

> When they heard that Jesus was alive and that she had seen him, they did not believe it.
>
> Mark 16:11

Annie is a thirty-seven-year-old woman who, by the world's standards, is mentally retarded and socially challenged. The morning's conversation had been engaging, causing Brenda to recall a similar dialogue from last year when Annie had looked up from her pancakes and quite deliberately asked, "What color is Jesus?"

Brenda had cautiously asked, "Why?"

"Well, in the Jesus movies, He's white. I think He's black!" was Annie's adamant response.

"Really? What makes you think Jesus is black?" had been Brenda's curious response.

"I saw Jesus!" Annie had animatedly said. "His hair isn't long either; it's short and curly!" Brenda had explained to Annie that Jesus, being a Jew, would have darker skin, curly hair, and, more than likely, He had dark brown eyes.

This morning's discussion gave Brenda a sudden inspiration; she prompted Annie, "I forget, Annie, when did you see Jesus?"

" 'member when I got my teeth pulled? I saw Jesus then. I wanted to go with Him, but He said it wasn't time, and I had to come back." Brenda remembered! Annie's blood pressure had plummeted from the anesthesia during her dental surgery. The surgeon had been extremely concerned.

Annie's recalling of last year's event had been word for word! Had Annie actually seen Jesus?

✝

Many people have related stories of Jesus appearing to them in a dream or vision; some claim to have seen Him in the flesh.

What causes us to struggle with Jesus appearing in the here and now? By and large, it's because just like the disciples, we doubt until He appears to us!

Most of us won't see Jesus face to face until the day He takes us home. It's difficult for us to deal with Jesus showing Himself to others and not us. It's an assault on our pride to allow someone else to see Him while we may not get to this side of heaven. And even though Scripture relates over forty days' worth of Jesus appearing to some five hundred people following the resurrection, not everyone saw Him.

He asks most of us to believe in faith and accept the witness of those, like Annie, who have seen Him.

Prayer

"Lord, help my faith be strong enough to not only not discount other people's claims of seeing You, but also to believe. Amen."

The Knife

June 2

Fathers, do not exasperate your children.

Ephesians 6:4

At fifteen, Allen had been trying to get his father's attention for as long as he could remember. All he'd wanted was to play catch, a video game, maybe go fishing or something. He just wanted to do anything with his dad, but his dad was always too busy.

On an impulse, Allen took one of his dad's special knives from his favorite collection and sold it to a kid at school. He couldn't tell you why he'd done it; all he knew was that he was angry at his dad.

His silent cry for attention went unchecked for several weeks until one day his dad asked, "Do you know where my knife is, Allen?"

"You mean the fancy hand-carved handled one in the case?" Allen baited his dad, a look of defiance on his face.

His father bristled at his insolence. "Where is it, Allen?" he demanded.

Allen continued the farce. "Yeah, I remember seeing it somewhere; now, where was that?"

"What'd you do with the knife, Allen?" his dad barked in response to Allen's attitude. He concluded with a consequence-inferred declaration, "You tell me right now or so help me…"

"I sold it! Okay?" Allen screamed, red faced, tears streaming down his cheeks. "So what? What're you gonna do to me?"

✝

Allen wanted what was rightfully his: love and attention from his father. And though his actions were misguided, he contrived to get his father's attention any way he could.

When we fail to give our children our time and attention, they go elsewhere to assuage their hunger for these inherent natural urges. Many substitute drugs, alcohol, sex, and gang life—almost anything for the love they crave.

In the busyness of our society, our children quite literally are fending for themselves. We shop them out to the closest family member or friend to give ourselves time to fit one more thing into our already over-stuffed schedules, only to find them disconnected, pregnant, and in trouble with the law.

Make no mistake: there is no replacement for our time. Our children need not suffer exasperation. Give of yourself to those who matter most.

Prayer

"Lord, help me provide the love my kids need—
in time and affection, in connectivity and bonding.
In Jesus' strength and Name, amen."

By Invitation Only

June 3

Blessed is the man who will eat at the feast in the kingdom of God.

Luke 14:15

She had not always been a popular woman. But today they were begging for an invitation to tonight's party. Reporters lined the sidewalks by the gate, waiting for her to appear and bless them with an invitation. They stood for hours, waiting.

When the owner of the estate made her appearance, it was brief.

She smiled and read a short, prewritten statement: "As none of you responded to my prior invitations, I have invited a select group to dine with me tonight. My guests will be arriving momentarily. Please be considerate and allow them to pass. Once again, this banquet is by invitation only. Please do not attempt to gain entrance or you will be arrested, and I will press charges against you." With that, she returned to the house.

Ten minutes later, limousines from every escort company in the city began pulling up to the gate. They provided proof of invitation and then drove to the large portico and presented their guests to the hostess.

To the paparazzi's amazement, the guests appeared to be beggars and homeless people. The hostess had them chauffeured from their cardboard homes as though they were royalty!

†

In the blink of an eye, all invitations to the feast in the kingdom will be sealed and no more will be issued. The King will determine that the banquet should begin, and there will be no admittance to those who do not have a personal invitation.

Until then, God continues to issue an open invitation to any and all who would receive Him. Because of the blood of Jesus we have the right to RSVP, which is to tell the Host whether or not we plan to attend.

Those who respond will partake of *all* the goodness of the kingdom. They will be seated in a position of prominence at the King's table.

And just like those in today's story, there will be many who will be turned away, never having accepted God's Son. Admittance to heaven is by invitation only. Have you sent your RSVP?

Prayer

"I gratefully accept Your invitation today, Lord. Thank You for sending Your Son to escort me to the dinner party. Amen."

170

The Hope Of Our Righteousness

June 4

... according to my righteousness; according to the cleanness of my hands he has rewarded me.

Psalm 18:20

The Simmons and Crafton families both appeared successful in the eyes of the world, yet were diametrically opposed in beliefs.

The Simmons devoted their lives to God's work. And God had blessed them financially.

Not because of their actions, but because of their hearts. They made mistakes, but their hearts were bent toward God; their lives began an ended in Christ.

The Craftons consistently ignored God's invitations to know Him. They were goal-setters, doing their best to amass as much wealth as possible, so they could own as much *stuff* as they could. They drove the right cars, entertained the most influential guests at the biggest parties, and worked for the most prestigious firms in town. When the economy tanked, both families experienced financial loss of a magnitude most people could not comprehend.

The Craftons were devastated, crushed by the thought that they had lost everything. Mrs. Crafton fell into deep depression, and in the ensuing weeks lost all hope. Mr. Crafton committed suicide, leaving his family to fend for themselves. The Simmons, on the other hand, understood that God had and would provide for every need. Though they may endure hardship, nothing could shake their security and hope in Jesus Christ. This security prompted them to extend the hope they possessed to the Craftons in their time of tragedy.

✝

Our belief, or disbelief in Jesus, and how we relate to Him, affects how we cope with the setbacks and tragedies we experience. Wealth and fame are fleeting. They will fade and fail in time. Yet a heart devoted to Jesus will stand the test of time. For God will forever take care of, and reward those who love Him.

In today's text, David, who was not faultless, was not boasting in his own righteousness, but rather, was proclaiming his heart's devotion to God, and God's faithfulness. Romans 3:22 says, "This righteousness from God comes through faith in Jesus Christ." Through Jesus Christ we can, like David, find hope in the righteousness of God.

Prayer

"Lord, our relationship is what matters most to me.
Teach me to live by faith, trusting in Your provision.
Help me be a good steward of all that You give me, that
my ways will be righteous in Your eyes. Amen."

Nothing Is Something

June 5

Lift your eyes and look to the heavens.

Isaiah 40:26

Jill's father turned his head toward her and quietly whispered, "It's close to bedtime, kiddo. Five more minutes then we gotta land this spacecraft, and you gotta hit the books." Jill's passion for lying under the night sky had been passed on to her by her father. He saw relevance in his and his daughter's stargazing.

His own father had not seen things that way. "Get in this house and get your homework done now!" he would scold. It seemed he couldn't understand his son's fascination. He said the same thing every time. "There's more to life than watchin' stars, boy. Go do somethin' worthwhile!"

"Well, Dad," he whispered into the night, "as far as I'm concerned, watching stars is doing something." He wished his father could have understood his interest. "And as long as Jill has a love for the heavens, I'm going to encourage her."

A few minutes later, Jill squealed with delight. A huge green blaze had just arced from one side of the sky to the other! "Oh, Daddy, that's the brightest shooting star ever! I'm glad we saw it together!" She couldn't see his smile but could hear him say, "Me too, honey! Me too. Maybe someday you'll get a closer look from space. You just keep lookin' up."

†

Doing things that to some appear senseless or serve no relevant purpose does not necessarily equate to doing nothing.

Not all of us are called to become astronauts, yet many of them had their interest piqued by watching the night sky. The stars are beautiful, and seeing a falling star fascinates each of us. You don't have to aspire to be launched into space to enjoy the stars.

Just because we don't see the value of something does not negate it. With an eternal perspective, seemingly meaningless things can have vast significance.

Prayer

"Lord, help me see the value in things that don't necessarily
interest me. Help me encourage others to seek the things
that bring them joy in Your kingdom. Amen."

Wherever I'm At

June 6

Whatever is true, whatever is noble, whatever is right, whatever is pure, whatever is lovely, whatever is admirable … think about such things.

Philippians 4:8

Brenan bumped in to Myrt at the post office. "How ya doin', Myrt?" he asked.

"Just marvelous, Brenan. The sun's not so hot just now!" she responded, referencing them having been seated beside each other at a football game the evening before. Early September games were played under the waning summer sun. It could, and often did, get into the nineties. Yesterday evening had been one such occasion.

Myrt was one of the community's long-term residents, having lived her entire life here. Brenan knew her to be cheery, with as positive an outlook as anyone he knew. He enjoyed *bumping* into her and spending time in conversation; she was well spoken, always upbeat, with constructive thought and an encouraging word for whomever she encountered.

As Brenan turned to leave, he said, "As always, Myrt, it was good to see you. Enjoy yourself today and have fun."

"Wherever I'm at, I have fun, Brenan!" she responded with a laugh. As he left, Brenan recognized the truth in her comment. He smiled as he thought to himself, *Yes, Myrt, life has never beaten you down. I have yet to hear you complain or speak negatively in all the years I've known you.*

✝

We have a choice in how we approach life, in how we portray ourselves to others, and our convictions are displayed in our attitude. We can, and do, display optimism or pessimism, hope, or hopelessness. Our outlook will help or hinder, encourage or discourage.

Unquestionably, people can read in our actions how we feel about matters we deem important or issues of consequence. So what are they hearing when our actions speak?

Though we should not allow what others think about us declare or define who we are, we should care that they have a brighter outlook upon leaving our presence.

Paul suggests we can do that by thinking about the right things. The axiom, "Garbage in, garbage out" is relevant 'wherever I'm at'.

Prayer

"Lord, let the light that comes from me be an illuminating
light and not a blinding one. In Jesus' Name, amen."

All-Star

June 7

…A people belonging to God…

1 Peter 2:9

He was the premiere player in the league; his followers numbered in the tens of millions. A good man and role model, every kid wanted to be just like him; most adults wanted to get to know him. Every corporate group wanted him to endorse their product. And for good reason. His devoted followers bought everything he put his name on.

His business manager had needed to hire an assistant to help with the enormous number of calls asking for an appearance from this sports phenom. His life had become a series of scheduled appointments. But he didn't mind; to him, it was part of his notoriety. He wanted to give back to the sport that had given him so much.

One night while walking through his old neighborhood, he was wounded in a drive-by shooting. His career was over.

When his sponsors found out he'd been partially paralyzed, his stock and appeal plummeted; the endorsements stopped coming.

Tragically, besides his sister, Sheena, only his closest friends stuck by him.

Sheena had always been there. Having kept him grounded in the fame, she continued to encourage him in this setback.

Slowly, with determination, he began to get better. As a Christian, the same inner strength that had served him in his sports career fueled his determination to rise above his so-called *disability*. He was, in fact, an all-star.

✝

When the dust settles on our lives, what's left is who we are. What each of us needs to know is that we belong to God. He has given each of us a unique gift, and we are expected to contribute to society. Just because we don't excel in sports, have a net worth in the millions, or do something exciting does not negate our usefulness.

We may not picture ourselves as a tremendous success, but that does not exclude nor exempt us from being productive members of society. Whatever your *disability*, perceived or real, you are to make an impact on those you come in contact with. You belong to a God big enough to make you an all-star. It's up to you to get in the game.

Prayer

"I want to feel like I make a difference, Lord.
Change my perspective of who I am and use me
to affect lives for Your kingdom. Amen."

The Beginning of Healing
June 8

Wine is a mocker and beer a brawler; whoever is led astray by them is not wise.

Proverbs 20:1

Sitting at the bar—well, slouching would have been a more accurate description—Gil realized he'd done it again. He was half drunk and couldn't tell you how or why it had happened. He'd stopped here with the intention of having one drink then going home.

Must be my sixth or seventh, he thought, looking at the amber liquid in his glass.

It had been two years since he'd had anything to drink. The last episode had seen him waking up in a holding cell, surrounded by a dozen other men. He'd served six days in the county lockup for his involvement in a bar fight and under the direction of the court, attended a few AA meetings.

I'm not a drunk, he'd thought at his first meeting. *I only drink once in a great while. How dare they associate me with a group like this! These people are mostly bums; some of them are even homeless!* This had been his egotistical attitude. Gil had lost his job as a result of his nefarious behavior and had sworn it would never happen again. *So much for never. If I get arrested again, Belle's gonna come unglued!* Then, another thought came unbidden. *I can't possibly be a drunk, can I? Maybe I need help.*

✝

Addiction is found in all walks of life—teachers, lawyers, preachers, engineers, public employees, sports writers, evangelists, steel workers, nuns, PTO moms. The list knows no boundaries.

As future citizens of heaven, we are to be disciplined. Constant obsession removes that ability. When we give in to cravings, it dishonors God and harms our witness.

Addictions come in many forms. *(Fill in the blank)* If you can't stop _____ when you want, if you find yourself in trouble each time you ____, if your family life, relationships, or job suffer when you ____, or if you can't control your behavior when you ____, you have a problem. Facing the truth and asking for help is the beginning of healing.

Prayer

"I submit my life and actions to Your care in this moment,
Lord. Renew my life and set me free. I'm good at hiding, Lord,
so cleanse me from the inside out. In Jesus' Name, amen."

June 9

I have loved you with an everlasting love.

Jeremiah 31:3

Sitting down at his computer, Randy immediately saw the note taped to his monitor. Handwritten on a piece of plain white paper was the acronym S.H.M.I.L.Y.

He smiled as he pulled it from the screen, folded the tape over the back, and placed it in his drawer alongside a mounting storehouse of affectionate compositions from his wife.

Randy and Shauna were forever leaving notes for each other. Neither left the house without leaving the other a note. Most notes revealed their whereabouts and when they would return. Many times they were terms of endearment, a reminder of their commitment and love for one another. S.H.M.I.L.Y. was one-such expression.

As Randy began his day's work, he thought about how to respond to Shauna's note. Settling on the one thing he knew would bring a smile to her face, he slipped away to the field behind the house and picked a bouquet of wildflowers an hour before she returned home from work. Arranging them in her favorite vase, he pulled this morning's note from his drawer, and added a two so it read: "S.H.M.I.L.Y. 2," and placed the vase on the kitchen counter and then returned to work.

They'd both meant every word: See How Much I Love You!

✝

Notes are a simple yet wonderful way to communicate with each other. Leaving them to be discovered in strategic locations can be a personal and inspirational way of declaring, "I care."

Taking time to pen our thoughts or feelings establishes our commitment to the one for which the note is intended.

God devoted a tremendous amount of work and time writing notes to us and has left them in strategic places for us to find.

His note to us in Jeremiah 31 says, "I have loved you with an everlasting love." Scripture is full of His wonder-filled and personal declarations.

In His note to us in John 17:24, at the climax of His earthly mission, Jesus prayed for us to be with Him and to see His glory. Translation: "See How Much I Love You!"

Prayer

"Lord, thank You for Your love that sustains me. Help me love
with a love that is selfless. May I bring affirmation to each
individual You place in my life today. In Jesus' Name, amen."

Dedicated to James and Myrtle Dobson

Be Prepared

June 10

Be prepared in season and out of season ... to discharge all the duties of your ministry.

2 Timothy 4:2, 5

Of the one hundred twenty-one merit badges young men can earn in the Boy Scouts, Lincoln had amassed ninety-five total badges. Each badge had increased his experience, knowledge, and skill in a specific discipline, spanning a broad spectrum from American business to woodworking. Lincoln needed only one more mandatory badge to meet the twelve-of-fifteen badge requirement necessary to attain the rank of Eagle Scout. Today's review for his Citizenship in the World merit badge would complete that objective.

However, unlike prior reviews, where he'd studied and restudied the relevant material, Lincoln hadn't spent much time preparing for this badge. He'd been pressed for time and had assumed he would be alright with a cursory examination of the issues. Finding he was unprepared, he approached his counselor, "I'm sorry, Mr. Barns. I've been so busy that I didn't take time to review the subject matter on international law," he admitted. "Can I please reschedule this review?"

"Alright, Lincoln, we'll reschedule for next week," Mr. Barns agreed. Then he added, "And when you come next week, do as our motto says: *Be Prepared.*"

Following a week of intense study, Lincoln passed his review, obtaining the rank of Eagle Scout. At the badge presentation, Mr. Barns spoke of the rescheduling, and the importance of being prepared, "Because you never know what life might bring."

✝

Like Lincoln, many of us put off preparing for upcoming events, relying on present knowledge to carry us through, sighting busyness as the reason for our lapse in judgment. The truth is ... we will make time for those things which are important to us. Un-preparedness, conscious or otherwise, will cause us to fail the testing of such knowledge.

Paul's charge to Timothy was that he be prepared for every eventuality in order that he might be able to discharge *all* the duties of his ministry.

Put in perspective: our failure to prepare may not only have us asking for a redo, we could very well miss an opportunity to minister to someone else.

Prayer

"Lord, show me what I need to focus on today to be ready for what comes my way. In Jesus' Name, amen."

High Anxiety

June 11

> Be careful, or your hearts will be weighed down with ... the anxieties
> of life.
>
> Luke 21:34

Nothing seemed to faze Merrill. "How can this not frustrate you?!" Vera demanded, more than a little irritated with her husband. "We owe the government 2,402 dollars, and you act as though things will be fine and everything will work out just peachy! Just where do you think we're going to get that kind of money on such short notice?"

"Vera, there's no need to get so worked up when something comes along unexpectedly." Merrill said quietly, trying to reason with his wife. "The world's not coming to an end."

"I can't believe this doesn't make you angry!" Vera was angry that Merrill was always able to take things in stride and remain calm, while she always stressed out over unforeseen events.

"Honey, right now, I'm not sure about this letter," he said, rereading it. "But fretting about it won't help. You know," he paused, "as I think about it, I'm not so sure we owe them anything. I'll call Barry and see what he thinks." And with that, Merrill picked up the phone and dialed his tax attorney's number. In less than five minutes Barry was able to ascertain that the IRS letter was in error. Vera's anxiety had been all for nothing.

✝

There are an innumerable amount of stressors in this world, most of which do not promote good health. Each one can induce a sense of instability, and anxiety; they can even release adrenaline into the bloodstream, causing our heart rate to accelerate!

Jesus suggests we learn to guard ourselves from unnecessary emotion; to remain alert to the things that matter, yet not become anxious over unanticipated events.

An apprehensive attitude leaves no room for peace or joy and hinders the Holy Spirit's work in our lives.

We can't predict the future. However, we can control our response to those things which catch us by surprise. If this is something you struggle with, ask God to quiet your heart and give you an optimistic outlook.

Prayer

"Calm my heart, Lord. Help me learn to take things in
stride and allow Your Spirit to work in my life. Cause
me to sense when I am relinquishing control to the
enemy so I can reclaim it. In Jesus' Name, amen."

That'll Never Happen!

June 12

The wisdom of the prudent is to give thought to their ways, but the folly of fools is deception.

Proverbs 14:8

"It's not a good idea, Granger," Steve said adamantly. "Your parents said no parties. What happens when they find out?"

Eddie Granger looked at his friend with a pained expression, "You're jokin'…right?! Besides, that'll never happen! They're seventeen hundred miles away on some secluded beach. They never caught me before!" he bragged.

So Eddie planned what he hoped would be the party of the year. After nailing down the details, he sent a mass-text, inviting everyone he knew.

Later that evening, with the party in full swing, Eddie took stock of his surroundings. There was plenty of alcohol and even some pot making the rounds. He was pleased with himself. *There must be well over two hundred people here!* he thought to himself. *I can't believe Steve didn't come! Oh well, his loss!*

A short while later, while enjoying the fruits of his labor, Eddie noticed it had suddenly gotten quiet. This realization was followed immediately by a familiar voice asking, "Where's my son?! Eddie?! Eddie! Where are you?!!!" his father hollered. *Nooooo! What are they doing here?! They're not supposed to be home until Sunday!*

✝

Eddie never figured on getting caught. He was so sure his parents wouldn't find out. *Never* is a fool's favorite word. It allows them to think only in terms of fulfilling insatiable desires and instant gratification, and keeps them from taking into account the possibility of undesirable consequences due to deceptive behavior.

Luke 12:2 says, "There is nothing concealed that will not be disclosed, or hidden that will not be made known." Our deception will be found out; if not immediately or publicly, then somewhere down the road. Our actions will not go unnoticed…or be inconsequential.

Sometimes it's hard doing the right thing; that's the nature of temptation. But doing what is right is always the best choice. When faced with tough choices we can either do as Eddie, eventually reaping destruction, or Steve, maintaining a clear conscience and avoiding unnecessary trouble. God expects us to put some thought into our actions.

Prayer

"Help me give thought to my ways, Lord. Guide my steps so I can avoid unnecessary and pain-filled consequences. In Jesus' Name, amen."

Necessary Corrections

June 13

A rebuke impresses a man of discernment more than a hundred lashes a fool.

Proverbs 17:10

It was his seventh day in population, and he was standing at his cell door for the midday count. Three times each day, the inmates were required to stand at their cell doors while guards established their presence.

It hadn't taken him long to learn to be at the barred door for count. The guards hated it when things didn't run smoothly. If you caused problems, it cost you. If an inmate wasn't present for count, he would incur the guards' wrath.

It was amazing how some inmates would deliberately lay in their bunks, in direct violation of the regulations. They knew the guards would punish them, but something within them wouldn't allow them to conform.

Troublemakers were given the most demeaning work in an effort to correct their behavior. This process was repeated until it broke their will. He'd found out on his second day when he'd overslept that morning's count. His sack time had cost him scrub time on the mess hall floors with only a hand brush and a bucket for company.

In three short days, he'd come to understand what the guards had told him: "You're here because you can't follow the rules. You are full of pride. We will assist you in making the necessary corrections."

✝

We discipline our children; we punish those who refuse to obey the law. When order is replaced by chaos, necessary steps must be taken to restore stability. When simple discipline fails, corrective measures must be taken to achieve the desired results.

Solomon attributes a spirit of discerning wisdom to those who receive discipline and make the necessary corrections. Similarly, he calls those who set themselves up against authority fools. It would seem our pride and an inner need to control our circumstances stand between us and a peace-filled life. Pride is one of the worst forms of rebellion and one of the most destructive.

Our rebellious behavior steals our peace, leaving us with a choice whether to respond and make the necessary corrections or continue on in frustration.

Prayer

"Help me rid myself of pride, Lord. I give You
permission to make the necessary corrections that will
restore peace in my life. In Jesus' Name, amen."

The Water Level

June 14

But Christ is faithful … and we are his house.

Hebrews 3:6

The new house had been delivered, and Dick had been given the job of building the piers upon which it would rest. As he loaded the truck, he noticed he was missing the one item he needed most. Not finding it in the shop, he called his boss. "Hey, Bob, do you know where the water level is?"

"The pieces are in the closet in my office," he directed.

Retrieving the items used to construct the tool, Dick headed for the site to complete the setup. Arriving on site, he put together the pieces that made up the water level. Once set up, this unique tool gave Dick the perfect point of reference without having to run a line level or set up a transit.

Dick began building twenty-four piers made of eight-by-sixteen-inch cinder blocks, positioning two side by side, and cross-stacking them four high. Then, using solid oak lumber and shims to fine-tune each one, he completed the erection of each pier. Two hours after he'd begun, the crane lifted the first half of the house into position, setting it down on twelve of the piers without a hitch. An hour later, the second half was sitting beside the first. As soon as he completed the interior work and connected utilities, the family could move in.

✝

A simple tool, yet extremely accurate, the water level provides a perfect point of reference to work by. The manufactured housing industry employs it because it is the most accurate tool available to ensure each pier is the exact same height. Without it, eventually the house would sag in the low spots and heave in the high spots, causing the interior walls to buckle. Doors would refuse to open or close, and the customer would become disgruntled.

Verse 4 of today's text says, "For every house is built by someone …" If we use anyone other than Jesus as the builder of our spiritual house, it will sag and buckle. Only by using Jesus as our *true* point of reference can we hope to rest on a secure foundation during the storms of life.

Prayer

"Lord, teach me to use Jesus as the foundation on which
I live. Keep me from using substitute reference points
that would lead to destruction. In Jesus' Name, amen."

Outside the Boat

June 15

Come.

Matthew 14:29

Standing in water up to his chest, Shamar encouraged his young son to jump into his arms. Standing along the edge at the deep end of the pool, Jamal was having second thoughts. Looking down at the water, he was suddenly worried. The shallow end was one thing; this was completely different! "I don't know, Daddy," Jamal began. "It's so deep. I'm afraid!"

"It's okay, Jamal. To be afraid, I mean. I was scared the first time I jumped off the end of the dock into your grandpa's arms at the pond on his farm. Grandpa understood my apprehension. He promised that he wouldn't let anything bad happen to me and that he would not let me drown. And I won't let anything bad happen either, buddy!" Shamar promised. "If you want to wait, it's okay. But I'm sure you can handle it. Just make up your mind to do it and jump! Come on, Jamal. You can do it," he encouraged.

You could see that Jamal had come to a decision. "Okay, Daddy. I trust you. Here goes!" he hollered. And with that, Jamal launched himself off the side of the pool and into a new level of faith.

✝

Faith is grown experientially. We all face difficult decisions. Our response will be determined by our faith in Jesus. Peter is remembered more for sinking in doubt than for the steps he took outside the boat. Yet he was the only disciple with enough faith to try! He knew that when Jesus said, "Come," things would be okay. He didn't think to ask how many steps Jesus would ensure. He didn't ask if his action would end in drowning. He simply stepped out of the boat.

Jesus is looking for those who would resolve in faith to discover how far they can walk with Him outside the boat. It's easy to remain faithful with assurance all around. It's another matter completely to take each step not knowing where our foot will land. Jesus bids us, "Come."

Prayer

"Sometimes I'm afraid, Papa. Help me answer Your
call with obedience built in faith. Cause my heart to
be strong in those moments of decision. Reach for me
as I step outside the boat. In Jesus' Name, amen."

A Great Follower

June 16

Come, follow me.

Matthew 4:19

Jesse was in his senior year of high school and still hadn't gained acceptance to one of the three major colleges on his wish list. He'd sent applications to two of the three but had been denied admittance due to what they stated was "a lack of leadership quality."

Deciding to try a different approach with the third school, he wrote on his application that he was quite sure they were looking for students who were great leaders. "Eventually I hope to become a great leader. However," he wrote, "I *am* a great follower." Depositing the envelope in the mailbox, he began the tedious wait for their response.

Three weeks later, his father handed him a letter that had arrived that morning. It was his response from the third school. Looking at it with apprehension, he felt this was his last opportunity for acceptance into an Ivy League college. Slowly, he opened the envelope, pulled the letter from it, and read his fate. "We are happy to announce that we have several openings for followers. We were inundated this year with applications from great leaders and needed to fill the requirements for each category. We congratulate you on your acceptance for enrollment."

Jesse smiled at the amusing response his comment had elicited.

†

Jesus wasn't looking for great leaders when he called the Twelve. And it's a good thing for us they didn't need to be. They were ordinary men with their own faults, yet they each had something that Jesus saw and intended to nurture.

If leadership skills were a requirement, then most likely none of them would have qualified for the position of apostle.

What a lesson for us! These ordinary men couldn't lead anyone anywhere when Jesus first asked them to leave everything behind and follow him. Yet each one of them dropped everything, deciding to see what this Man could show them.

They were the epitome of the term *follower*. And over the next three years, they were transformed into great leaders who changed the world.

Before we can become great leaders, we must learn to be great followers.

Prayer

"Lord Jesus, take my hand and lead me. I
want to be a great follower. Amen."

I Trust You

June 17

And my God will meet all your needs according to his glorious riches in Christ Jesus.

Philippians 4:19

They had paid what they could; yet four hundred fifty dollars of debt remained. As their son secretly listened, they lifted this need together before the Lord. The next evening, the pastor and his family headed for the small country church where he'd been filling in during the last month. He'd been preaching there on Sunday evenings so he could preach at his own three-church circuit on Sunday mornings.

Following the service, one of the elders pulled the pastor aside, handing him an envelope, "We collected a love offering before you came tonight. It's not much, but we'd like you to have it. We sure appreciate your filling in while Pastor Johnson was gone." As the pastor stood at the back of the church saying goodnight to people as they left, a grizzled old man with a gruff voice and a sharp wit approached. He shook the pastor's hand and winked, pressing something into it, saying, "Young man, you're a blessing, but I won't tell anyone if you don't!"

Opening the envelope upon returning home, the young couple found $449.50. It was then the pastor remembered the old man's handshake. Reaching in his pocket, he pulled out a fifty-cent piece, bringing the total to four hundred fifty dollars.

✝

Trusting God for everything comes by experience. It's not automatic, and it requires development. Retrospect causes us to shake our heads, wondering how we could have ever doubted.

The young pastor and his wife would live to experience many more blessings in ways they couldn't quite comprehend. That's how a big God does things—in little, intimate ways. We remember it when He stoops low enough that we feel His breath on our face. That's when we learn about faith and trust. The God who moves mountains moves people to action and, in turn, moves us to trust Him. Divine moments are just that—divine. Learning to recognize them as such comes with experience.

Prayer

"Precious Father, teach me to trust You for everything
in my life. Help me to know the difference between
wants and needs and use me to help You meet those
needs in others' lives. In Jesus' Name, amen."

Give Thanks

June 18

You are my God, and I will give you thanks.

Psalm 118:28

Hurricane Ike made his presence felt in the Ohio Valley. Four hours of seventy- to eighty-miles-per-hour wind gusts had resulted in widespread power outages and property damage across much of the Great Lakes Region. They had expected torrential rain, but high winds had come in its place. And now some two million homes across Ohio alone were without power.

Ralph had faired better than most, but he had sustained damage nonetheless. He felt that having to clean up tree limbs and debris was nothing compared to the problems faced by those along the Texas-Louisiana coast, especially those on Galveston Island, where there had been loss of life and catastrophic destruction.

Ralph's compassionate heart battled a sense of guilt regarding his anxiety over the fuel cost of the generator keeping him and two of his neighbors up and running.

Many who hadn't lost anything except power openly complained about the high cost of fuel to run their generators. Ralph tried to understand their complaints, but it was a struggle. He realized how blessed he was to have weathered the storm. And to that end, he continually gave thanks to God.

✝

Finding something to grumble about is easy. And sadly it comes a bit too naturally to a self-indulgent mind-set.

In a world filled with death and destruction, our hearts can become burdened to the point we see only the negative. Instead of a thankful heart for making it through the storm, we find ourselves asking God, "Why did You let this happen?"

Having a sense of entitlement can easily cause us to complain at the slightest inconvenience instead of declaring our gratitude for the things we do have.

Developing a grateful heart by giving thanks requires conscious effort if we're not used to looking on the brighter side of life. But it pays dividends.

Praising our Creator brings encouragement to our soul. There is much good in our lives, and our attitude and mood improve when we acknowledge it. Learning to praise God through adversity changes us. It lifts us from discouragement to enlightenment.

Prayer

"When I get sidetracked by life, Lord, help me remember what's
important and where to focus my attention. Help me learn
to be grateful more often than not. In Jesus' Name, amen."

Cleansed in Surrender

June 19

"Follow me," Jesus said to him, and Levi got up, left everything, and followed him.

Luke 5:27–28

He waved good-bye to his little girl as his estranged wife drove away. As her SUV vanished from sight, his shoulders sagged and his head fell toward his chest. The weight of his circumstances settled heavily as he sensed his world crumbling.

He'd brought this upon himself, but that didn't make the heartache any less painful. They'd been through this before: him getting drunk and losing control, she taking their daughter and staying at her sister's for a few days. Then her resolve would melt under his charismatic charm, and they would live in fragility, awaiting the next incident. Until now. He had crossed a line even she wouldn't tolerate. This was the final good-bye. Children's services and attorneys would determine how often he would or wouldn't see his daughter now.

It didn't take a psychologist to see his regret was genuine; he was truly sorry for his actions. But previous pain hadn't been enough to bring about lasting change. Turning back into his now empty house, he realized it was no longer a home.

As his wife's parting words echoed in his head, he fell to his knees seeking God's intervention. "If you would give God as much attention as you give that bottle, He could show you who you truly are. Unless you give *Him* control, you'll always struggle with alcohol."

✝

To worry and heartache, we give consideration; pain we mostly obey. And yet, even agonizing pain sometimes isn't enough of a motivator to rid us of unwanted behavior. For that there is only one cure: the love and grace of Jesus Christ.

Matthew (Levi) was a tax collector, a publican, one of the vilest of sinners, taxing unscrupulously every person coming to Capernaum. Because of his Roman licensure, Matthew was considered a traitor by the Jews. When Jesus showed up, he must have felt so dirty. But when the Master said, "Follow Me," the cleansing was complete and immediate. Matthew was changed forever.

There is nothing that does not fall under the grace of our Savior. His simple forgiveness comes in one two-word supplication: "Follow Me." It only requires our surrender. He promises to do the cleansing.

Prayer

"Help me, Lord! Amen."

Fully Awake

June 20

But when they became fully awake, they saw his glory.

Luke 9:32

Slowly, over a period of minutes, if not hours—I can't honestly tell you which it was—awareness pushed its way to the surface. Understanding began to replace uncertainty. I was in the hospital and had just undergone major surgery, and the only reason I knew that was because that's what my recovery nurse told me each time I awakened to ask, "Where am I?" Then back to sleep, wake up a while later, and do it all over again until I could finally fend off the weariness and apathy the anesthesia was causing. The same medication that helped me endure surgery conspired to rob me of coherent thought.

Years after the accident I still remember how thick the confusion was, trying to figure out where I was, why I was in this shape—whatever shape this was—and why I couldn't maintain consciousness for more than a few seconds at a time.

When released from the hospital four days later, I was still suffering from the sluggish behavior brought on by the anesthesia. It was more than a week before I felt fully awake and in control of all my faculties, completely free of the effects of the drugs.

✝

Scripture describes Peter, James, and John as "very sleepy" and that until they became "fully awake," they could not see what was taking place. They had not noticed the transfiguration of Jesus, nor had they discovered the presence of Moses and Elijah! It wasn't until the heaviness of sleep was washed away that events began to register.

What a perfect picture of the veil of deception Satan uses. Until we become fully awake to Jesus Christ, we cannot sense His glory or realize our potential for His kingdom. Satan wants to keep us asleep and constantly seeks to administer anesthesia through temptation. When we give into temptation, we become lethargic and apathetic to the cause of Christ. We must remain vigilant so we do not fall back to sleep, becoming indistinguishable from the world. We have a choice of whether to fight for complete awareness or be content to sleepwalk our way through life.

Prayer

"Awaken me fully, Lord, that I may be set free
from the veil of spiritual slumber. Amen."

Who's Spirit Is Showing?
June 21

We have not received the spirit of the world but the Spirit who is from God, that we may understand what God has freely given us.

1 Corinthians 2:12

It was like watching an aerial dogfight. As soon as one gained the upper hand, another attacked from a different quadrant of the sky. Hovering near their food source, little wings beating one thousand times a second, the hummingbirds defended their territory. Time and again they would hover over the feeder, dipping their beaks into the little yellow flower.

If alone, they would take the perch while eating. Whether they stayed there was determined by which of their neighbors showed up.

Catching them on film had become a challenge. Trying to capture their acrobatic antics had become as entertaining as reading or watching TV, even to the point of naming them.

Skinny had become our favorite. We found ourselves rooting for her, watching her fend off all comers. As her name would imply, she was of slender build, about half the size of most of the birds who visited our feeder. Yet she possessed a fierceness the others didn't. Only one bird challenged her belief that she was boss—a ruby-throated male named Ralph. Yet even Ralph gave ground when Skinny pushed the fight.

✝

Regrettably, the same traits displayed by these tiny, feathered helicopters are present in the church. We fight and bicker over denominational issues, proud that we have it all figured out! And in doing so, good-willed people place pride ahead of grace.

As much as I loved to watch Skinny triumph, I had to admit that she was selfish, narrow-minded, and domineering. She didn't need to expend this negative energy. There was plenty of food if she would only share. But she couldn't seem to put aside her domineering attitude. There was an incessant animosity that would not be denied.

We were given God's Holy Spirit that we might learn to be gentle in grace, showing others a true reflection of Christ. Yet to our disgrace, there are times when there are no signs of His presence.

Prayer

"Lord, forgive my petty attitude. May You find me willing
to overlook inconsequential differences and ready to build
bridges instead of burning them. In Jesus' Name, amen."

Too Tired

June 22

Let us throw off everything that hinders and the sin that so easily entangles.

Hebrews 12:1

As Trey rolled over, he was trying to decide whether to stay home or go church this morning. *I don't feel so good* was his initial thought. The *truth* was he was just tired, and it would be easier to stay home.

Lying in bed, he remembered what had happened the last time he'd stayed home. "You missed an awesome service, honey!" Marla had told him. She'd come home all pumped up, sharing how the pastor had deviated from his original sermon.

He'd preached a powerful message on living for God, giving an alter call at the conclusion. "Bring all your needs to the Lord," he'd urged. And they had. Three people had received Jesus Christ as their Savior; one woman had been healed of breast cancer, and two teens were set free from addiction! Trey had kicked himself for three days after missing out on the *God encounter,* as he'd labeled it.

Well, he thought, *I'm not gonna kick myself again!* And getting out of bed, he smiled, realizing he wasn't all that tired anyway.

✝

Tired isn't a good reason to miss church; it's an excuse; one Satan gives us to use to stay home. And church isn't about showing up to fill a pew because it makes us look good. It's about a relationship with Jesus Christ…our relationship.

Following Jesus isn't always easy. It is necessary to discipline ourselves to push through and gain a new level in our relationship with Christ.

Satan fears our walk with God, and he'll use something as simple as our weariness to derail that relationship. When he whispers, "You're just too tired; it's okay to stay in bed," simply ask yourself, "If this were a football game, a movie, or some other social event I enjoy, would I go?

Tell Satan to go to hell; you don't want his input and then throw off the covers and get moving in the *right* direction!

Prayer

"Help me not be lazy when it comes to our relationship,
Lord. Help me to never allow myself to be too tired
to join You in church. In Jesus' Name, amen."

Hmm...

June 23

> Husbands, love your wives ... and the wife must respect the husband.
>
> Ephesians 5:25, 33

Most evenings found Mark and Tina reading. One would invariably come across something interesting enough to share, and would utter a soft "Hmm..." It was an invitation to listen; it meant "I really want to share this with you! Are you interested?"

The *Hmm* hadn't always been endearing. It had initially been viewed as an inconsiderate interruption. Yet over time, they grew fond of these moments of sharing. It promoted laughter, and strengthened their relationship. The "Hmm..." had taught them to be considerate of each other; to place the other's needs above their own. It became a tender, affectionate bonding that strengthened their marriage.

Their now positive response to the "Hmm..." was a result of learning to be unselfish. They had discovered that their willingness to put the other first paid huge rewards in maturing their love. Over the years God used the "Hmm..." to teach them the importance of validation through attentive listening.

So tonight, when Mark heard Tina's soft, "Hmm..." he grinned, inserted his bookmark, laid the book aside, and turning toward Tina with a knowing grin, said, "Okay, what?"

Tina, now the center of Mark's world, smiled brightly, as if to say, "I knew you loved me," and began to relate what had elicited her discreet interruption.

✝

God made men and women different: women naturally love; men naturally respect. Doing the opposite does not come naturally; we must be taught.

If we want deep, long-lasting relationships, we will do as God commands in today's text. Through submitting to God's wisdom we learn the importance of honor above self.

When we begin to genuinely enjoy finding out what interests each other, instead of selfishly looking at these opportunities as inconsiderate interruptions, we grow and mature spiritually.

Our spouse is to be held in high esteem. When we dismiss their "Hmm..." as insignificant they hear, "You do not matter to me right now. Please wait until I am no longer busy before you bother me again."

1Corinthians 13:4–7 says, "Love is patient, love is kind ... it is not self-seeking ... it always protects." This then, is how we are to respond to each other's "Hmm..."

Prayer

"Help me place my spouse's need for validation above my
need for undisturbed peace. In Jesus' Name, amen."

An Uncommon Servant

June 24

For to me, to live is Christ and to die is gain.

Philippians 1:21

George lived out loud. There was no façade, no exterior trimming; what you saw is who he was—and mostly you saw Jesus. Some said his approach to sharing the Gospel was a bit over-the-top, and that he needn't be so forthright. You see, George did nothing quietly... his unambiguous passion was conspicuous. George *always* greeted the Brethren with a holy kiss (Romans 16:16). "Victory!" and "Wonderful!" were staples in his inspirational vocabulary.

When George prayed or sang, he did it with his whole heart at the top of his lungs, holding nothing back. And because of his fervency and enthusiasm some felt a bit uncomfortable around him. But for those who called George, *Friend,* they expected nothing less. They understood how George felt about Jesus... he was in love. And this love is what George exhibited unconditionally; in this he was uncommon.

George lived passionately until he died. So much so that the staff at the hospital where he went home to be with Jesus will never forget how he introduced himself to each one: he grabbed their hands, and asked "Is there anything you need prayer for?!" He prayed unashamedly, speaking to his Father on their behalf. He was an uncommon servant, living completely, squeezing every ounce of life from each day, leaving nothing in reserve.

†

George and Paul are much alike; while on earth they loved Jesus with all their hearts, and didn't care how they looked doing it! They both longed for the day they would begin the face-to-face portion of eternity; yet while among the living, they lived lives of purpose, speaking on behalf of their King, telling everyone they met about His love and saving grace.

As Christians—recipients of God's Greatest Gift—our purpose is to carry the cross of Calvary wherever we go, telling people about the Man Who hung there on our behalf, and the cleansing power of His blood. We should not sit idly by, waiting to die to be with Jesus. We, as George, should be passionately living for Him as uncommon servants.

Prayer

"Lord Jesus, help me to be uncommon in Your service.
Cause the world to disappear in light of Your presence
that I might witness Your love without reserve. Amen."

At the End of Each Day
June 25

We have different gifts according to the grace given us.

Romans 12:6

"How do you deal with the accolades?" John asked Marlie. "I've always felt like I was supposed to downplay my part. You know, give all the glory to God."

Marlie chuckled. "I struggled too until my father gave me this advice. 'Just say thank you. I love to sing, and it blesses me when someone is touched through my gift.' Then give the glory to the One Who deserves it at the end of each day." Marlie continued, "If we declare, 'It wasn't me,' we negate the gift of God, a gift we are meant to share. It also extinguishes the work of the Holy Spirit. But if we allow them to share what God has done through us, we give credibility to the gift."

She continued, "Paul taught that we have different gifts, and we are to use them. Our songs are a source of encouragement to many. Through our singing, people are lifted above their trials and into the worship of His presence. If you were a renowned artist and someone told you that your painting stirred him deeply, would you feel a need to say, 'I didn't paint this; it was God'? Of course not. Just remember, when you lie down for the night, tell Him thanks and that you're ready to do it all again any time He calls."

✝

Every good gift comes from God. Not one of us could perform in our daily lives apart from His grace. He has gifted us, equipped us for the work He ordained for us to do.

To the banker who works late hours making sure the figures balance, you are to take comfort in the fact that without your abilities given by God, our financial institutions would suffer collapse. To the waitress who smiles for each customer, you bring lighthearted joy to someone who may be going through a rough time; you are a servant.

Whatever your gift, say thank you and give glory to the One Who deserves it at the end of each day.

Prayer

"For what You do through me, Lord, thank You. I give
You the praise I have received this day. Continue to bless
and use this gift of Your grace. In Jesus' Name, amen."

Make Me Pure Again, Lord

June 26

Create in me a pure heart, O God.

Psalm 51:10

Russell turned off the computer, feeling defeated. It had been six weeks since he'd given into the temptation, and now he felt horrible. He didn't understand how he could love his wife and still do this.

He tried to control his impulses, yet he couldn't seem to help himself. He always seemed to end up at a porn site, committing adultery with women he would never meet. And when it was over, guilt and shame replaced denial and desire; he hated not being able to resist the temptation.

The next morning, he called a friend who happened to be a Christian counselor. "I don't understand this, Paul. I get this urge that won't be satisfied until I give in. I love Barb. Why can't I stop?"

"It's a complex problem, Russ," Paul began. "Men are visually stimulated. They catalogue every image they see. If the image stimulates sufficiently, it is retained. Pornographic images cause a hormonal flood in the brain, which creates heightened desire because it alerts the procreation instinct, which feels the need to respond immediately. It's the same as being addicted to heroine. The only way to stop the process is to delete the images from your memory, and that's not humanly possible. Only God can recreate your mind and remove those images from your memory. Let's set an appointment to talk further."

✝

Pornographic images stimulate and trigger the release of adrenaline, testosterone, endorphins, and oxytocin, a stimulus package sufficient to cause tremendous euphoria. Pleasure receptors override common sense. Once viewed, you cannot stop uncensored recall of the images. Only blocking the ability to remember can inhibit recall.

Had David taken the images of Bathsheba to God when he saw her bathing (2 Samuel 11:2), he may not have given in to his sexual desire. Instead he chose to entertain them, and he and many others paid the price. In his sorrow, David asked God to renew his heart.

As with David, God would set us free if we would ask. For those who fight this battle, Christian counseling is a good place to begin.

Prayer

"Make me pure again, Lord. Lead me in the steps necessary
to bring about true freedom. In Jesus' Name, amen."

Check the Salt

June 27

But if the salt loses its saltiness…it is no longer good for anything.

Matthew 5:13

"Ahhhh!" Rebecca was infuriated. "When was the last time you put salt in the softener?" she hollered.

Instantly, Hank knew what had happened. *Oh, no! Rust spots in the white clothes! Way to go, Hank!* He derided himself for not checking the salt level in the softener recently. Actually, he wasn't as concerned about the rust-spotted clothes as he was the grief his oversight created. The next week would be miserable; that was about how long it took Rebecca to forgive him.

Getting out of the chair, he headed to survey the damage that would certainly be referred to as his fault. He decided to sow a seed of goodwill, an olive branch of sorts. "Honey, I'm really sorry," he said ahead of his arrival. "It just slipped my mind."

As he entered the laundry room, he realized his apology had been a mistake. It was having little to no effect. "How bad is it?" he asked, making his second mistake.

Her answer had all the earmarks of a torch for his olive branch. "Not too bad…if you enjoy wearing orange underwear!" she said, holding a pair aloft. They were a mottled mess of reddish-brown and rusty white.

Realizing there was only one thing he could do, he said, "I'll take care of it right now." And with that, he sheepishly turned and headed to the basement to dump a couple bags of salt into the brine tank.

✝

In the same way a constant source of salt is needed to condition rusty water, our spiritual lives need a constant filtering to keep unwanted impurities from soiling our spiritual being.

The level of salt must be maintained in a water conditioner, just as the intake of godly things in a Christian's life must be maintained.

By reading God's Word regularly and meeting on a regular basis with other Christians for encouragement and insight, we can stop the accumulation of unsavory buildups that cause us to lose our solid footing and effectiveness.

We must regularly check the level in our spiritual salt tank.

Prayer

"Thank You for Your Word that provides life-giving wisdom. Help me to be diligent in my actions concerning my Christian walk so others and I might benefit. Amen."

Before We Speak

June 28

The tongue is also a fire.

James 3:6

"Have you heard about Jeremy?" Katrina asked her brother. "No. What's up?" Phil responded. "Well, I'm not sure …" she hesitated, then said, "I heard he was back on pain pills."

"That's too bad. I like Jeremy," Phil replied.

A week later, Jeremy was called into his employer's office and immediately terminated. They gave him no explanation other than *he was no longer a good fit for the company.* Jeremy repeatedly asked for a more defined explanation but they would say no more.

Shaken, Jeremy determined to put it behind him. But finding suitable employment during the economic downturn took more than six months. In that time he lost his car and used up his entire savings as well as his retirement fund.

Two years later, Jeremy ran into a co-worker from his former employer. In the course of their conversation, the man asked Jeremy if he was still having trouble with pills.

A little surprised by the question, Jeremy told him, "No, I'm great. I've been clean for six years."

The man seemed surprised by the *'six years'* and proceeded to tell Jeremy that he'd been part of a conversation with Jeremy's old boss and Katrina's brother, Phil, the week of Jeremy's termination. "Phil told the boss you were back on drugs. I guess he assumed Phil knew what he was talking about and didn't think it warranted further investigation. I'm really sorry man. I always enjoyed working with you."

Jeremy was sorry, too. But at least now he had the truth.

†

We are never to be careless with our words. Yet, many find fulfillment in spreading gossip. Although untrue, Jeremy's life was devastatingly impacted by gossip. When we speak without concern for the consequence of our words, we are taking someone's integrity, welfare, and quite possibly their life in our own hands.

Proverbs 18:21 says, *"The tongue has the power of life and death."* When we hear gossip we have two choices: to lovingly confront the gossip, suggesting they refrain from the practice of spreading rumors; or remove ourselves from their presence, refusing to take part. What we say matters. At the peril of others, we must consider our words.

Prayer

"Lord, guard my lips that I would not harm
another. In Jesus' Name, amen."

Laughter-Filled Prayer

June 29

A cheerful heart is good medicine.

Proverbs 17:22

This group was a sampling of the community: pastors and their wives, church members from several different denominations, laymen and women alike. And everyone was welcome.

This group believed that corporate prayer with likeminded people was more important to their community than their inconsequential doctrinal differences. A testament to their commitment was that they had been meeting together for over eight years.

But there was something even more compelling at work that drew them together each Tuesday at noon; they loved each other with the love of the Father, and they laughed a lot, and not just the occasional chuckle or smile. These people knew how to laugh together. They had grown to love each other so deeply that it showed in the way they picked on one another. No one was exempt from spending time in the hot seat. And none of them seemed to mind.

They had learned to share their lives, the victories and defeats. This was a close-knit group. And the more they laughed, the more they loved. The more they loved, the closer they got. They spent time praising the Lord and lifting the needs of the community before the throne. They were dead serious when it came to what they felt God had called them to. But they were never far from the laughter.

✝

It's not a sin to laugh, even during prayer. Today's text directs us to have a cheerful heart. It's hard to imagine being any cheerier than when we're laughing. God loves to hear us laugh. He is not affronted by, nor does He disapprove of, laughter-filled prayer.

When we come before the throne, we are to come in reverence. My dictionary defines reverence this way: "A feeling of awe and respect and often of love." None of the three are out of line with laughter. When we laugh with our friends, it's not an act of irreverence; it's sharing our joy.

God wants to be our closest friend. Prayer is spending quality time with Someone we love. And although there are times to be somber as we approach His throne, God wants to share our laughter too.

Prayer

"Lord, You are the author of laughter. May you find
me willing to share mine with you. Amen."

Life's Roller Coasters

June 30

Great are your purposes and mighty are your deeds.

Jeremiah 32:19

"How've you been, Oren?" Tyrel said as he hugged his friend, eager to catch up on what had happened since they'd last seen each other.

"Good," Oren responded. "But it's been a little disappointing. I recently lost an opportunity to expand my business. I met with a new investor several times, and everyone seemed satisfied. They called, saying things were almost complete on their end. That was four months ago. I haven't heard from them since."

"I'm sorry, Oren. But don't give up. Who knows? Maybe they'll call today." He tried to encourage his friend with a metaphor. "It sounds as if you've been on a roller coaster ride. They're thrilling *and* frustrating. But we learn a lot from taking the ride." He continued, "Just seeing the coaster elicits a thrill! Kinda like you, looking forward to growing the business. The first big hill is scary, but anticipating the drop is thrilling! The next thing we know, we're falling at breakneck speed. We involuntarily scream and feel like we're losing control. We get freaked out and want to jump. But that would be suicide! Oren, the hardest part of the ride is trusting the operator. God knows what's best for your life. Just hang on and trust Him."

"I do. But sometimes I wish the ride wasn't so wild," Oren said.

✝

We can all identify with Oren. We've been on life's roller coasters, where the rides have been some of the toughest lessons we've ever learned. Yet apart from these disappointments, we gain no appreciable experience, and our spiritual growth becomes stunted. Learning to lose gracefully pays dividends.

Coaster rides are difficult, frustrating, and sometimes even perilous.

But know this: God will never harm us. He wants to purpose our lives by leading us to the center of His will. Sometimes that means riding the coaster when it's the last thing we want to do. Have faith! His Word assures us that He is trustworthy.

Would you risk a wild ride with God for His promise of great and mighty things?

Prayer

"Sometimes life scares me, Lord. I need reassurance.
Take away my fear and replace it with the faith that
knows You're near. In Jesus' Name, amen."

The Art of Listening
July 1

Listen to advice and accept instruction.

Proverbs 19:20

Gary's patience was being tested. His young trainee continually interrupted his instruction, trying to finish Gary's sentences. Yet each time he spoke out of turn, he found himself embarrassed as Gary showed him the error in his assumptions.

"Look, Bobby, I know you're intelligent," Gary began. "But every time you interrupt, you display an inability to listen to instruction, and you extend the length of this training session. Please listen and hold your responses and questions until we complete each phase. All right?"

"I'm sorry, sir. I just get kinda nervous in these situations. I want you to know I'll be able to handle whatever you give me to do. I don't want to upset you. I really want this job and want to impress you. I guess that was a crash and burn effort."

"Look, Bobby," Gary confided, "we don't mind training someone who is willing to learn. That type of person takes instruction well. And that's who we're looking for."

"I understand. If I promise to listen, will you give me another chance?" he asked, his countenance showing he meant what he said.

Gary was sensitive to the young man's uneasiness. "Sure, Bobby. It's understandable that you're a little bit nervous. But in the future ... I suggest you train yourself to listen. You'll learn a lot more."

✝

Listening is a discipline. Bobby is not unique. We've all spoken out of turn only to find out we were wrong. It's easy to want to showcase our experience. But in our eagerness to succeed, we can speak when we should be listening. A willingness to show ourselves teachable is far more attractive than continually trying to outguess or impress someone.

Active listening is the art of controlling our emotions and our tongue, trading our silence for knowledge we might not possess. Failure to listen robs us of vital knowledge that may benefit us in the future. It also shows us as immature and impulsive. It is better for us to remain silent and be thought a fool than to open our mouths and confirm it.

Prayer

"Help me learn to listen, Lord. Still my tongue and
open the ears of my heart. In Jesus' Name, amen."

The Benefactor

July 2

They gave to anyone as he had need.

Acts 2:45

Deon had been injured ten months ago in an industrial accident but had received no financial compensation due to his employer's continued appeals. They held that Deon's own negligence had caused his injuries.

Rubber mill rollers had snagged his shirttail, pulling him toward certain death. Deon had resisted until the shirt ripped from his body. Most of the soft tissue in his back and rib cage suffered extensive trauma. He would be off work for an extended period of time. It seemed the worst injury was that he wasn't going to receive any financial assistance.

Ten months with no income had depleted their savings, as well as their children's college fund. They had hoped worker's compensation would restore at least the fund. Now it appeared that wasn't going to happen.

One morning in prayer, Deon sensed God say, "I am sending a benefactor." So Deon and his wife looked up the definition of *benefactor:* one who bestows a gift.

They agreed this seemed a bit far-fetched, yet prayed and continued to trust God for their welfare.

Two weeks later, in the midst of foreclosure on the house, an anonymous donor provided a large check earmarked for their mortgage. Over the next six months, checks sufficient to cover expenses showed up in their account. They would never discover who their benefactor was, but they never stopped asking God to bless their anonymous supporter.

✝

What a tremendous modern-day demonstration of today's text—God using His children to meet some of His other children's needs! In this same situation, would we give out of our abundance or even believe for the benefactor?

Believing God in the lean times does not come natural. It requires faith that He exists, that He cares, that He can do all things, and that He will always act in our best interest.

If He asked for all our earthly possessions, would our salvation through Christ Jesus be enough? Trusting God in times of plenty is not remarkable.

Job said, "Though He slay me, yet will I hope in him." Would we echo Job's sentiment?

Prayer

"Teach me how to trust You, Lord. When I get discouraged,
show me that You're there. May I come to know that
You are my true benefactor. In Jesus' Name, amen."

Before We Get on the Bus

July 3

Listen to my instruction and be wise; do not ignore it.

Proverbs 8:33

"Can I ask you something, Rueben?" Holly asked. "What do you do for devotions? Which books do you use and what do you consider to be the most important part?"

He said without hesitation, "For me, it's not which books as much as it is spending time with God each morning, Holly. Don't get me wrong; books are good, but He enjoys spending time with me. And I've found He's always ready to listen or talk. He loves having input in my day. Let me ask *you* a question," he said, turning the tables. "When your children were in grade school, did you expect them to get themselves up each morning and get ready for school? Did you want them to fix their own breakfast and make sure they had their lunches packed and didn't miss the bus so you could sleep? Did you care who they got a ride home with if they'd had an after school activity? The truth is that in the same way you wanted to be involved in your children's lives, God wants to take an active role in yours. He wants to hear what happened yesterday at work and how you feel about today. He's a hands-on kind of parent. Before we get on the bus, He'd like to have breakfast with us and send us on our way with wisdom and a hug. But it's our choice."

✝

Spending time with God is not mandatory. He will not force us to listen to wise counsel that would benefit us throughout the course of events we will face today. Nor will He lean on us with instruction, regardless of the fact it may save us untold grief or unnecessary detours. He has given us the freedom to share as much of our lives with Him as we wish in whatever capacity we choose.

God knows relationships cannot be forced. He understands we can't hear what He has to say unless we listen willingly. We would be wise to seek His instruction on a daily basis.

Prayer

"Create in me a hunger to meet with You, Lord. Help me become wise enough to seek Your instruction daily. Then help me learn to listen to what You say. Amen."

Set Them Free

July 4

For God did not send his Son into the world to condemn the world, but to save the world through him.

John 3:17

Kevin had been the sole survivor of an attack on his M2 Bradley tank. Tears began to build in Lauren's eyes as she listened to her brother's story. "The IED came out of nowhere. One minute we're haulin' along, the next there's this deafening explosion, and there's fire everywhere!" Then his voice lowered. "Guys were screaming."

Fighting for composure, he went on. "Next thing I remember is waking up in Walter Reed. That's where I found out I was the only one that made it; someone from the Humvee behind us had pulled me free." Kevin's face mirrored the loss he was feeling. "They were my friends," he whispered. "Why them and not me? Why'd they have to die?"

"I don't know the answer to your question, Kev," his dad quietly answered. "But sometimes good people die so that others might live." He continued, "Freedom will always have its casualties. War is a reality in the world in which we live. When tyranny sets itself up to steal freedom from those who hold it precious, there will be conflict. Your willingness to fight and set others free was shared by each of your friends, son. Remember them. Never forget they understood the sacrifice of freedom, just like you, and paid the ultimate price. When others are held captive, our freedom, if it means anything at all, must rise up and defend them in their weakness. We must set them free."

✝

When Satan set himself up against his Creator, he began the work of pitting man against man, good against evil. Since then there have been casualties of war. Sadly, there will be more.

Seeing what mankind had done to His plan, God undertook the means by which we are set free. He submitted Himself to the hardships of a war He could have won with the utterance of one word. Yet with a love so deep that He could not bring Himself to destroy His Creation, He spoke to His Son, "We must set them free." And in one act of love, They set us free!

Prayer

"Mighty God, thank You for Jesus. May we never take His sacrifice for granted. Amen."

Absolutely!
July 5

Praise the LORD ... who redeems your life from the pit.

Psalm 103:1, 4

As the professor began presenting his theory on black holes, he surveyed this newest group of would-be physics majors. "Black Holes 101," he began. "Nothing escapes a black hole. Once past the event horizon, matter cannot reemerge." He continued expounding. "An event horizon is the boundary in space-time past which matter cannot escape a black hole's gravity. The weight of the mass within the hole is billions of times greater than the mass outside the horizon, causing a gravitational pull almost unimaginable. So great, even light itself is trapped and cannot escape." The professor pointed to thousands of galaxies shown on his celestial map. "Each galaxy you see is believed to contain a black hole near its galactic center. Though we cannot directly view black holes, effects on the matter surrounding them infer their presence. Once matter falls past the event horizon of a black hole, no escape velocity is sufficient to break its grip. The type of horizon we are studying today is an *absolute* horizon. This is when anything that passes through the horizon from the observer's side is never seen again."

✝

People fall beyond absolute horizons every day. They disappear from existence, never to be seen or heard from again. And the truth is that many of them, if not all, could have been saved. For some there is still time.

There is a dynamic difference between galactic black holes and the black holes some of us face each day. In our daily lives, there are no event horizons distinguishing an absolute point of no return. We may drop off the radar, but there is still hope.

God can rescue us from what we believe is beyond the point of no return. No one is outside God's power to save. He is able to rescue us from the deepest pit and restore us completely.

There is absolutely nothing we can do that is beyond His great love. His hand is extended to anyone who would take hold and be lifted out of their pain-filled circumstances.

Prayer

"Lord, I absolutely need Your help! This mess I'm in
has stolen my life, and I want it back! Lift me out of
this pit and redeem my life. In Jesus' Name, amen."

If I Were King

July 6

We are therefore Christ's ambassadors.

2 Corinthians 5:20

"Look, if you don't want this assignment, I'll give it to someone else," Carl's editor said. "Look at it this way. It'll give you an opportunity to present your case."

Carl was being sent to interview a nationally known talk show host whose stance against God's existence and religion, Christianity in particular, was widely known. The interview was to be part of an upcoming segment on faith, or the lack of it.

"Oh, I want it, Ruthie. It's just that I don't understand how people can ignore the presence of a Creator, let alone take the stance this guy takes. You have to admit, he displays an unusual intolerance for Christianity." Carl felt the man's snubbing of God bordered on hatred and foreshadowed his eternal damnation. "I don't get how you miss it that badly."

Ruth posed the question, "So what would you do with this guy if you were king?"

Carl thought a moment and then responded, "I have to say I'm glad I don't have that responsibility. I deserve judgment myself. But because of Christ, I'm assured of salvation." He paused a moment and concluded, "Not all that long ago, I'd have cut myself slack while meeting out horrific sentences to those I disagree with. I'm not qualified to make those decisions. Nor do I want to. Pray I look like Christ to this guy."

✝

Pride is an insidious evil. It tells us we've got it all together and have every right to stand in judgment of those who don't believe as we do. It's so easy to set ourselves up as king of creation, when the truth is we tend to forget where we'd be if it weren't for God's loving mercy and grace.

We are to be Christ's ambassadors, not His Supreme Court justices.

Paul wrote to Corinth to help them understand God wants to reconcile our sins, not count them against us. So if the God of Creation extends such a warm welcome to those who are spiritually dying, how much more, as His ambassadors, should we do the same?

Prayer

"Father God, You alone are to judge the nations. I
never want to be the reason someone feels he is not
worthy of salvation. Help me be Your ambassador
and not someone's judge. In Jesus' Name, amen."

The Secret

July 7

I have learned the secret of being content in any and every situation.

Philippians 4:12

In light of her circumstances, Elsie had a tremendous outlook on life. Her secret? She looked for the brightest part of each day and refused to let circumstances dictate her attitude. She certainly had reason to do otherwise.

Elsie's multiple myloma had resurfaced after twenty years of remission, and she'd just come through colon cancer that had required several surgical procedures. Right now, her doctor was advising her to undergo chemotherapy on top of her radiation treatment. Having been through this before, Elsie took a moment before she responded to the doctor's suggested course of treatment.

"What do you think, Tommy? Are you up for this again?" she asked her husband.

Tom said, "I'm up for whatever you decide, Els. No matter what, God'll get us through this."

She looked at her surgeon. "Can we have a couple days to discuss things and pray about it, Doc? I'm involved with the kids at the hospice center. If I undergo therapy, it'll mean giving that up for a while. I want to be sure."

He was inspired by Elsie's concern for others in the midst of considering her own welfare. She motivated him to approach life with tenacity. He smiled, "Sure, Elsie. You and Tom take whatever time you need. Then call me with your decision."

✝

How we live gives witness to what we believe. Others read us like a book. So what do they see? Contentedness or contention?

Elsie knew this was something God would handle and guide her through. It was evident God had her trust, and He was in control of her life.

A grouch is not difficult to spot. Neither is someone who inspires us to live above defeat and despondency.

Paul discovered what Jesus already knew: by looking to our ultimate future, we are better able to walk through today with hope in our hearts.

Elsie's thoughts? "Live like heaven begins tomorrow; sing like no one is listening; dance like no one is watching; and love like you've never been hurt before." Sounds like a good place to start.

Prayer

"Teach me the secret, Lord, of being content by trusting
You for everything in my life. In Jesus' Name, amen."

Shocked to His Senses

July 8

Teach us to number our days aright, that we may gain a heart of wisdom.

Psalm 90:12

Jim regained consciousness. He was dazed and confused but alive. He'd been filling the grain silos. With one silo full, he was moving the boom of the elevator over to the next silo. As the boom swung, it came in contact with a bare power line. Thousands of volts of electricity shot through his body, discharging through his toes into the ground. The resulting shock knocked him unconscious. Awakening, Jim crawled to his neighbor's. He was transported to the county hospital where he received treatment and was later released.

The following week, Jim received a visit from a local pastor. He had come to invite Jim to church. "I can talk to God anytime I want right out there in the fields," Jim said, swinging his arm expansively.

The pastor asked, "But do you? If you had died that day, do you know if your soul would be in heaven?"

Jim had to admit he didn't. As for talking to God while out in the fields ... He took the pastor up on his offer.

✝

Jim's true relationship with God began the day he was introduced to his own mortality. That relationship grew over time as he came to know the One Who saved his life. He eventually became the pastor of a local church.

Instead of harvesting grain, Jim began to reap souls for the kingdom. And though now with the Lord, Jim's legacy of harvest continues through his family and parishioners.

One significant moment can bring change to our lives and the lives of countless others. Today's text says that we have the ability to gain wisdom by our actions, the act of learning from God what He has in store for our lives. Do we continue on in false ignorance?

Prayer

"Lord, teach us to number our days according to Your
Word. And to walk uprightly in relationship with
You. Guide us into wisdom that is pertinent in our
lives and Your kingdom. In Jesus' Name, amen."

The Last Place We Look

July 9

Look to the LORD and his strength; seek his face always.

Psalm 105:3

They split up to cover more ground.

"Where'd you wear it last? And how long ago was that?" Tony hollered up the stairs. He and Jill had been searching for her butterfly necklace for half an hour.

Jill was determined to find it, even if that meant being late for their dinner engagement. *It's the perfect necklace for the gown I'm wearing.*

Tony had checked the kitchen and downstairs bathroom. Nothing! He'd pulled the cushions from each piece of furniture and reached into every crack but had come up empty. Now in the guestroom, he began looking through drawers while asking God for patience. *This is not my favorite pastime, Lord!*

Jill continued searching through jewelry boxes. Still no necklace. "Any luck yet?" she hollered.

Tony reined in his frustration. "Not yet."

Then, "I found it!" Jill hollered triumphantly and whispered, "Thank you, Jesus!" As she worked the clasp, she explained, "It was in the zipper compartment of one of my backup purses! Wouldn't you know it, it was in the last place I looked!"

Tony couldn't help himself, "Of course it was in the last place you looked!" he said. "You wouldn't continue looking once you found it, would you?"

✝

If we knew exactly where we'd lost something of value, we wouldn't waste time looking for it somewhere else. We would go straight to that spot and retrieve the lost item.

So why is it that God is frequently our *last resort?*

Self-sufficiency is a form of pride. Yet generations have been raised by the maxims: "Stand on your own two feet," "Buck up," "Get in there," "No one is going to do it for you." We've become a do-it-yourself society without a lot of God sufficiency. What are we teaching our children?

David, for all his faults, constantly sought God's wisdom and strength. No matter how many mistakes he made, David relied on God's loving guidance until the day he died.

It is not God's desire to be found in the last place we look.

Prayer

"I need help today and every day, Lord. Help me
come quickly to stand in Your strength. Amen."

What Is Faith?

July 10

Now faith is being sure of … what we do not see.

Hebrews 11:1

Helen was agnostic. "How can you believe in God?" she asked. "And how are you so sure He exists?"

Ronnie chose her words carefully. "I see God in nature and in the details of life. I've personally seen Him work in the circumstances of my life, and I hear Him when He speaks to my spirit, Helen."

"So now you're saying God talks to you? Yeah right!" Helen's comment was dripping with sarcasm. She refused to believe in God because she had never witnessed conclusive proof of His existence.

Ignoring Helen's remark, Ronnie went on. "Answer this question, Helen. Can you prove God doesn't exist? For example, you can't see the wind, but you know it's there. When you flip on a light switch, you expect there to be light. And you know the sun will come up tomorrow no matter what. Each requires an act of faith. Why is it such a stretch to believe in a Creator?"

Helen didn't like where this was headed. "Each of those can be proven scientifically. What's your point?"

"My point is that faith fails to be faith when we have tangible proof. You demand tangible proof of God's existence, and unless you get it, you will continue to reject the possibility that there is Someone outside your control in control of your life. God asks us to believe without seeing."

✝

The thought of being subject to Someone else's authority has caused multitudes great anguish. God's existence challenges our life choices.

Any religion that denies Christ's deity, meaning Jesus is the only way to heaven, shares an inability to believe God would condemn. They refuse to believe they are condemned, not by God, but by their own choices, and so they choose to disbelieve. In their unrighteous and unholy living, there is no room for admitting a Holy God cannot abide their actions.

Christians believe solely on His Word, the circumstantial evidence surrounding us and our ability to reason.

Our stance on whether or not He exists will not change that He does.

Faith is making an informed decision, aware that where we spend eternity hangs in the balance.

Prayer

"Give me words of truth to speak into
nonbeliever's doubt, Lord. Amen."

Not By Sight
July 11

Walk by faith, not by sight.

2 Corinthians 5:7

Sandy's mother, Gladys, was legally blind. Now in her eighties, Sandy helped care for her.

"Mom," Sandy said. "Do you remember the day you sent me to school for the first time?"

"Oh, honey! That's a day I will never forget! It's funny you should ask," Gladys responded with delight.

"Whaddya mean?" Sandy asked.

"I was thinking about that just last week. I felt so bad making you get on that bus. I cried most of the morning. I called your father and told him he'd have to stay home from work and send you himself if the crying continued!" She laughed. "I made it through those first few weeks with a lot of tissues and prayer. And I grew to trust God." Gladys's eyes were blind, but you could tell she was seeing those days in a way blindness couldn't alter.

"Many a time I thanked the good Lord for His constant assurance. Not knowing the reasons for some of the trials we went through made it difficult. And though I didn't always understand what He was up to, I learned to trust Him. As I trusted God, He proved faithful. Those lessons have come in handy. If I didn't trust Him, I'd have become angry or bitter about my blindness. Knowing He has His reasons has allowed me to look past the obstacle and lean on His strength as I face each new day."

✝

God rarely explains the reasons for His actions. And we have a choice in response: anger and frustration or submission and trust.

Faith requires risk. When we take a calculated risk, we have some idea of how things will turn out. Yet sometimes we have no idea what God is up to. And that can be disconcerting if we dwell on what's next.

Gladys could easily have spent her days questioning God about her blindness. Instead, because of her experience and years of walking with Him, she chose to believe that He would bring blessings out of difficulty. Having emerged victorious through the trials of her life gave her hope for the future.

Prayer

"Lord, teach me to trust. Show me how to have
faith instead of giving in to the natural tendency
to cut and run. In Jesus' Name, amen."

Be Still

July 12

Be still, and know that I am God.

Psalm 46:10

As Dell's parents left the neurologist's office, they were coming to grips with the truth that Dell wasn't going to outgrow this.

He had just been diagnosed with Tourette's syndrome, a neurological disorder that manifests itself through various involuntary motor tics and vocalizations. The head jerking and rapid eye blinking now had a name.

As time passed, they helped Dell adjust to each new tic and the frustration it brought. They helped him develop coping skills for everything from homework to sleeping habits. It seemed like the battles would never end. And when they asked for a tutor at school, their request was denied because Tourette's was not yet recognized as a learning disability. They were stunned.

It was difficult for Carolyn and Mark to watched Dell struggle, estranged from his peers because of his tics, belittled because he was *different*.

As months turned into years, they continued to ask God to take away this trying disorder that brought ridicule and tears. All God seemed to say was, "Be still," and in place of healing came grace.

As Dell matured, God's purpose emerged, and the desired healing was forgotten. Dell was a man of compassion with deep conviction. An accomplished musician, Dell graduated college with a degree in communications and music. God had elevated Dell above his struggles.

✝

It's easy to overlook the silver lining because we're focused on the trial. Believing God has our best interest at heart can be a difficult thing, especially when it involves our children. It's easy to forget that God intimately understands our heartache where our children are concerned.

How many of us would willingly have sent our only child to die for something he didn't do, especially knowing he was going to die in place of the guilty party?

When storms hammer us, it's natural to cry out for deliverance. It's not natural to believe God would allow this to happen. So when we cry out only to hear Him say, "Be still," it doesn't make much sense. Have faith.

God is inviting us, like the psalmist, to focus on Him. And though the earth gives way...to not fear.

Prayer

"Lord, I have trouble trusting You when I can't see Your purpose. Help me to trust You. In Jesus' Name, amen."

For the Ages

July 13

Do not remove an ancient boundary stone set up by your forefathers.

Proverbs 22:28

Lawrence was having a revelation as he leafed through the magazine. Beautiful, well-manicured farms were showcased in this month's issue. Two in particular stood out as his favorites, their moss-covered boundaries bringing nostalgic reminiscence.

His father had cautioned him to leave the stone fences outlining the property intact. "You'll miss them someday if you don't, Lawrence," he'd said. "And an awful lot of work went into erecting them. It'd be a shame to lose 'em."

The local stone quarry was paying good money for pallets of stone. They bought the stones because it removed the raw harvest portion from the process at the quarry, saving them machine usage and man-hours. They were more than willing to pay for stones from the fences of the countryside. The fences would always offer a quick way to make money.

Well, Lawrence hadn't listened to his father. Constantly repairing the gaps in the rocks where livestock tried to escape had been an aggravation. The same year he inherited the farm, he began hauling away the stones. He wanted to replace the rocks with up-to-date fences. "And besides," he told himself, "the money will help make the necessary upgrades." The truth was, he still had to mend fences. Broken wire didn't stop wandering animals either.

✝

Each generation believes it has a better plan. So we set about re-laying the foundations laid before us. And without much thought as to the why, we set our minds to the task of making it ours! In the process, we sometimes lose precious ground our forefathers labored to gain on our behalf.

Youth is wonderful, yet impetuous. We have the curiosity and desire to do great things, yet have not gained enough wisdom to temper our actions. We haven't lived enough to understand that some things should be left alone.

Heritage is a gift to be cherished, not a slight against our character. We are to build *upon* the past in hopes of providing a better future. If we must make it ours, then we should do it in connection with the past, not in place of it.

Prayer

"Thank You for my heritage, Lord. Upon it, with Your guidance, we shall build a future for the ages. Amen. "

Fidelity

July 14

He who loves his wife loves himself.

Ephesians 5:28

"Flirting, however harmless you might feel about it, is still being unfaithful to Gretchen," Cal said. "It's a temptation to take it a step further. Yes, it can make you feel alive. It wouldn't be tempting if it didn't. But it's wrong, Randy. Gretchen deserves better. So do you."

"But I don't *feel* in love anymore," Randy argued. "This other woman makes me feel appreciated and understood. I don't get that from Gretchen. I'm tired of going through the motions."

"You know, Randy, Patty and I felt the same way years ago. We'd lost the spark, and it felt too much like work to pretend. But we stuck it out and allowed God to lead us through counseling where we found out things had begun to overshadow our love; we'd stopped communicating.

"Randy, when someone of the opposite sex pays attention to us in a way our spouse hasn't, we can easily form an unhealthy emotional bond. It *feels* right, and it tempts us to give up in spite of the covenant we made. You've got to fight the temptation," Cal urged.

"How'd you get through it?" Randy asked.

"With a lot of work in God's strength, and understanding that issues will always raise themselves up to assault our marriage. We fought for what we knew was right. And in the fighting, we learned that our love hadn't died; it had become bogged down by the issues we faced."

✝

No-fault divorce, disillusionments, and annulments are easily granted and too widely accepted. "If you aren't happy, move on," we say, putting our happiness ahead of our spouse, our children, and our commitment.

Marriage is meant to be forever, not until we get tired.

Fidelity is standing in God's strength instead of our own, holding ground not meant to be given up. It's where integrity is discovered and selfish ambitions are laid to rest.

Fifty percent of today's marriages end in divorce. Statistics say that eighty percent of those who remarry will divorce again. You will take each unattended issue wherever you go. Great reward can come from not giving in to selfish desires. Stay and fight for what God ordained.

Prayer

"Weld my marriage to You, Lord. Help us stand
and fight instead of giving in to the temptations
of infidelity. In Jesus' Name, amen."

A Pound of Salt

July 15

Let your conversation be … seasoned with salt, so that you may know how to answer everyone.

Colossians 4:6

Neil had been looking for ways to witness to his neighbors. So when he saw one of them using a rickety stepladder to remove a broken tree limb, he grabbed one of his sturdy work ladders and headed over to help.

"Hey, Jeff? I saw you using that old ladder and decided I couldn't let you do that when I have a much safer one. Here, let me help." And with that, he set up his six-foot fiberglass stepladder, positioned it where Jeff could safely reach the big limb, and said, "Go ahead, I'll hold it for you."

Jeff asked one of his sons to lift the end of the heavy limb to remove pressure at the cut so the saw wouldn't bind. Neil, trying to help, told the young man how to lift the limb. When instruction failed to bring the desired results, Neil grabbed the limb and held it aloft, showing the young man what he'd meant.

The limb was removed and dragged away. Neil took his ladder and returned home, believing he had just shared the love of Christ.

Two days later, he met the son while walking, and when he spoke, the boy did not answer. Disturbed, he asked what the problem was. The young man admitted he had been embarrassed when Neil had taken over.

Neil had done the opposite of what he had intended.

†

Too much salt tastes worse than none. Our best intentions, if not carefully considered, can bring harm. Neil's offer of the ladder, though well-intended, exuded arrogance.

In his spontaneity, he hadn't thought out how best to approach the opportunity. His desire to help was good, but he was ill advised in taking control of circumstances. Instead of a dash of salt, he dumped out the whole shaker.

Our actions need filtered through the question, *How will what I do affect others?*

What we do in the Lord's name is meant to have a profound, positive effect. We must take care to season and not saturate.

Prayer

"Lord, I never want to offend where I intend to show people Your love. Help me listen for Your guidance instead of rushing in ahead of You. Amen."

Help Me Remain Humble

July 16

Have mercy on us, O Lord … for we have endured … much ridicule
from the proud … much contempt from the arrogant.

Psalm 123:3, 4

Kendal's business partner was one of the most obstinate people he'd ever met.
The fact that he was his brother-in-law only made matters worse. Try as he
might, Kendal couldn't seem to understand the man's what-I-say-goes attitude.
He dominated the office; absolutely nobody tested his resolve. Because of his
oppressive demeanor, they had lost several good employees over the past year.

No one, including Kendal, could reason with him. He would listen to what
you had to say and then look you straight in the eye and say, "If you have a
problem doing what I told you, I can get someone else in here to do your job!"

Kendal confided to his wife that her brother's attitude had become so bad
that he didn't know how much longer he could continue working in the stress-
filled atmosphere.

"Honey, I wake up each day not sure whether to say, 'Good morning,
Lord' or 'Good Lord, it's morning.' I don't look forward to my work anymore."
His brother-in-law's attitude was emotionally draining, and he wasn't willing
to compromise his sanity much longer. "Help me remain humble, Lord!" he
prayed.

✝

Many of us have worked for or know domineering employers who do not
understand how relationships are meant to work from an authority stand-
point. Somewhere along the line, they developed a need to dominate instead
of nurture.

In today's text, the psalmist petitions God for mercy from the position of
a slave to his master on behalf of a people who have endured rough treatment
at the hand of oppressors.

We are not told how God answered their plea or what action they took, if
any, against those who abused them. We only know they were oppressed.

When faced with heavy-handed authority, Paul instructs us, for the sake
of the oppressors, to gracefully endure persecution (1 Corinthians 4:12), leaving
retribution to God so that He might bring change.

It is okay to cry out to God for relief as long as we remember our *humble*
witness may be needed a little bit longer.

Prayer

"Save me from oppression, Lord. And until that day,
give me grace to endure. In Jesus' Name, amen."

As Is

July 17

Buy the truth and do not sell it; get wisdom.

Proverbs 23:23

The price was attractive, but something didn't feel right. It could be either a blessing or a sham. "I don't know, Michael. This car should cost almost twice the asking price," Brice warned. "I can't tell you what, but something's not right."

"Aw, you're just jealous 'cause I found such a sweet deal! I'm buying this car." Having made up his mind, Michael secured a loan and purchased the vehicle.

Three weeks later, the transmission began to slip. Taking the car to a local dealership, he discovered the previous owner had taken steps to temporarily hide the mechanical problem in order to sell the car.

Angry at being played for a fool, Michael called the man. "I'm returning the car! You deceived me!" he accused.

Unfazed, the man responded, "You bought that car as is. As it is now yours, I don't care what you do with it. Sell it for all I care!" he said, chuckling as he hung up.

What had looked like such a sweet deal had become one of the worst deals Michael had ever made. He should have listened to the wisdom of his friend and at least had the vehicle checked out before buying it.

✝

We live in a world where Satan influences some of the most harmless-looking people. When we fail to be wise or refuse to listen to wise counsel, we can be taken in. And to make matters worse, Satan gets us to attack ourselves. "You deserve a break. Look how sweet this deal is!" he whispers. We shove aside our doubts and bury the truth in denial for the glitter of the moment.

And when we've made the deal, he sits back, laughing. "You knew what you were getting into. You bought the package as is. Now live with it!"

It's tempting to sell ourselves short when something appealing, yet toxic, appears. God exhorts us to purchase the truth and not exchange it for a seductive lie, to get wisdom and hang on to it with a relentless grip.

Prayer

"Help me listen for the truth in the midst of all the
lies, Lord. Then help me hang on to it. Amen."

It Ceases to Be a Gift

July 18

We have different gifts, according to the grace given us ... if it is con-tributing to the needs of others, let him give generously.

Romans 12:6,8

Bobby was fifty-three and single. He owed two thousand dollars on student loans, had three credit cards maxed out, and two signature loans totaling several thousand dollars. The remarkable thing about his financial situation was that all this debt was on behalf of other people. Bobby had literally taken on the cash flow problems of others in an effort to help them out during tough times. Bobby was a giver; he was always helping others out. People assumed Bobby was wealthy; no one ever suspected he was going into debt on his or her behalf.

He'd gotten started in this back-door philanthropy by helping his younger brother pay off a high-interest loan.

A bean counter of sorts, Bobby enjoyed seeing people set free from the financial burdens holding them back. When word would come about someone in need, Bobby offered a gift large enough to meet the need. His credit report was spotless, so he never had trouble financing his ministry.

One prior beneficiary had gone on to secure a home loan because of Bobby's generosity. He offered to pay everything back, but Bobby had declined his offer, saying, "If I allow you to pay me back, it ceases to be a gift."

✝

Not many people would consider a small mountain of debt a blessing. But Bobby did. And each day he went looking for ways to use his gift. Out of the generosity of his heart, Bobby lifted the burdens of family, friends, and strangers alike, anonymously giving through third parties when practical.

Today's text says that each of us is gifted in some way. In it, Paul points out that we are to use that gift to make other's lives better. It is God's desire that we discover what our gift is, and that we put it to use.

Prayer

*"Lord, show me what my gift is, then lead me to
a place of selfless desire to give of myself in light
of Your Great Gift. In Jesus' Name, amen."*

Hope with a Smile
July 19

By this all men will know that you are my disciples, if you love one another.

John 13:35

Sally awakened at 4:00 a.m., said a hearty "Good morning, Father" as her feet hit the floor, and headed for the shower. She dressed and headed for the kitchen to fix breakfast for herself and Tiger. "Hiya, kiddo," she greeted the big cat, stroking his sleek fur.

Eggs cooking, she spooned tuna delight into Tiger's dish. "Eat it all now!" she said in mock sternness, then chuckled as Tiger cocked his head at her. Dishes done, she headed out the door, ready to meet the day. She loved the short drive to work as it often afforded her a beautiful sunrise or a full moon hanging in the waning night sky.

Sally volunteered in the day surgery unit of the local hospital.

With a smile on her face and a servant's heart, she set about putting things in order. "I love the quiet," she would say. "When I arrive, there's no one here but me. I like that." Arranging doctors' charts and nurses' orders, preparing each room by making sure everything was ready was Sally's way of ministering to the staff.

Those rounds complete, Sally took her station in the lobby, greeting every-one scheduled for surgery. She took names and met needs, adding quiet words of encouragement and comfort or a prayer offered from a heart that had felt their pain and known their fears. Sally was the bright spot in their day; she gave them hope with a smile.

✝

A servant's heart is a precious thing. Out of it flows kindness with compassion and tenderness through encouragement. It's born of a deep love for others, a selfless love like Jesus showed us on Calvary.

Servanthood is this great ability to rid others of their heartache and fear, rejection and pain, if only for a little while.

Jesus calls those who give of themselves in this way His disciples. And for good reason. They love with abandon, holding nothing back, lifting others above the struggles they face. Such an extravagant love makes a remarkable impact, and it begins with a mind-set that brings hope with a smile.

Prayer

"Help me love like You do, Lord. Use me to brighten someone else's day. In Your Name, I pray. Amen."

Then Who?

July 20

If anyone … sees his brother in need but has no pity … how can the love of God be in him?

1 John 3:17

The little girl looked so forlorn. Her mother looked as though she were fighting back tears. A covert glance revealed smudged faces and dirty clothes.

Lord, please send someone to minister to whatever problems they're facing. Meet their needs, Sherry silently prayed as the elevator stopped on her floor.

"Why not you?" God softly invited.

Oh, Lord, I've got to get to work, she rationalized and stepped off the elevator.

"If not you, then who?" God whispered.

What am I supposed to say? Their personal issues are none of my business, she argued.

"Compassion is everyone's business," came the soft reprisal.

Turning back, Sherry hesitantly spoke. "Excuse me. I don't want to offend you, but it appears as though you could use some help. Is there something I can do?"

The tears refused to be held back any longer. "I'm sorry," the mother began. "It's been so difficult lately. I lost my job. Cyndi and I have been living in homeless shelters. I came here in hopes of getting a job, but the way I look, I'm afraid no one would hire me."

Reaching into her purse, Sherry pulled out a brush and began brushing the little girl's hair, listening as the mother told her story. "Maybe I can help," Sherry began.

✝

We may not own a business and be able to hire the unemployed or have spare rooms to offer, but we can still reach out to those in need in whatever capacity we are able. Whether we choose to see it or not, hardship surrounds us.

The third chapter of John's first letter deals with how we are to respond to God's love. He invites us to mercifully emulate that love to a world in need.

It may take a few extra minutes, and we may be a bit uncomfortable, but when we encounter someone in need, we should mentally trade places, as if we ourselves were the one in need. And then remember God's challenging appeal: if not you, then who?

Prayer

"Father, thank You for the loving sacrifice that made
me right with You. May You find in me a willingness
to be Your hand of mercy when You call. Amen."

Clear Conscience

July 21

But even if you should suffer for what is right, you are blessed.

1 Peter 3:14

They called him a whistle blower. As they agency's head accountant, Wes had called for an investigation into alleged improprieties. Everyone felt he had betrayed the agency. They didn't know what Wes knew. He had discovered that three of the top executives had embezzled 2.3 million dollars in company retirement funds.

He'd figured it out while doing an in-depth cross-check of the last two years' books. Someone had *cooked* the books to show bogus market exchanges after the year-to-date expenditures had been signed off on.

Someone had slanted the books to make it appear the firm had spent millions on a new office building in the downtown district and that each employee was a contributing shareholder.

He'd uncovered a trail where thousands of dollars at a time had been siphoned from the money market investments without anyone's knowledge. Wes ran across the discrepancies by checking deposit dates against phony real estate entries.

When the two-month external investigation proved Wes had been right, the whistleblower label was replaced with pats on the back and a huge debt of thanks. Wes had done what was right. In his mind, he couldn't have done otherwise.

✝

Sometimes doing the right thing requires taking some abuse. But that should never be the deciding factor in how we proceed. To look the other way when things are not as they should be is to forfeit character, honesty, and integrity.

Wes could have chosen to ignore his discovery. He could have simply resigned his position and gone to another agency. He was aware that by implicating those in authority he was taking a chance on having his character dragged through the mud. After all, he'd only been with the company a little over a year, and it was his word against theirs. For a while, it had been a very lonely stand.

It is better to suffer a while for what is right than live with a troubled heart. There is no substitute for a clear conscience.

Prayer

"I want to be a person of great integrity, Lord. Help
me to put what's right ahead of my comfort no matter
the circumstances. In Jesus' Name, amen. "

Evil's House

July 22

If a man pays back evil for good, evil will never leave his house.

Proverbs 17:13

Flynn said good-bye to his last guest and closed the door. "Wow! What a night," he said, smiling at his wife, Leslie. The grim look on her face alerted him to something amiss. "What is it?" he asked.

"Someone has taken the cookie jar fund," came her somber reply. "As I began washing the dessert dishes, I noticed the lid on the jar was a little crooked. So out of curiosity I lifted the lid. The money is gone. I know it was there right before the dinner because I dropped in some change from my purse right after I got home from the grocery store." Then she added, "I didn't want to say anything while the guests were here because I didn't want to offend the innocent parties. What should we do?"

After a moment of thought, Flynn said, "I don't know that we should do anything, honey. To find out who took it would require asking each person if he or she knew anything about the missing money. We would be putting everyone's integrity in question, and I'm not sure I'm willing to do that. I'm thinking that whoever took it will have to deal with his guilty conscience and that God will convict him of his evil actions. Let's just let God handle it," Flynn suggested. "We can replace what's missing so the kids don't suffer for someone else's poor choices and leave it at that."

✝

To repay someone's generosity by stealing from him is to ensure evil a place in our heart and house. Evil acts, regardless of the act, give Satan a foothold he will exploit in an effort to turn it into a stronghold.

If the person remains unrepentant, evil will eventually become a fortress seeping into every part of his life. It will ultimately bring total destruction to the entire household, leaving no one unaffected.

Solomon says that the one who commits evil will never be free from it. The only way to escape evil's house and Satan's grip is to bring our actions before the Lord in repentance. Then follow His leading.

Prayer

"Keep evil from my doorstep and my heart, Lord. Amen."

Daddy's Charge
July 23

So now I charge you in the sight of all Israel and of the assembly of the Lord, and in the hearing of our God: Be careful to follow all the commands of the Lord your God, that you may possess this good land and pass it on as an inheritance to your descendants forever.

1 Chronicles 28:8

As they circled the dance floor, he held her close. His little girl had grown too fast. He felt so blessed, so proud of who she had become. He was feeling the separation that comes when our children come of age. Beautiful beyond words, she smiled a tear-filled smile, Daddy's girl all the way! The dance ended too soon. Roles had changed in less than an hour. He had gone from provider and protector to sometimes advisor and prayerful encourager—advisor only when solicited.

He thought back to the ceremony when he'd charged his new son, "Today, I present to you my daughter. I charge you with the nurturing love of a mother and the fearless protection of a father. May you be strong when necessary and gentle in times of tears. And may God bless this union."

Back in the present, he thought, *Funny how life screams by at light-speed when it involves our children.* He caught his wife's knowing smile over the crowd. He was pretty sure she was saying, "Now you know how my dad felt." He had a new perspective.

✝

Responsibility brings with it promise. In this text's pronouncement, Israel, if they followed God's commands, would inherit the land set aside for them for all generations.

We are to not only follow God's commands, but to faithfully instruct our offspring. They are to be nurtured, able to leave us, moving into the next season of their lives. We are charged with calling them to accountability.

As with the father in this story, we are to charge those who inherit the care of those entrusted to us. We are not to do this with ambiguity. We are to actively speak truth of responsibility to the next generation.

Prayer

"You charge us this day, to follow Your commands, Lord.
Teach us to be faithful in response to that responsibility
as we follow Your leading. In Jesus' Name, amen."

So, What Do You Think?

July 24

They are darkened in their understanding and separated from the life of God because of … ignorance.

Ephesians 4:18

Gwen's transformation from atheism to Christianity began in a local coffee bar when an engaging young man named Britt asked her, "So, what do you think is going to happen to you when you die?"

Gwen had given him the answer she'd used hundreds of times to defend her position. "I will cease to exist, end of story."

A few espressos later, Britt had convinced Gwen to attend church with him the following Sunday. She heard the gospel message in a way that made sense. And for the first time she began to doubt her position. She began to pray and asked God to reveal Himself.

Britt challenged her to read the Bible. Within two weeks, Gwen became convinced there was a God, and she wanted to know Him. Giving her life to Christ had been life-changing. Having a new perspective on eternity, Gwen felt an urgency to share her newfound faith with those who had shared her ungodly skepticism. She now realized that the alternative to not asking the tough question was eternal death for those with whom she had shared her ignorance. Though she felt a twinge of fear each time, she refused to allow it to stop her from asking each one, "So, what do you think is going to happen to you when you die?"

✝

Sharing our faith can be confrontational. The truth is most of us don't like confrontation. The other side of the coin is having the knowledge we asked the question and gave someone an opportunity to say yes to Jesus. If *we* don't ask them the question, who will? This is not someone else's job.

Approximately 150,000 people die each day worldwide, many of them never knowing Christ for lack of someone asking them the tough question.

If this Jesus we follow and trust with our eternal lives is Who He says He is and Who we believe He is, how can we allow the question to go unasked?

Prayer

"Lord, I know I will survive the embarrassment and
discomfort of sharing my faith with unbelievers. May
I find the courage to take as many people to heaven
with me as I can. In Jesus' mighty Name, amen!"

Take Time to Laugh

July 25

A time to laugh…

Ecclesiastes 3:4

Lindsay walked through the front door and did a double take. *Jack never leaves the house looking like this,* she thought; there were dirty dishes on the kitchen counter, the stove, and in the sink. Two comforters lay haphazardly on the living room carpet, and dirty clothes littered the laundry room floor. She'd only been gone for one day! This was completely uncharacteristic of Jack. *He's got some explaining to do,* she thought.

Setting aside her briefcase and hanging her coat on the wall peg, she set out to find her husband.

As she headed down the hall toward the toy room, she caught muffled laughter. Curious, she silently made her way to the room and stood outside the closed door, listening. *Beth!* She smiled as she recognized her youngest daughter's squeal.

"Stop, Daddy! Quit tickling me!" Then Jenny's laugh joined the mix, followed by Jack's gruff voice. "The tickling continues until you both surrender!"

"We surrender! We surrender!" they said in unison.

As Lindsay listened, her heart began to melt. It thawed completely when Jenny said, "Thanks for playing with us today, Daddy! This has been the bestest day ever!" "Yeah, Daddy, the bestest!" Beth agreed.

All the irritation vanished in light of the truth: some things are more important than a spotless home.

✝

There truly is a time for every season and activity. Housework is important; but so is laughter! Our children are only young once, and many opportunities to teach them the importance of spending time doing the right thing at the right time vanish with their youth.

When teachable moments present themselves, we must seize the opportunity to teach and instruct and not allow the moment to slip away because we were too busy being busy.

Being too rigid will find us standing on the wrong side of many issues. Not only will it bring dissention among the ranks, but our children and their children will ultimately pay the price. Lighten up and laugh a little. The work will still be there when the laughter fades.

Prayer

"Lord, keep me from being too busy when it's time
to laugh. Reset the attitude of my heart so I will
recognize what time it is. In Jesus' Name, amen."

Don't Gloat

July 26

Do not gloat when your enemy falls; when he stumbles do not let your heart rejoice.

Proverbs 24:17

"What did I tell you about taking pleasure in other people's misfortune?" Steve posed the question to his daughter, Karla. "Phil works hard providing for his family. And now that he's lost his job, they'll have a rough go of it."

"I don't care how rough they have it!" Karla said vehemently. "He's a jerk, Daddy. I can't believe you're taking his side after what he did to Sheila," she spat.

"Listen, Karla, I don't approve of your attitude or how he treated Sheila when he broke up with her. She's my little girl just like you, and it hurt when that happened. But that was fifteen years ago. You need to forgive him and let God work it out," he advised. "It's just as wrong for you to gloat over him losing his job as it was for him to cheat on Sheila. It bothers me to see you taking pleasure in his family's suffering."

"I'm sorry, Daddy. But he's still a jerk!" was all she would say.

"You know, Karla, sometimes I wonder what you're thinking. I'm your father, not your judge. But you profess to have a heart of forgiveness, yet when someone you dislike encounters problems, you find it amusing. That's not how God wants us to respond. And remember, what goes around comes around."

"I'll take my chances," she said and left the room.

✝

It's tempting and natural to take pleasure in the misfortune of our enemy. It's also wrong. We are to love our enemies and do good to those who hate us. A true test of forgiveness is not in forgiving someone with whom we have a good relationship, but rather, when it is someone we dislike.

It's easy to find satisfaction when someone we dislike has fallen on hard times. That's why God instructs us not to gloat when it happens. He asks us to have a spirit of forgiveness and leave retribution, if any is required, to Him.

Prayer

"Help me forgive my enemies, Lord. Teach me to put the past behind me and look to bring healing to their lives instead of rejoicing in their pain. In Jesus' Name, amen."

Point of Impact
July 27

All of us who are mature should take such a view of things.

Philippians 3:15

Mark Pendleton was forty-something, slightly built, and showing signs of balding. Yet there was a quiet confidence about him that caused people to take a second look.

Proceeding with his demonstration, Mark shared that as a young man he'd gotten into trouble. Then a friend had introduced him to Jesus, and he began learning about God's plan for his life.

Through the martial arts, God taught Mark where to direct his attention in matters of importance and how to harness the strength necessary to demolish any obstacles the enemy placed in his way.

"In order to break these blocks," Mark explained, "I must first establish the correct point of impact, then visualize my punch reaching that point. To be successful, I must focus on the bottom of the stack. I visualize the completed punch having reached a point at which the blocks will have broken."

The crowd watched as Mark began his mental focus routine. Standing two feet behind the blocks, Mark slowly rotated his fist, driving his arm and shoulders in a downward, slow motion punch to the bottom of the stack. When he was finished with his preparation, Mark stepped up to the blocks, and with a loud "hiya," he executed one more punch, completely shattering all six blocks!

†

As we mature, we set out to make our mark on society. Many of us succeed, obtaining goal after goal, never looking back.

In contrast, many of us fall short of the success we envisioned, hopelessly lost in failure. For the vast majority of us, it's because our goals were not set correctly, and our point of impact was unclear. In order to successfully reach our intended goal, we must determine the correct point of impact.

Paul told the Philippians to forget their past failures and press on. We too must forget the past and set new goals.

Wisdom suggests we set attainable goals in order to not become discouraged. Then we must visualize completion of the goal. Most importantly, we must rely on God's strength and instruction when determining the point of impact.

Prayer

"Lord, guide me along life's path and help me look for the right point of impact within my realm of influence. In Jesus' Name, amen."

In My Time
July 28

Look up at the heavens and count the stars … so shall your offspring be.

Genesis 15:5

In the midst of doubt, Shane still knew God was there. But that didn't bring much comfort right now. Having stepped out in faith, Shane was still awaiting the manifestation of God's promise. "Answer this call and I will sustain you. Trust Me."

Shane had answered the call. Yet it was going on seven months and there was no evidence of God's provision. His financial situation was getting desperate. Bills were overdue; he was stressed out; his faith was being tested. "I can't do this much longer, Lord!" he shouted.

Shane didn't doubt God's leading. Yet for him to be struggling like this didn't make sense. It felt as if he were missing something God was trying to tell him.

"I don't believe this is what You promised, Lord. If I'm missing something, please show me what it is." He was completely perplexed. "I refuse to give up!" he shouted. "But I need some direction here, Lord." Shane listened into the silence that followed. No answer came.

Deciding to wait no matter how long it took God to show up, he wearily said, "You know, Lord, I get a sense of what Abraham and Sarah must have felt like when they doubted Your promise."

✝

Seven months is a bit short of Abraham's twenty-year wait; but doubt is doubt, and many of us have walked in faith with doubt as a close companion. God understands and continues to guide us, like Abraham, to a place of complete dependence on Him.

Abraham failed this test of faith by having Hagar bear Ishmael. Yet God, in His infinite mercy, kept His promise, and Sarah bore Isaac.

And so it is with us: we fail and God remains faithful.

God is looking for a heart of obedience, completely turned to Him, a heart that will wait for His perfect timing, serving as though they had already received the promise.

As we draw closer to God, we realize that great faith comes by overcoming great doubt. God says, "I have given you My promise; will you wait for it in My time?"

Prayer

"Strengthen my resolve to trust You, Lord. Guide me
into an unshakable faith. In Jesus' Name, amen."

Stuck in Saturday

July 29

> I tell you the truth ... you will grieve, but your grief will turn to joy.
>
> John 16:20

Penny lay awake, the heartache tonight not much less than a year ago. She hadn't slept much since Richard had died.

Married only six months, Richard had died when his car skidded on a patch of ice. The vehicle had gone over the guardrail above a deep gorge, rolling several times before coming to rest at the bottom. It had been several hours before he was found, and it had taken several more to remove him from the wreckage; he'd lived for two days before succumbing to his injuries.

Penny was numb, yet her brain never shut down. She rarely went a full ten minutes without it all playing back in her mind: the scene at the trauma center, the two days in ICU, the funeral, and the emptiness. It seemed her life was stuck on replay.

Penny cried out to God for answers, answers that probably wouldn't relieve the ache or make this any easier.

Family and friends felt she was stuck in her grief. They continued to minister to her in love, praying that her outlook would brighten, bringing this profound grief to an end.

✝

Anyone who has lost a loved one or a friend knows the depth of Penny's heartache. Their absence creates a hole in us that refuses to be refilled; we've lost someone so precious that to think otherwise would feel like betrayal.

Jesus, on the night he was betrayed, did what He could to reassure His disciples of His resurrection. But on Good Friday nothing could take away the sting, the shock, or the pain in their chests. And all day Saturday they tried unsuccessfully to console themselves.

Then came Sunday!

The truth is if we live long enough, we will experience Penny's pain. If we love deeply, we will grieve the same way. But someday our grief will turn to joy. It's Jesus' resurrection that keeps us from getting stuck in Saturday.

Death came on Friday, resurrection on Sunday, but there was a very long day in between. It's okay to grieve. But do it with hope.

Prayer

"Give us strength to walk on in the pain, Lord. Thank You
that, because of Jesus, this pain will turn to joy. Amen."

Saving for a Future

July 30

> But he who gathers money little by little makes it grow.
>
> Proverbs 13:11

Patty and Glenna were twins. But that's where any similarities ended. Patty was a vigilant, careful saver.

Glenna had never learned the fine art of financial prudence.

Patty had gotten her driver's license and was checking out cars on the Internet, looking for a good deal.

Glenna never seemed to be able to pass up the latest fashion trend, DVD, or techno gadget.

While Patty saved enough money to make a sizable down payment on a dependable vehicle, Glenna gave no thought to the future. Her peers teased her that she would need to marry into money if she expected to continue her gotta-have-it lifestyle.

Patty put aside what she received for birthdays and Christmas, as well as wages earned working evenings for a local department store.

Glenna, on the other hand, was spontaneous and rarely thought past her next impulse purchase. Every time Apple came out with a new phone or iPod, Glenna just had to have it. Consequently, when she needed a loan, she had no credit established and was denied without a cosigner. Patty was also wise enough to tell Glenna no when she asked if she would cosign.

✝

Squandering money can be as harmful as worshiping it.

Setting and working toward financial goals builds discipline and allows us to defer our need-it-now mentality.

Financial discipline can be difficult for many people; some because they don't believe it's possible to save money on a limited income; others because they cannot quell their desire to possess everything they see.

Many impulsive people can't view saving as a long-term prospect and have a hard time putting "A lot of little investments makes a lot of money" in perspective.

Yet for those who have practiced this principal, they have found it works very well.

Saving is a learned behavior. Preparing for the future requires restraint. By setting goals and working toward them, we find it's not as hard as we thought, and it works. Saving a little at a time for the future will pay huge dividends.

Prayer

"Lord, help me reign in my desire to spend
when it's not necessary. Teach me to save a little
at a time and watch it grow. Amen."

Does It Matter to Me?

July 31

Train a child in the way he should go …

Proverbs 22:6

"Look, Gretchen, if you want to fight with the school board over this smut, book-in-the-library issue, that's your business. But don't involve me because it's not my fight!" Luther said heatedly. "I don't happen to agree with your perspective about our freedoms being taking away!" he said emphatically.

Gretchen was astonished. "How can you say that with a clear conscience? By not taking a stand against the removal of God from every part of our society or when they try to pass off smut for legitimate reading material, you passively take their side!" she fired at him.

"I have taught my children the difference between creationism and evolution, I'll have you know!" he fired back. "And they know about those books too. I've forbidden them to read them!" He argued. "If more people took care of these things at home, it wouldn't matter what these liberal-minded lobbyists did. And we wouldn't be having this battle!" he finished, face flushed in irritation.

"Your children may know the difference," she interjected. "But what about your grandchildren? What makes you think your kids won't read those books anyway? Or don't you care?" Gretchen couldn't believe how anyone could explain away his responsibility to take a stand against the advancement of evil.

†

Silence among the Christian community has been the greatest proponent to the propagation of evolution and removal of our entire belief system from not only our public schools, but society as a whole. There are very few times we have the option on whether to engage the enemy or not.

The it's-not-my-fight mentality, where we neither have the time nor wish to be connected to anything that might make us look like a zealot, is too prevalent in the body of Christ today. We say ridiculous things like, "I don't want to make anybody angry; I just want to be Jesus to them."

Be assured: Jesus would not tolerate what we allow because of our fear of man! And to that we must ask ourselves: *does it matter to me?*

Prayer

"Lord, give me the sense and courage to take a stand and be willing to defend our freedom of religion. In Jesus' Name, amen."

August

Alive and Free

August 1

If the Son sets you free, you will be free indeed.

John 8:36

Peter wasn't sure if he was reaching these men. Only two of them had given their lives to Christ in the time since he'd begun this Thursday night Bible study at a prison just outside his community. He wasn't too impressed with his conversion versus attendance ratio. Right now he was waiting for the prisoners to show up for tonight's meeting following nine o'clock count.

Peter knew firsthand how these men felt, as he'd done a stretch of time five years before. Released and delivered, Peter wanted to give other men the opportunity he'd been given. He warmly remembered the day when that big brute of a man, Ben Johnson, had looked him in the eye and said, "I'm not dead or incarcerated, and I could be either. The reason I'm not is Jesus Christ! Because of Him I'm alive and free!" The smile on his face seemed to fit. There was an evident sincerity in his eyes that said, "This freedom thing is awesome!"

Snapping back to the moment, Peter watched as the men began filing in and taking their seats. When they were settled, he welcomed them and asked them to join him in prayer. "Lord, each of these men has a story, and many should be dead. I thank You that instead they're alive. Help them see what they can have in You. Show them how being one of Your children can conquer any problem they face and how Your love can set them free. Amen."

✝

Prisons come in all forms, and death of the soul can take place long before our physical expiration. Jesus wants to set us free.

Walking through life with burdens we were never meant to carry erects walls of confinement. Any lifestyle that runs in opposition to God's will keeps us from experiencing the fullness of life, the joy and freedom we receive in the Holy Spirit, and leaves us in jeopardy of losing our eternal life. As long as you still breathe, there's a chance to experience these things.

Ben said, "Because of Him I'm alive and free!" The antithesis is dead and incarcerated.

Prayer

"Lord, set me free from this prison I'm in. Release
the chains of bondage and set me free! Amen."

Connect the Dots

August 2

Your word is a lamp to my feet, and a light for my path.

Psalm 119:105

"Come look at my zebra, Mom!" Will called.

"Let me see," Sheena said. "That's great, honey!" she added, impressed with the precision with which he had completed the connect-the-dots drawing.

"Thanks!" said the nine-year-old, the pride of accomplishment evident in his demeanor. "An' look at this! The stripes look like four scrunched letter Zs!" he remarked, tracing each letter to emphasize his point.

What a vivid imagination, Sheena thought, wondering if she would have noticed it herself. "You know, Will, your Uncle Ralph loved connect the dots. And now he's an architectural engineer." Realizing Will needed a simple definition to make the connection from one to the other, she added, "An engineer uses scientific knowledge and principles of how things work to construct buildings, bridges, and other structures."

"I could draw a bridge, Mom!" Will said enthusiastically and began immediately to draw a basic, one-dimensional blueprint with ruler and pencil. Five minutes later, he held aloft the drafting job he had carefully completed. In truth, it bore a striking resemblance to the intended subject matter, quite impressive for a nine-year-old. Who knew? Perhaps her son might just follow in her brother's footsteps.

✝

Connect-the-dot drawings do not provide entertainment alone. They teach the basics in perceptual thinking. As a child, I eagerly guided my pencil from one dot to the next, connecting each corresponding number to the next, revealing the secret of the numbers. These simple drawings taught me the concept of visualization and gave me the ability to understand how critical a sequence of events and following directions are.

God's Word is similar in nature. His written account of history provides a starting point for our spiritual education and leads us through the steps of maturation from infancy, where we are taught His precepts, to maturity in Christ and how we are to conduct ourselves in His service. Each lesson has its own built-in navigation system; as we complete one lesson in life, God's light illuminates our path to the next.

Prayer

"Lord, thank You for Your version of connect the dots. Lead me as I trace my way through each lesson. Help me visualize the path You have laid out for me. In Jesus' Name, amen."

Sticks and Stones

August 3

Whenever Hannah went up to the house of the LORD, her rival provoked her till she wept and would not eat.

1 Samuel 1:7

Laura wiped at her tears as she walked up the drive; she didn't want Dick to see she'd been crying. "I hate mean people!" she vehemently cursed under her breath, not noticing or caring as the bus faded into the distance.

Thoughts from today's trip whirled through her head. *Why does this always happen? Why are people so mean? And why can't people just leave me alone?* She would never get used to the stares and the names. *I never hurt any of them, and still they call me hurtful names, staring at me as if I'm some kind of monster!* The tears began anew.

At seventeen, Laura had been in an explosion involving a gas grill. It had left her with burns over thirty percent of her body. The right side of her face had required extensive cosmetic surgery, leaving disfigurement that could not be hidden. She was still receiving monthly treatments to stretch ongoing skin grafts.

Laura hated visits to the city. Because no matter how much she prayed, she always saw *that look* and heard *those comments.*

Why couldn't people see past the scars? "Why couldn't You have just let me die in that explosion?" she challenged God for the hundredth time.

✝

"Sticks and stones may break my bones, but names will never hurt me." Most of us have used this comeback as a form of protection for lack of a better defense. The idiom is a lie; name-calling hurts.

And for good reason. It undermines our personal confidence while telling us we are defective and unacceptable; it wounds a heart longing to be loved.

Hannah was so affected by name-calling that she wept until she couldn't eat! But God heard Hannah's cry. And he hears ours too. Like Hannah, we too might endure ridicule we do not deserve, but, in the end, our sorrow will turn to joy. There is no guarantee that our situation will soon change, as there is no shortage of mean-spirited people. But God hears our cry. And in time He will take away our pain.

Prayer

"Lord, help me bring healing instead of pain. Guard
my tongue and words. In Jesus' Name, amen."

Dumber than Dogs

August 4

As a dog returns to vomit, so a fool repeats his folly.

Proverbs 26:11

Jeff considered himself a daredevil. His friends considered him foolish.

Jeff, and the rough crowd he hung with, thought it was a true act of courage to go *swerving;* a game in which two friends, upon recognizing the other's vehicle approaching in their direction, *swerved* into the other's lane, passing each other on the wrong side of the road. It didn't matter to them whether it was a city street, highway, or country road.

Jeff and his boys had done this on many occasions. As a matter of fact, they had done it so many times that it had become boring. So they decided to change the rules. Instead of swerving when you saw a friend, you just picked a target vehicle coming your way and swerved into its lane, forcing the unsuspecting driver to slam on his brakes or yield his right of way by pulling off the road. The boys considered it exciting and kept a running total of their *swerves.*

Jeff's wiser friends tried to persuade him to stop his foolish ways, but Jeff just laughed it off, saying, "It makes me feel alive!"

Two days later, the headline in the local paper read: Teen Escapes Death in Auto Accident!

✝

A dog that eats his vomit doesn't know any better. We, on the other hand, should. God instilled in each of us a certain amount of common sense that He expects us to use. To know the consequences ahead of time and choose to complete the act is nothing short of rebellion and is a direct snub to God. To knowingly endanger ourselves or others is not some fun game; it is only foolishness.

We are responsible for our actions. We should not tempt God nor continue doing foolish things for the sake of an adrenaline rush while denying the possibility of great disaster. If we continue in our folly, we are dumber than dogs and will certainly end up paying a higher price than we ever thought possible.

Prayer

"Loving Father, I am capable of doing foolish things. Please help me realize the error in my thought process before someone pays a price he was never meant to pay. In Jesus' Name, amen."

Broken

August 5

The sacrifices of God are a broken spirit...

Psalm 51:17

The Sunday service had begun as it did each week with the worship team leading the congregation in praise and worship. Nothing unusual there, the people's praises inviting God into the atmosphere.

Then God showed up, and it was personal.

Conrad loved singing and praising God. Suddenly, in the midst of worship, he felt an enveloping presence, a fullness he'd never experienced before. From deep inside his being he heard a voice speak.

Jerking his head up and looking around to see who was watching, Conrad was momentarily stunned. Seeing no one looking his way, he closed his eyes once more. As he did, he realized the voice had come from *inside.* And the moment that realization hit him, he heard it again. "Broken. You must come broken."

To say Conrad was startled was a gross understatement! God had never spoken to him like this! Regaining his thoughts, he whispered, "What do You mean, *broken?*"

"You are holding on to burdens that are not yours. But unless you are broken, I cannot take them." The Holy Spirit continued, "I want all of you. Even the deeply hidden things, Conrad. You must be broken to be made whole."

Conrad hesitated only a moment. "Take my heart, Lord. Make me whole."

✝

Completely broken in spirit, yielded to God at the purest level, requires our desires to take a back seat to God's will. Scary, but it's actually where we are the safest.

Satan says otherwise. He whispers, "It's too great a risk; you will be humiliated."

Satan is a liar. Complete submission to God can be intimidating; voluntary vulnerability is not natural. But it is where pride yields to God's Sovereignty in such a way that He can heal the deepest, darkest wounds of our heart.

God wants to take our broken pieces and fit them together in such a way as to make us whole. He wants to set us free of the bondage of secret sin. To risk our heart this way is to leave ourselves bare before the Lord. But the benefits are worth any possible risk.

Our Savior is gentle and loving. He does not humiliate His children. He's asking us today, "Will you come broken in spirit?"

Prayer

"I sacrifice my broken spirit, Lord. Make me whole. Amen."

Instruments of Grace

August 6

Each one … faithfully administering God's grace.

1 Peter 4:10

At seventeen, Kellen was a repeat offender.

Marshal was his newest probation officer. "You tired of the juvy system yet? 'Cause if you keep shopliftin', you're gonna find out what it's like to be tried as an adult. And they'll introduce you to our wonderful prison system."

Silence.

"I don't get you, Kellen." That wasn't exactly true, but he wasn't ready to tell his story. "You're a good-looking kid, star athlete, good grades, then *bang!* You throw it all away. What for? A few trinkets?"

"Like you care," came his smug reply.

Marshal spoke softly. "What makes you think I don't?"

"No one else ever did. What makes you different?" Kellen shot back.

"Look, Kellen, you may find it hard to believe, but I *do* care. I've a better understanding of your life than you might think." What Kellen didn't know was that Marshal had done time for petty theft as a teen. Then someone had taken an interest in his future. They had cared enough to reach out; it had changed Marshal's life.

He continued, "I've been where you are, Kellen. And someone cared enough to get involved. Things were screwed up on the inside of me. My stealing was a cry for help. And because they understood that, things changed. It can happen for you too if you want it to. How about it? Can you try to trust me?"

"I don't know why I do it," Kellen finally responded honestly.

"Now that, I believe," said Marshal.

✝

Moral and ethical patterns are set at an early age. What we learn or don't learn in our youth shapes our values. Under ideal circumstances, we grow and mature and make adjustments to those values until they are tempered with wisdom and integrity. But most kids don't grow up in an ideal world.

Today's society throws pitches to our children they are not ready to hit. And their immaturity doesn't stop them from swinging. Mistakes are made; consequences arise.

But the mistakes need not be permanent or the consequences life-ending. We can reach out in grace and compassion with an offer to lead those who would otherwise remain lost, into the saving grace of God.

Prayer

"Make me an instrument of your love and grace,
Lord. Use me to affect change. Amen."

Hidden or Bare?

August 7

Nothing...is hidden from God's sight. Everything is uncovered and laid bare.

Hebrews 4:13

Jeremy had been dealing from the bottom of the deck, so to speak, living a life committed to Christ on the outside while entertaining a hidden secret. He loved Jesus but seemed unable to resist the temptation of gambling. He wasn't sneaking off to the local casinos or playing online poker; Jeremy was addicted to lotto tickets. Things had gotten out of hand. He'd purchased more than three hundred dollars worth in the past month. Bills were being ignored, and his stress level had spiked.

He'd run into a few members of his congregation at the local convenience store while buying tickets, but had covered up by lying, saying he was getting them for a neighbor.

As it turned out, a recovering gambler had observed him scratching tickets in the parking lot. Sensing God's leading, the man approached Jeremy's car. He tapped on the window, causing Jeremy to jump as if stung; the shock and distress on his face told the man all he needed to know.

Caught and embarrassed, Jeremy's immediate thought was, *This is none of his business!* But he kept it to himself. "Hey, Mark. What's up?" he said.

"Hey Jeremy, how's this lotto ticket thing working out for you?" Caught off guard by Mark's candidness, Jeremy just sat in stunned silence, unable to answer. And in a moment of clarity, Jeremy realized God was giving him an opportunity for freedom. He'd sent Mark, who knew a little something about this corner of hell.

✝

If we believe the evil we do will not be uncovered, we are deceived. God's Word declares He sees everything. But the deceit-filled heart whispers, "You will not be found out or required to pay the consequences of your indiscretion." We buy the lie, living in blissful ignorance until it all comes crashing down around us.

There is a depravity in hidden sin. It can convince and pervert the purest of hearts, successfully convincing us that God isn't really watching.

But His Word says otherwise. Anything hidden will be spoken of from the rooftops (Luke 12:3).

Prayer

"You alone know everything about my life, Lord.
Cleanse my heart and keep me from the lies
of hidden sin. In Jesus' Name, amen."

It's the Filling That Matters

August 8

Like a coating of glaze over earthenware are fervent lips with an evil heart.

Proverbs 26:23

Five feet nine inches tall, long auburn hair, and deep green eyes, she was stunning! Clark almost tripped as he turned to get a second look at the woman he'd just walked past. "Wow! I'd love to get to know her," he said, nudging his buddy, Brad.

"No, you wouldn't," came Brad's unexpected reply. "She's a snob, Clark," he said.

"Aw, you're just jealous," he quipped.

"Let me tell you a true story, Clark," Brad said and proceeded. "Everywhere this woman goes, she commands attention. Everyone who sees her jockeys to meet her and to be seen with her. Yet few ever get the chance. Those who do usually regret ever wasting time trying." Looking to see if he was making any impression, he continued. "My father was present on one occasion when a young man about her age approached her at a dinner party. He shyly asked her to have a drink with him in the restaurant bar. Dad said the woman briefly looked at him and with disdain in her voice, said, 'It would be a tremendous waste of my time, and I would die before I would be seen with the likes of you.' And with that, she turned her attention back to her sycophant admirers. Clark, I'm telling you, she's as vile on the inside as she is beautiful on the outside."

✝

Created in God's image, there are, regrettably, times we don't resemble Him in the slightest. Our exterior may be bright and shiny, but our soul can be riddled with poison, leaching out into our surroundings, polluting everything it touches.

It isn't enough to look the part of a Christian. We must share similarities with our Creator. And the similarities must penetrate deeper than the surface of our existence. God, unlike us, is concerned with the heart. He barely slows down to see how we look on the outside.

What people see when they meet us is important, because Who we represent can be seen in our attitude. But the shell is not as important as the filling.

Prayer

"Make me beautiful on the inside, Lord. And help me look
past other's shell to find the goodness within. Amen."

Deeply Within

August 9

I have hidden your word in my heart.

Psalm 119:11

"Okay, now repeat after me," Ms. B instructed her Sunday school class. "You did not choose me ..."

"You did not choose me ..." the children echoed.

"But I chose you ..." Ms. B smiled as she saw the look of determination on one young boy's face.

"But I chose you ..." He was squinting his eyes to help focus.

"And appointed you ..." It was difficult to hold her laughter as she looked from face to face.

"And appointed you ..." The volume was increasing. You could see their hearts were completely given to this memorization exercise.

"To go and bear fruit." She almost whispered it to see their response.

"To go and bear fruit." Giggling could be heard as they followed suit and whispered their responsive statement.

"Can anyone tell me what fruit Jesus is talking about?" Ms. B asked.

"Bananas!" one child hollered.

"Apples!" came another. Fruits of every kind were being hollered out.

Finally, Ms. B, laughing and smiling, held up her hand and called for silence. "Those *are* all fruits and good answers," she said, smiling brightly. "But the fruit Jesus is talking about in this verse is about how we live our lives and how other people know we belong to Jesus because of how we act" (Galatians 5:22).

✝

There are times each day that we could benefit from God's words. They are meant to bring us strength, joy, and purpose.

Scripture memorization is essential to our spiritual well-being. Each verse we commit to memory can comfort us in times of trouble and sorrow, be used to fend off attacks in times of temptation, and enrich our walk with God, but only if they have been planted deeply within. If they are not there to begin with, we cannot recall them when we want or need to.

When Jesus was tempted in the wilderness, the words He memorized as a young boy were used to counter the attacks of Satan. Jesus knew He needed His Father's words to resist the devil. Do we need more reason than this?

Prayer

"Lord, help me begin to hide Your Word deep in my
heart, so it will be there when I not only need it, but
when I want to meditate on it. In Jesus' Name, amen."

Payment on Demand

August 10

You fool. This very night your life will be demanded from you.

Luke 12:20

Luke's credit was tanked. Unable to get the financial assistance he needed from a legitimate lending institution, Luke decided to borrow the money from a shady source. Now the note was due. But Luke didn't have the money. He'd made the initial investment he'd borrowed the cash for; he'd even made a small profit. But Luke had gotten foolish.

Having discovered online poker, Luke began playing regularly. *It's no big deal,* he told himself. *I'm just having a little fun.*

After success in a few online matches, Luke decided to multiply his holdings by entering a high-stakes game. So, taking his winnings, along with the balance of his borrowed investment, Luke did just that.

But things hadn't gone his way; he'd lost it all. And now he was in trouble. The financer was demanding payment.

Nervously, he pleaded with the financer to give him more time to come up with the money, a grace period of sorts, he'd called it. The financer finally decided Luke wasn't worth the risk and had two of his associates teach Luke a lesson. The problem was they got carried away, and Luke died two days later as a result of his injuries.

✝

Today's text reveals there is a payment coming due for each of us. Those who foolishly choose to ignore the demand will suffer for eternity.

We have the ability to ask Jesus Christ to pay the due penalty or put it off right up until the moment we die. After that, all bets are off.

Scripture says we are but a vapor, and then we are gone. We do not know the time of God's demand on our life.

We can do as Luke did, putting off life's most crucial decision until it's too late, or we can turn to the One who has the ability to wipe our slate clean, leaving the balance paid in full. The choice is ours alone.

Prayer

"Lord Jesus, I want and need Your sacrifice to
cover my sin. Cleanse me now with the payment
that only Your blood can cover. Amen."

What Do You See?

August 11

Lift your eyes and look to the heavens: Who created all these? He who brings out the starry host one by one, and calls them each by name. Because of his great power and mighty strength, not one of them is missing.

Isaiah 40:26

Watching the night sky, they were enjoying one of their favorite pastimes: stargazing. Tonight the whole family was there. The kids were lying in the middle of the hood of the car, Mom and Dad on the sides, all of them bundled in blankets, their heads cushioned by pillows. They were looking for meteors. Terry loved the stars. He always felt close to God when surveying the wonders of the universe. Tonight and tomorrow night, August 11 and 12, were the peak nights to observe the Purseid meteor shower.

They had driven up on Coe Hill in the wee hours of the morning, their hearts building with anticipation and excitement to witness hundreds of brilliant green and white vapor trails streaking across the sky as the little pieces of dust lit up the atmosphere!

It began around 4:00 a.m. with just a few at a time and then built to what seemed like hundreds coming in from every direction! They were privileged to see one of the most awesome displays of fireworks God had ever provided! All for the meager price of a couple hours of sleep. It was a night they would cherish and speak of often.

✝

How is it that some people look at the sky and see God while others see only stars?

As Terry lay there, he was reminded of the *Apollo* 11 moon landing in July 1969 as Neil Armstrong spoke those immortal words: "One small step for man. One giant leap for mankind." Many people aren't aware of what Buzz Aldrin was doing; he was taking communion and reading Scripture, but was unable to broadcast it because of a legal battle NASA was in at the time.

The world touted man's accomplishment; Aldrin silently proclaimed the power of God.

Prayer

"Father of the heavens, I am awed by Your mighty power.
I don't know the names of all the people in my town, yet
You know my name and the name of every star. How
immeasurable is Your glory! Thank You for Creation! Amen."

Will You?

August 12

If one of you says to him, "Go, I wish you well; keep warm and well
fed," but does nothing about his physical needs, what good is it?

James 2:16

Quinn had lost his job and hadn't been able to find suitable employment in
over four months. They had used Charlotte's most recent paycheck to keep
the electric and gas on, but their mortgage, as well as a signature loan, was two
months delinquent. The slumping economy and Quinn's disability had only
added to their struggle. This morning found them pouring out their hearts to
God, asking for divine intervention.

Around noon, Charlotte received a call from a couple in their congregation. They felt God leading them to share some food with them. "How much
room do you have in your freezer?" came the question.

An hour later, the credit union called. Quinn assumed they were notifying
him of collection proceedings and prayed for strength to deal with this situation. However, when he got on the line, the account manager said, "Mr. R,
an anonymous provider has stopped by our office this morning and paid your
mortgage accounts current. They have asked we not divulge their identity, but
that we inform you so you can best use the finances you have available." Quinn
was numb with wonder as he hung up the phone. It took a full minute before
he was able to relate the nature of the call to Charlotte.

✝

At a time when society trusts their 401(k) or stock portfolio to provide for
tomorrow, God is asking us to trust *Him* and not yield to the temptation to
lean on ourselves for the future.

Giving God permission to reposition His money through us is not an easy
thing to do. It requires faith that He truly is a debtor to no man.

Today's text is clear; we are not to stand idly by and give lip service to
situations that demand attention. Giving out of our abundance requires an act
of will. Will you?

Prayer

"Lord, help me to bare the essence of Your love. Help
me hang on loosely to the things You have given
me. May I never see a brother in need and fail to do
everything I can to meet it. In Jesus' Name, amen. "

With Jesus

August 13

When they saw the courage of Peter and John ... they took note that these men had been with Jesus.

Acts 4:13

Dewey held up his hand, asking for silence. "I understand your doubt, folks. But"—he paused for emphasis—"if we fail to take this stand, our children and their children will pay the price of our indifference."

"What makes you so sure they won't rule against us anyway?" challenged one dissenter. "I, for one, am not in favor of rocking the boat. They'll just use this as a platform to build a stronger case against us!" the man argued. He was alluding to city council's removal of all God-related materials from public buildings and property over the last year. Tonight's meeting had been called because council was now legislating new ordinance against open-air gatherings of a religious nature.

"Look, I hear you," Dewey acknowledged. "But I believe you're dead wrong. It's that very attitude that allowed God to be removed from our schools. We did nothing to stand up for the free exercise of our religious rights the Constitution gives us. We must stand now."

The man sat back down, red-faced and fuming.

Dewey continued, "Sitting still and *hoping* the enemy retreats is the equivalent of saying, 'Go ahead, take all my rights.'"

He finished with, "Look, if we believe Jesus is Who He says He is, then it's our responsibility to take the same action He would take if He were here."

✝

Would a stranger know we've been anywhere near Jesus? Or do we, instead, blend in with the world through our words and actions?

As Christians, there ought to be a visible difference, something tangible that causes others to take notice when they see us, something that causes them to ask what that *difference* is. The only way others will know that we have been with Jesus is by the giving over of our right to ourselves and into the control of the Holy Spirit, by dying to self so Christ can shine through.

Peter and John displayed a countenance of courage after the Holy Spirit's presence was evident in their lives. That same Spirit wants to grow us into the likeness of Christ.

Prayer

"Help me put to death anything that would keep me from looking like You, Lord Jesus. Amen."

Understanding Comfort

August 14

Comfort…with the comfort we ourselves have received.

2 Corinthians 1:4

Danny was a commercial construction contractor. His firm built low-rise structures in and around the downtown area. He and his wife, Susan, their three children, Ammie, Ben, and Chris, lived in the suburbs.

This morning, Danny was running a bit late, but that was okay because it was Saturday, and he would be the only one at the jobsite anyway. He and Susan had stayed up late to watch *It's a Wonderful Life* last night, Susan giggling at George and Mary's whirlwind romance, teasing Danny and saying, "If you treated me the way George treats Mary, we'd never have a bad day." Susan would remember, with heart-wrenching clarity, her comment in the days to come.

As Danny jumped in his truck, Susan waved good-bye through the side door. Neither of them saw Chris playing behind his father's truck, and in one horrifying moment, Danny put the truck in reverse and backed out of the garage, running over his five-year-old son, killing him instantly.

In the weeks that followed, they were surrounded by friends and family who tried to comfort them. But no comfort could be found. Danny couldn't sleep; Susan blamed herself and Danny for the loss of her son.

The blame would shift from themselves to God and back over the next two years. Their faith would ultimately hold them together, and grief counseling would bring a measure of healing. But not before the enemy had his way for awhile.

✝

What do we do when tragedy of this magnitude invades our lives? It seems so unfair, and the anger over a life taken long before its time runs deep. "How could a loving God allow something like this to happen?"

We say, "Bad things happen to good people." And this is true but woefully inadequate for these situations.

The truth is bad things do happen, and sometimes they happen to us instead of somebody else. And we need the understanding comfort only God and those who have lost a child can bring. If you are bearing this grief, reach out. If you have lived through this nightmare, comfort those whose pain is still raw.

Prayer

"My life is Yours, Lord. But today that doesn't
help. Show me how to grieve this unspeakable loss.
Bring healing to my broken heart. Amen."

Superficial
August 15

Let another praise you, and not your own mouth.

Proverbs 27:2

Reed had just brokered the largest deal in sports history. His client was now the Breakers' newest running back.

Reed had landed Gerald Humphries a multimillion-dollar contract with the largest signing bonus ever demanded. Not only would his client be set for life, so would he. But aside from business, no one seemed to gravitate to Reed; his attitude alienated everyone who knew him, and those who didn't quickly learned how big his ego was.

The press prompted Humphries, wanting to quickly get the details of the contract so they could write their stories and make deadline. One reporter asked a pointed question about his lightning speed only to have Reed interrupt and make the following statement: "Humphries is fast. But his ability isn't unique. There are many athletes with his ability. But nobody on the planet could have closed this deal except me. I'm the reason this kid's getting the largest signing bonus this team ever paid!" It didn't occur to Reed that he was a distinct turnoff or that they really didn't want to hear about *his* personal triumphs. It didn't register that he was smugly touting his own achievements instead of directing questions to his client, who was standing beside him with a look of complete amazement on his face. And it never occurred to Reed how his arrogance was received until, following the press conference, Humphries fired him.

✝

When we set out to exalt ourselves, we will, at the very least, be reviled and at worst, humbled by God.

Our God-given talent is to be used in helping *others* rise to new levels of success and service. We should never promote ourselves. Self-promotion is vain conceit.

And there is no surer way of alienating ourselves from God and the relationships He intends us to share with others. It is difficult to enjoy the company of someone who constantly exalts themselves. It reeks of narcissism.

We should instead look for opportunities to elevate others and their accomplishments, not looking for personal gain or recognition.

Prayer

"Keep me humble, Lord. Help me to seek not to
elevate myself in the eyes of men and to do what
is right in Your eyes. In Jesus' Name, amen."

Cryin' Saints

August 16

And he who searches our hearts … intercedes for the saints.

Romans 8:27

It would be thirty years before the boy would understand what he'd witnessed that night.

It was the church's weekly prayer meeting, and elders, spiritual leaders, and many members of the congregation, as well as the senior and associate pastors, were present in the Fireside Chapel.

The young boy didn't want to be there. But he was the associate pastor's son, and when Dad went to church, he went to church.

As he sat in one of the comfy chairs in the back of the chapel, he watched and listened. For over an hour they prayed. The boy was beginning to fidget. Then he heard crying from the altar; he wasn't sure what to make of that. He'd never heard anyone cry when they prayed. And this wasn't just normal crying either. Whoever it was, they were sobbing!

Curious, he stood on his chair to take a look. His curiosity was rewarded as he discovered it was the senior pastor.

On the way home, the boy questioned his father. "Why was Reverend Wilber cryin', Dad?"

His father paused and then tried his best to explain how the Holy Spirit moves on the hearts of His saints when they're in desperate prayer. "When that happens, the emotion can sometimes be overwhelming. And sometimes people even cry," his father had said.

The young boy looked through the darkness at his father and asked in complete innocence, "So Reverend Wilber is a cryin' saint?"

✝

The Holy Spirit intercedes for His saints when they don't know what to pray. And *we* are His saints.

I've known many who believe the term *saint* is reserved for those who have gone before us in death or for those whose contribution to the faith has raised them to a loftier salvation than our own. But plainly, saints are people who have separated themselves from the world and consecrated themselves to the worship and service of God.

Many of us have needed God's urgent intervention and were at a loss for words. A "cryin' saint" is someone given over to the Holy Spirit's examination, asking Him to take the need before the throne of God when we can't.

Prayer

"When I can't pray, Lord, please take over and
speak to the Father on my behalf. Amen."

Never Grow Weary

August 17

Do not become weary … for at the proper time we will reap a harvest
if we do not give up.

Galatians 6:9

Charles and Lucille had been married twenty-eight years. "Lord, you promised
Charles would come to You if I was diligent in prayer. I have been praying
faithfully all these years. Please show me that my prayers are making a difference. Just a morsel, Lord!" she implored.

That night, Lucille had a dream. In the dream she saw a lamb. God spoke
to her, "Pay attention. Look!" She looked again; the lamb had become a sheep.
God said again, "Pay attention. Look!" She looked once more to see that the
sheep had become dirty and was peeking around the corner, poking its head
in and out. God then said, "This is Charles at the door, wanting to come in.
Continue to pray!"

Two weeks later, Charles gave Lucille an unexpected gift. Lucille opened
the package to find a praise and worship CD; she was elated! "Thank You,
Lord!" she said, grateful for another morsel.

Lucille listened to the CD repeatedly, gaining inspiration in the knowledge God was changing Charles's heart. One evening, she walked into the
house to find Charles not only listening to the CD but also singing along! "Oh,
Lord! Thank You!" she whispered.

Three weeks later, Charles began attending church with Lucille; within six
weeks, Charles gave his life to Christ!

✝

Lucille's perseverance in prayer is a lesson for us all. Many, if not all of us, have
unsaved family members. Though they may not respond to our direct influence,
we can affect change by lifting them to the throne consistently, praying for the
veil to be lifted and God's light to penetrate the darkness.

Today's text encourages us to not give up in our weariness. God hears our
prayers and responds by drawing them unto Himself.

Twenty-eight years is a considerable amount of time to pray without evidence of an answer. Yet it pales in comparison to eternity and eternal separation from Christ. We must not grow weary; it is not hopeless.

Do you want a harvest? Persevere in prayer!

Prayer

"Lord, hear my prayer. Draw all those in my family
who don't know You to Your side. Help me to never
give up on them. In Jesus' Name, amen."

The Last Supper at Breakfast
August 18

When evening came Jesus was reclining at the table with the twelve.

Matthew 26:20

While eating breakfast, Rachel noticed the painting of *The Last Supper* and asked, "Do you know what that painting means, Uncle Ed?"

"No," he responded.

His response caused her to ask, "Have you ever accepted Jesus as your Savior?"

"I don't know how," was his strained response.

Continuing to pursue this line of questioning, Rachel asked, "Do you know Who Jesus is?"

"No, not really," he admitted. "Did you ever attend church?" she asked.

"No," he began. "I can't read, you know, and I was afraid the preacher would call on me for answers. So I stayed home…" He trailed off, a note of shame in his voice.

Where do I start, Lord? she thought. *I can't ask him if he wants a Savior he doesn't know.*

"At the beginning," God replied. So for an hour, Rachel related biblical events: Creation, the flood and Noah, Moses, the exodus to the promised land, concluding with Jesus' birth, death, and resurrection. When she finished, Ed said, "Come with me." He led her to the bedroom where he brought out a book of Bible stories. It contained the very stories she'd just shared!

Taking God's cue, Rachel asked; "Would you like to ask Jesus into your heart?" she said.

"Oh, yes, yes, yes!" he responded.

✝

Ed is now with his Savior. Rachel's sensitivity enabled her to present the invitation.

We should never *assume* that people *know* Jesus, even if they have religious material around the house. Had Rachel accepted the painting as proof of Ed's salvation, he could have spent eternity in hell.

The truth is there are many *unsuspecting people* on their way to hell; many because we assume they've heard about Jesus, so we don't go out of our way to ask them, "Do you know Who Jesus is?"

We may be required to give explanation of the events from Creation through the resurrection; people should understand the decision they're making. And this may require doing some things we're not comfortable with. In light of the alternative, we must put aside our discomfort and never *assume* they know the truth.

Prayer

"Make me sensitive to those who don't know You, Lord. Help me help them to know Who You are. In Jesus' Name, amen."

Enemy-Occupied Territory

August 19

The god of this age has blinded the minds of unbelievers.

2 Corinthians 4:4

Jennifer and Karen were having the age-old discussion. "How can a loving God let bad things happen to good people?"

"In war after war, innocent men, women, and children die senseless deaths. And for what?" Karen demanded. "Are you going to tell me that it's *God's judgment* for a nation's disobedience?!"

"Karen, no matter what I say, it probably won't change your belief of God turning a blind eye to injustice. I understand your frustration and at one time shared your misconceptions about how God can say He loves us yet stand by and let people suffer. How do you rationalize cancer or AIDS?" The softness in Jennifer's voice did little to diffuse Karen's anger. When her husband died of leukemia, Karen blamed God for not answering her prayers. She'd turned away from God and hadn't returned since Randy's death.

"Karen, you mentioned wars and how innocent people die needless deaths. The truth is we were born into war. And we live in enemy-occupied territory. This is not the earth God created. That all changed when Adam ate the forbidden fruit. And until Jesus comes to judge the Earth, and all those in it, we will live under the enemy's occupation."

†

It is inconceivable—apart from faith in God's redemptive nature—that evil reigns on Earth. Yet, Adam had a choice: say no to temptation and retain dominion or eat the fruit and usher in a season of mankind possessing knowledge we were never meant to have. When that happened, sin, in the form of illness, lustful desire, and myriad forms of idolatry entered the heart of man, and death was required so we would not live *forever in our sin.*

Those who believe there should be no evil among us are living under a veil of deception. The enemy manipulates the hearts of those who will listen to his sordid lies.

Bad things do happen to good and bad alike. In this world, God does not promise we will not endure hardship and loss, but that while in enemy-occupied territory, He will provide shelter.

Prayer

"Lord, we pray for the removal of the veil from
the minds of those who blame You for the evil
in this world. In Jesus' Name, amen."

The Three Whys

August 20

No one comes to the Father except through me.

John 14:6

"Okay, Mr. Know-It-All," Marvin challenged. "What makes you so sure *you* have the right answers? I may not be the sharpest knife in the drawer, but what makes *your* beliefs right and *mine* wrong?" The heat was evident in his tone.

"Marvin," Chris began softly. "I don't have all the answers, and you are right sometimes. But when it comes to *those* three questions, there is truth, and there are lies. I believe each of us is faced with a choice: believe and follow Jesus or reject Him and spend eternity in hell."

"Yeah, I got that!" There was no give in Marvin. "Your belief says that God is where I came from, God is why I'm here, and God wants me to know where I'm going!" Sarcasm dripped from his words. "So," Marvin goaded, "God is the answer to *everything!*"

"Marvin, just because you choose not to believe in God doesn't make Him nonexistent. The proof is all around you." Chris had a thought. "Take gravity, for instance," he baited. "You can say you don't believe in it. Yet, if you were to put your belief to the test from the top of a ten-story building, your belief wouldn't keep you from dying."

"No one's stupid enough to do something that ignorant when the proof is so apparent," Marvin interjected.

"Right!" Chris said. "Seeing makes it easy to believe. But faith believes without undisputable proof," Chris finished.

"Well, until I have proof of God's existence, I'm not buyin' it!" The conversation died an uncomfortable death.

✝

God created us for a relationship with Him. His desire is that we choose to spend eternity with *Him.*

And the world hates Him for it. They can't abide His conditions that we accept the sacrifice of His Son on Calvary's cross as the propitiation for our sinful living, asking His forgiveness, and turning from sin.

They revile and reject God's one-way atonement, demanding, "How can a benevolent Father make such a demand?"

And to that there's only one answer: Jesus died to present us faultless before God.

Whether we choose to believe Him or not has no relevance to the truth.

Prayer

"Lord, use me to help others see the truth in You. Amen."

Walking It Out
August 21

How beautiful are the feet of those who bring good news.

Romans 10:15

Sandra and Ginny had been friends for almost ten years. In that time, they had shared their lives. The most important thing they shared was a deep love for Jesus, and for over nine years, they had committed to deepening that relationship.

Two years into their friendship, God led them to begin prayer-walking their neighborhood, rising in the predawn hours to walk and lift their neighbors and their needs to God.

They watched in wonder as God brought neighbors into their lives with critical timing: someone facing a tremendous struggle or the loss of a family member. They were able to witness God's love and spend time with each one in prayer. They simply followed God's lead.

They had been prayer-walking for three years when they felt God asking them to *assemble* the neighborhood so He could weave their lives together. So they set to work planning the first block night Sharp Road would ever experience. They dropped off invitations to every family, asking them to bring one covered dish, lawn chairs, and an appetite. That inaugural evening had been a remarkable success!

Five years later, they still gather monthly at a home determined the prior month. Volunteers are never in short supply, and the fellowship is sweet.

Sandra and Ginny count it a privilege to be part of the movement of God that has seen seven people, to date, accept Jesus as their Savior.

✝

Paul's prayer at the beginning of chapter ten is that the Israelites might be saved. He makes the case that *anyone* believing on the name of Jesus *will be saved.* Then he sets about challenging their conviction and commitment to Christ. "And how can they believe in one of whom they have not heard?" He's asking them to go tell others about Jesus.

Knowing Jesus is only the beginning for those who are saved. Telling others about the freedom and joy we have in Christ should be, like Paul, the desire of our heart.

Walking it out means taking each opportunity God provides to share His Son.

Prayer

"Lord, lead me to those who have never heard of You. Guide my feet to who needs to hear about You next. In Jesus' Name, amen."

The Egg Minister

August 22

Each man should give what he has decided in his heart to give.

2 Corinthians 9:7

The two-story Cape Cod blended well into the surrounding countryside. And the 6.2 acres of land it sat on was sufficient to allow the boys room to grow. Ron and Rochelle had purchased this little piece of *country* for the expressed purpose of raising their three boys outside the lights of the city.

Ron had built two outbuildings, a kennel for the dogs, and a workshop for himself. One day, Rochelle asked Ron to add a chicken coup to the side of the dog kennel. Standing on the porch, Rochelle smiled as she fondly remembered that day two years ago when God had called her into the ministry. Not just any ministry, mind you; He'd called her into the egg ministry. Ron had thought it a strange request but had built it nonetheless, saying, "Chickens you want, chickens you get."

Rochelle hadn't immediately explained her plans, mostly because she wasn't quite sure what those plans were exactly. All she knew for sure was that God had given her a desire to own a few laying hens. It seemed a reasonable desire; they would enjoy fresh eggs, and the boys would learn about raising chickens.

As the hens began to lay, Rochelle discovered they had more eggs than they could use. With this unexpected bounty, Rochelle realized she could bless a few of the neighboring families. And so it began, a ministry that now saw Rochelle giving dozens of eggs to family and friends.

✝

Such simple projects generate a tremendous impact. Giving of our lives is the most personal service we can offer. To give money is good; we are all supposed to assist in financing the kingdom of God.

But when we give something for which we have labored, it tells others we have taken time to share our lives.

Not all of us are called to move to the country and raise chickens. But we do each have the ability to step outside ourselves, seeking new and unique ways to serve. Ministry begins when God plants a desire in our heart. It's up to us to make it grow.

Prayer

"I want to be about Your business, Lord. Show me
where I might be of service. In Jesus' Name, amen."

Waiting in Fear

August 23

The wicked man flees though no one pursues...

Proverbs 28:1

Day after day he waited for the phone to ring or for the police to knock on his door. Ever since he'd found that wallet, he'd been living in a constant state of fear. He knew he should have returned it to the owner when he'd found it. But when he discovered those six one-hundred-dollar bills, something had come over him.

He'd removed the cash and thrown the wallet, credit cards, driver's license, and all into the Potomac River. He hadn't had a good night's sleep since! He just knew someone was going to figure it out; then they'd come calling.

Finally, unable to deal with the constant pressure of waiting to be caught, he'd gone to the forty-seventh precinct and turned himself in, saying he wanted to repay the money he'd found, but he couldn't remember the man's name.

Unable to substantiate his statement due to the lack of evidence, the detective had finished taking the report and told him, "If anyone files a report about a lost wallet, and if he chooses to file charges, we'll be in touch. Without someone pressing charges, we have no reason to hold you."

Leaving the station, he felt worse than before. He had no idea if someone would ever claim the lost wallet or not. He'd sacrificed his clear conscience in the heat of the moment, and now he couldn't get free from the guilt of his actions.

✝

When we begin to do the wrong thing, our conscience automatically responds by alerting us. *This is not right!* If we fail to respond correctly, the Holy Spirit convicts our heart in an effort to bring repentance and return us to a right relationship with God.

What we do in that moment will determine whether we walk in integrity, without the constant over-the-shoulder looks, or wait in fear for the phone to ring.

Unscrupulous behavior breeds evil and fear. If left unchecked, it desensitizes our hearts, building an uncrossable chasm between us and God.

It is far better to repent and face the consequences than it is to live waiting in fear.

Prayer

"Lord, Help me resist temptation when I'm weak or
unprepared. Keep my heart pure. In Jesus' Name, amen."

Unobservant

August 24

The disciples came to him..."Tell us," they said...what will be the sign of your coming?"

Matthew 24:3

Craig pulled in the driveway, thankful to be home from vacation. He was tired. The kids were asleep in the back; Marie was out cold too. He decided to unload the car before waking anyone. *No sense in them being awake at 3:00 a.m.*

He'd walked past the living room three times, taking each piece of luggage to the appropriate room. This time, however, on his way out the front door, he glanced into the living room and realized something wasn't right. *Strange,* he thought, *something's different, but what? Oh well.* He'd figure it out eventually.

Finished unloading the car, he carried each child to their bedroom, got them into pajamas, and kissed each on the forehead as he covered them up.

Returning to the car, he woke Marie and assisted her into the house. Half bleary eyed, Marie walked through the front door, took one look into the living room, and jolted wide-awake, a shock replacing her sleep-filled eyes, "We've been robbed!" she blurted out.

"What?" Craig said in surprise. Then it registered: the TV, DVD player, MP3 player, and Bose stereo were all gone! *How could I have missed that?* he thought, followed by Marie's question, "Didn't you notice there was no TV when you turned the light on in here?" she asked incredulously.

"I noticed something was different; I just didn't know what," he said sheepishly.

✝

In truth, we, like Craig, are prone to miss things once in awhile. Especially in spiritual matters. Granted, to miss being robbed is a biggie, but consider this: even the disciples missed what Jesus was trying to say. So much so that He warned them to "keep watch" (verse 42), knowing they would probably let their guard down without His encouragement.

End-time signs are all around us: "Wars and rumors of wars; Nation rising against nation; famines and earthquakes...the beginning of birth pains."

But whether Christ comes in the next ten minutes or ten thousand years, we are to watch and interpret the signs, preparing for His coming by sharing the gospel.

Prayer

"Lord, help me be sensitive to everything important
that's going on. Show me where to focus my efforts
for Your kingdom. In Jesus' Name, amen."

Beetle Boots and Levis

August 25

If anyone says to you, "Look, here is the Christ…do not believe it.
For false Christs and false prophets will appear."

Matthew 24:23

It was two days and counting; summer vacation was over. "You never get us the original!" Elliott said with the frustration of a fifteen-year-old. "Everybody else in school will have genuine Levis and Beetle Boots. Not some lame knockoffs like these!"

"Honey," his mother began, "we can't afford the originals. Those boots and jeans are three times as much as these, and they don't fit our budget. This is the best we can do." Had Elliott been thinking about anything but himself, he would have been able to see the hurt in his mother's eyes. But he wasn't, and he didn't. All he could see were cheap imitations that would elicit ridicule from his peers at school. They'd take one look at these off-brand jeans and low-heeled boots with the zipper on the side instead of in the back, and they'd say what they always said, "Whutsamatter, Bennett? Mommy still dressing you?" Kids could be cruel, and these lessons seemed unfair.

With that thought in his head, Elliott headed for his room. *I've gotta figure a way to get what I want or everyone'll think I'm uncool!* And with that, he slammed his bedroom door on the world.

†

There is a knockoff for everything; someone has counterfeited the original and is looking to profit from it. And in most cases it's not life threatening.

However, there is one counterfeit that we must not buy, and regardless of the cost, we must purchase the original!

Satan has staked his claim to the throne of God and comes deceiving those who would listen to his sales pitch. His minions tell us we're uncool and won't be accepted unless we buy what they're selling.

Jesus, knowing sin is tempting in the early stages because it feels good, warns us so we will be on guard, because there are always consequences. To make the wrong choice in this case will be eternally fatal.

Jesus is the original; there is no other way to salvation.

Prayer

"Lord, help me see past all the bells and whistles
when Satan comes to deceive. Help me discern the
lies and seek the truth. In Jesus' Name, amen. "

Assembly Line Christianity
August 26

Be imitators of God.

Ephesians 5:1

Jessie's passion meter was stuck on "I'm here" and didn't seem to register any higher. It wasn't so much that he didn't want a deeper relationship with Jesus; he just wasn't sure how to go about getting it. And six months of attending this church hadn't helped. It was "Come as you are, we'll accept you. Do as we tell you and everything will be wonderful!" Yet, he didn't seem to know any more about Jesus than he had when he'd first started here.

"Everything here seems tailored to mold people into some kind of automaton," he'd shared with another newbie, as they were referred to in the membership class. "Doesn't this feel kinda *plastic* to you?" he suddenly asked.

"I guess I never thought about it," was the man's casual reply. "What do you mean?" he countered.

"Well," Jessie began, "I feel like we're all on this big assembly line headed for the final production stage with nothing but superficial understanding. It's like a cookie-cutter mentality. As if they're just trying to *turn out* Christians, and there's no understanding required to graduate." Feeling the need to qualify his comment, Jessie added, "Don't get me wrong, I'm not saying they don't love Jesus, but it's like there's nothing required for membership. We're not required to share what we believe or why. Do you know what I'm getting at?" Jessie asked.

✝

Whose likeness are we trying to imitate? Are we looking for the truth, or are we playing follow the leader, regardless of where the leader is headed?

Many of today's churches offer a brand of religion that falls short of God's example in Jesus Christ. And people blindly follow, thinking, "If it walks like a duck and talks like a duck, it must be a duck," never understanding they are ignorantly tempting hell.

It *absolutely* matters what we believe and why because simply saying the name of Jesus will not gain us entrance into heaven. If we do not confess Jesus as Lord and are not required to ask forgiveness through repentance where there is no turning from sin (understanding we will not do this perfectly), then we are deceived. We will be held accountable, regardless of our professed ignorance.

Prayer

"Lead me on the one true path of salvation, Lord.
Show me the way. In Jesus' Name, amen."

We Are the Prodigal

August 27

Father, I have sinned against heaven and against you.

Luke 15:18

Shell had kept her distance from the zealots in her family for years. Her thought? *If you want to believe in Jesus, fine. Just leave me alone.* Then something had happened that she couldn't explain in rational, humanly possible terms. It had God's handprint all over it; she could no longer deny the truth. "There is a God, and He cares!"

With this newfound realization came understanding: she'd been selfishly doing as she pleased because she wasn't going to live by anyone's rules but her own! Now she understood how blatantly she had snubbed her nose at God! *Oh, what have I done in my arrogant belligerence,* she thought. Not knowing what to do, she called her mom. Through tears of joy, her mother assured her that God could and would forgive her of everything if she just asked Him.

In stark contrast to how she had lived her life, she knelt beside the couch and said through tears, "I know now that I'm a sinner, Lord Jesus. And you have no reason to forgive me, but everyone who knows You says I can ask and You'll forgive every wrong thing I've done. So I'm asking now that You forgive me and come into my heart and make me clean, show me how to live a life worthy of Your sacrifice. Amen." Mother and daughter alternated between laughter and tears, both thanking God for His infinite mercy and grace.

✝

Each of us has sinned against God and need His forgiveness. Many of us have made a lifestyle of it, thinking we could escape judgment. Others want salvation but are under the impression they don't deserve another chance. Neither statement is valid.

We cannot unashamedly reject Jesus Christ and expect mercy, nor are we beyond the depth of His grace if we turn and invite Him into our heart.

As in the story of the prodigal, we have been separated from God by sin. And as the prodigal's father, God is waiting to run to us the moment we turn and head in His direction.

Prayer

"Lord, sometimes I do foolish things and get lost. Lead
me home to where You are. In Jesus' Name, amen."

Let Me Help

August 28

So after ten years … Sarai his wife took … Hagar and gave her to her
husband to be his wife.

Genesis 16:3

"I don't care what you say," Grace challenged. "I think we need to give Stephanie the money." Ralph, on the other hand, felt their daughter needed to learn from her carefree lifestyle and rampant spending.

Protection mode kicked in. "I can't believe you could possibly want her to have to suffer through the long process of reestablishing her credit!" she said diplomatically.

But Ralph felt he needed to stand firm on this issue. "Grace," he began, reining in his frustration in light of her opposition. "What would we be telling her by bailing her out? The truth is," he blurted, "that's just what she believes we're going to do!" Sorry he'd momentarily lost the battle over his emotions, he regrouped, saying, "Honey, she's been way too cavalier about doing as she pleases. I believe she needs to resolve this issue on her own." Attempting to lessen Grace's heartache, he pulled her toward him and held her close as he said, "We had to learn on our own too, you know. No one could tell us what to do at that age either."

"Oh, Ralph." She sighed in resignation. "She's my little girl. I just want to help."

"Me too," he said with an affectionate squeeze.

✝

It can be tremendously difficult to stand aside and allow our children to suffer when any interference on our part would be wrong.

Restraint at a time when someone wants our intervention requires wisdom. Only by seeking God's guidance will we make the right choice.

We might actually be doing our children a disservice by taking action. We may be helping them out of the very situation God intended to use to bring them to an understanding of their improprieties.

When we get in God's way, as Abraham did when he fathered Ishmael, we are taking matters into our own hands instead of allowing God to work things out in His way. Abraham's disobedience has caused two nations to remain in constant contention. We can hurt our children if we're not careful.

Prayer

"Teach me the difference between hindering and
helping, Lord. Show me when to stay out of other
people's business. In Jesus' Name, amen."

Divine Q-tips

August 29

And after the fire came a gentle whisper.

1 Kings 19:12

"Did you hear what I said?" Kelly broke in on his wife's reverie.

"What? Did you say something?" Her startled response told Kelly that Denise hadn't heard a word he'd said.

Always the jokester, Kelly decided to have a little fun at his wife's expense. "You never listen to me!" he wailed in mock frustration, wiping a pretend tear from his eye. "You need to clean your ears out with Q-tips!" He forced himself to keep from laughing, "You don't give me the time of day anymore! I slave my life away for you and what do I get in return? I'll tell you what: nothing! A great big nothing!" He couldn't hold back the laughter anymore.

"You big doofus!" she said, swinging and missing her prankster husband. "I'm sooooo sorry!" She almost touched the floor in a benevolent, servant-style bow, as if humbling herself before her master. "What, pray tell, can this lowly waif do for his highness?" The words dripped with sarcasm.

"Okay, okay," he surrendered. "We could do this all night. But I seriously thought you were listening when I asked if you minded that I go golfing with the guys tonight? I mean, I know you don't care. I was just wondering if you had any plans."

"Nope, nothing that would require the king to stay home guarding his kingdom." She teased. "Have fun, my dear. Hey, would you call Bruce and have him ask Patty to come over while you're gone, please?"

✝

We complain about never hearing from God when, in reality, we haven't been tuned in to the sound of His voice.

We desire some ground-shaking form of correspondence, something more tangible than a whisper and easier to recognize. God, in His sovereignty, would rather we learn how to listen for the gentle whisper of the Holy Spirit.

In truth, there are times when we can't hear God because we don't want to, so we pretend He is mute. The truth is we are deaf, and what our spiritual ears need a good cleaning with divine Q-tips.

Have you ever dug too deep with a Q-tip? It hurts! The more attentive we are, the less digging is required.

Prayer

"Clean my spiritual ears, Lord, so I can
hear You when You speak. Amen."

Conscious Effort

August 30

Think on these things.

Philippians 4:9

Another using dream. Gibb wondered what was going on and what it meant. He couldn't get the images out of his head.

He'd been free from addiction for over five years and hadn't had to deal with the seduction or obsession since then. Yet this dream felt so real; he'd been searching through medicine cabinets in houses that weren't his. When he awoke, his relief was profound. But he was disturbed that he'd not only found pills during his search, he'd taken some! Knowing it would end in him hurting those he loved and terrorizing people he didn't know, he couldn't figure out why, after all these years, the dreams had surfaced again.

Searching for a reason, Gibb realized he'd slacked off in his morning devotions recently. He'd begun to hurry through the readings. He hadn't been as consistent in his prayer time either. Getting out of bed, Gibb decided to change his devotional routine to see if the dreams stopped.

After brushing his teeth, he headed for the living room. Bending his heart to God, Gibb simply asked, "What are the dreams about, Lord?" He received an astonishingly immediate response. "Your life of leisure, Gibson. You have taken things for granted lately, and the enemy has responded. When I told you to think on these things, I meant *all the time.*" Grateful that God had redirected him, and knowing this would end the dreams, Gibb bowed his head in thanksgiving.

✝

We can become neglectful of our relationship with God and end up losing the closeness where we find refuge. It may not necessarily be a fatal mistake, but left unchecked, it can cause needless suffering. Prolonged distancing will cause us to cut ourselves off from our shield of protection. When that happens, we must return to the basics, recommitting our hearts in an effort to draw closer to God. Having gotten sloppy in our approach, it will usually require conscious effort to reestablish our relationship without establishing just a *familiar* routine.

Paul advised the Philippians to think about wholesome things in order to keep their minds stayed on God. We would do well to do the same and not allow ourselves to become slipshod in our spiritual discipline. Conscious effort will be rewarded with closeness in relationship.

Prayer

"I'm prone to becoming lazy, Lord. Help me
recommit my heart and mind to Your care. Draw
me ever closer. In Jesus' Name, amen."

Saddle the Donkey

August 31

Abraham got up and saddled his donkey.

Genesis 22:3

    Carl and Ruth were tired. Working tirelessly for twenty-six years, they had served on almost every board and committee in the church. Someone had told them early in their Christian walk, "God wants us to be spiritually exhausted at the end of each day!" They had taken it to heart, and many times they had sacrificed personal activities in an effort to be where they thought God expected them to be; they just wanted to please God.

    Then one fall Sunday morning, on a rare vacation, they attended worship at a quaint little church in a picturesque little town in the South. The pastor brought a message regarding purposeful service. He explained that our reason for being is to serve the Lord.

    Amen, thought Carl and Ruth.

    Then he said something they'd never heard before. "When God calls us to service, it is to be *His* call, on *His* terms, for *His* purpose. We are not to serve for the sake of service. When God called Abraham to sacrifice Isaac, it was *God's* call. Abraham did not awaken one morning and tell Sarah, 'I think we should sacrifice Isaac. What do you think, Sarah?' He would never have set out to do that on his own!" The pastor went on to say, "We set out to please God by doing things in His name. Many times those things are not what He would have us do."

✝

It is our reasonable sacrifice to serve God. He created us for service. But *what* we do is as important as *why* we do it.

    How many times have we found ourselves *serving* God only to be completely frustrated and at wits' end? If we were to ask, we might hear God say, "I appreciate your hard work, but that's not what I wanted you to do." Many times we begin an act of service, not instigated by God, asking Him to bless it, never connecting our frustration to the fact He wants us doing something else.

    Our self-assigned sacrifice may look good, but we really should make sure God wants us to saddle the donkey.

Prayer

"Lord, please show me what You want me
doing right now. In Jesus' Name, amen."

September

Miles of Preparation
September 1

Being confident of this, that he who began a good work in you will carry it on to completion until the day of Christ Jesus.

Philippians 1:6

As he read the e-mail, he could actually picture the tears running down his daughter's face. In her freshman year at college, she was struggling with separation anxiety. So was her daddy. Separated by two hundred miles, it felt like ten thousand.

That first year marked the beginning of new levels of growth for the family. Visits by both student and parents alike marked their progress. After a couple years of saying good-bye, they didn't hang on to each other quite so long, and the heartache was a little less intense. As the four years passed, there was measurable growth. There were struggles and disappointments: Daddy would undergo bypass surgery, and his daughter would begin to lean on the other man in her life. Her boyfriend of four years would become her fiancé. They would graduate with their bachelor's degrees, return home, and as planned over the past two years, get married. Then new levels of growth would bring new pain.

✝

There is pain attached to most meaningful growth. In childbirth, both mother and child experience trauma. But that trauma gives way to joy and delight. As children grow, they begin to assert their individuality. Falling, they get back up, sometimes crying in pain and needing comfort, sometimes stubbornly moving forward without much thought to the fall.

As God's creation, we have an inherent need to seek and learn and grow. God's good work prepares us for the future. Though our parents provide much of the knowledge we seek, experience is the teacher we learn from the most, because hands-on learning imprints itself deeper in our mind.

As we ourselves have grown, we must allow our children to go it alone, gaining their own experience, trusting in today's text that God began this good work in their hearts. He alone can draw them into a relationship that will guide them as they grow. His preparation brings a certain amount of pain. With that pain comes growth.

Prayer

"I don't really like pain, Abba. But I trust You. Walk me through the pain. Continue this good work in me. In Jesus' Name, amen."

Proven Character

September 2

We also rejoice in our sufferings, because we know that suffering produces perseverance; perseverance, character; and character, hope.

Romans 5:3, 4

Cody was a C- and D student in his freshman and sophomore years of high school. The university he was applying to required a 2.8 GPA for enrollment. His cumulative 2.4 wasn't going to get him in. But someone had watched Cody change over the past two years, and he believed in him. He wrote a letter to the dean of admissions, enlightening him with regard to Cody's accomplishments and his 3.24 GPA in his final two years of school. He asked that the university take into consideration this change of behavior when determining whether this young man should be given an opportunity to prove himself at their institution.

To their credit, they allowed Cody to enroll at their branch campus, promising that a 2.8 GPA in his first year of studies would make him eligible for transfer to the main campus the following semester. To his credit, Cody carried a 3.1 GPA that first year and was allowed to transfer. He graduated with a 3.45 GPA, a bachelor's degree in psychology, and a minor in criminal law.

✝

Cody is reminiscent of those who for one reason or another have applied themselves in their latter years. Sadly, many who make these positive changes are never reaffirmed.

But unlike our peers, God doesn't see us as unfit because we made poor choices in our early years. He is pleased that the changes take place. Cody was fortunate that someone saw the change taking place in him and believed it to be genuine.

God also wants to champion our cause, to stand up for us in the face of opposition. Abba Father wants us to know that He sees us. He knows the truth and urges us to persevere by overcoming hopelessness. He wants us to know and feel the satisfaction of positive change in our lives. He whispers, "It is possible to build character at any point during your life." We need only choose to believe and follow His lead.

Prayer

"Lord, please raise up advocates for those who are genuinely trying to make a better life. Bind those who would stand against them and restore hope to the hearts of Your people. In Jesus' Name, amen."

Deep-Seeded Desires

September 3

Each one is tempted, when by his own evil desire, he is dragged away and enticed.

James 1:14

Taylor was beautiful. Gary had tried—unsuccessfully—to land a date with her for almost two years. So when she stopped by his office on Tuesday and said with a smile, "I'm free Friday night if you don't have any plans," Gary immediately secured the date. The problem was he actually did have plans. And his plan's name was Wendy. Gary and Wendy had been dating for about a month.

Gary, realizing his dilemma, called Wendy and told her something had come up, and he wouldn't be able to keep their date on Friday. Wendy had assured him it was okay and that she would take a rain check.

All day Friday, Gary played out his perfect scenario of how the evening would go: a quiet dinner over on the east side at Carrillo's, a ride in a Handsome Cab through the Old Town, followed by a romantic walk down by the pier. He couldn't believe his luck; he had finally gotten a date with Taylor!

They arrived at Carrillo's around 7:00. Upon entering the restaurant, Gary walked straight into his worst nightmare. There stood Wendy and her father, waiting to be seated. When their eyes met, Wendy's smile disappeared and was replaced by a look of horror and humiliation. Suddenly, Gary realized in his desire to date Taylor he had made a self-centered decision. His regret was profound, immediate, and too late.

✝

Our value systems become compromised when we cloak selfish, indulgent behavior in lies and choose to give in to deep-seeded desires that are morally or ethically wrong. When temptation rears its ugly head, we must look for a way of escape instead of allowing the thought room to breed and grow.

Temptation in itself is not sin. But, as James describes, we get carried away when we don't immediately reject its offer. When we entertain the temptation, we are taking steps to consummate the agreement brought by the enemy. Instead, we should be running in the opposite direction. Remember, no temptation has taken us that we cannot overcome if we choose (1 Corinthians 10:13).

Prayer

"Lord, help me live a righteous life. Cause me to
be aware of the danger in entertaining evil desires,
even momentarily. In Jesus' Name, amen."

Once Upon a Time

September 4

O Lord, open his eyes so he may see.

2 Kings 6:17

"Tell me a bedtime story, Daddy!" squealed Jennifer Rose.

"Okay, but just a short one," Dale said as he lay his daughter in her bed. "Let's see," he began. "There once was a little girl who had a great big guardian angel. One day, as the little girl walked along a path beside a swift-flowing creek, she slipped in the mud, falling headlong into the water. Now, the water was deep and the undertow was strong! The little girl screamed 'Help! Help!' as she struggled against the current. She stroked with all her might, pulling herself closer and closer to the edge of the creek.

Unseen by the little girl, her guardian angel gently pushed her with his huge hand, nudging her toward safety until finally she reached the bank.

Well, that little girl clawed her way onto dry ground; thankful God had heard her cry. She raced home and told her mother about her harrowing experience!

Relieved that her daughter was safe, the mother scolded her for running off on her own. She warned the little girl to never go near the creek alone!

The little girl said, 'I'm sorry, Mommy,' then added, 'But I'm never alone. My guardian angel is always with me! He's the one who saved me!'

Her mother answered, 'That's nice, honey. Now go get changed.' And the little girl lived happily ever after.

Okay, end of story, time to go to sleep." He kissed Jennifer on the forehead and turned out the light.

✝

Most bedtime stories are make-believe and fictional, the equivalent of a fairy tale. But what about today's story? Do we believe, like the little girl, that angels are watching over us in the heavenly realm? Are there otherworldly warriors fending off the enemy as we journey through life? Do we believe, as the Bible declares, that the air around us is filled with a raging battle?

Or do we, like the world, believe that it's just a good story in an outdated book?

We either believe it or we don't. There is no middle ground. So what *do* we believe? Truth or fairy tale?

Prayer

"Reveal the truth to those who doubt in the heavenly realm,
Lord. Like Elisha's servant, open their eyes. Amen."

Intellect or Wisdom?

September 5

A rich man may be wise in his own eyes, but a poor man who has discernment sees through him.

Proverbs 28:11

J.D. Artweller had amassed a fortune. His holdings included three of the high-rise structures visible along Chicago's skyline, one of which housed the eighty-second floor, corner office he was sitting in. He held partnership in two banks and owned the local ALS team. Nobody really knew the true extent to which he was involved.

"Martha!" Artweller hollered at his receptionist. "Is Flanerty here yet?"…"Time is money," he grumbled to himself.

"Yes, Mr. Artweller," Martha answered.

"Then send him in!" came his clipped command.

She smiled across her desk at J.D.'s 2:30 appointment, hoping to alleviate any tension her boss's crassness might be causing.

J.D. didn't seem to care about people other than what they could do to increase his holdings. Embarrassed for the man, she said apologetically, "You may go in now, Mr. Flanerty."

She needn't have been worried. John Flanerty wasn't fazed by Artweller's demeanor. He'd had dealings with J.D. in the past. He knew him to be a very lonely man beneath the rough-barked exterior, and had determined when he'd first met J.D. to show him unconditional kindness by treating him in such a way that it would be in keeping with the nature of Jesus. Perhaps those seeds would sprout and choke out the bitterness entangling his heart.

✝

For reasons unknown to most of us, there are people who have been wounded so deeply that they have turned to the god of wealth for their validation. They hold the misconception that accumulated riches equates to great wisdom. But there is a distinct difference between great wisdom and intellectual and financial cunning. And those who are discerning know the difference, they see right through the J.D.s of the world.

Matthew 6:24 says, "You cannot serve both God and money." This world and everything in it is God's. When we greedily hoard stuff or money we set our hearts against God. To be rich and wise in our own eyes is to be lost. Not just in thought or position, but in spirit. There are no riches worth such cost.

Prayer

"Help me to not be possessive of what You've given me,
Lord. Guide my heart to distribute Your wealth where
it will do the most good. In Jesus' Name, amen."

Soldiers of Love

September 6

As a mother comforts her child, so I will comfort you.

Isaiah 66:13

J.J. had juvenile diabetes. His father pricked his little, four-and-a-half-year-old finger to see if he needed an insulin injection, a process that was repeated four times each day. J.J.'s mom was in charge of making sure he ate the right foods at the right times.

Blindsided two years ago by the diagnosis, Aaron and Megan had managed to make the necessary adjustments, ensuring their son would lead as normal a life as possible.

A professional musician, Aaron was on the road much of the time. Home for a few days, he loved spending time with the kids.

In a recent interview, he'd been asked how Megan managed the home with him on the road so much. "I head home if there's a crisis," he'd said wryly. "But meeting J.J.'s everyday needs falls to Megan. She's a real trooper! Up at seven every morning, she tests J.J.'s blood sugar and fixes breakfast accordingly. She balances the demands of J.J.'s daily routine while Kaylie, our three-month-old, vies for her attention. Megan never gets a day off and never complains." He summed up his thoughts. "Moms are soldiers of love. They're the ones who handle the continuously changing needs." He added, "Dads are the warriors; we kill the giants. But moms? Moms are forever! When our kids get sick or fall and skin their knees, there's only one person they want. And it's not me! I respect my wife. I could never do what she does."

✝

Mothers are a special breed. They faithfully go the extra mile without thought of compensation. If you tried to reward them, they would be offended.

Men may be the spiritual leaders of the household, but mothers are the glue that bonds the family together. It is said, "A father will go to war for his children; a mother will die."

Jesus compared a mother's love to His own. There is no greater compliment than to be compared to the Savior of the world. And the epitome of His love is revealed in the touch of a mother. They truly are soldiers of love.

Prayer

"Thank You, Lord, for mothers, for their compassion,
tenderness, self-sacrifice, and thank You for
creating them to love like Jesus. Amen."

I'm Christ's Alone

September 7

For in Him we move and live and have our being.

Acts 17:28

Many of the songs he'd written were inspired by the trials he'd faced. This song had become his mission statement, so to speak.

Jon had tested the waters of life. But there hadn't been much wisdom in Jon's selection process. He'd just headed out with the belief that he was *entitled* to have some fun. When confronted about his cavalier lifestyle, Jon smugly answered, "If it was good enough for Solomon, then it's good enough for me!" So Jon set out to pleasure himself for the purpose of gaining self-awareness, an experiment of sorts, he called it. After years of the more sordid things of life, he'd gotten tired of the casual life. Redirecting his efforts, Jon pursued a more spiritual awakening, using mind-altering chemicals to assist in gaining nirvana.

One evening while high on crystal meth, Jon sideswiped an abandoned vehicle along the side of the road. His vehicle had rolled twice and come to rest in the ditch. Suffering life-threatening injuries, Jon had somehow survived.

Over the next ten weeks, he labored in the rehabilitation ward at the OSU Medical Center. Layer by layer, God peeled away Jon's rebellion. One of his rehab nurses spoke to Jon about how blessed he was to have survived. She spoke about the hope she had found in Jesus Christ. The week before Jon left Dodd Hall, he gave his life to Christ, writing the words that would later become the song "I'm Christ's Alone."

✝

Many of us have traveled through life taking our own little detours from God's designated path, recklessly experimenting with dangerous things, so we could experience life on our own terms. Most, if not all of us found nothing but emptiness.

Luke, in today's text, sums up Paul's words to the Romans about the freedom to be found in a relationship with Jesus Christ. Paul told them that God gives all men life, breath, and everything else, so that they might seek and find His Son. Like Jon, God is always willing to meet us at our point of surrender. Unlike Jon, we needn't take life's detours.

Prayer

"Lord Jesus, I'm tired of running. Lead me into a life better lived through Your Spirit. In Your Name I pray, amen."

No Compromise

September 8

His divine power has given us everything we need for life and
godliness.

2 Peter 1:3

There were two packages sitting on the porch when Trent and Sheila arrived
home. One contained a portable DVD player, the other an in-house DVD
player. "I thought we were only supposed to get the portable player. Maybe they
sent two by accident, and they aren't aware of their mistake," Trent reasoned.

"I don't know, but we'd better find out," Sheila responded.

Trent located the customer service number for the company, and dialed.
"These automated services drive me nuts!" he said, putting it on speakerphone
so he could make use of his time while waiting for them to respond. To his surprise, a customer service representative responded almost immediately. Trent
explained to the rep that he believed they had received an extra item by mistake.
"We got the portable DVD player we were supposed to get, but we received
an in-house DVD player as well. Can you tell me what happened?" he asked.

The CSR asked Trent to wait a moment while she checked. Coming back
on the line, she said, "We sent the second DVD player as a token of our appreciation because you waited for over ten weeks for your initial order due to
multiple back orders."

Trent said, "So you're saying we get to keep them both?"

"Yes, sir!" the CSR said cheerfully. "Thanks for shopping with us."

✝

It would have been easy to keep the second item, no questions asked, and no
one the wiser. But integrity doesn't check itself at the door on occasion.

To have virtue is to have moral and ethical standards that don't yield or
compromise. They are standards grounded in righteousness and sustained
through spiritual discipline.

Peter urged those of precious faith to be diligent in seeking good moral
character, as it would serve them well in fending off corruption and temptation. Too many times we enjoy flirting with trouble only to have it shackle us.
A match is more easily extinguished than a bonfire. Virtue is a deterrent to
spiritual slippage.

Prayer

"It's so easy to give in to small temptations, Lord. Stir in me
a desire to remain pure before You. Create in me a hunger for
the godliness You desire in my life. In Jesus' Name, amen."

A Language of Faith

September 9

I have been reminded of your sincere faith, which first lived in your grandmother Lois.

2Timothy 1:5

Grandma Doris never liked hearing the words *shut up*. She said they hurt her ears and her heart. So when Grandma Doris was around, you said, "hush" or "be quiet." If she heard anything else, you were in for a major scolding!

Grandma Doris emigrated from England in 1904 at the tender age of seven. She brought with her all her worldly possessions and an already deep faith in Jesus Christ. She married Grandpa Earnest, a preacher, and together they passed on the inherent traits of a pioneer: press ahead in kindness and never look back in regret. The legacy passed on by Grandma Doris was given to her by her father and his father before him. In the lineage of both Grandma Doris and Grandpa Earnest there is a history of profound faith in Jesus Christ. For at least six generations before and the two since, there have been preachers and lay leaders serving God, great men and women of faith.

Grandma Doris's death left a hole in people's hearts but not their faith. That heritage lives on and is testament to what was important to Grandma Doris: loving Jesus and using words to edify and not impair the lives of those we meet.

✝

It seems like such a simple thing, teaching children the value of using kinder language rather than harmful words. But it's in the simple things that we discover our true character.

How we treat others, such as which words we use, speaks volumes of who we are and what we believe. Harsh language says we are not concerned about how we gain the results we are seeking.

Paul wrote to Timothy in regard to testifying with power. He said to testify in love and self-discipline, letting God do the convicting.

Too many times our society uses words with shock value to make a point. Paul tells us that kind words, full of grace, will accomplish the task. We are to testify of Jesus' love and do it in a language of faith passed on from generation to generation.

Prayer

"Lead me to speak kindly in faith, Lord. May I always testify to Your love with words of grace. In Jesus' Name, amen."

Flatter or Favor?

September 10

He who rebukes a man will in the end gain more favor than he who has a flattering tongue.

Proverbs 28:23

Carlos's role in the corporation's steady growth over the past two quarters had earned him the lead on one of their largest projects. At the moment, he was meeting with a team of advisors to determine what the company should do next in preparation for launching the twenty-five-thousand-dollar ad campaign.

"Our target audience is twenty-two to forty-five-year-old females," he said, directing everyone's attention to the built-in monitors in the conference table. "Okay, sounds good." "That sounds about right." "Great!" "You're the man," came responses from the ingratiating group.

"All right. Let's move on," said Carlos, believing the matter was settled.

"Hold on a minute," interrupted Brendan. "I'm not sure we should limit our ad to females. I believe we'd be missing a large portion of potential customers if we target them alone."

Conversation immediately ceased as everyone waited for this ad exec wannabe to get shut down.

But to their amazement, Carlos simply asked, "Okay, what do you have in mind?"

"Well," he pressed, "we're coming into the Christmas season. I believe that if we include our target audience's counterpart, twenty-two to forty-five-year-old males, we can increase sales by targeting their purchases for their spouses and girlfriends."

"I like it," he said. "Let's figure out how to incorporate them into this marketing strategy. Good work, Bishop."

✝

Carlos hadn't gotten where he was by figuring it out all on his own. Realizing he didn't have all the answers, he was open to criticism. We would do well to follow his lead. By refusing to listen to or give useful criticism, we are cutting ourselves and others off from useful correction. We also must not accept everything presented to us as accurate or just. We must assess each situation and speak up where necessary.

If we approach each situation with sensitivity, we will discover a greater capacity for understanding in which we can both hear and be the voice of reason by departing from a closed-minded mentality. Do we want to flatter or gain favor?

Prayer

"Lord, help me recognize when I need to listen to criticism or confront certain issues in love. Give me the wisdom I need to do what's right. In Jesus' Name, amen."

That Day

September 11

Righteousness and justice are the foundation of your throne.

Psalm 89:14

"Have you seen what's happening?" Mark asked Collette over the phone.

"Yes, we have the TV on, and I can see the smoke on the horizon. What's going on, Mark? Who would do something like this?" she asked as they watched smoke billow from the Twin Towers. Mark from his office in Midtown, she from Queens. Then came the news that the Pentagon had been hit. Anger mixed with fear brought the unbidden question: *How many planes do they have?*

There was so much confusion that day—citizens running away from the chaos, first responders running into burning buildings.

Life changed that day as people looked on with a mixture of horror and fascination.

And in the time it took for those acts of terrorism to unfold, a nation resolved to pursue with determination those responsible.

In the ensuing years, there has been waning support; life has resumed; many have forgotten the reality of that day. But the question of that day still lingers: where were You that day, God?

✝

On September 11, 2001, our innocence was forever soiled. That day when the towers fell; that day when brave men and women gave their lives; that day when children became orphans; that day when evil appeared to have won; that day when we had an overwhelming need to know…where were You, God?

He was there, reaching down in love to comfort those who were suffering in the planes and the towers, the Pentagon, and on Flight 93; He was there, leading brave men and women into burning buildings while others were running for their lives; He was there, receiving each of His children who made that journey into eternity; He was there, catching the tears of every man, woman, and child overcome with fear and uncertainty.

We live in a world where everyone has free will; bad things happen to good and bad people alike.

Where was God on that day? Where He was the day His Son died and has always been—on His throne. And someday soon He will judge the nations. On that day, justice will reign.

Prayer

"O Lord, may we never lose sight of You just because evil
has threatened our faith. We stand secure in the knowledge
that You are always here and that we are not alone. Amen."

Afflicted
September 12

It was good for me to be afflicted so that I might learn your decrees.

Psalm 119:71

Rolf had contracted Acquired Immune Deficiency Syndrome from a blood transfusion he'd received in the early eighties, before the CDC began testing for the AIDS virus. He'd lived independently for quite a long time, but recent increased severity in his symptoms had forced Rolf to give up the freedom he cherished and move into a nursing facility. He was a straight-talking kinda guy, used to saying what was on his mind; today he was saying he didn't like this confounded nursing home he was confined to! His caseworker, Kari, had taken an instant liking to him.

During the intake, she'd asked Rolf how he'd contracted AIDS. He'd told her he'd gotten the virus through a transfusion he received during a surgery in 1982. Unaware the blood was contaminated, the virus had been discovered through a blood test in 1997 when Rolf had had an extended bronchial infection.

He told Kari he'd spent the first year angry at the world. Then someone had given him a Bible, and he'd begun reading it. He confided to Kari that had it not been for the AIDS virus, he might never have found Jesus Christ. Reaching over to his nightstand, Rolf grabbed that very Bible and, looking directly into Kari's eyes, said, "I want you to have this. Read it and ask God to show you what it means. I promise you He will."

She did, and He had. Kari cried tears of joy and sorrow at Rolf's funeral, thankful God had sent him to show her the way to Jesus.

✝

Affliction can be devastating. But it can also be life changing. When we've been brought to the end of our own strength, we must learn to rely on someone greater than ourselves, as in Rolf's case, God.

In truth, we are all afflicted. Every one of us has a deadly disease that we cannot cure ourselves: sin. And only God can take away this affliction and that can only happen once we discover our need and ask for healing. Have you asked God to heal your affliction?

Prayer

"Lord, set me free from the affliction of sin. Remove all vestiges of it from my life by the blood of Your Son, Jesus. Amen."

With Confidence?

September 13

Let us then approach the throne of grace with confidence.

Hebrews 4:16

Jennifer had heard it all before. "God answers prayer." Well, it never happened for her! She was listening while her best friend Rachel asked God for a specific answer to her prayer. A hurricane had blown the roof off her house, and she was asking God to send someone who would not take advantage of her. She had insurance, but so many homes had been affected that the reputable contractors were busy. In the past, fly-by-night contractors had descended on the areas hardest hit. They had given people low bids to entice them to sign on the dotted line; and then they'd taken their cash and never returned.

As Rachel ended her prayer, she saw the scorn in Jen's eyes. "Before you start doubting, watch and see how God answers my prayer."

"I'm sorry. I just don't have the confidence that He really cares!" Rachel said skeptically. "I've never seen Him answer any of my prayers!" she blurted, which sounded more like hope-filled defiance.

That evening, a contractor from Ohio knocked on Rachel's door asking if she had found someone to facilitate repairs. He provided written testimonies from people he had done work for following prior storms and explained that this was his way of serving God. He would drive from Ohio after each storm, spend time working for half his normal rate, repairing as many homes as he could, and then return home.

✝

God answers every prayer whether we see the answer or not. The only difference between Rachel and Jennifer was experiential faith. Rachel had seen God's answers; Jennifer had not. Perhaps because God had chosen to answer in a way she had not expected, possibly the answer wasn't one she wanted.

Scripture says God's grace is for each of us; it does not respect who we are or what we've done. But it does favor those who approach the throne with confidence. Witnessing God's response develops our faith. That faith causes us to expect an answer. The more we develop that faith, the easier it is to see how God answers prayer.

Prayer

"Help me see how You respond to my prayers, God. Give me the confidence to trust You. I want to know that You are working in my life. In Jesus' Name, amen."

The Kindness of Kindness

September 14

He who gives to the poor will lack nothing.

Proverbs 28:27

Jonathan and Gloria's fiftieth wedding anniversary was fast approaching, but they hadn't made plans for a celebration because they couldn't afford much more than cards for each other. Deciding finances were just too tight, they agreed that they would settle for cards. After fifty years together, they didn't really need anything else.

Friends in the community found out and set about organizing a secret fund to rectify the situation. In just two weeks, they raised enough to pay for reservations for a weekend at Salt Fork Lodge.

The Carringtons would be able to enjoy some much needed time alone, away from the farm and daily chores. People had taken to the idea with great enthusiasm! The love within the community was apparent. The fund had grown so quickly that there was several hundred dollars left over after the reservations were paid for. The remainder was allotted for dining out, dancing, and a couple of shows. There would even be enough left over for each to buy a present for the other!

The day the surprise was unveiled almost the entire community showed up. They presented their gift to the Carringtons after church the Sunday before their anniversary. Jonathan's best man was given the privilege of presenting them a check for six hundred eighty-seven dollars, a room confirmation number, and a gas card to cover the fuel for their trip.

Speechless, the Carringtons wiped tears from their eyes as they surveyed the smiles on the faces of those in attendance.

✝

Kindness is an act of love and obedience. When we give unselfishly to those in need, we fulfill God's purpose, and it pleases Him. By giving of ourselves we do God's work, we become His hands and feet.

We should always be mindful of those who are less fortunate.

Giving helps us remain unselfish, and it focuses our faith and trust where it should be: on God.

This is one of God's promises: we will never be in need if we provide for those who are. He asks and then leaves the kindness up to us.

Prayer

"May You find in me a willingness to always give of
myself, whether it be time or money. Help me be
selfless for Your purpose. In Jesus' Name, amen."

He Will Welcome Me

September 15

And you will receive a rich welcome into the eternal kingdom of our Lord and Savior Jesus Christ.

2 Peter 1:11

"I'm sorry about your father, David." Nancy offered her condolences on the loss of his father. "How are you and your mother doing?"

David had been born at a time when society missed the blessing of Down's syndrome children and institutionalized them instead. But Dick and Betty Lou had refused to yield to a worldview that discarded children in an effort to justify not dealing with the responsibility and challenges that special needs children pose. They raised David to believe he could succeed, and he had! He not only learned to care for himself, but for others as well, his passion for life driven entirely by a greater passion for Jesus.

"Thank you," he said, halting and then continuing with solemnity. "We are coping."

"If there's anything you need, please call us," Nancy offered.

It was evident that David's response to Nancy's genuine concern was heartfelt. "Thank you very much. I will relay that to my mother." Then David shared, "My Dad's in heaven, and someday we will join him."

"Yes, but not soon, right?" Nancy was sure David was not alluding to a premature reunion.

"No, not soon," he replied with understanding. "But someday." And then David declared with certainty, "I am his only son, and he will welcome me!"

What profound insight, Nancy thought. "Yes, David, he will be standing at the portal of heaven, waiting to present you to Jesus."

†

What a startling image of our arrival to our true home! We who die in Christ will not just awaken in heaven to stand before God (although this would surely be enough). Our arrival will be celebrated by the Host of heaven, and we will see those who have long since slipped from our memories.

Peter speaks of a rich welcome, when time will be no more, and the constraints we live with on earth will vanish in that moment! All of heaven's attention will be trained upon two people: the One who made it possible and us. In that moment, we will be His only child, and He will surely welcome us.

Prayer

"Lord, I long for the day when You celebrate my arrival and I see You face to face. Until then, lead me in Your grace. Amen."

Can I Talk to Nannaw?

September 16

Blessed are the pure in heart, for they shall see God.

Matthew 5:8

The little girl climbed into her father's lap as he sat reading the newspaper. His startled look didn't faze her in the least; she was on a mission. "Daddy, can Nannaw hear me when I pray?" Daddy was thinking of how to respond and what to tell her, not really knowing if God allows views from the portals of heaven, when she broke his concentration once again, excitedly saying, "I know she can, 'cause Babbaw Nelson said he would keep watch over me when he went to be with Jesus. So if he can see me from up there, then Nannaw can hear me! Babbaw said so!"

✝

There is something pure in a child's faith. When they are taught by someone they trust, they believe. As we age, there is a real danger of becoming cynical. We can lose the purity of heart we once enjoyed as a child. We use phrases like, "That's so childish" or "Now that I'm older," to rationalize our mature yet awkward relationship with God. Purity is a matter of the heart, not age. Our hearts end up jailed as we lose that childlike trust. Over time, other things crowd out our innocence, and the world comes crashing in upon our unprotected heart. "But," Jesus said, "take heart! I have overcome the world." Our hearts can be reclaimed! It requires a decision to turn things over to Christ, seeking help in dealing with the accusing whispers of the enemy while reaching up in childlike faith. When we cry out to see God, listening in the ensuing quiet, He is revealed to us. The return from cynical maturity to a pure heart is possible. God wants to be seen by us. Would you believe?

Prayer

"Papa God, I cry out to you in my pain with a childlike innocence. Please reveal to me your restoring power, the power that can give me my heart back. Lead me into healing and peace. Send someone to help me walk this out because I can't do it alone. In Jesus' Name, amen."

Who's Your Model?

September 17

To this you were called, because Christ suffered for you, leaving you an example, that you should follow in his steps.

1 Peter 1:21

Sitting around the backyard fire pit, Jimmy posed the question to J.D. "I know some of your story, but when did you finally decide to follow Jesus?"

"Well," J.D. began, "I've mentioned before that I gave my heart to Christ at the tender age of twelve, and I meant it too!" he said decisively. "But when I turned fifteen, we moved and I began running with a group of guys four years older than me. They were pretty rough, and God didn't fit into their lifestyle, so I ditched Him too. Within a year, I'd started hanging with two guys in particular; I eventually rewrote my moral and ethical standards. I was young and impressionable; I looked up to them. Well, life got pretty wild. It wasn't all bad. As a matter of fact, some of it felt great! But thirty years of that lifestyle wears on you. I got tired of living day to day with no goals or significant motivation. So I told God, 'If you don't help me stop, I'm not gonna stop.' I meant that too!"

"So what happened?" Jimmy asked with a grin.

"No joke, Jimmy. I felt God tell me to stop looking at the world as a model for success. So right there I asked Jesus to lead me out of that prison I called freedom. I've been following Him ever since."

✝

The world can be an attractive example of what it means to live. But it's not the right one.

In our hunger for acceptance and attention, we sometimes choose spiritually unhealthy, nonbeneficial lifestyles, refusing the truth of where we're headed in order to rationalize doing things we know to be wrong.

When we model our life after the world, we're choosing to go our own way; that flies in the face of God's sacrifice.

Life is about Who we choose to follow and why. God will not force His will for our lives on us. But a life lived in the shadow of Jesus' example yields eternal life, a life that begins the moment we choose to follow *in His steps*.

Prayer

"Lord Jesus, You lead, I'll follow. Draw me into a relationship that is life changing. Amen."

Complete Rest

September 18

Then I heard a voice from heaven say, "Write: Blessed are those who die in the Lord from now on … they will rest from their labor … "

Revelation 14:13

"Can you imagine never having to deal with temptation again?" Phil asked incredulously. "It's almost inconceivable. But that's exactly what Jesus means when he says, 'Well done, good and faithful servant. Come and share in your master's happiness!'"

Phil was speaking at a teen conference, enlightening them on benefits of living a sanctified life. "That means never feeling the need to give in to torment, never feeling the allure of premarital sex, never having to say no to drugs because there won't be any!"

"Do you really believe that?" one young man challenged. "I mean, like, we're really gonna live without temptation of any kind?" His skepticism was shared by many nodding heads.

"Yes, I do believe it!" Phil said with a passion and assurance that transcended their doubt. "Jesus said it, and I believe Him! If you believe *anything* Jesus said, you have to believe it *all*." He gave them a moment to digest that and then said, "Jesus said, 'Great is your reward in heaven.' Complete peace is part of the reward for living for Jesus! Don't you see it?" He had them thinking. "To live *for* Him *here*, saying no to evil and yes to righteousness, means when we live *with* Him, *there* it will really be heaven!"

†

Temptation has a way of making us believe we need what it's selling right now! But Jesus asks us to defer short-term self-satisfaction so that we may enjoy His long-term eternal reward.

It's not easy saying no when giving in would feel good for a while. And that's the catch: it only feels good for a while and then come the consequences.

To consecrate our life to Christ is not to say we will never fail. It means we care enough to die to ourselves.

To refuse is to say we don't believe in or want what Jesus says is waiting for us: complete and utter peace.

Jesus said, "They will rest from their labor." Labor means work. The opposite of work means never having to fight against evil ever! Live for His rest!

Prayer

"Help me say no when temptation is near, Lord Jesus.
Thank You for Your promise of complete rest. Amen."

Evil's Insidious Nature

September 19

When an evil spirit comes out of a man … it says, "I will return to the house I left … then it takes with it seven other spirits more wicked than itself…"

Matthew 12:43, 44

Peter had never seen anything like this. A pastor for over twelve years, he believed in and had dealt with demonic influence. This was different.

Carol had been involved in the occult but had, at some point, denounced the lifestyle and began attending church. Recently, something had changed. She was exhibiting different personalities; they would come and go, schizophrenic in nature.

Carol's husband had worked with Peter before he'd entered the ministry, so it seemed only natural to ask for his help. "Pete, I don't know what to do. Carol's acting crazy. She sits and rocks, then jumps up and runs around screaming unintelligibly. Can you help?"

Peter agreed to counsel Carol. That agreement began a month-long spiritual war unequaled by anything in his past.

Each time he spoke with Carol she manifested different personalities. One refused to hold a Bible, screeching wildly when Peter held one near her. Others cursed violently or attacked Peter physically. One even caused Carol to run from the sanctuary during praise and worship, screaming obscenities. Over a difficult, battle-ridden month, Peter discovered she had revisited the occult. Eventually, Peter brought each demon under Jesus' authority and cast them out.

Clear eyed, Carol sought to fill the cleansed places of her heart through the Holy Spirit's instruction.

†

Today's story, though names have been changed, is true. Demonic influence is real. But Satan wants you to think it's all fairytale and make-believe.

We were born into a world of evil, and its nature is to insidiously destroy as many lives as it can. And whether we choose to believe in this evil or not determines the effect it will have on us.

By choosing to deny evil's existence, we give Satan and his minions the freedom to destroy with blatant disregard to Jesus' warning in Scripture.

We have been given authority over the enemy. But we must believe he is real before we can engage him in battle.

Prayer

"Lord, show me the truth of spiritual warfare.
Implant in my heart courage to face this evil
and, in Your power, deny it room. Amen."

Do We Resonate?

September 20

Sing and make music in your heart to the Lord.

Ephesians 5:19

Wendy was a busy fourth grader with a penchant for making noise. Fortunately for her, Mr. Wren was an imaginative teacher. One day after class, he pulled Wendy aside. "How would you like to learn to play a musical instrument, Wendy?" he asked. "I believe you would make a wonderful musician." He encouraged, "What do you say? Want to give it a try?"

"I don't know, Mr. Wren." Her voice was strained as she struggled to relate the battle within her. "Mom says we don't have enough money to even rent an instrument, let alone buy one." Her disappointment was obvious. "I want to play the violin, but ..." Her small voice trailed off a moment. Then something came alive within her. "I really love the way the music resonates when the bow glides over the strings."

He could see the glint of a fire in her eyes as he wondered, *Where did she come up with* resonates? He shook his head in amazement, smiled, and said, "Come with me."

Taking her hand, he led her to Ms. Ostrander's music room. Entering the empty classroom, Mr. Wren explained, "We have a new program, Wendy, where any student who wants to learn to play an instrument can join the band or orchestra, and the school will provide the instrument. If the school provided a violin, would you want to learn to play?"

"Ohhh." Her small hands clasped together in a wishful pose. "Do you mean it?" she squealed.

"Yes, Wendy. What do you say?" he asked.

"Yes! Yes! Ohhh, yes!" Wendy practically screamed.

✝

To resonate means to have a *full* and *pleasing* sound.

As the rosined bow is drawn across the violin's strings, it creates vibrant sound. When in the hands of a master, the sound is *full* and *pleasing*. Yet, in the hands of an apprentice, the noises emanating from the instrument are somewhat less enchanting.

Only through much practice does the violinist become proficient in producing sounds that make the heart glad. If, however, we would attempt to become more proficient by practicing, both sounds are pleasing to the Lord.

Prayer

"May the music of my heart be pleasing to You, Lord. Teach me to resonate with fullness for Your pleasure. Amen."

Imitate the Father

September 21

In everything, do to others what you would have them do to you.

Matthew 7:12

Crystie and Andrew were still reeling from shock. They had just discovered that their investment firm had become involved in shady marketing strategies and had lost all their holdings.

"What are we going do, Andy?" The hurt and anger were apparent in her voice. "They can't get away with this!"

"I don't know, Crystie," Andrew said, his own thoughts scrambled. Their broker was supposedly one of their best friends. *How could this have happened?*

Trying to order his thoughts, Andrew wondered if there was any legal action they could take that would allow them to recoup their losses. "I'll contact Jay and ask him what they intend to do for the shareholders. Maybe it's not as bad as it appears." He wasn't nearly as hopeful as he tried to sound.

"Do you think Jay is mixed up in this too? I mean..." She just let it drop in midsentence.

Andrew was quickened in his spirit, remembering how this had all begun. "Listen, we prayed about this. We were sure God said to move forward. He's still in control, and we have to believe He'll work this out. As far as Jay, I don't want to believe he would be involved directly, but regardless, we're gonna get through it." He drew Crystie close and kissed the top of her head.

✝

In the parable of the gifts of the Father, Jesus says we have a choice in how we treat others; He suggests we are capable of doing good.

Some in today's society are willing to risk other people's livelihood in an attempt to profit, not caring how they do so in order to attain their goal.

How we treat each other has to do with where we get our strength and Who, if anyone other than ourselves, we trust in.

Jesus told those listening to consider how they treated others. He was saying, regardless of how others treat us, we have a choice in how we treat them. He's suggesting we imitate the Father.

Prayer

"Lord, it's not easy dealing with someone who intentionally sets out to deceive us. Help me extend mercy and grace so that peace will reign in my heart. In Jesus' Name, amen."

The Cost of Grace

September 22

Shall we go on sinning so that grace may increase? By no means!

Romans 6:1, 2

"Where do you get off telling me I need to make changes?" Trip asked heatedly. "And what's so wrong with me looking at this anyway! It's not as if I'm cheating on you!" He threw the magazine across the coffee table and sat back in his chair, smoldering.

"You wait just a minute, Trip. I didn't make that statement! You said you wanted to change," Kerry reminded her husband. "Every time I see you looking at those women, I feel cheap and dirty." She picked the magazine up off the floor, holding it toward him. "Do you really think it shouldn't bother me?" Tears began to well up. "This can be forgiven. But if you're going to live closer to Christ, like you professed you wanted to, you're going to have to make real changes. Do you think God approves of this magazine?" she asked, raising it higher.

That hit home. He'd said he wanted to change, and he'd meant it. *But was this so wrong?* No sooner had he posed the question in his mind than he had his answer. No matter how he wanted to justify his actions, he just couldn't picture Jesus flipping through those pages. "I'm sorry," he said, all the fire gone out of him.

Kerry said softly, "I forgive you. But maybe you'd do better telling God."

✝

We can be sure that when we submit our lives to Christ and His care,
we will be convicted by those things that do not merit our attention.
To continue in doing things that mock God is to solicit evil.

Paul was absolutely clear that grace covers every sin we repent of. But he was also adamant that we do not have licensure to continue living in our old nature with blatant disregard for Christ-like behavior.

Grace cost God His Son. To repeat our past is to mock the cross. When we do that, it guarantees moral struggle and dire consequences. Because as much as God loves us, He hates sin.

Prayer

"Lord, help me put to death anything that is an affront
to You. Forgive me in my weakness and give me strength
to kill any sin that remains. In Jesus' Name, amen."

Poor in Christ

September 23

But the Son of Man has no place to lay his head.

Matthew 8:20

Napoleon was neat, clean, and well dressed. But upon closer inspection, you'd have found that his clothes, although clean and pressed, were threadbare and meticulously hand patched from within, hiding small holes.

He drove a nondescript sedan with worn tires and duct tape holding the driver-side mirror in place. Napoleon had been a teacher of music, music being his second love, Jesus his first.

Napoleon tuned pianos most evenings. He was an interesting man, knowledgeable and well spoken, yet modest, and was often heard to say, "Oh, I just can't wait!" and when asked for what, he'd say, "Well, for the day I see Jesus! Don't you know?"

I'm not sure where Napoleon lived, but I am sure it was a modest home, nothing extravagant. You see, not too many people knew of what his love for Jesus and others led him to do. His meager stipend as a teacher paid *his* bills; his piano-tuning money paid *others'* bills.

Napoleon was filled with goodwill; he couldn't seem to give enough to assuage the desire of his heart. As I said, not too many people knew of his generosity, for it had all been done anonymously. I'm sure that's why there were only six people at his graveside service. To him it wouldn't have mattered; he wouldn't have wanted accolades he felt were meant for Another.

†

Jesus had no material ties to this world, and for good reason. He knew the work He had to do before His death must be void of distractions.

Napoleon felt the same way. He was a simple man who'd taken literally what Jesus had said about the cost of following.

Are there things we hang onto a little too tightly, that if asked to give up we might hesitate?

Jesus didn't say we had to be poor to follow Him; He did say we had to be ready to let go of things upon request and to listen for requests.

Do we have any needless distractions? Blessings held on to cease to be blessings. Are there areas in our lives in which Christ would have us become poor?

Prayer

"What I have, You provided. Is there anything
You would have me give away for You or learn
to use more in a kingdom way? Amen."

Model of Integrity

September 24

In everything set them an example ... show integrity

Titus 2:6, 7

The last thing Russ needed was a three-inch rock through his windshield. But last thing or not, here it came! It shattered the windshield with a loud *crack,* creating a lightning-bolt effect across the entire windshield. "You've gotta be kidding!" he groaned. *This'll raise my insurance premiums,* was his first thought. Then he had a second thought and followed the truck until he was able to pull alongside and motion the driver to pull over.

When stopped, Russ said, "Hey, I'm sorry to bother you, but your trailer just threw a rock through my windshield."

"Oh, man. I'm sorry," the driver said. "I just left a muddy jobsite. Musta picked it up there. Look, call my boss, Mr. Keen," he said, scribbling his boss's number on a company business card. "He'll make it right."

Skeptical, yet thanking the man, Russ got back in his car and dialed the number. "Yeah, hi, my name's Russ Bettencourt. You don't know me, but one of your trucks just threw a rock through my windshield. Your driver gave me this number and said to call you."

"I'm very sorry Mr. Bettencourt. Do you live in the area?" Keen asked.

Russ answered, "I do," surprised that the man's response seemed truly genuine.

"Good," he said. "I'll call Strang and schedule the repairs. Let's see if we can't get it repaired within the week. Can you be reached at the number on my caller ID?" he asked.

"Yes," Russ answered.

"Then I'll call you later with a time and date," he said, and they both hung up. True to his word, the new windshield was installed two days later.

✝

Integrity is a priceless teacher. When least expected, it will not only bring a welcome surprise, it will create goodwill, leaving an example of how to respond under difficult conditions.

Mr. Keen could easily have advised Russ to turn the claim in on his vehicle insurance, yet he chose to do what he'd been taught: treat people with respect and exhibit integrity, leave them a model to follow when dealing with others in the future.

Prayer

"Help me to be a person of integrity, Lord, so
that others will follow the example You provide
them through me. In Jesus' Name, amen."

1-800-Who Cares?

September 25

Those who are pure in their own eyes...those whose teeth are swords...

Proverbs 30:12, 14

"Excuse me, young man. Could you tell me if there—" The elderly gentleman began, but was immediately cut off!

"Do I look like a tour guide?" the young man said condescendingly. "Look, old man, if you want directions, call 1-800-WHO-CARES!" And with that, he reburied his head in the book he was reading.

Taken aback, the gentleman looked about the mall's concourse to determine if there was a pharmacy in the complex; his wife was having an angina attack. She'd forgotten her pills and needed nitro to relieve the pain and tightness in her chest!

Deciding to try once more, he began, "Young man, I don't understand your attitude, nor do I care at this moment to teach you how to respect your elders, but my wife is in need of medication *immediately,* and I need to know if there is a pharmacy in the mall!"

"Oh, dude, I'm sorry. I didn't know. Yeah, there's one down that hall," he said, pointing to his right, "about half way down on the right."

With that, the gentleman headed that direction, focused on bringing his wife the care she needed, but determined to revisit the young man if he was still there when this was over.

✝

Every generation has a group of people whose world is so small that they believe they are the epicenter. Conversely, each generation has become increasingly disrespectful. They have graduated *summa cum I couldn't care less,* responding viciously to those who have done them no harm.

The truth is they are a result of our own teaching. We have relaxed the boundaries of discipline to the point that we allow blatant disrespect within our classrooms in deference to lawsuits against well-intended educators in the name of civil rights. This epidemic has run amok! We have forfeited the right to *civility* because we do not wish to deal with the responsibility of changing matters, leaving it to be inherited by each ensuing generation.

There is not ample room to address this issue correctly here; to say *discipline begins at home* is a good start.

Prayer

"Help me care about raising caring, respectful children, Lord. Guide me as I guide them. In Jesus' Name, amen."

Strong, Powerful, and Breakable

September 26

If anyone speaks, he should do it as one speaking the very words of
God.

1 Peter 4:11

Dale and Kieran, two good-willed people, stomped off in different directions following an exchange of words meant to wound each other. It didn't matter that they hadn't meant what they'd said or that they couldn't tell you why they'd said such hurtful things.

Kieran ran to the bedroom, wondering if Dale really loved her while Dale, angry with himself, slammed the sliding glass door on his way outside.

He just didn't get it. He loved Kieran with all his heart, yet he couldn't seem to stop himself from blurting out injurious words, words he really didn't mean. He didn't blame Kieran; he knew she was just responding to his hurtful words.

Twenty minutes into his thoughts, he walked back in the house, went to the bedroom, and pulled a sobbing Kieran into his arms. "Honey, I'm so sorry. I don't know why I said what I said. Can you forgive me?"

"Dale, you make my heart hurt when you speak to me that way," she shared through the tears.

✝

It's really quite amazing the amount of physical protection God gave our heart. It is encased within an intricate cage of flexible bone, perfectly designed to shield it from injury, wrapped in sinewy, soft tissue, which is resilient and powerful. Centered between both lungs and liver, it is the strongest muscle in the body, forcing life-giving blood through miles of arteries and capillaries. It requires a tremendous amount of trauma to the chest to damage the heart.

And yet a simple word can completely break it.

We have all experienced heartache or heartbreak at some time in our lives, the empty feeling we think will never go away.

Some wounds take a long time to heal, and relationships can become strained.

In the worst of cases, the wound may never heal completely.

Peter says we have a choice of what comes out of our mouth. A heart bent toward God and a disciplined tongue will save unnecessary wounds.

Prayer

"Lord, help me guard my words. The enemy wants
my sharp tongue to surface. Please help me think
ahead before I speak. In Jesus' Name, amen."

Over-the-Road Hospitality

September 27

Even though they are strangers to you ... show hospitality.

3 John 8

Jeff was a long-haul trucker by profession, a servant by nature. His wife, Debra, was both gracious and longsuffering when it came to her husband's *unique* ministry.

It had been two years since Jeff had brought home their last *houseguest.* The man had stayed on for two weeks before stealing away in the middle of the night with some of their possessions.

Jeff was on his way home, pulling an empty trailer, carrying an unanticipated passenger. Home typified small-town America, where everyone knew everyone else—and their business. So it was no secret that Jeff was known as the purveyor of hospitality within the sleepy little community.

Over the years, Jeff and Deb had taken in strangers, providing food and shelter for as long as they needed, offering motivation to rise above the circumstances that had brought them to Jeff's attention.

Notwithstanding their last guest had betrayed their trust, at no time had Jeff or Deb considered ending their over-the-road ministry. As God continued bringing people their way, they continued ministering the love of Jesus Christ.

With chagrin, Jeff remembered the lesson he'd learned about showing up with someone unannounced. So, in light of that bit of hard-earned wisdom, he called home while his passenger was grabbing them some coffee. "Hey, Deb. I picked up a fellow that's down on his luck. You okay with me bringing him home?" he asked.

Deb didn't hesitate. "I'll have the guest room ready with clean sheets, towels, and washcloths when you get here. Be safe," she responded, infinitely touched by her husband's compassion.

✝

We are passing through this life in preparation for eternity. Jesus, although He had nowhere to lay His own head, was big on hospitality, to the extent He advised His disciples to shake the dust from their feet if they were refused welcome during their travels.

We are to extend welcome to those in need—whether acquaintances or strangers. With all the crime and mistrust today, showing hospitality can be a daunting, if not dangerous, proposition. Yet, we are to seize the opportunity when God solicits our hospitality, trusting He will provide for every eventuality.

Prayer

"Lord, teach me to be hospitable. Show me how to
extend the hand of kindness in Jesus' Name. Amen."

Stubborn Pride

September 28

I will break down your stubborn pride.

Leviticus 26:19

They pulled their motorcycles in the drive, hung up their helmets, and headed for the backyard. They found the girls deep in conversation.

Unexpectedly, Connie turned on Mac; her eyes were like two lasers; her body language screamed *I'm far from happy!*

Wary and on guard, Mac realized he wouldn't have to wait long to find out why.

"You know something?" Her tongue borrowed the fire from her eyes. "You have *back* problems!" she finished vehemently and then let it hang there.

Embarrassed, Mac responded defensively, "What the heck are you talking about? My back is just fine!" Among his racing thoughts was *What is she talkin' about?*

Interrupting those thoughts, she spat out, "It must not be…because every time you say 'I'll be right back,' you leave, and I don't see you for hours!"

His pride now fully under attack, Mac remained defensive. "Now just wait a minute—" But Connie cut him off. "You've been gone for seven hours, Mac!" There was no mistaking her frustration. "I'm tired of you dropping me off wherever," she said, waving her arms expansively, "leaving me at your mercy with no vehicle, to await your return while you go play!"

He realized the truth of her statement, but his pride was unrelenting. "Oh, bull! That's not true," he denied, wondering how lame he sounded.

With tears in her eyes, Connie simply said, "You know the truth, Mac."

Finally, with the truth undeniable, Mac relented. "I'm sorry. I didn't want to admit I was being so insensitive."

✝

Mac realized there was no excuse for his actions. And so it is when our pride meets the light of God's truth: all of our arguments are hollow—any defense of our stubborn pride meets that light and is seen for what it really is: rebellion.

God warned the Israelites He would break their stubborn pride if they failed to obey His commands. God brings us warning when we exhibit a prideful attitude. We have a choice: choose humility over pride, or God Himself will humble us.

Prayer

"Lord, help me lay down my pride so I can see the path
You have chosen for me. Help me treat others with the
love and respect they deserve. In Jesus' Name, amen."

I Understand

September 29

For we do not have a high priest who is unable to sympathize with our weaknesses.

Hebrews 4:15

As Bart began the long drive back home, sadness descended upon him. His wife, Jenny, had died two years ago, and now this. He had just left his son, Trenton's, basic training graduation. Bart had remained strong for Trenton as they'd released each other in embrace, saying good-bye for who knew how long. Trent had orders to ship out for the Persian Gulf tomorrow, and the weight of that was hitting Bart like a sledge to the chest.

Arriving home, Bart listened to the one message on his answering machine. "Hey, Bart, it's Gary. Give me a call. I reserved a tee time for six-o'clock at Apple Valley. Doug and Chris are gonna round out the foursome."

Gary's son had been killed in a firefight when the army's Third Infantry, along with the 101st Airborne, had made the initial assault on Baghdad in 2003.

As they teed off, just the presence of these three military fathers brought Bart comfort. They understood his heart. He didn't need to say anything if he didn't want to, but that unspoken support told him that he would find understanding with any of them when times became difficult.

✝

Gary's sensitivity to Bart's situation told him loud and clear, "I understand what you're feeling." Bart knew that Gary's arranging the golf outing was his way of saying, "If you need anything, bro, we're here."

We all need someone in our lives who understands what we're going through, and God is faithful. He quickens the spirit of those who have suffered similar situations, those who are acquainted with our troubled heart, when we need encouragement. And, as Gary did for Bart, others step up to comfort us.

Yet, even if no one completely understands, there is One Who truly knows what our heart needs most. That One is Jesus. Without a doubt, He can say, "I understand." Hold out your wounded heart today and find peace.

Prayer

"Jesus, my heart has known sorrow. My heart has known
pain. I thank You for bringing peace and comfort
when I need it most. Help me reach out to others in
that same way whenever I see a need. Amen."

I Don't Want This Bed

September 30

Humble yourselves … under God's mighty hand, that he may lift you up.

1 Peter 5:5, 6

Reuben, struggling to roll over while trying to not wake his wife, finally made it and then sat up on the edge of the bed. He tentatively reached behind himself with both hands and began rubbing his lower back. *I hate this bed! This thing's killin' my back! I hate my back too. Hey, God, how about a touch,* he asked silently. He'd been asking God for healing for almost thirty years now. *My thorn, I guess,* was his first thought, followed by his second, *This bed's gotta go!*

He made his way to the shower and just stood there, allowing the hot water to massage his aching muscles.

June emerged from the bedroom a half hour later, whistling and ready for the day.

Reuben looked at her and said, "We're getting a new bed today." Then he added, "I refuse to sleep on that slab of rock one more night!"

"I'm sorry, honey," June said with a bit of a chuckle. "But do you really think the next mattress is going to be any better than the last four?"

Reuben was determined to try at least one more time. "I won't be able to answer that question until we try the new one we're buying today." And following breakfast, they jumped in the pickup truck and headed for the Discount Wholesale Furniture Warehouse.

✝

Society often uses the idiom, "You made your bed, now lie in it!" But God says He can lift us out of difficult circumstances.

It is within each of us to make spiritual changes based on what God is able to do for us. We are not hindered from asking Him to show us the way to a better life. We are limited only by our courage to humbly ask Him to show us how to bring about such improvement.

When we make the effort to lift ourselves day by day to a new spiritual level, God provides what's necessary to attain that life. Though it may require temporary discomfort, we need not suffer a negative attitude that is clouded by our physical circumstances.

Prayer

"Lord, I come to You asking for guidance. Show me how to improve my mind-set and to look to You instead for my daily bread. Amen."

October

Sludge Free
October 1

You must live no longer as the Gentiles do.

Ephesians 4:17

There was no longer any friendly banter. The politicians had pulled out all the stops, and the gloves had come off. They were running smear campaigns and defaming each other. It didn't matter what damage was done or that they had stooped to new lows; they wanted to win. Character assassination was the order of the day.

"Can you believe this?" Melodie said, laying down the newspaper. "Neither of them is standing on godly principals. All they want is to make his opponent look bad. I can't, in good conscience, vote for either one of them."

Kyle sighed. "They're both walking in darkness. Both have consistently voted against moral legislation. They've made this election about money and who's going to bring the economy back in line. You know, if we would honor God's laws, we wouldn't be in this financial crisis. There doesn't seem to be a politician on the Hill that's standing for what God wants. It's getting so even the lesser of two evils is totally evil!" Kyle looked toward the ceiling and voiced his concerns. "Forgive our nation, Lord, and those of us who allowed things to get to this point. Raise up men and women to carry the fight to Washington and right this sinking ship. Lift us out of the darkness that has spread itself over our nation like sludge. Amen."

✝

The New Living Translation uses the word *ungodly* in place of *Gentiles,* denoting Gentiles as anyone not living a godly life.

The world is full of people seeking personal gain in a godless manner. Among them are many of our politicians. They seek to further and empower their party's worldview regardless of the cost.

Paul is precise in his instruction of how we are to respond. We are to avoid such living while trying to influence those who choose this lifestyle in a godly manner. We may find ourselves with opportunities to share our faith, yet we are instructed to not live as they do. Paul knew that our own spirituality will become contaminated if we swim in sludge.

Prayer

"Lord, keep me under Your watch and care. Help
me refrain from anything that fails to line up
with Your will. In Jesus' Name, amen."

Forever!

October 2

But he who feeds on this bread will live forever.

John 6:58

For whom blackest darkness has been reserved forever.

Jude 1:13

"So you're telling me that when I die I'll continue to live, not in physical form, but live nonetheless?" Jack could see Stan's skepticism. "And you believe that?" Stan asked.

"To the best of my ability," was Jack's honest answer. "Look, Stan, I admit that I don't fully understand everything the term *forever* means, but Scripture says that we will live forever in heaven or hell. I believe that."

Stan thought about that for a minute and then said, "I don't know if I can wrap my mind around that enough to believe it."

"You can't wrap your mind *around* the things of God, Stan," Jack tried to explain. "God is so much bigger than us. Just ask Him for the faith to believe now instead of trying to figure it all out before you accept His offer of salvation."

Stan was unmoved.

"Look, Stan, I'm just saying it requires faith to believe in something we can't categorically prove here and now. I'm also saying that *I* believe even though I have some questions about how *forever* actually works. Forever is a term we really don't understand. But not understanding it completely has no effect on the truth that we *will* live forever."

†

We tend to fear things outside our control, disbelieving what we don't understand. We live from day to day, taking life as it comes. We're not acquainted with more than a temporal existence, so it's hard to grasp the nature of eternity.

Trying to completely understand eternity is like trying to remember what it was like breathing amniotic fluid. We know it happened; yet we don't understand it much, if at all.

The word *forever* conjures thoughts of living with physical, emotional, or mental limitations for the rest of time. But throughout eternity there will be no curse, and those limits will cease to exist.

Faith requires belief in an *Infinite Someone* bigger than our finite mind truly understands. Our not understanding *forever* does not make it untrue.

Prayer

"Lord, give me faith to believe in forever so that
my choices here are based on where I want to
spend all that time. In Jesus' Name, amen."

Enough to Send His Son

October 3

> This is love: not that we loved God, but that he loved us and sent his Son ... for our sins.
>
> 1 John 4:10

"What makes you so sure?" Jenna's question about God loving us apart from our performance was valid. She wanted to know why God didn't require good behavior a prerequisite to salvation.

"God told us through His Word, Jenna," Shari explained, opening her Bible and reading, 'This is love: not that we loved God, but that He loved us.'"

Shari searched for the right words. "Jenna, we could never measure up to God's standards. His holiness requires perfection, and we aren't perfect. Scripture says, 'All have sinned.' That means we needed a perfect sacrifice to save us. That was God's Son. God's love is so fierce that He would rather send Jesus to die in our place than allow us to spend eternity apart from Him." Shari felt it was time to ask Jenna to make a decision. "Would you like to know such love?"

"You know," Jenna began, "I've watched you and Walt, and I see something." She paused. "You have such a peace, even when things aren't going so great. I'd really like to know that peace in my life."

Shari silently asked for the right words. "Jenna, God wants you to know that peace too. All you need to do is accept His Son into your heart. You can't earn salvation; it's a free gift given at a high price." Seeing tears begin to form in Jenna's eyes, she pressed on. "Just ask Jesus to take over from today on. Tell Him you know you're a sinner in need of His sacrifice."

Jenna bowed her head, and Jesus became her Lord and Savior.

✝

There is nothing we can do to earn God's love or approval. He showed us His love on the cross of Calvary.

He does require a humble heart, a heart turned to Him, a heart willing to *accept* His great love and not one trying to earn it.

It costs us nothing. It cost Him everything because He cared enough to send His Son.

Prayer

"Father God, I lift my life to You in this moment
and commit it to You. Wash my sins white as snow
with Your Son's blood. In Jesus' Name, amen."

We Must Ask

October 4

Therefore wisdom and knowledge will be given you.

2 Chronicles 1:12

It had been a year since the couple had battled issues of infidelity, and he was wondering how his younger brother and his wife were doing. On the surface, everything appeared fine. But he knew that the early stages of temptation rarely show outward signs.

"Have you spoken to Gail about how she and Jeremy are doing lately?" he asked his wife. "They appear to be okay. I just wonder if they really are."

"Actually, I asked her last week. She assures me things are great," she responded.

He remembered his own battle with infidelity; it had almost ruined his marriage in the early years. He'd given in to temptation and made a terrible mistake. Fortunately, his wife believed in their marriage vows in a way he would later come to understand, and they had worked through the pain of his indiscretion.

He had become accountable back then by giving two men permission to ask personal questions about his faithfulness and to take any measures necessary to remind him of his commitment to one woman. He'd needed that help because the enemy had visited with the temptation of desire until he gained victory through perseverance. He thanked God once again for the commitment of those two men; for without them asking, "Are you experiencing any sexual temptation?" he would have been left alone to resist the temptation. He prayed that God would send someone to keep his brother and sister-in-law accountable.

✝

We all face some nature of temptation; none are exempt. We need accountability with someone we are comfortable confiding in because self-sufficiency in spiritual matters will eventually result in our failure to resist.

Solomon asked God for wisdom instead of wealth, riches, or honor. Because of that, God granted his desire. He also gave him wealth, riches, and honor.

But wisdom is the key. Without it, we have no basis for understanding with which to make sound decisions.

If someone we know has fallen to temptation in the past, the question is, "Dare we ask him how things are today?" The answer is yes. Wisdom says we must ask.

Prayer

"Help me be a friend that helps others avoid temptation, Lord. And please send someone to help guide me along the path of wisdom. Amen."

The Mantle

October 5

When they had crossed, Elijah said to Elisha, "Tell me, what can I do for you before I am taken from you?" "Let me inherit a double portion of your spirit," Elisha replied.

2 Kings 2:9

From the mezzanine, they watched the crowd filtering in. The well-known evangelist placed his hand on the boy's shoulder. He spoke softly, yet passionately, "Each one of these people here tonight has needs, son." Pointing, he asked, "Do you see that man in the red shirt, son?" "Yes, sir," the boy of eleven answered. "How about the lady with the blue coat?" "Yes, sir. I see her," came his reply. "And how about the girl with the ponytails, there in the second row?" "I see her, sir." Then this man of God spoke with an even deeper passion. "Ask God to show you what they need. Ask Him to show you their hearts, son!" He paused a moment and then continued, "I always survey the crowd before speaking. Then I ask God to speak through me what they need to hear." The boy looked up, awed that this man had taken time out of his busy schedule to share his heart with him. The evangelist had found out this boy felt God's call to become a pastor. He understood the importance of nurturing the vision. In those few moments, he did for this young man what no one else could. He passed on the mantle.

✝

God bestows His mantle upon those He calls. This godly man understood the privilege he'd been given. He remembered his father doing this very thing with *him* when *he* had answered God's call to the ministry. This was a night the young boy would never forget. He was ready to answer the call. God equips everyone for ministry. He provides all the skills we need for each situation we find ourselves in. He will never send us out to do anything we aren't ready for. We may feel apprehensive, but if we move forward in faith, we will find that the Holy Spirit is right there giving us courage and strength.

Prayer

"Sometimes I'm afraid of the unknown, Lord. I'm uncomfortable about being embarrassed. Help me put aside the fear so I might teach others about You. In Jesus' Name, amen."

Just One Thing

October 6

But one thing I do.

Philippians 3:13b

Byron had asked Shane to run for a seat on city council. "Look, Shane, I understand your reluctance, but think about it."

"I hear what you're saying. I'm just not sure I agree. There'll be many opposed to my holding political office if they find out about my past. You know campaigns are anything but private, and the other camp will surely dredge it up."

Shane wasn't afraid of being found out; he just didn't want to drag his family through an unnecessary mudslinging contest.

Sixteen years ago, he'd been arrested for possession of marijuana and cocaine and had done a short stint in the county jail. He'd gotten clean and stayed that way. Yet he knew society could be a cruel reminder.

But Byron had witnessed the change in Shane and appreciated how he approached life today. "At least discuss it with Carol and see how she feels."

That evening, Shane posed the question to his wife. "What would you think about me running for the vacant city council seat next November?"

"I think you will be a good councilman," she said with finality and a twinkle in her eye. She understood his concern; she just wasn't going to let it dictate their lives. If it came up, so be it. It was what he did, not who he was.

Shane was sworn in on a windy and cold January evening and would faithfully serve the City of Grayson, being reelected to six consecutive terms.

✝

We all have pasts and have fallen short of the mark. Too many of us let those mistakes define who we are today. If our personal sin were laid bare for all to see, we would cease throwing stones of incrimination, and we would judge less critically.

Paul was aware of his shortcomings to the point of listing many of them in the hope that others would understand the importance of not allowing past mistakes to affect present performance. So I emphasize his words for you: "Forgetting what is behind, and straining forward, I press on!" Do just that one thing; press on!

Prayer

"Forgive my mistakes, Lord. Help me not allow what I've done
in the past dictate who I am in You. In Jesus' Name, amen."

Redeemed

October 7

> It was not with perishable things ... that you were redeemed.
>
> 1 Peter 1:18

Sally had been attending services for about two months when the pastor and an elder dropped by to visit her husband, Bob. They brought him an information packet that included a CD of the most recent sermon. Following an extended visit, they said good-bye, and invited for Bob to come check them out.

"Vietnam left deep scars on too many good men and women," the elder remarked, alluding to Bob's comments about taking part in the fighting and his struggles with God since then.

The following Sunday, Sally showed up alone. The pastor asked, "Do you think Bob will come?"

"I don't know. Maybe someday. But not today," she said with deep sadness.

"Don't give up," the pastor encouraged.

Halfway through praise and worship, Bob walked through the door. And that very day, he gave his life to Christ!

There was a church picnic that afternoon right across the street from Bob and Sally's home. Midway through the picnic, Bob appeared from the house and approached the pastor. "I wasn't going to come today," he began. "As a matter of fact, I turned around three times. But I wanted to see if you were as good in person as you were on the CD," he said sheepishly. Growing serious, he reached in his pocket and stretched his closed hand toward the pastor. "I want you to have this. I *was* going to use it. But I don't need it anymore." And with that, he dropped a nine-millimeter bullet with his name written on it into the pastor's hand.

Since that day, Bob has grown to know the One Who saved him with His redeeming power.

✝

Nothing of intrinsic value could have redeemed us. The price sin required was Jesus' blood.

Some believe they've done too much, committed too heinous a crime to be of any use to God. But no matter where we've been or what we've done, Jesus' blood is sufficient to cover that sin.

God wants us to know our worthiness has nothing to do with salvation through His Son. He just calls us to come and be redeemed.

Prayer

"Lord, I feel unworthy. But Your Word says if I
accept Your Son, You will redeem me anyway. Forgive
me, Lord. I want to be redeemed. Amen."

Unsuspecting Martyrs

October 8

Isaac spoke up and said … "Father?"

Genesis 22:7

Gabriel watched in horror as the woman in front of him pulled into oncoming traffic. He wasn't sure whether it was a mistake or intentional. And there wasn't much he could do to stop it from happening. Honking his horn for lack of another option, Gabriel prayed she wouldn't be hit.

The first two oncoming vehicles reacted instinctively, slamming on their brakes and swerving to miss her. Those following closely behind were faced with snap judgments. Many responded defensively, pulling over in time to allow the wrong-way vehicle to pass by, unharmed yet unyielding.

Gabriel watched as car after car avoided her. Then, without warning, the woman pointed her car right at the overpass abutment and slammed into it at somewhere around seventy miles an hour.

Paramedics responded quickly but were unable to save the woman. She had not been wearing her seatbelt and had been ejected through the windshield. State patrol investigators later determined the woman was mentally unstable. They found a suicide note on the passenger seat, the distraught woman saying she could no longer live without her children. Further investigation revealed they had been killed in an accident seven years before. She had been driving.

✝

Life can be cruel. And many suffer for reasons not of their own making.

Just like Isaac, this woman's children did not ask for their fate. Yet tragedies happen, and we must do our best to deal with the loss.

But what of the unsuspecting martyr and what of those times we suffer when we feel it isn't fair? Jesus told us we would have trials in this world. He did not make the statement to scare us, rather to prepare us to choose how we will respond as we meet life's trials in our walk with Him.

If we find ourselves walking a road full of peace and prosperity, walk in grace. If, however, we find ourselves on a road marked with sorrow and grief, walk in communion with God, trusting Him to go through it with you.

Prayer

"Walk with me, Lord. Help me cope with the troubles
of today. Show me how to be gracious in the good times
and to lean on You in the bad. In Jesus' Name, amen."

Listen to God, Then Do What He Says

October 9

To prepare God's people for works of service …

Ephesians 4:12

It had been a rough year. Medical issues had left a seemingly insurmountable amount of debt. Yet they trusted in the Lord's provision. This morning's mail brought an unexpected bill. Molly had forgotten to include the quarterly water bill in the budget. She prayed, asking God to meet the need. Then Molly sent her pastor an e-mail asking if the church's benevolence fund might cover half the water bill; they could handle the rest.

The phone rang. It was the bank asking Molly to please come and pick up an envelope someone had left for her.

So, grabbing her coat, she headed out. Upon arriving, she was handed a nondescript, white envelope. Thanking the young woman, she returned to the car to open it. To her amazement, she found two five-hundred-dollar money orders with an unsigned note. "Molly, we know how God uses you and how you say, 'Listen to God, then do what He says.' We are listening to God. Please receive this gift and use it as you see fit."

Molly, tears in her eyes, ran back into the bank and asked the young lady, "Who did this?"

"I'm sorry, but they asked to remain anonymous," the girl answered.

In her excitement, she drove to the church to share the miracle with her pastor! Unknown to her, he had responded to her e-mail, telling her to drop by with the bill so they could pay it. When she showed up, he assumed she was bringing the bill.

His smile grew as Molly shared her story of how God had moved on the hearts of His people to meet her need before it was known.

✝

God wants to move us to do good works on His behalf. He's given us Scripture to help us understand how to hear His voice. He has also raised up others to aide us in distinguishing between His voice and the world.

Through their instruction, His Word, the gift of the Holy Spirit, and with persistent practice, we can learn to filter out the world's noise.

The Father's desire is for us to listen to His voice and then do what He says.

Prayer

"Speak, Lord. Then help me do what You say. Amen."

The Enemy Within
October 10

Who am I?

Exodus 3:11

"Why did you just up and quit?" Reece was trying to understand how someone with Tim's drive and intuition would abandon his life's goal. So far he hadn't figured it out. So once again, he asked, "Why'd you pull up short, Tim? And why now?"

"You really want the truth?" Tim seemed to resent the questioning of his motives.

But as Reece looked into Tim's eyes, he recognized something from having seen it in the mirror himself: fear.

"You're afraid, aren't you?" he said, bewildered. "I can't believe it. You of all people, afraid of what the future holds. So you're pulling the plug before you lose control?"

Reece was dumbfounded. He'd never suspected his closest friend wasn't as sure of himself on the inside as he appeared on the outside.

This had him stymied. "Tim…" He struggled for the right words with which to encourage his friend. "I've watched you take on challenges that would have brought many a good man to his knees. You always stressed that to believe in myself only required the knowledge that God's always got my back. You gonna tell me now that you really don't believe that?"

"It's not that simple," Tim blurted. "What if people don't respond favorably? Then what?"

"Well, my best friend is always telling me, 'Just put one foot in front of the other and see where God leads you.'" Reece said, knowing that had been what Tim needed to hear.

✝

Our greatest enemy to accomplishing God's tasks is the one within. We all, at some level, fight Moses' battle against inner fear. Satan introduces doubt couched in the fear of rejection and failure or even our past. He intends to use them as a means to stop us from reaching for a higher level of accomplishment.

Self-sufficiency is a weighty and dangerous thing. Only when we realize that God will equip us *completely* for His work will we forge ahead.

Only God can defeat this enemy within. And then it's only if we allow Him into the battle.

Prayer

"Lord, I hate being afraid. And I don't readily admit to fear.
Please send someone to encourage me to reach higher for
Your purposes if I begin to falter. In Jesus' Name, amen."

Words of Life!
October 11

The words I have spoken to you are spirit and they are life.

John 6:63

"Mom?" Steph said, calling for her attention. "Jesus said that our flesh counts for nothing and that only the Spirit gives us life. Then He said the words He spoke are spirit and life. Is He referring to the written word alone? Or do His spoken words have more meaning for us?" Steph had been given a religion class assignment to explain what spiritual life meant to her. She'd focused on the New Testament, the red-lettered spoken words of Jesus, to be more precise.

"Well, what do you think He's saying?" her mom prompted, wanting her answer the question for herself before she received any outside influence.

"I guess I think it's a combination of both," she said with a tinge of unresolved doubt.

"So why do you feel He meant both?" Mom asked.

"Well, first of all, I believe He's talking about the natural life versus the spiritual life, specifically, eternal life versus eternal damnation. And that if we rely on ourselves for all the answers, we'll become introspective and self-deceived by thinking we can walk through life apart from God without any need of a Savior." Then she added, "I believe when we speak God's written word, it comes alive, you know, sharper than any two-edged sword. So what do you think?" she asked.

"Sounds to me like you've got things well in hand, honey," Steph's mom said, noting the twinkle of satisfaction in her daughter's eyes.

✝

How many times have you read, read, and reread the same verse of Scripture only to have it jump off the pages in one blindingly revealing moment? Everyone who has ever been a student of Scripture will have this phenomenon occur many times over his or her studies of the Bible. It is the inherent Word of God, our lifeblood, which the Holy Spirit opens for our understanding as we prayerfully read. God intended us to study His Word in order that we would, through that nourishing act, receive the life of the Spirit.

Prayer

"Lord, reveal spirit and life to me as I read Your
written account of the story of Your love for me
and all mankind. In Jesus' Name, amen."

The Coming Storm
October 12

> The rain came down, the streams rose, and the winds beat against the house; yet it did not fall.

Matthew 7:25

Her husband had always known what to do: stay and ride it out or to seek shelter inland, away from the fury of the storm. Yet he had died six years ago, and this decision was hers alone.

As the surf pounded the sand with increasing intensity, she sensed the fury of the coming storm. And although the storm was still hundreds of miles out, she realized it might be a direct hit. They'd prepared for storms many times over the years, closing shutters against the strong winds. They had even rebuilt twice, saying, "We will not give in to this unwanted aggressor."

She watched the waves pound with a force that belied the storm's awesome power and knew this one would be bad. Having been through some rough storms in the past, she decided to board up and head inland, taking the kids to her sister's, not risking their lives to protect inanimate objects.

The storm bore down on the coast, rending wooden structures as if they were made of cardboard. When she was finally granted access to her neighborhood, she found only piles of debris shoved up against the palms; not one shred of the house was left standing.

Only now did she realize with clarity how important the decisions of life could be. She was thankful for having made the right one.

✝

Many times, spiritual storms strike without advance warning, giving no sign of the coming struggle. They develop quickly, like a tornado out of a supercell thunderstorm, leaving no time to prepare or run for shelter.

Because of this frequent lack of warning, we must take steps ahead of time to shore up the structures most vulnerable and valuable: our spiritual being.

Jesus says the only way to assure survival from these storms is to build our lives on a solid foundation by immersing ourselves in His Word, spending time with Him in prayer, and meeting with others of like mind. We *can* prepare for the coming storm.

Prayer

"I need Your protection, Lord Jesus. Teach me
how to stand on You and Your Word as the
Foundation for everything I do. Amen."

The Root of Jesse

October 13

From his roots a Branch will bear fruit.

Isaiah 11:1

They planted the sapling in the corner of the yard. "Daddy," his young daughter questioned, "can we use it for a Christmas tree someday?"

He chuckled at her optimism; she saw potential in this small, vulnerable sapling. "You bet, honey. We'll nurture it to make it the best Christmas tree ever."

She cocked her head curiously. "What does nurture mean, Daddy?"

"It means we'll need to love this tiny tree, honey, and treat it with tenderness. We'll need to cut away dead branches and unwanted growth. We'll have to make sure the roots have a chance to grow deep so it will grow big and strong."

Then, as an afterthought, he added, "The weather will actually cause the roots to grow deeper. As the wind and rain, sun, and cold weather beat down on the sapling above ground, the little tree will tell its roots to grow deeper, giving it the ability to stand against the harshest weather."

So for eight years they nurtured the tree, shaping it by cutting back unwanted growth.

Over time, the pine grew strong and tall. Then something unexpected happened. Birds began building their nests in the tree's sheltering branches and ate its pine nuts for life-giving nourishment.

When the time came to harvest the tree, the girl decided to leave it for God's wildlife. And instead of cutting it down, they decorated it right where it stood, giving the birds the most beautiful home in the neighborhood.

✝

Our heavenly Father is also optimistic when He looks at us. He sees great potential in each of us. He wants to be our refuge when spiritual winds blow, nurturing us, growing us to maturity.

When we are assaulted by spiritual elements, He patiently waits for us to seek His assistance. As we come, He prunes away unwanted, sinful growth, leaving us stronger and better equipped to stand against the trials of life.

As we grow, we can see *our roots* being anchored in the root of Jesse. Only there will we find the spiritual nourishment necessary for our own sustenance and be able to bear fruit for His kingdom.

Prayer

"Lord, grow my roots deeper. Make me a strong branch, able
to bear fruit for those in need. In Jesus' Name, amen."

In Times of Need
October 14

> Are not all angels ministering spirits sent to serve those who will inherit salvation?
>
> Hebrews 1:14

Lew had outlived his three-month life expectancy by two years before hospice was called in. For those two years, Lew *lived*: visiting museums, taking walks with his beloved, Patty, and working in his garden from time to time.

On the eve of his death, Lew kept calling for Judy. Judy was, as she put it, Lew's wash girl; her ministry had been to tenderly meet Lew's bathing needs. Knowing Judy wasn't scheduled to work that day, Patty called hospice, asking that they send her anyway. "Lew is asking for Judy. Please tell her."

When later the doorbell rang, Patty was pleasantly surprised to find Brenda, Lew's RN, smiling through the door at her! "I just left the Healing Hands of Christ seminar and felt led to stop by and see Lew. Would that be okay?" she asked.

"Oh, yes!" Patty exclaimed, welcoming Brenda with a hug.

After simmering a pot of hyssop, frankincense, and myrrh, Brenda anointed Lew with the spices, salving his hands and feet and head while hymns softly played. As she finished, Lew lifted his right hand, pointing toward the corner of the room.

"Do you see someone, Lew?" Brenda asked. His head nodded yes. "Is this someone you know?" she prompted. He shook his head no. "Is this someone speaking to you?" she asked.

"Can't you hear him?" Lew said in wonder.

"No, we can't," they replied.

"It's the Angel of the Lord, come to take me home." Trying to sit up, Lew remarked, "You can't take a trip lying down!"

✝

God's conspicuous attention through the persons of Judy and Brenda, as well as revealing His Angel's presence as He took Lew home, was personal.

And this is the hope we have in Christ Jesus when we choose to accept Him as our Lord and Savior.

It is appointed unto man once to die; we will not escape this life alive. But we can take great comfort in the knowledge that having made the choice to become one of God's children, in times of need, we will be tended by ministering spirits.

Prayer

"Loving Father, be near to those who are in need today, regardless of the reason. In Jesus' Name, amen."

Extinguished Flames

October 15

The devil prowls ... like a roaring lion

1 Peter 5:8

As the pastor and his family returned home, he found an envelope tacked to the parsonage's front door.

Curious, he pulled it from the door and read. As he read, his face turned ashen; the shock and confusion on his face caused his wife to ask what was wrong. There were no words to soften this blow:

> We, the leadership of the church, no longer require your services. We therefore inform you that you have one week to vacate the parsonage. We will find your replacement in due time and do not wish any future contact with you.
>
> Signed,
> The Leadership

With no further explanation forthcoming and in total shock with inexplicable heartache, they complied with the request, leaving the little church God had called them to.

The young pastor agonized. *Haven't I spoken the true Word of God? Hasn't the community responded affirmatively since my appointment? And hasn't God shown me areas of needed growth I've been addressing?* With astounding clarity, he understood; he had made the leadership uncomfortable, requiring growth and a new level of commitment. He had become a threat to *their* little church.

Rumors spread by his accusers followed the young pastor, and he was unable to secure future appointments. Jaded, he returned to secular work, never to minister again from the pulpit.

✝

What a profound loss. What an egregious act of abhorrent behavior. What an insidious use of God's children by Satan. Our enemy prowls, just as today's text tells us, *like a roaring lion.* But he also slips subtly in and out of our lives, undetected and unidentified, using good-willed people to extinguish the fire of God from the hearts of men. Failure to recognize or admit Satan's influence in our lives will prolong our struggles. Without giving evil more power than it deserves, we must be aware of Satan's willingness to use us against each other.

Satan is real; he hates the things and people of God, and he will use us to attack each other. We must learn to recognize his tactics and then resist him!

Prayer

"Lord, make me aware of the enemy's subtle
attacks. Help me to resist them. And use me as an
instrument of grace. In Jesus' Name, amen."

The Selfish Trinity

October 16

Do not think of yourself more highly than you ought.

Romans 12:3

During a work session to repair a parishioner's house, the pastor pulled one volunteer aside, away from listening ears. "John, I need to speak with you about something."

Having John's undivided attention, he forged ahead. "God wants to use each of us, and your assistance here is very much appreciated."

He noticed a look of boredom dawn in John's eyes. "John, your attitude and actions scream, "Look at me!" You make people uncomfortable, and you effectively steal the blessing God—"

"Look, Pastor," John cut him off. "I hear you. But quite honestly, I do things the way I want, or I don't do them. Is that a problem?" You could tell he expected the pastor to back off, believing they couldn't get along without him.

What happened next took John by surprise. "It's a big problem, John. And I surely won't force you to make changes you're not willing to make. But if you choose to continue treating others with disdain, I must ask you to leave. And I mean our church, John, not just this project."

Taken aback, John responded in anger. "Fine! I don't need your high-and-mighty church!" he said forcefully and left, slamming the door on the way out.

The mood in the house changed almost immediately; it was as though a dark cloud had been lifted.

✝

John suffers from a case of the selfish trinity: *me, myself, and I.*

Some would say the pastor was too strict. On the contrary: pride is a sinister root, which if allowed to propagate, will pollute and choke out healthy roots.

It led to the fall of mankind; Satan decided to elevate himself above the throne of God and in doing so set in motion a series of events that led to his and a third of the angels' eviction from heaven; thus sin entered the world.

It is so subtle that we rarely, if ever, realize our own pride.

So in His mercy, God sends His Spirit to convict us. When convicted of *any* pride in our lives, we should humble ourselves before God and deal with the issue.

Prayer

"Is there any pride in me, Lord? If so, help me put it to
death so I might be humble before You. Amen."

Abstinence Is Work

October 17

> Abstain from sinful desires, which war against your soul.
>
> 1 Peter 2:11

"I feel like I'm in this constant battle," Carlene said incredulously. "It's like I'm constantly faced with decisions of right and wrong," she confided.

Rochelle understood her friend's quandary. "I know. You see, before you came to Christ, you lived your life apart from God; you were ignorant of His ways." Rochelle let that sink in.

"When we give our lives to Christ, He gives us His Holy Spirit. The Spirit convicts us of actions we failed to recognize as sinful before." Rochelle watched as the realization of what that meant dawned on Carlene.

"This isn't easy," Carlene remarked woefully. "It's like this constant battle rages inside me. I feel"—she paused, searching for just the right word—"*dirty* when I do some of the things I used to do. Does that make any sense?"

"It makes perfect sense," Rochelle answered. "Living a godly life comes with its battles. It's all part of learning to live for God instead of ourselves. The things that we want are filtered through God's Spirit. When it's something God considers sin, it registers on our heart, letting us know we should resist and not give in to the desire."

"I'm gonna need a lot of help," Carlene said, a mixture of wit and worry in her voice.

"God always provides assistance when we ask for it," Rochelle assured her. "But it's our responsibility to ask. God isn't some genie Who makes life easy for us. He's a loving Father Who instructs His children in what's best and then allows them to make informed choices."

✝

Sin is sensual and seductive. And Peter instructs us to engage in the battle instead of passively giving in.

The Christian life is not one of ease; it demands a life of physical and spiritual discipline, one of abstinence in which we actively war *against* Satan and his tempting offers.

Although our salvation may be complete when we give our life to Jesus, we've only begun to take on His likeness. The more we abstain from sinful temptation, the closer the resemblance gets.

Peter encourages us to be built up into a spiritual house, one that looks like Christ.

Prayer

"Lord, give me wisdom and strength to wage war
against the enemy. In Jesus' Name, amen."

I'll Never!

October 18

Children, obey your parents in the Lord.

Ephesians 6:1

"I hate you!" Benny screamed at his dad. "When I have kids, I'll never treat 'em like this!" And with that, he slammed his door.

Geneva looked at her husband and impishly said, "Sounds like the boy I met in high school. Whatever happened to him?" she teased, hoping to ease her husband's frustration at having his son stomp off in rebellion.

"For two cents…" He decided not to finish a statement he knew he didn't mean. "Yeah, I was an awful lot like him, wasn't I?" He reminisced. "I even remember saying the exact same thing to my dad." Then it hit him. "Am I just like my dad?" he asked.

"Well, I happen to love your father—" she began.

"You weren't his son." He parried.

"No, but he's a good man, Paul. And you could do much worse than to emulate your father. As a matter of fact, you are very much like him: kind, compassionate, loving, tender, thoughtful, and considerate. Those are wonderful attributes, and I hope Benny inherits every one of them," she said with conviction.

Paul knew she meant every word. "I guess those traits got lost in the discipline. Yes, Dad is a good man. I guess Benny is just like me; I never liked the word *no* either," he lightheartedly said.

✝

Our parents love us. And because they do, they seek to keep us from harm. Rules serve a necessary purpose. That we don't like them remains irrelevant to the fact we need them.

Sometimes the rules can be imposing. And in the midst of that imposition, we can get out of sorts, forgetting that although everything is permissible, not everything is beneficial (1 Corinthians 10:23).

Most, if not all, of us have made the claim, "I'll never treat my kids like this!" And with few exceptions, we've treated them exactly that way: with love and concern for their well-being. To do otherwise would be to fail them. So when you find yourself facing an obstinate child, consider this: you were once just like them; then try to smile as you enforce the rules.

Prayer

"Father of grace, teach me to be the parent I
need to be. Guide my actions and help me to not
exasperate my children. In Jesus' Name, amen."

Refuse to Quit
October 19

I will strengthen you and help you.

Isaiah 41:10

Darla slouched at the piano, discouraged; her little fingers didn't stretch far enough. Each time she tried to play full chords, a sour note resounded from the piano. "I'll never get it right," she said in distress. "My hands are just too small."

With complete understanding, Mrs. Netching placed her arm around Darla's shoulders and said, "Darla, when I was your age, my fingers didn't reach either, and I wanted to quit. But my mother wouldn't allow it. She told me I would one day appreciate the hard work of today. So I determined to make the best of things by playing well the things I could, understanding that someday my fingers would grow long enough to reach all the keys. I want to share with you what my piano teacher taught me." Rising from the bench, she stood behind Darla, reached around her, and asked her to play the single-note melody for the music in front of her.

As Darla began to play the simple notes, Mrs. Netching began to accompany her, adding the chords that were impossible for Darla to play. The resulting harmony was beautiful!

"Can we do that again?" Darla asked, excited by the rich sound they had created.

"Why sure, honey," Mrs. Netching responded. "Just remember this day when your lessons are hard. Don't let today's limitations dictate tomorrow's potential. Keep practicing; commit yourself to doing the best you can. Refuse to quit, and I promise someday you will be an accomplished musician."

✝

Life is full of difficult lessons. And there are moments that the only thing we want is to quit. But quitting in the midst of trouble is accepting defeat without bringing all the power of heaven to bear on our situation.

Like Mrs. Netching, God wants to orchestrate our lives, accompanying and encouraging us until we are capable of reaching further in faith.

As the Master comes alongside us, it's *His* skill that causes our lives to become something beautiful. And the music is heard the way it's meant to be. God wants us to fight when things get rough and refuse to quit.

Prayer

"I need an awful lot of help, Lord. Please be patient with me while I get this thing called life right. Amen."

Offhanded Prejudice
October 20

Out of the same mouth come praise and cursing…this should not be.

James 3:10

"Okay," Kevin started his joke. "There was a Jew, a German, and a blonde—"

"Wait a minute, Kevin," Martin interrupted. "Look, I know you're just trying to be funny, and maybe you don't mean anything by it, but I don't appreciate those kinds of jokes, and I'd appreciate it if you'd not finish it."

"Yeah, me too," said Carlos. "To be honest," he continued, "I used to think it was okay. But then I realized that it's a form of implied prejudice hidden in unsavory humor. It's a slam against individuals or a race of people meant to generate laughter. I have to admit that when someone told a Hispanic joke in my presence, it made me angry."

"Excuuuuse me!" Kevin dragged the word out for effect. "I didn't realize you two were too good to listen to a simple joke anymore."

"Not too good, Kevin," Martin gently corrected. "I'm just trying to be more thoughtful of the language and words I use these days. You yourself know that I used to freely slander ethnic groups and blondes because it got laughs. But then God showed me that these people I'd been slamming are no different than me; they're actually just like me, and they're undeserving of my offhanded prejudice. Whether you believe it or not, what we say influences others toward those we speak. And I, for one, don't want to be responsible for planting seeds of prejudice anymore."

†

If confronted, many of us would do as Kevin did and immediately defend ourselves. "It's just a joke for goodness sake!" we'd say. But that's just not true. It is an audible statement of opinion—whether unconscious or otherwise—and we are responsible for it.

James addressed this issue two thousand years ago: double-talk, or what society now calls being two-faced—saying one thing while pretending to say something else.

If in the future you are tempted to use this form of prejudice or are present when others do, remember God's exhortation through James and have nothing to do with it.

Prayer

"Lord, reveal to me the consequences of offhanded prejudice so that I might know in my heart how wrong this form of insensitivity really is. In Jesus' Name, amen."

The Cancer of Greed
October 21

Put to death…sexual immorality, impurity, lust, evil desires and greed, which is idolatry.

Colossians 3:5

Kenny was executor of the estate when his father died. His mother's passing a few years before meant the entire estate would now need to be settled. It was a sizable estate to be settled among the three children: Kenny, his older sister, Kate, and their younger brother, Kurt.

For years Kenny had dreaded this day, but now that it was here he saw an unexpected opportunity. With startling clarity, he realized the will was rather generic in nature, and there was room for interpretation.

Having lost his life savings in a recent securities venture, Kenny was financially insolvent, completely broke. Here was an opportunity to recoup his financial losses by siphoning off funds from the estate.

So, deciding to make the most of it, Kenny fudged the books to reflect fictitious debt his father had accumulated. By filtering the finances to cover those debts, Kenny would make a substantial amount of money and receive three times more than his siblings in the settlement.

His plan almost worked. Kenny was unaware that his father had taken Kurt into his confidence weeks before his death because he was afraid of this very thing happening. When confronted, Kenny initially denied any improprieties. The resulting feud tore the family apart. Kenny was unremorseful over his veiled attempt to defraud his own family, and greed claimed another victory.

✝

Greed is a cancerous evil. It changes a person's character, gradually increasing its grip, claiming more and more of the person's heart, until finally he or she is consumed by it.

Greed tells us we are deserving, subtly gaining our allegiance, all the while making it harder to recognize its influence in our own lives.

And it doesn't always show itself in a deliberate manner as in today's story; it frequently comes cloaked in possessive behavior such as stinginess or entitlement.

Paul tells us to kill it.

Through prayer and purposeful giving, without thought of personal gain, we can resolve any issues of greed in our lives. By committing random, anonymous acts of generosity, we put to death the idol of greed.

Prayer

"Help me hold on loosely to what You've given
me, Lord. Teach me to have a giving heart instead
of a selfish one. In Jesus' Name, amen. "

The Greatest Acquisition

October 22

Do not store up treasures on earth.

Matthew 6:19

You could describe the Connor family in two words: scuba fanatics. They spent much of their free time diving along the Carolina coast, one location in particular.

"Can we go diving tonight, Dad?" Rafe asked.

"Sure," Logan said. "I was actually thinking about making another dive this morning. A little more treasure, and we'll cash in."

Rafe's father, Logan, had been a merchant marine when he was younger. He'd listened closely to his co-workers' endless tales and folklore of bygone years as they'd recounted fables of buried treasure along the eastern seaboard.

After several years, Logan decided to take a stab at treasure hunting. On one of his forays he'd actually found treasure: two pieces of eight, to be precise. He'd stumbled upon the location quite by accident. He had staked a pseudo-claim according to maritime law, but lived in fear of someone finding his secret cache. So far no one had. Weekend dives provided small amounts of treasure that were kept in the family safe.

On the day they cashed in, the Connor family found out their claim held no legal bearing. News of the discovery spread quickly. Salvage crews scrambled to stake legal claim to the wreckage. One crew managed to procure legal claim and went on to discover some 2.5 million dollars in treasure, none of which the Connor family shared.

✝

Our devotion to the acquisition of material goods is staggering; we place personal wealth ahead of the needs of others yet wonder at the broad-based suffering throughout the world today.

As with the Connor family, we can lay claim to future riches only to find out too late that what we hoped in could be taken away.

Jesus spoke clearly where wealth is concerned, instructing us to invest heavily in heavenly endeavors, endeavors that cannot be stolen.

By seeking earthly wealth, we stake our future in material possessions instead of relying on God for our daily needs.

God's promise is that if we acquire the hope in His Son Jesus Christ, it will never be taken away.

Prayer

"I like being comfortable, Lord. Help me change
that mind-set to one of helping meet others' needs
instead of amassing great wealth on earth. Show me
what You'd have me do. In Jesus' Name, amen."

Genuine Reproductions
October 23

As water reflects a face, so a man's heart reflects a man.

Proverbs 27:19

The three-hundred-foot covered bridge was located on an old railroad bed turned horse trail that traversed the Mohican River Valley in north central Ohio. Glen stood on the bridge, taking pictures of the colorful fall foliage.

He leaned through one of the bridge's windows and directed the camera toward the water, snapping frame after frame. The scene was breathtaking; all the colors of the surrounding hillsides were mimicked in reflection, not quite as brilliant, yet showing two images: genuine and reproduction. The reflection was marred only by the ripples in the current as the water flowed downstream.

While Glen was drinking in the wild beauty of his surroundings, a bald eagle soared up the river valley toward his location. As the majestic bird glided closer, it suddenly dived toward the surface of the water. Glen snapped frame after frame, hoping to capture the bird's hunting prowess. In one swift motion, the eagle grabbed a fish in its talons, disappeared under the bridge, and flew from sight.

At home, with photos transferred to the computer, Glen was ecstatic; he'd caught it all! He'd gotten several incredible photos for his portfolio.

As he brought the images up on the monitor, he was fascinated by one photo in particular. It was the frame in which the eagle's talons sliced into the water after its prey. In the troubled water, the eagle's reflection was anything but majestic; it appeared distorted and grotesque. Shaking his head in wonder, Glen catalogued it along with the rest.

✝

As Christians, we are the image bearers of Christ. When people look at us, they should see grace and compassion, love and understanding. Yet, is that what they see in us? Do we, by the life we live, have a Christlike appearance? Or, like the image of the eagle, does the reflection appear distorted and grotesque?

The choices we make are reflected in the way we live. What's sown into our heart is apparent to the world.

Only by sowing grace and love with the help of the Holy Spirit can we become a genuine reproduction of Christ's image.

Prayer

"Father, find in me the likeness of Your Son and bring it to the surface so my reflection is pleasing to You and those whose lives I touch. Amen."

Absolutes

October 24

Then they can train the younger women to ... be self-controlled and pure.

Titus 2:4

Shania realized she'd made a terrible mistake accepting Reggie's offer of a ride home. She grabbed his hand, pulling it away from her breast. "No!" she said adamantly. "Stop it!" The timbre in her voice left no doubt that she meant what she'd said. "I want to go home now!"

"Aw, c'mon, Shania. What's wrong with a little exploration?" Reggie's hormones were cranked, and he wasn't going to be easily dissuaded. "You didn't mind it when we kissed. What's the big deal?" he asked, genuinely perplexed.

But as she scooted away, he sensed his expectations dying an emotion-filled death. *This doesn't make any sense.* He thought. *After all, she kissed me, didn't she? What's up with that?*

"What makes this so wrong?" he said, confusion and frustration driving him.

"I'm a Christian, Reggie," she stated with conviction. "I made a commitment to Jesus not to have sex before marriage. I want my husband to be the only man I ever have sex with, and I don't intend to break that vow. You offered me a ride home," she reminded him, "not a sexual encounter. Now, please take me home."

Completely baffled but resigned not to push her anymore, Reggie restarted the car and drove Shania home.

✝

It's difficult for teens to remain pure until marriage while television and blockbuster movies are constantly sending the message, "Everybody's having sex!"

Society has removed moral absolutes because of their restrictions, yet refuses to make the connection to the rising rate of teen pregnancy, teen abortion, teen rape, and teen suicide.

When we fail to teach the spiritual reason for abstinence, we remove the ability to understand why morality matters. The consequences of sex outside of marriage can run the gambit from disease to unwanted pregnancy, not to mention being open to spiritual assault.

Paul instructed the older women to train the young ones. Sadly, many have failed in their responsibilities by modeling a life of promiscuity, so the cycle repeats itself.

The cycle will end when those who understand absolutes step up and show our young women how to reclaim their purity.

Prayer

"Forgive our turn from moral absolutes, Lord. Help us
reestablish them in our homes so our children might understand
Your purpose for their lives. In Jesus' Name, amen."

Inconsequential
October 25

And even the very hairs of your head are all numbered…you are worth more than many sparrows.

Matthew 10:30, 31

Bethany was fourteen when she tried to take her own life. She saw herself as a disappointment and felt she had no choice but to end her life by hanging herself from the rafters in the garage. Divine intervention brought her brother to the garage at the very moment she stepped off the chair. Grabbing her around the legs, he stepped onto the chair and supported her with one hand while removing the rope with the other.

Bethany later admitted that she felt inconsequential and unsuccessful—neither of which was true—and saw everything through a pass or fail lens; in her mind, there had been no room for error.

Her parents were shocked and horrified to learn their youngest daughter had thought of herself as a failure or that she believed death was the answer.

†

We no longer allow our children to be *average*. And because of this mind-set, our children are choosing to end their lives because they don't measure up in their own eyes.

Teen suicide is a growing epidemic and in large part is a result of being subjected to irrational ideals that create irreconcilable dilemmas teens are neither emotionally nor spiritually mature enough to handle.

Irreconcilable dilemmas create depression that, if unrecognized, causes excessive withdrawal and isolation. These symptoms can be misunderstood as a need for personal space. Quiet withdrawal is not always a downtime thing needed to regroup.

Bethany eventually learned that self-imposed, irrational expectations could overwhelm anyone. No one person is capable of carrying the weight of such demands.

Christian counseling brought Bethany to a place where her overwhelming sense of a need to succeed no longer overshadowed rational thought.

We must not fail to recognize signs of depression. They can be as subtle as they are destructive. There are abundant recourses available; Christian psychiatry can be beneficial; the local library and online medical sites have a wealth of information.

But as valuable as these are, God's Word is priceless. Our children must know they matter. And we must not fail to tell them.

Prayer

"Lord, save our children from the lie of inconsequence. Help us end this epidemic by revealing Your great love for them through those who know the truth. In Jesus' Name, amen."

Self-Imposed Ignorance
October 26

Therefore this generation will be held responsible for the blood of all the prophets.

Luke 11:50

"Did you hear about the Reager boy?" Janet asked but didn't pause long enough to allow Tom time to answer. "Kali told me he missed school this week because his father beat him, and he doesn't want anyone to see the marks."

"Janet, I swear. You listen to too much gossip," Tom said. "I can't believe George would lay a hand on his kids." What he was actually thinking was, *I'm not about to get involved in some other family's affairs. It's none of our business as far as I'm concerned.*

But Janet didn't let it go. "Tom Sherman! I can't believe you'd ignore this to keep from getting involved. Shame on you!"

"What proof do you have anyway? Where did Kali hear about it?" he said defensively. "And even if it's true, what are we supposed to do?" he demanded. "That's a job for children's services or the police."

"If they don't know about it, they can't do anything!" Janet said adamantly.

"So why do we have to be the ones to tell them?" he argued.

"Because we're the ones who know," she said quietly.

In that final statement, Tom knew she was right and decided that to do nothing was to allow it to continue. He picked up the phone and dialed children's services.

✝

Self-imposed ignorance is a form of denial. If denial lasts long enough, great tragedy will occur.

In the 1940s, the Germans heard rumors of evil being committed in their midst, yet they refused to investigate for themselves in order to remain ignorant and therefore not responsible to take action. At the end of the war, Allied troops marched German citizens through concentration camps and also forced them to look upon mass graves in hopes that they would never again allow ignorance to perpetuate evil.

In today's text, God assigned blame for the blood of the prophets on those who turned a blind eye to brutality and murder.

Self-imposed ignorance is no excuse. We are responsible for the knowledge we possess, and we can only claim ignorance once. Once enlightened, we have a responsibility to take action.

Prayer

"Lord, cause me to do what is right when I become aware of wrong. In Jesus' Name, amen."

When Christ Comes

October 27

If anyone is in Christ, he is a new creation.

2 Corinthians 5:17

Ray wasn't so much uncaring as he was self-preservation driven. He did what he thought was best for him. "Look, if we don't jump on this, we may not get another opportunity." He was adamantly defending purchasing stock options without a thorough background check of the company they were looking at. It was a merger buyout—the perfect opportunity to make a quick buck—and Ray couldn't understand their hesitation. "Why is it so important that you know how the money is being used?"

"Shelly and I don't want to unknowingly fund groups whose secular worldview and agendas don't align with our biblical worldview," his brother-in-law Peter answered. Shelly reminded Ray, "Do you remember when I spoke to you about our perspective in regard to finances?" Receiving a blank stare, she continued. "We believe our finances are God-given for the purpose of growing His kingdom, not for our own personal gain. Anything that goes against His will is not where we want our money."

"Whatever." His condescending attitude was dripping with sarcasm. "Just don't cry to me because you missed out on a good deal."

Peter never hesitated. "Ray, the last thing we would do is blame you for a poor choice on our part. So until we know what our investment is being used for, we have no intention of taking part in the merger, huge returns or not."

✝

Until Christ comes into our lives, our decisions are based on selfish choices, mostly by how those choices relate to our perceived personal desires and possible accomplishment.

When Christ comes into our lives, our lives are Holy Spirit directed, and we begin to view things through kingdom lenses. Now we realize our responsibility in making spiritually correct choices.

For the most part, this does not happen automatically; we must persevere in spiritual discipline by asking God for His input in every aspect of our lives. No issue is too small; no problem is too big. To get rid of the old nature requires taking an active part in killing the old. Once we understand God's sacrifice, it becomes a blessing to do the will of the Lord.

Prayer

"Father, show me what's right for my life. Teach
me to ask for Your advice and speak to me
through others. In Jesus' Name, amen."

Big, Mean Bully

October 28

The LORD disciplines those he loves.

Proverbs 3:12

As the story unfolded, the boys related how they'd found some "giant ant hills." And, as boys do, they decided to rid the neighborhood of them. Having procured some gasoline and stick matches, they saturated the hills with gas, stood back, and threw a lighted match. The ensuing explosion sent embers flying in every direction, hence the large grassfire. Running to the nearest house, they had alerted the owner, who called 911.

As the fire trucks pulled away, Jamie, standing beside his father, asked, "Is God gonna punish me for startin' that fire?"

Looking at his nine-year-old son, Luther wondered, *Where do we get this picture of a big, mean God waiting to punish us?*

He said, "No, Jamie, God is not going to punish you. But do you understand all three of you could have been badly burned or killed today? And you could have burned people's homes to the ground."

They walked a little farther, and Luther said, "God isn't going to punish you, Jamie. I, however, am. Because of your little escapade, you're grounded for two weeks. No contact with Bruce or Stevie during that time. And you will call Mr. Breece to see if he wants you to help him clean up his property. Is that understood?"

"Yes. I'm sorry. We were just tryin' to kill those ants was all." He sounded so forlorn; Luther had to turn his head to keep Jamie from seeing his smile.

✝

God is not a big, mean bully, arbitrarily punishing us for our mistakes. He does, however, discipline those He calls sons and daughters. I've not met a loving father who didn't reprimand his children when they've done wrong.

Like Luther with Jamie, God disciplines us to keep us from harming others or ourselves. His discipline is not indiscriminate or ambiguous. It is intended to teach us how to eliminate unnecessary trouble from our lives.

To do that, God first instructs us; when instruction fails, He is forced to gain our attention with love-driven discipline.

Rebellion and mistakes have consequences. Most, if not all, could be avoided by heeding our Father's instruction.

Prayer

"Father God, teach me to listen to Your instruction. Discipline me for my own sake when I'm rebellious. In Jesus' Name, amen."

What's the Difference?
October 29

Keep your servant from willful sins.

Psalm 19:13

"What's the difference if I make a mistake once in a while?" Jean asked. "I mean, it's not like I did it intentionally, you know ..." Her voice trailed off.

Her argument sounded good, but Carolann knew the truth. "You know as well as I do that it matters. And you know why. You knew that what you were doing was wrong, yet you chose to do it anyway. That's a choice, not a mistake."

She continued to correct Jean in love. "Making an honest mistake is one thing; blatant disregard for moral and ethical standards is another."

Jean bristled at Carolann's words. "I'm not perfect like *some* people I know!" she said, angry at having been rebuked when she'd shared the confidential information on her own. "I didn't have to tell you, ya know," she insisted. "God's not going to strike me down because I made one mistake," she challenged defensively. "And I am better than I used to be."

"No, He won't. And yes, you are growing. But remember, God knows what's in our heart when *mistakes* are made. More than that," Carolann emphasized, "being a Christian means we're supposed to look and act differently than the world. Do you understand?"

"Yes," Jean acknowledged. "If it's any consolation, I didn't get any pleasure out of it anyway," she admitted sheepishly.

"You asked, 'What's the difference?' The difference is, when Jesus comes into our life, sin no longer has the same appeal. And once we begin to live for Christ, we begin to look and feel different."

✝

God's instruction leads to life. Yet our moral consciousness is flawed and imperfect. This means we can sin without understanding it is sin. However, there are times we knowingly and willfully go against the nature and will of God—sins of commission.

Unless there is a change of heart, there will be no discernable difference in how we feel toward sin or look to the world. Giving our lives to Christ does not mean sin no longer exists in our lives. It means when we sin, convicting discomfort sets in, and we have another choice to make.

Prayer

"Father, show me the sin in my life. Give me
a heart of discernment that I might not sin
against You. In Jesus' Name, amen."

Giving Our All

October 30

Whatever you do, do it all for the glory of God. Do not cause anyone to stumble.

1 Corinthians 10:31, 32

"How much longer are we gonna be here?" Jensen hated physical labor and wasn't hiding the fact he didn't enjoy being here. He'd been subjecting everyone to a steady monologue about "getting roped into this project."

"I don't enjoy comin' to Hicksville doin' work for somebody I don't know, let alone doin' it for free!"

He was deriding his church's *Resurrection!* outreach program; they repaired homes in underprivileged neighborhoods.

Simon had listened to all the complaining he could take. "What's your problem? This is a community service to show Christ's love. If you didn't want to do it, why'd you sign up?" He was concerned that if Jensen continued complaining, the homeowner might hear them and take offense. "You may not get it, Jensen, but we enjoy doing this. We figure we're on God's clock, and it's His choice to reward us. But that's not why we do it."

"So why do you?" Jensen asked with a true sense of sincerity.

"Because Jesus says we should help those less fortunate." Simon put his hand on Jensen's shoulder. "Look, man, this may not be your idea of working for the kingdom. If not, then find out what lights you up for Jesus and do it. But for today, could you just try to see the good in what we're doing and commit yourself to the work?"

"I never thought about it like that," Jensen responded. "Yeah, I can do that." And with that, he went to work with a new perspective of why he was there.

✝

Giving our all means serving without restraint. When we serve our fellowman, it is a service to God. And our attitude in regard to service speaks loud and clear.

Kingdom work is not meant to bring *us* glory. If we complain when we serve, even silently, then maybe we should examine our motives. Because if we serve with a chip on our shoulder, the world will know; and we will build a wall where a bridge is meant to be.

Prayer

"I sometimes fall short when it comes to serving
without complaint, Lord. Help me build bridges
instead of walls. In Jesus' Name, amen. "

In Light of the Truth

October 31

But when he, the Spirit of truth, comes, he will guide you into all truth.

John 16:13

Out of the blue, Mark said, "You know, Britt, some of the things I learned growing up don't serve me well today."

"What do you mean?" Britt asked.

"Well, some of what I learned was actually counterproductive and discriminatory in nature. Some of the things I did were unsavory. They were done in ignorance."

"So how did you figure out what things no longer, as you put it, serve you well?" Britt asked.

"Well, through studying the Bible and spending time in prayer, God has opened my eyes by showing me that some things I once believed to be harmless were actually extremely destructive. He made me aware of the negative influence they had in my life and those around me."

Britt was intrigued. "So what kind of *things* are you talking about?"

"Well, one example would be my habitual use of foul language. I could, as they say, swear like a sailor. But then I realized how terrible a witness profanity is and how it offends God when those words are spoken."

Britt smiled and asked, "So how'd you stop swearing?"

"I no longer justified the behavior in light of the truth. I disciplined myself to preappraise my speech. It's a retraining process that's not always easy. But I've found that if I'm willing to change, God will equip me for the challenge."

✝

With few exceptions, our parents did the best they knew how when it came to raising us. In truth, many things we picked up on our own, without our parents' knowledge. Had they known, they would have blistered our behinds!

As we mature, we come under new influence; our perceptions change. And although profanity is used in today's scenario, the list of sin's exposure to truth is broad-based. When we do things we shouldn't, we notice a *catch* in our spirit, a Holy Spirit alert.

Heeding God's Spirit is always the correct course of action. However, we don't always take the road less traveled. Just remember: the more we seek the truth, the more we discover.

Prayer

"Help me sort through what I believe and why I believe it. Show me what needs to go, and renew my mind to Your precepts. In Jesus' Name, amen."

November

Rehashing the Past
November 1

I…am he who blots out your transgressions…and remembers your
sins no more.

Isaiah 43:25

"But you don't know what I've done!" Cassandra asserted, sobs wracking her
body.

"And I don't need to," Julie said. "God isn't as concerned with your past as
He is with your today, Cassie. He loves you so much that He's willing to forgive
you of anything if you'll just bring it to Him. Repentance brings forgiveness.
And once God forgives, that sin is gone forever; He refuses to hold it against
us."

"But it can't be that easy," she argued. "Not after what I've done."

As sure as Julie was of the truth, she knew Cassandra couldn't fathom the
depth of God's grace right now. So she said, "The Bible assures us of God's
complete forgiveness, Cassie—an everlasting, unconditional forgiveness that,
although we may not understand, is perfect in every way. I've experienced it
myself." And Julie had! What Cassie didn't know was that Julie had once been
a working girl. "If I were to let my past rule my today, I'd be telling God He's
incapable of forgiving sin. And that's not what the Bible says. If we allow Satan
and his followers to sell us the lie of unforgiveness, we are walking without
faith and hope."

"But I don't feel forgiven," she said.

"Forgiveness isn't about feelings, Cassie. It's about God redeeming things
that are lost: parts of our soul. And it requires taking God at His word."

"I'd like to do that," Cassandra said. And with hope in her heart, she con-
fessed her sins, asking God to forgive them.

✝

God wants us in the present, ready to do His good will. But if we continue
rehashing our past, we can't join Him, thereby destroying our ability to effectively work in the present for His kingdom.

In Isaiah 43:18 God tells us to, "Forget the former things; do not dwell on
the past." We do well to heed His words.

Forgiveness covers every part of our past; not part, but all. He wants to
bring us into the present with that forgiveness. Would you come join Him?

Prayer

"Lord, help me believe that my sins are forgiven. Speak
to me in ways I can understand. And help me forgive
myself that I might join You in the present. Amen."

Absolute Rebellion

November 2

The LORD is slow to anger, abounding in love and forgiving sin and rebellion. Yet he does not leave the guilty unpunished.

Numbers 14:18

Joe was still fuming about what just happened when Kathy, his girlfriend, climbed in the car. "I'm done with them," he asserted, "and their closed-minded religion. It's old school with obsolete morals. This is the twentieth century for God's sake!" He slammed his fist against the steering wheel.

Kathy tried to assuage his smoldering anger. "But it's what they believe, Joe. You may not adhere to their faith anymore, but surely you can understand why they said no. I do." Kathy was speaking to the point of Joe's contention. Joe's parents believed sleeping together outside of marriage was a sin and had just refused to allow Joe and Kathy to stay the night sleeping together under their roof. The night had immediately deteriorated as Joe had stormed from the house with Kathy apologizing before catching up.

Joe said, "No! I don't understand! Christianity is archaic! Times have changed! Can't they see that?"

Kathy was concerned this fallout might place a wedge between Joe and his parents if he couldn't come to grips with this.

As it turned out, Kathy's concerns were well founded. They broke up shortly thereafter, and it took seventeen years before Joe darkened the door of his childhood home. Even then, his visits were overshadowed by an awkward civility. Joe held himself at arm's length while his parents continued praying for him, hoping the Light of Life would pierce the darkness their son was walking in.

✝

In a world where increasingly liberal philosophy has no patience for, understanding of, or care to know why moral absolutes matter, we find rebellion against God on the increase.

Satan and his angels devise schemes to advance his kingdom through moral corruption, sexual perversion, deception, and a myriad of other forms of evil. Still in possession of their power, malevolent angels attempt to destroy God's creation (Romans 11:29; Ephesians 6:12).

As slow as God is to anger, He will be swift to judge those who die in their rebellion! There are absolutes. We will all be judged accordingly.

Prayer

"Lord, in this ever darkening world, help me live a life
of righteousness. Give me courage to stand against those
who rebel against Your decrees. In Jesus' Name, amen."

Defending the Weak

November 3

Defend the cause of the weak... and oppressed.

Psalm 82:3

Marla sat in the corner of the lunchroom, away from the other kids. She was unpopular and constantly reviled by her peers.

Teresa hated the insensitivity of her classmates. Angered by their actions, she began sitting with Marla, which in turn, caused them to turn on her, too.

During an exceptionally unpleasant day, Marla asked her, "Why do you stick up for me? Now they make fun of you as much as they do me."

"For a couple reasons," Teresa said. "One: what they're doing is wrong. Two: they're ganging up on you. I refuse to let you stand against them alone. As far as I know, you've never done anything to deserve their ridicule. Besides"—she leaned closer—"something inside me burns when bullies attack in groups."

"But don't they hurt? You know, the words and gestures?" Marla asked. "Aren't you afraid?"

Teresa said, "Sure, it hurts when they call us names and make those vile gestures. But I'm not afraid." She saw Marla's eyebrows rise. "Marla, don't get me wrong, I don't like it. They're cowards masquerading as thugs. But I don't get my affirmation from them. I get it from God. I'm not afraid because God has given me peace about it. Yes, the words hurt. But I'm not who they say I am and neither are you. I know that because of God's loving encouragement. He protects my heart from their insensitivity. God loves them too and wants them to change. Until they do, He's asked me to take a stand against small-minded people."

✝

Without exception, we have all been bullies and been bullied. Someone or something has paid the price of our insecurity, receiving undue ridicule, or we ourselves have been on the receiving end.

Defending the rights of the weak is everyone's responsibility. Yet fear of man prevents many of us from taking the necessary action. It can be uncomfortable, unpleasant work standing up for someone not directly involved in our life.

When faced with injustice, ask yourself: "If this were my sister, my brother, or my child, would I stand aside and do nothing?"

Prayer

"Lord, may I never again be the oppressor. Help me to always defend the rights of those who are weak and oppressed. In Jesus' Name, amen."

Age Doesn't Matter

November 4

God our Savior, who wants all men to be saved.

1 Timothy 2:3, 4

Beth had steeled herself against a day like this. Five months pregnant and holding her three-year-old daughter's hand, she gazed at her husband's coffin one last time. You could almost hear her heart. *You weren't supposed to go yet!*

Aaron had been thirty-one when he died tragically, leaving them to carry on alone. He'd been a good man. There had been about him a charismatic charm; his smile was disarming; his gracious attitude sincere. He was well liked and deeply loved.

Aaron just couldn't seem to escape evil's grip. And on that New Year's Eve, after ringing in hope for the future, it cost him his life.

Beth had spoken at the funeral. She wanted everyone to understand the reality of not being guaranteed our next breath.

She spoke openly about Aaron's faith in God; his asking Jesus into his heart, and his love of family. "Although *we* may believe we have all the time in the world, it's a fleeting hope. You see," she pleaded, "age doesn't matter. At thirty-one, Aaron thought he would live forever. But death respects no one, regardless of age or station in life. When we die, our eternity is set in stone."

She challenged those in attendance to "make a choice for Jesus today, before that choice is revoked in death. I am compelled to ask; if you die today, where will you spend your eternity?" And with that, she took her seat.

†

Studies show that in the short time it takes to read today's devotion, some twelve hundred people have died. Most, if not all, had no idea death was coming. Sadly, only an approximate seven percent of them went to heaven.

That means if these statistics are correct, 1,116 deaths unnecessarily ended in the penalty of eternal separation from God in hell.

God wants none to perish. Sadly, a great many do. So knowing how unforeseen death can be, can we elect to put off a choice so critical?

Poor choices can hasten preventable death. If you have never made Jesus Lord and Savior, please take this moment to assure yourself eternal life.

Prayer

"Forgive the sin in my life, Jesus. Please come into my heart
and lead me into a loving relationship with You. Amen."

Resolved in Christ

November 5

For I resolved to know nothing … except Jesus Christ.

1 Corinthians 2:2

"Your brother never shuts up about Jesus!" Peyton complained.

"Why should that bother you?" Chase asked, wondering what brought this up.

"He embarrasses me, constantly asking people where they're planning to spend eternity!" She was more than a little agitated.

"Nathanial is a good man, Peyton. He believes that our chances of dying are one hundred percent and that we live on spiritually in either heaven or hell. He wants to take as many people to heaven as he can. Asking people about eternity is his effort to do that."

"Well, I don't like it!" she stated.

Chase saw his date in a new light. It appeared she really couldn't comprehend Nathanial's actions. Did she really believe what she professed, salvation and eternal life in Jesus Christ?

"So let me get this straight." Chase was beginning to have his own doubts but not about Jesus. "You say you believe in Jesus, but you don't want to be around when the good news of the gospel is being shared?"

"That's not what I'm saying!" she responded defensively. "I just don't believe it's appropriate to talk about such a personal issue unless you're asked."

"So how does that work exactly?" Chase asked incredulously. "I mean, if we don't talk about Jesus, how are we going to find out if they know Him?" There was an awkward moment, and Chase said, "I agree we need to reach out in love, Peyton. But we have a responsibility to reach out."

"Well, I, for one, have no intention of offending people by badgering them about their beliefs." The finality of her statement shocked Chase. This would be their last date.

†

There are doubtless more Peytons than Nathanials in the world. But we should not lose heart. Paul was but one man and look at the impact he is still having for the kingdom of Christ!

The truth is that in order to have any measurable impact for Jesus, we must resolve to know Him so intimately that we no longer worry about what the world thinks when we ask the question, *'Where are you planning to spend eternity?'*

Prayer

"Help me be bold, Lord. Help me care less about
being embarrassed than allowing others to perish.
I ask this in Your Name, Jesus, amen."

So, What Now?

November 6

The LORD is in his holy temple; the LORD is on his heavenly throne.

Psalm 11:4

The race was over; the election hadn't gone their way. "So, what now?" Peter asked Nathan.

"We keep doing what God tells us," was his brother's simple reply. "Look, Pete, God is still on His throne, and each day when my feet hit the floor, I'm going to continue doing what God called me to."

"How can you be so calm about this, Nate?" Peter's frustration was obvious.

"Pete, more than ever, what we need to be right now is calm. Getting upset and frustrated will only cause confusion, which is exactly what the enemy wants. When we're frustrated and confused, it's harder to hear what God is saying."

Nate's response sounded reasonable, yet Peter was angry at the lack of group effort from the Christian community.

Nathan continued, "Do you think God fell off His throne when the winner was announced?"

"Well, no, I don't suppose He did," Peter admitted. "But in the same breath, I don't think it made Him too happy that many professing Christians sat idly by and did nothing to stop this from happening."

"Maybe, but we can't change that. What we can do is make the best of what we have. God allowed it, Pete. I trust Him." With that, Nathan slapped Peter on the back and went back to work.

✝

In today's text, David makes a wise observation: although his adversaries appeared to have the upper hand, God remained in control and would prevail.

Our righteous God sees His righteous people and does not forget them in their time of trouble. Jesus himself said that there will be trouble (John 16). He also said He has overcome it.

When we face adversity, we need to remember and believe that God is never taken by surprise and will always stand with us to see us through to the other side of our problems. We stand in a place of victory. The time in between now and realizing the fulfillment of that truth will be better spent listening as we ask God the question, "So, what now, Lord?"

Prayer

"Lead me on in Your strength and assurance, Lord.
Help me focus on Your agenda instead of being
distracted by the world. In Jesus' Name, amen."

Messengers

November 7

I will send my messenger.

Malachi 3:1

Thoroughly distracted, Michaela continued waiting tables. She'd just received the news that she was being laid off, and she'd been given one week's notice before the layoff took effect.

Like everyone else, Michaela and her family lived day-to-day, dependant on her and her husband's weekly wages.

Lord, what are we supposed to do? she silently prayed. *You know we don't have any savings. And Melvin's wages won't support us. How are we supposed to manage?* In her spirit, she felt God answer. *I will provide. Trust Me.* Somewhat encouraged, she went about her business. Yet unsure of how His provision would manifest itself, she remained a little unsettled.

As Michaela took an order from a middle-aged couple, they asked if she had any prayer needs. She couldn't believe it! Briefly, she shared what had happened. Even more unexpected, when she'd concluded her story, the couple took her hands and prayed for her, right there, right then! Her hope restored, Michaela thanked them and returned to work.

Later, as the couple left, they hugged Michaela and told her to have faith.

After they departed, Michaela returned to clean their table and found an envelope with her name on it. Opening it, she was awestruck to find five hundred dollars and a simple note. "God sent us here today with a message of hope for you. Never doubt that He has His eye on you!"

✝

God knew the worry that threatened Michaela's heart, so He sent messengers to confirm His unseen provision.

Although God sends us messages all the time, the message and messengers aren't always easily recognized. Many times we fail to notice the visit until sometime later, after we've had a chance to assimilate the message.

God's use of His children, as well as all Creation, is well documented in Scripture. He uses His messengers to show us that He knows what we need and is paying attention. Not all messages are as definable as today's story. Sometimes the message is subtle; other times it's as clear as audible conversation.

Each of them is timely and perfect if we watch for them.

Prayer

"Help me trust in You for all my needs, Papa. And
when I doubt, help me recognize Your messenger
so I can better hear the message. Amen."

Our Best Behavior

November 8

Woe to those who go to great depths to hide their plans from the LORD.

Isaiah 29:15

David was a different person when his father wasn't around. He openly opposed his mother, defying her authority. But when his father was home, he was on his best behavior. So when his mother broached the subject to her husband about their son's increasing disrespect, he had a hard time believing her accusations of insolence.

"I'm sorry, Tammy," Trace said doubtfully, "but I can't imagine David intends you such disrespect. Are you sure you're not just misjudging his actions?"

"Do you seriously think I would lie about something like this?" she asked. "I'm not doing this to get attention. Our son is treating me like dirt!"

Trace knew he'd said the wrong thing. He headed for work, unsure of what to do. Deciding to show up unannounced to see if he could discover the truth, he left work a couple hours early that evening. Arriving home, he slipped in the back door. In complete shock, he arrived just in time to hear David call his mother a vulgar name, telling her he didn't have to do what she said!

"Mister." Trace saw panic in David's eyes as he stepped into the room. "If you ever say anything like that to your mother again, it'll be the last thing out of your mouth for a long time!" He was livid. He couldn't believe what he'd just heard his son say; even worse, he couldn't believe he'd doubted his wife. "You apologize right now. Then you and I are going upstairs."

✝

When we remember God is watching, we, like David, are on our best behavior. However, our forgetters work very well. During those times we become an alter ego of our best-behavior self, slandering and cursing those around us. We do unseemly things that affect our relationship with God and those we love.

It is unbelievable the depths to which we descend when we forget that God is watching. And when reminded of that fact during our worse than abhorrent behavior, we experience shame and repentance.

We all share this weakness. But through conscious effort, we can minimize the resurgence of our evil selves.

Prayer

"Lord, forgive me when I act unreasonable. Remind me when I fail to remember You never turn away. Amen."

Are We a Threat?

November 9

I urge you to live a life worthy of the calling you have received.

Ephesians 4:1

"You're not much of a threat to Satan these days, Mike." Shaw brought the indictment against his friend.

"What are you talking about?" Mike didn't like the allegation.

"I mean that lately your lifestyle doesn't bless heaven or threaten hell. You're kind of ambiguous," Shaw said matter-of-factly. "You're a professing Christian, yet if a stranger were to watch you for twenty-four hours, I'm not sure he'd know it."

"Where the hell do you get off judging me?" Mike was incensed.

"See, that's exactly what I'm talking about," Shaw said, staring at his friend.

"What, exactly, are you talking about?" Mike said, exasperated.

"I'm talking about your angry attitude. You know, the one you used to swear at me in the process of denying my claim?" Shaw softened his approach, trying to make a point, not an enemy. "Look, I'm not your judge. And I don't want you to think that's what this is about. But Satan's not threatened at all by you lately. You don't represent any imminent danger to his kingdom. And you don't shed much light in God's either."

Arrested by the truth of Shaw's statement, Mike was suddenly overcome with conviction. He was indeed a professing Christian. But he had to admit he hadn't been living a life that brought much glory to God recently.

✝

Satan doesn't need to pay much attention to many of today's professing Christians. They just don't represent a real threat to his kingdom. Many Christians go about living their lives, doing pretty much what they did prior to asking Jesus to save them. In other words, they're not advancing the kingdom of Christ. Therefore, they're no threat to Satan's.

It's not always easy to *live* for Christ. And sometimes we need a kick in the pants to get us back on track. Not many of us are capable of living a righteous life without good friends to help remind us of our commitments.

Prayer

"Lord, I love You. But sometimes I do a lousy job of showing
it. Forgive my inattentiveness to the life You died to give me.
Help me become who You created me to be. And thanks for
good friends who help me live the life. In Jesus' Name, amen."

Change Bait
November 10

"Come, follow me," Jesus said, "and I will make you fishers of men."

Matthew 4:19

Marvin was ready to bait his hook. "Toss me the dough ball, would ya, Duane? I think I'll try to catch a few catfish."

Duane retrieved the jar of thick paste from the tackle box, tossed it to Marvin, and remarked, "I'm gonna see if I can catch a few bass before I join you in bottom fishing." He reached back into the tackle box and grabbed a top-water plug, attached it to his line, and began casting.

Poppers, as they're known, are a perfect late-evening bait for large-mouth bass. The fish see the plug jump across the water and identify it as a frog or some other water-skipping prey. They strike with extreme force, making an exciting experience for the angler (unless they're not biting).

An hour and zero bites later, Marvin decided to try his luck at cat fishing. "Must not be a bass for twenty miles," he proclaimed. "Otherwise, my stringer would be full!"

"Riiight." Marvin dragged the word out, letting Duane know he wasn't buying his rhetoric. Then he decided to tease him a little. "And you know that how? Oh, yes," he snickered, "I forgot. You are such a legend in fishing circles that the fish just can't wait to jump on your hook!" He ducked as a piece of dough ball came flying his direction.

✝

Fishing for men can be frustrating at times too. We might cast and cast and cast only to come up empty. Perhaps we're using the wrong bait.

Men, like fish, aren't always attracted by the same bait. For that reason, we must be willing to change bait.

Accomplished anglers constantly test different baits, always looking to find which bait works best at any given moment. They will change lures all night long in an effort to find just the right bait. And when they do, they have great success.

And so it is with fishers of men. They must be willing to change bait when one isn't working.

There are different ways to present the gospel, and being willing to change our approach will result in catching more men for the kingdom.

Prayer

"Lord Jesus, teach me to expand my casting techniques. Show me what bait will work the best in each situation. Amen."

Betrayal

November 11

Jesus would not entrust himself to them ... for he knew what was in man.

John 2.23

Ben and Kurt were childhood friends. There friendship spanned sixteen years of disagreements and reconciliations; until the day Kurt betrayed Ben's trust when he learned Ben liked Melodie Wilson.

Ben confided to Kurt that he would like to date Melodie and asked Kurt if he would *test the waters* for him, so to speak. He prefaced this favor with the condition that Kurt not talk to her directly. Instead, he asked Kurt to talk to her friends to see if Melodie had ever mentioned him in conversation; and more importantly, if she liked him.

Teenage boys are likely to discard every other relationship in lieu of their first love! And that's exactly what happened because Kurt himself was smitten by Melodie. In the blink of an eye Ben got kicked to the curb. Kurt began spreading rumors about Ben among Melodie's friends. He even lied to Melodie, telling her that Ben only wanted to get her into bed. He, on the other hand, declared his honorable intentions. In the end, neither won her heart.

Sadly, Ben and Kurt went their separate ways, a life-long relationship abandoned because Kurt's impetuous heart wanted what it wanted, and Ben couldn't find it in his heart to forgive the pain of betrayal.

✝

In all trust there is the possibility of betrayal. Once betrayed, the heart rejects immediate forgiveness. Instead, it becomes wary ... of everyone and everything. If left unforgiven, the rift will widen, and a spirit of cynicism will plant seeds of doubt until they grow into a lifestyle of suspicion, influencing our every thought. Nothing and no one is exempt from its vile destruction. The heart will protect itself at all costs; *you will never get close enough to hurt me again!* In a doubt-ridden mind trust and forgiveness are not open for discussion. Our hearts need Jesus.

And Jesus, knowing what is within man, is never cynical. He perfectly understands our nature and what He can do for us. He openly invites us to trust in Him without the possibility of betrayal or abandonment.

Prayer

"I've been wounded many times, Lord Jesus. And sometimes it's even been by friends. But I come today, trusting You to bring healing instead of betrayal or abandonment. Amen."

What Are We to Do?

November 12

You will always have the poor among you.

John 12:8

Walt and Erin were headed out for their annual Christmas shopping day. Each year, they set aside one day in November to go shopping with their Christmas club fund they'd so faithfully contributed to all year long.

As they drove toward their destination, Erin shared some misgivings. "I don't feel right about spending all this money on ourselves and the family when there are so many people who don't have anything. So many kids will wake up Christmas morning and not get a single gift." The quiver in her voice betrayed her sincerity.

"Look, Erin, I understand what you're saying," Walt gently began. "But it's not like we're stingy or uncaring." Stopped at a streetlight, he looked over and reached for Erin's hand. "The truth is I feel a little that way myself."

As the light changed, Walt continued, "But we do tithe each week; we sponsor Emily in Haiti; we've set aside the emergency fund for those times we see someone with a need." After a minute's pause, he glanced at her and said, "Even Jesus said, 'You will always have the poor.' And as much as we'd like to, we can't help them all. I believe that no matter what we do, there will always be a need that we could use this money for."

✝

Anyone who loves the Lord struggles at one time or another over what to do regarding this issue.

When brought into the light of "it's all God's money to begin with," we must then answer the question: "What am I to do with what He gives *me?*"

This is a personal decision meant to be brought before the Lord in prayer and discussed with those who share in the decision.

Our decision is just that, *ours.* We should not judge harshly the choices others make and be careful of our own.

Are you struggling with this question? Pray, seek His will in all your financial matters. We all have a part; ask Him what yours is.

Prayer

"Lord, I know there will always be the poor. And I struggle
with having more than my share sometimes. Please lead
me to a place of understanding in what You want me
to do with Your money. In Jesus' Name, amen. "

Future Reward

November 13

He causes the sun to rise on the evil and the good, and sends rain on the righteous and the unrighteous.

Matthew 5:45

"I understand the free will thing and how bad things happen to good people," Gabe said. "But how is it that so many nasty people have so much? How come God allows bad people to have good things?" Gabe wasn't just complaining. He wanted an answer.

"Well," Grant said, "Scripture says that God's rain falls on the just and the unjust alike, Gabe. He shows love to everyone without distinction or favor. He allows us all to sense that love so we have the chance to know and follow Him. He doesn't want anyone to perish. So He blesses some with wealth, hoping they will understand where the blessings come from and give Him glory."

"It just doesn't seem fair. They get all the stuff, and I get hard work and frustration." Now Gabe *was* complaining.

Grant continued, "Gabe, Jesus also said, 'For what good is it for a man to gain the whole world, yet forfeit his soul?' (Matthew 16:36). You see, although they may have wealth and material possessions, they have lost the most important thing we can hope to have: eternal life with God. Would you want their riches if you had to pay their consequences?" he asked.

"No," Gabe said, noticeably subdued. He was contemplating the enormity of the truth as it became clear.

†

Great wealth can cause great envy. Our finite minds conjure the image of God randomly blessing people who have no intention of giving Him credit for their wealth while we struggle to make ends meet. Without the entire picture, we can come to the wrong conclusion and resent God for His liberal lavishness.

But if God, in His infinite wisdom, brings rain on the unjust, could it possibly be because He knows something we don't? And if that is true, shouldn't we give Him leeway to do as He pleases without lodging complaints?

As believers, our future reward is based on our inheritance: salvation in Christ Jesus. Having such a promise and reward, how can we envy those who have gained wealth and possessions yet are perishing?

Prayer

"Forgive me when I envy wealth and prosperity, Lord. Help me remain focused on my future reward in heaven. Amen."

Return to the Father

November 14

He ran to his son, threw his arms around him and kissed him.

Luke 15:20

As the young evangelist looked out over those who had come to mourn, he spoke of eternal life through Jesus Christ. At one point, he paused and appeared to be wrestling with something. As he lifted his head, you could sense the battle within was over. "I've struggled over whether to share this or not, but I've decided I must.

"In my short time of pastoring, I've not performed many funerals. Yet, in that short time, I have performed way too many for men from Brinkhaven."

Weeping could be heard as an acknowledging murmur ran through the church; family members of those he had preached funerals for were present today.

"I've decided that to remain silent while young men choose to go their own way, rejecting God's offer of salvation, would be wrong. Men, today you have a chance to change that. You can return to the Father as the prodigal did, asking Him to make you one of His own; not a second-rate citizen, but one of His own, an heir to His throne!" His voice broke with the passion of his plea. It wasn't hard to grasp that he did not wish to preside over another unnecessary death.

"Frank was a man of faith, his life dedicated to God. Is yours? If not, I ask that you do something about that today before it's too late."

"Amen!" and "That's right!" echoed through the sanctuary as the evangelist nodded his head. God had taken what the enemy meant for evil and had used it for good.

✝

Premature death is too frequently the consequence of poor choices, consequences that are not mandatory. Pride and rebellion are costly, deadly if we treat with impunity God's offer of eternal life.

That offer remains on the table until we take our final breath. At that moment, we lose any chance of choosing where we will spend eternity.

Until that time, God waits with arms wide open, watching for those who are lost to return.

Prayer

"Lord, I'm weary from all the mistakes I've made. I want a new life in Jesus. Forgive my sins and make me one of Your own. In Jesus' Name and by His blood, I surrender my life today. Amen."

Spiritual ADD

November 15

> [Aaron] took what they handed him and made it into an idol cast in the shape of a calf.
>
> Exodus 32:4

Nick was just like every other kid in his class: high energy, fun loving, even a bit of a prankster. Nick had recently been diagnosed with attention deficit disorder. His attention span was much shorter than his peers due to what his neurologists called a short circuit in his brain's hard wiring. This *short* created an inability to tune out outside stimuli.

Nick's parents knew his actions weren't just a ploy to avoid homework or chores because they'd observed the same distracted behavior on the baseball field.

Nick played second base. At any given moment, you might catch him looking around the outfield while the pitcher was in his windup. Or he'd be drawing pictures in the dirt when he should have been chanting, "Hey, batter, batter, batter."

It was difficult for Nick to concentrate on his lessons for more than ten minutes at a time; there were just too many things vying for his attention. His parents and teachers were instructed to be patient and allow for his inattentiveness. They were told that long-suffering persistence would eventually help Nick overcome his inability to focus for extended periods of time. Nick learned coping strategies that helped fend off the unwanted interference, helping him direct his focus on things at hand.

✝

Israel had a severe case of spiritual ADD. Although God was constantly with them, they were unable to focus on Him for more than a few days at a time. The miracles He had done on their behalf were forgotten, and they went right back to complaining. It cost them forty years in a desolate land.

But before we judge the Israelites too harshly, we should admit that we don't retain the goodness of God any longer than they did. We, like Israel, get distracted by the enemy. We gripe and complain about our circumstances and God's failure to meet our needs.

Like Nick, we need to develop coping strategies to tune out unwanted influence. By listening to God's instruction, we can shorten our time in the wilderness.

Prayer

"Thank You, loving Father, for putting up with my impatient behavior. Help me shut out the world's interference so I can focus my attention where it needs to be. In Jesus' Name, amen."

In Spite of the Giants

November 16

All the people we saw there are of great size.

Numbers 13:32

Bresden's intention was to motivate his teammates. "We can win this game!" the senior point guard confidently claimed.

His teammates looked skeptical. One echoed their collective doubt. "We've never beaten them before. What makes you think we can do it tonight?" They were remembering the last two seasons, seasons in which this team had totally annihilated them.

"Look," Bresden responded. "We've worked hard and played well all season! They're not invincible. If we leave it all on the court, we can beat them!" You could see their confidence grow. "Let's get Coach the win!" Bresden challenged. And with that, they took the court.

It was their best game of the season! The score changed hands fifteen times and was tied five. Nobody could remember seeing Tremont play with this level of enthusiasm. No matter what they threw up, their shots dropped. Basket after basket ripped the net—three-pointers, layups, it didn't matter. It was so awe-inspiring that the crowd was on their feet for most of the game. When the final buzzer sounded, Tremont walked off the court victorious!

In his final game, Dan Bresden had inspired his team to greatness; they believed what he told them, and because they believed, they had come away with the victory.

✝

What we believe has a tremendous effect on how we respond to adversity. Who we believe in matters even more.

When faced with imposing odds, we can be tempted to admit defeat before we've even entered the battle.

God sent spies to survey the land, not the enemy (13:1). Sadly, eight of the ten forgot that. All they saw was the size of the enemy. They lost all confidence in God's ability to deliver the enemy into their hands.

God will never send us into a battle we can't win. And it's our responsibility to remember with Whose power we fight.

Nevertheless, all the pep talks in the world won't convince us unless we first believe, "If God is for us, who can be against us" (Romans 8:31).

Prayer

"Anchor my faith in You alone, Lord. Keep my
feet planted firmly for battle instead of ready to
run. Remind me that with You I can stand against
the fiercest enemy. In Jesus' Name, amen."

Knowledge Without Wisdom

November 17

The fear of the LORD is the beginning of knowledge, but fools despise wisdom.

Proverbs 1:7

Kendall was blessed with an incredible amount of knowledge ranging from thermodynamics to mechanical engineering; the list was extensive and quite impressive. He actually was a *know-it-all.*

But Kendall lacked humility. Benevolent use of his intellect was not his strong suit. He wielded his achievements like a sword. In short, Kendall mistook his vast amount of knowledge for wisdom.

Kendall was privileged to receive an invitation to a think tank conference with some very influential men. One man's reputation, in particular, preceded him. Whatever he did succeeded and was done correctly. He was respected and well liked.

He was Kendall's contemporary in every way but one: where Kendall was haughty and self-promoting, he was considerate and reflective. When asked for input, he provided the shortest, most concise answers possible, forgoing the need to display his intellect.

Curious, Kendall asked for a moment of his time. "Mr. Pendleton, you are so much smarter than these men. Why do you address them as equals?" His question was sincere, if indiscreet.

"Young man," he said, "I have learned that knowledge without wisdom is always found lacking. I am not the wisest man in the world. But we have been sharing the room with several of them. What they desire of me is knowledge. What I receive from them is wisdom. Together, we create solutions. To presume my knowledge outranks their wisdom would be to imply that I neither want nor need their assistance. Only a fool would believe that."

✝

Knowledge is of great value, yet in itself is incomplete; in its basic form, it is only information.

To be wise is to be able to apply such information with understanding. Without wisdom, we will remain incomplete. We may learn to compensate without it but will always fall short of achieving the desired results or best conclusion.

To reject wisdom is to sacrifice understanding. We would be foolish to do something so irrational. Because without wisdom, we will come to believe in our own accomplishments, not in the One who gave us the knowledge.

Prayer

"Teach me to respect wisdom, Lord. Teach me to use every resource You've given me. Open my eyes to any part of me that resists Your guidance. In Jesus' Name, amen."

Set Apart
November 18

Paul, a servant of Jesus Christ … set apart for the gospel of God.

Romans 1:1

"What's your greatest barrier to telling people about Jesus?" Craig asked his friend Charlie.

Halfway through his excuse, Charlie got a sense of how lame he must have sounded by the look on Craig's face. "Okay! Stop looking at me like that. You really want to know why?" He sighed. "A lot of the time it's because I don't feel very spiritual. You know, like I don't measure up on the 'Spiro-meter.' So I think, 'Why should people listen to me?'"

Craig understood his friend's dilemma. He'd shared those same misgivings. Then God had convicted him that gaining our silence is one of Satan's attempts to keep us from spreading the gospel.

Craig shared his revelation, concluding with, "If I let how I feel dictate when and where I say something, I wouldn't spread much of the gospel. If I remain silent because I don't *feel* like speaking up, then most of the time I'd be robbing people of the chance to accept God's love. Satan will lie and tell me any number of reasons I shouldn't speak on God's behalf—guilt and shame, inadequacy, shyness, being tired, or sick. The list is endless; but the results are the same. I fail to share the gospel. And Satan wins that round!" He emphasized his last remark. "I've found that if I respond when God leads by beginning to witness, the words come, and my hesitancy disappears."

✝

Until we come face to face with the reality and permanence of hell, we will fail to understand what our witness means; and, we will continue to succumb to Satan's attempts to keep us quiet.

Fear of man and the threat of ridicule keep many Christians from sharing what God has done in their lives. Without this testimony, many may never hear what they need to hear to make a decision for Christ.

We are set apart for God's kingdom. We cannot remain neutral in the battle for souls. It should be our privilege to stand up and proclaim the love and salvation to be found in Christ!

Prayer

"Help me, Lord Jesus, to share Your love. Give me
the words to show what You've done in my life so
others might find salvation in You. Amen."

Mom's Cookies and the Term Paper

November 19

Turn your ear to wisdom … search for it as hidden treasure.

Proverbs 2:1, 4

Where's that term paper? Christopher had used most of Saturday morning to turn his dorm room upside down to no avail. The paper was due in two weeks, and he needed to edit the final draft. All his notes were on that printed copy.

His cell phone interrupted his search. "Hi, Mom," he said. "I don't have time to talk." On a hunch, he asked, "Do you remember seeing that term paper I showed you and Dad when you were here a couple weeks ago?"

"Christopher? Did you forget asking me about that Tuesday when we spoke? I told you I read it and gave it back. Maybe it's under something in your apartment. Ask God where it is, honey."

A holy lecture, great! "You ask Him, Mom!" he shot back. "I need to keep looking."

She asked a meaning-filled question, "Did you take that box of cookies to church last Sunday?"

"Mom!" He was exasperated. "I need to find this paper … gotta go … love you." And he hung up.

She glanced across the kitchen table at her husband as she closed the cell phone. He knew there was a story behind her grin. "Okay, what's up?"

"Remember me asking Christopher if he'd been attending church during our last visit?" Getting an affirmative nod, she continued, "He told us he's been attending regularly." Another nod. "I decided to see *how* regularly." There was a mischievous glint in her eye. "All he has to do is deliver those cookies. I laid the box on the kitchen counter … right on top of the paper he's searching for. He's got another week before it's due. If he doesn't call by tomorrow evening, I'll give him a call."

✝

Church fellowship is critical. Of much importance is the *godly wisdom* to be found there. Separation from that fellowship causes *spiritual slippage*.

God gave us moms; they are priceless and wise beyond their children's years! Many a return from the separation of such a necessary relationship can be attributed to mothers as they pray and attempt to guide their wayward children.

Regardless of age, we can benefit from listening to our mothers' hidden treasure.

Prayer

"Help me place godly wisdom high on the ladder
of importance in my life, Lord. Amen."

Snipers

November 20

A gossip separates close friends.

Proverbs 16:28

Ted used sarcasm when he talked about his friends. Present or absent, he still had something to say that should have been left unsaid.

"You know, I really like Jack. He's a good carpenter. Builds some top-of-the-line houses, he does. Ain't much of a singer though. You ever hear him sing? Screech is what I ought to say! Oh man! I mean catlike!" he said and laughed.

One day his friend Terry confronted him about his slanderous comments. "Ted, you ever think before you speak?"

It was an honest question. But Ted didn't understand it. "Whaddya mean?" he asked, looking puzzled.

"I mean," Terry proceeded, "when you talk about people, do you ever think about what you're going to say, or does it just come out on its own?"

"What do you mean, 'the way you talk about people'?" He was genuinely at a loss and also getting genuinely upset. "Just how *do* you think I talk about people?"

"You may not recognize it as such, but your offhanded sarcasm is hurtful," Terry said, letting that statement sink in.

"I resent that!" he said. "What offhanded sarcasm are you talking about?"

"Remember your comment about Jack's singing the other day?" Terry countered.

"You can't be serious!" He was incredulous. "I didn't mean anything by that." He defended his actions.

"But it was negative nonetheless, Ted. That's the issue. Offhanded comments, or friendly banter, as you call it, create tension. Carelessness like that has been known to break up friendships. Is that what you want?" Terry asked.

"I never thought about that. You know I don't mean anything by it," he argued. But Terry had made his point.

✝

There are some who, like snipers, pick others off using words as weapons. Some of them mean harm; others don't understand the negative affect of their words. Sometimes thoughtless, innocent-seeming words can cause irreparable damage to lifelong relationships.

We must be conscious of the affect our words have on others before we speak. Casual words spoken with no ill intent can have devastating consequences.

If we can't use language befitting true friendship—encouraging and edifying—we should remain silent.

Prayer

"Help me choose my words wisely, Lord. May
I always be conscious of their affect before they
are spoken. In Jesus' Name, amen."

Upside Down

November 21

You turn things upside down, as if the potter were … the clay!

Isaiah 29:16

Driving home from a business trip, Kathy noticed that some of the billboards and bumper stickers she saw shared a common theme. As the theme sank in, its message disturbed her: "Save Our Planet. Stop Off-Shore Drilling!" and "Save A Tree—Kill A Lumberjack!" one proudly proclaimed. "Animals Have Rights—Spay or Neuter Your Vet!" They were all geared toward elevating the earth and its creatures to the top of the world's to-do list. These special interest groups were out to save everything but humans.

Kathy decided to document as many of these "counter-humanity messages" as she could during the remainder of her trip. In all, she compiled over one hundred and fifty pro-planet billboard and bumper sticker slogans.

Upon returning home, she decided to do an Internet search. Typing in the words "Save the Earth," she was astonished to find over sixty-two million listings!

Investigating further, she found that many groups received some form of government funding while their Web sites listed numerous ways one could contribute to their efforts. Millions, if not billions, of taxpayer dollars were being used to fund the efforts of their "planet above people" campaigns.

With startling clarity, Kathy realized Creation had been turned upside down in light of God's commission to Adam: "Fill the earth and subdue it … rule over every living creature."

†

While I believe ravaging our planet and cruel disregard for animal welfare is not what God intended, He left no doubt as to which has dominion and is meant to survive.

Since the fall in the garden of Eden, Satan has done his best to deceive us. Special interest groups are one form of deceit that is gaining popularity in today's worldview market. They are more concerned with our use of resources and animal rights than with genocide, tyranny, or starvation. They elevate the earth and its creatures above God and the needs of humanity. This is exactly opposite the commission given in the garden.

In a world where many no longer consider God our Creator, it is reprehensible, yet no surprise, to find creation being elevated above the Creator.

Prayer

"Creator of all things, forgive our ignorant pride that causes
us to disregard Your commands. Cause us to repent and once
again worship the Creator instead of creation. Amen."

Pieces of Hope
November 22

For I know the plans I have for you...plans to give you hope and a future.

Jeremiah 29:11

Merrill had stopped looking in mirrors several months ago. He couldn't deal with the pain of even the slightest glance. Morbidly overweight, he began isolating himself, limiting all social activities. He quit his job, alleging he was too sick to work. He did his grocery shopping in the middle of the night when everyone else was asleep. He eventually stopped going out in public altogether. And when his health really did begin to deteriorate, Merrill couldn't compel himself to seek medical attention.

Merrill languished between shame and self-loathing, constantly thinking of himself as a loser with no hope of ever returning to a life of joy and happiness.

Fortunately, Merrill's pastor wasn't the kind to let someone disappear off the grid without finding out why.

Merrill was horrified the day his pastor showed up at his front door. But a momentary sense of hope outranked his shame, and Merrill allowed him in. One visit turned into many. With each opportunity, the pastor spoke to Merrill of God's love for him and assured him that if he would trust God, God would change his life. But first he had to allow God to change his heart, change how he thought God saw him and how he should perceive himself.

Over time, Merrill responded, dealing with the issues that clouded his self-perception. He rediscovered God's love and returned to life among the living.

†

Our lives begin as an unassembled puzzle. As children, we never hesitate asking our parents for help in putting the pieces together. But as we age, pieces of us can get torn or even lost. Sometimes the puzzle falls apart completely.

Many times, in secret, we attempt to fix things on our own, denying ourselves beneficial assistance.

God wants to help us fit the pieces of our lives together correctly. He knows where each piece is and where it fits.

We cannot hope to change our lives unless we first give God the ability to change our heart. And for Him to do so, we must give Him *all* the pieces.

Prayer

"Loving Father, I bring to You every piece there is of me.
Take my life and make it whole. In Jesus' Name, amen."

Wait Right Here
November 23

But they that wait upon the LORD...

Isaiah 40:31 (KJV)

Slipping off his shoes, Joel reflected on the day's events, one delay after another. But what an awesome conclusion!

He'd taken the morning off for a dental appointment. The appointment had run an hour late. Leaving the dentist, he'd climbed into his car to discover a dead battery, costing him an additional hour waiting for AAA.

Needing to eat, Joel went to a local restaurant. After eating a soft, dentist-approved lunch, he'd walked out of the restaurant to find his right front tire flat! Fighting the urge to scream, Joel prayed instead. "Lord, I can't take anymore of this. I'm all out of patience." In his spirit, he heard God say, "Wait right here."

As he was sorting out God's nudge, a young man came walking up. He glanced at the tire, looked at Joel, and offered, "I'll change that tire if you buy me lunch."

God said, "This is what you've been waiting for. Take the deal."

With the flat changed, Joel sat and watched while Brice ravenously devoured his lunch. As they talked, Brice's story emerged. He'd been trying to get home from college to see his ailing father. With no money, he'd had to hitchhike. It had been two days thus far with two hundred miles to go.

Nudged once again, Joel took the young man to the bus station, bought him a ticket home, and saw him off.

Just ten minutes ago he'd received a call from Brice's mother, thanking him through tears of gratitude for his compassion and generosity.

✝

In this fast-paced world, most delays feel like obstacles to be vaulted over on our way to our next engagement. But what if it actually is God asking permission to meddle in our lives? And what if we're moving too fast to listen and we miss His call? It's hard to hear at ninety miles per hour.

It may not be a life-changing moment like Joel's. It may just be God's attempt to slow us down a bit. But wouldn't it be great to know? Wait right here and listen.

Prayer

"Lord, I give You permission to slow me down when
I refuse to do it on my own. Help me listen closely
so I don't miss my purpose for each day. Amen."

Are We Compelled?

November 24

For Christ's love compels us.

2 Corinthians 5:14

It was hard to miss the man perched eight feet above the ground, standing on the highest level of the fountain. A sizeable crowd had gathered to listen. His voice was rich and strong and could be heard over quite a distance.

He spoke a message of love and commitment to God, to family, and to each other.

And the longer he spoke, the more impassioned he became.

He hoped they were listening, hearing his words of counsel. "God loves us unconditionally! But if we continue to disregard His decrees and continue living without moral restrictions, He cannot ignore our rebellion!"

Many stopped just long enough to hear the message. Some shook their heads in disgust; some offered harsh comments; each went their own way.

Others, constrained by the message, were held captive by its unblemished truth. This nondescript street preacher was speaking to any and all who would listen. And unmindful of their response, he spoke from his heart.

"We are trampling on God's love! We rebel and dare Him to show us His judgment!" He held nothing back, yet his manner was nonjudgmental. It was as if you could hear his soul crying out, "Please, listen! The Lord cannot allow us to go unpunished! His holiness cannot abide our sin. His love will not let us go!"

It was as if Christ Himself were speaking to the masses. And just like in Jesus' day, the people were divided.

✝

Paul brought a message of reconciliation to Corinth. His message, much like this street preacher's, fell on both fertile and barren soil alike. Yet he could not remain silent. Christ's love so compelled him that he cared nothing of what they thought of him, only the message.

I have known a few who were compelled to this level of devotion; gripped so desperately by the truth of what awaits those who refuse to accept the cross of Calvary and the One Who paid the price for their salvation that they throw all caution to the wind to bring this message.

We are compelled by Christ, and in light of the truth, we should refuse to remain silent.

Prayer

"Give me words to speak, Lord. Compel me to tell others of Your great love. In Jesus' Name, amen."

Arch the Angel
November 25

And do not hinder them, for the kingdom of God belongs to such as these.

Luke 18:16

They'd been practicing for the school's Christmas play for a week, and Mrs. Doty still hadn't made a decision regarding the lead character. "Lord, I know whoever I choose will do a wonderful job, but I feel like Arch is supposed to be someone specific. Help me choose the right child."

Putting it out of her mind long enough to read this morning's entries in her students' daily journals, she smiled, marveling at nine-year-olds' perspectives on what was important. She could hear each little voice as she read their entry. How precious each child was to her. She spent her life nurturing little hearts and minds because of her love for children and teaching.

Finally, she came to Pete's journal. "I love God. He is my Lord," this morning's entry read. A preordained moment—she had asked, and here was the answer!

Three weeks later, Mrs. Doty's third-grade class took the stage in what was to be one of the most memorable performances of her tenure. Arch stole the show. The smallest boy in the class, Pete was wonderfully animated as he glided across the stage singing, "I can zoom, and I can hover when I'm workin' under cover, and folks never seem to see the likes of me."

†

Children are approximately forty percent of our population—and one hundred percent of our future. The generation we are raising up for tomorrow should be the focus of today.

A child's heart is a rough gem in need of polishing. Many of us have been blessed by the strong hand of a father, the attentive love of a mother, and the extra polishing by the Mrs. Dotys in life.

Sadly, others have never known the dedication of someone devoted to cultivating their spirit. Instead, they heard they were no good and would never amount to anything.

Innocence yields to direction. It learns to treat in keeping with how it is treated.

"Do not hinder them" is a directive.

Prayer

"Help me polish my kids correctly, Lord. Give me the wisdom and patience to bring a precious gemstone from these rough-cut stones You have entrusted to me. In Jesus' name. Amen."

Where's Your Heart Set?

November 26

Set your hearts on things above...

Colossians 3:2

The story goes that an old man was sitting at the edge of town, whittling, when a traveler appeared. "I'm a stranger hereabouts, just kinda passin' through." Then the traveler asked, "What are the people like here in this town?"

The old whittler paused a moment, looked up, and asked, "What were they like where you came from?"

Taken aback, he answered, "They were kinda mean and nasty. Wouldn't lift a finger ta help you."

The old whittler gave him a long look, shook his head sadly, and said, "Well, you'll find that's what they're like here."

The traveler responded cynically, "Kinda what I figured!" and walked on into town.

As the man disappeared, a second traveler walked up to the old whittler and said, "I'm looking for a place to settle down. This looks like a nice town. What are the people like?"

Once again the old whittler asked, "What were they like where you came from?"

The traveler responded, "Oh, they were wonderful. People went out of their way to be kind. If there was a need, someone was always ready to lend a hand."

The old whittler nodded and said, "Well, you'll find that's exactly what they're like here!"

"Wonderful!" the traveler responded and headed into town.

†

Two travelers with the very same question regarding the very same people in the very same town received two very different answers. Why? Because the old whittler knew they would find what they were used to looking for.

Our outlook on life sets the tone for our expectations. What we come to expect, we will experience. If we project these expectations long enough, they will become the rule of thumb by which we judge everything.

When we look for the good in people, we will find it. Likewise, when we look for their faults, they will become evident.

Christ died to fill our hearts with hope, not irritability. We can choose what we experience. It is a matter of disciplining our hearts to look for the right things. Where is your heart set?

Prayer

"Lord, give me eyes to see the good in others, not only
the bad. Develop in me a right attitude so I might be
a blessing to this world. In Jesus' Name, amen."

November 27

Praise be to … God … he has given us new birth … through the resurrection of Jesus Christ …

1 Peter 1:3

It was in the cold predawn of Thanksgiving Day that found Jack poised to forget about the festivities scheduled for later that day. *This must have been what
Ebenezer Scrooge felt like.*

Jack had been up all night. The routine was always the same: cough violently for two to three hours, spitting up blood several times during the cough-
ing fits. He'd been dealing pretty well with these episodes up until last night.
This one had lasted almost five hours; he was exhausted. *It's only been two weeks
since the last episode. Why so soon?* he wondered. *And why on Thanksgiving? Are
You testing my thank-o-meter?* he asked God.

Actually, the episodes had been pretty regular, one every three or four
months. So, to have another one so soon brought concern as he contemplated
the possibilities. Several reasons came to mind, but the one that prevailed was
it's getting worse. His doctors had told him that at some point symptoms would
accelerate and then things would happen pretty fast. *Give me grace for today,
Lord. Give me a heart of gladness instead of gloom.*

If this was to be his last Thanksgiving, Jack was determined to make it one
of the most thank-filled days of his life.

✝

There are enough negative things to focus on in the world to allow us to live
in despair, cursing the day. But because of Jesus' sacrifice, we can choose to live
a life of victory, reminded that this is not our home. He took care of all our
tomorrows, and someday soon we will be with Him in heaven.

This world is a temporal place; it is not our home. And we have the promise of life beyond our pain. What we deal with today is real, and sometimes it
stinks. But we can maintain a thankful heart in the midst of our struggles if we
lay claim to a permanent life in Christ.

The greatest reason for our *Thankstobegiven* is Salvation unto eternal life.
Once received, nothing can take it away!

Prayer

"I don't want to whine, Lord. Keep me focused on things
to be thankful for. May I always be filled with thanks
because of the gift of Your Son! In His Name, amen."

Peace... At Whose Expense?
November 28

Blessed are the peacemakers, for they will be called sons of God.

Matthew 5:9

The brothers had been estranged for years. Neither felt they were wrong. For a fact, they each felt the other was to blame. Consequently, neither of them took the initiative to resolve the issues keeping them apart, so small in light of the impact it had on these once-close siblings. A childhood friend had been praying for them for a few years when he had a revelation: talk to them individually about the joy they had shared growing up, the laughter and tears, all of it. He got them to recall times of swimming in the farm pond, camping in the mountains, even the time they had hitchhiked to a rock concert in '76. As they continued to remember the wonderful times they'd had, they began to gain a renewed perspective. Warmth replaced bitterness; forgiveness replaced anger. The chasm melted away in light of the truth; it wasn't bigger than their love. Because of the devotion of a friend, they learned to share their lives once again.

✝

Unresolved wounds breed. They never give in or go away. If we choose to embrace the wound, we give it life, and it takes hold in our heart. Untreated, it can become a stronghold of bitterness. Most of the time, we can't even recall what the initial offense was; we just want vindication! Self-vindication never heals. This friend decided to take positive action that would hopefully lead to reconciliation. The action required the brothers to recall the better, more important times. No offense should outweigh the value of the relationship. We are asked to become peacemakers, to place relationships above anything that would threaten them. Peacemakers are sons of God because they understand how priceless relationship is to the Father; without it, we are damned.

Prayer

"Lord, Thank you for the peacemakers in my life. I admit
that it's hard for me to forgive and be the one to ask for
forgiveness for any part I played in the rifts of my life.
Help me understand that being a peacemaker starts the
beginning of healing in my life. Please give me strength
as I take that first step. In Jesus' Name, amen."

Not Unlike My Own

November 29

For we do not have a high priest who is unable to sympathize … we have one who has been tempted in every way.

Hebrews 4:15

As Gary shared with Preston about an ongoing temptation he was dealing with, he said, "Nobody understands what I'm going through."

"I hear what you're saying, Gary," Preston said. "But your struggle is not unlike my own. Not necessarily literally, but we all deal with some kind of temptation." He shared briefly of his battle with vanity.

Happily married, Preston was a handsome man. But he turned women's heads in public. It created a tug-of-war between his pride and ego and his faith. "Believe me when I say it required God's intervention to get victory over my pride."

"So how'd you work it out?" Gary asked. "You know, how'd you stop looking in the mirror all the time?"

Preston chuckled. "I still look in the mirror, Gary. I have to shave," he joked. "But seriously, I had to be humbled myself. And as God humbled me, He adjusted my attitude. What I look like does not define who I am. It does, however, present temptation. And that's the point I'm trying to make. We're all tempted." He paused and then added, "But the great part is that Jesus *knows* how we feel. He's been tempted the same way we're being tempted. You're neither alone nor unique. And if you're willing to seek His guidance, Jesus is willing to help with the victory."

†

When we're under attack and can't free ourselves on our own, it's hard to admit that others have been where we are and gained a victory. It's easier to believe that no one else has ever experienced the kind of trial we're in. It's one of the ways Satan keeps us where we are. And if successful, he'll continue using it against us.

God put on skin so we would know He could relate to our human suffering. Jesus knows exactly what we're going through. He *is* the way of escape and wants to help. And if we cry out to Jesus, He'll answer, "Your battle is not unlike My own was. I know how to help you."

Prayer

"Lord Jesus, I need Your help. Give me wisdom beyond
my own; lead me into a victorious life. Amen."

Seal of Approval
November 30

On him God the Father has placed his seal of approval.

John 6:27

Each June, area churches work together in conjunction with a local bakery, and pass out free loves of fresh bread to the community.

The day begins early with runners, as they are titled, shuttling bread between the bakery and drop off sites. Trucks full of bread, dinner rolls, croissants, and flatbread arrive throughout the day.

Deliverers are assigned designated sections of the community. They pick up supplies and go door to door passing out the baked goods, offering words of God's love and encouragement.

There are pick up sites where people from outlying areas come for bread as well. No limits are placed on how many items one may receive (up until the bakery runs out). If you have great need, you receive an amount equal to that need.

When asked, "Why do you do this?" by recipients, they tell them of Jesus' love and how He is the Bread of Life and how this act is symbolic of that gift.

Some ask, "Is the bread stale?" and are guaranteed, "Each item has the *freshness* seal of approval."

Some life-changing stories shared during this day are truly inspirational. Men and women alike cry, telling the deliverer they had no food in the house.

Bread of Life changes lives on both sides of the effort. For no one can ever be the same after witnessing or having a desperate need met.

✝

Such outreach for Jesus is a tremendous thing. Yet we do not have to wait for one day in June to deliver the Bread of Life to our communities.

Even as some are in desperate need of the physical nourishment this type of event provides, everyone in the world is in need of God's spiritual gift of life through His Son. So much so that God put in His written Word His seal of approval on what His Son did on our behalf.

We are to be light and salt in a dark and tasteless world. This is one example of how to do that. We have God-given creative ability. Put it to use for His kingdom.

Prayer

"Lord of all Creation, show me how I can make a
difference in my community. Give me the vessel with
which to help transform lives. In Jesus' Name, amen."

Decemeber

Prophet and Provider

December 1

Surely this is the Prophet who is come into the world.

John 6:14

Gwen stood completely still, not wanting to disturb the deer that had come to the saltlick in her backyard. She had come out on the deck to replenish the bird feeders and discovered a doe and her two yearlings eating hungrily from one of the mineral blocks Gwen's husband, Shaun, had set out for the wildlife in light of the harsh winter months.

The doe finally noticed Gwen, yet somehow recognized she was not a threat and therefore didn't respond in the normal preservation-driven act of flight. They nibbled away as Gwen watched. From time to time one would surreptitiously watch the human in the funny-looking tree and then return to eating. Their acceptance of Gwen's close proximity made her wonder if they somehow knew this human was the provider of the life-giving substance they so hungrily accepted.

As Gwen began to feel chilled, she slowly retreated to the warmth of her kitchen to observe the deer until they had eaten their fill. Watching their struggle for survival triggered a deep sense of awe in Gwen. She was moved by the knowledge that God was using her and Shaun to provide sustenance for His Creation.

✝

The crowds on the shores of the Sea of Galilee were enamored with Jesus because of the great works he had done. Feeding over five thousand men, not to mention women and children, was something to take notice of! They believed this work showed Jesus to be the great prophet who would be like Moses (Deuteronomy 18:15).

And because He had met their physical need, they missed His true identity. And that's what Jesus told them when, the very next day, they came looking for Him.

He proclaimed a new message: that what He came to provide was life everlasting; more than physical, it was spiritually eternal.

Jesus came to provide nourishment that endures forever. And the food He provides never spoils. He has come so that we no longer have to hunger and thirst for eternity. As we partake of His Living Word, we are nourished and well fed.

Prayer

"Thank You, Father, for Your perfect provision in Jesus
Christ. Create in me a desire to continually feed on
Your Living Word. Thank You for Jesus. Amen."

What's Algegra?
December 2

> She is a tree of life to those who embrace her.
>
> Proverbs 3:18

Matt raised his hand and asked, "What's algegra? I heard my sister talkin' 'bout it last night, an' she said she hates it! Is it like spinach or somethin'?"

Ms. Dennis pursed her lips tightly until her laughter was under control. "I believe your sister was speaking of *algebra*, Matt," she enunciated. "It is a form of mathematics," she said, writing the word on the blackboard so they could see the correct spelling.

Taking advantage of this teachable moment, she explained that algebra is the use of numbers in sets. She made the lesson comprehensive to first graders, finishing with, "And yes, Matt, some people hate it as much as spinach. But math, like spinach, is good for you, even if it leaves a bad taste in your mouth."

Arriving home, Matt told his sister, "You need to do your algegra." (He hadn't taken notes.) "I hate spinach. But Ms. Dennis said I should eat my spinach, and you should do your algegra 'cause it's good for us," he concluded.

Looking at him through squinted eyes, she asked, "What in the world are you talking about?"

"I heard you say last night you hate algegra," he said innocently. "So I asked Ms. Dennis 'bout it."

Amused by her little brother, she ruffled his hair and said, "Okay, you eat the spinach; I'll do the algegra."

✝

God wants to reveal to us the intricacies of life. As babies we have beginner-level comprehension. As we mature, we are able to assimilate more complicated matters. The more mature, the deeper our understanding.

Nowhere in Scripture is retirement mentioned. The reasoning behind our self-imposed work stoppage is flawed; it creates a stop-learning mentality.

No, I am not suggesting you never retire. But...

Knowledge is the accumulation of experience. Wisdom is the ability to apply that knowledge. When we cease to learn, our brains begin to deteriorate for lack of stimuli.

God's desire is that we embrace learning until the day we die. And although to some it's like eating spinach, we should always strive to learn. Because, in Matt's words, "It's good for us."

Prayer

"Lord, may I never stop learning the things You
have set before me. Stimulate my mind to be
sharp and sensible. In Jesus' Name, amen."

Carved by the Master

December 3

Your works are wonderful.

Psalm 139:14

Bob Birney had plied his trade for more than a few decades, turning out works of art unparalleled by his peers. Such was his gift that his works were sought by other woodcarvers from around the globe.

The tools of his trade were intricate and razor sharp. He knew how to use each one. As he made each cut, removing what didn't belong, a masterpiece began to emerge.

On this occasion, he was carving the bark of a cottonwood tree. It was the perfect media for small carvings. Two and a half inches thick, its heavily lined structure required great imagination and steady hands to reveal the beauty hidden within. Bob was equal to the task. As he carved, he whispered to himself, "This piece does not fit. It must give way," and, "You cannot hide. I have seen you for what you are."

Some found his manor a bit quirky; others understood. The master was at work. He could see things others could not. He was revealing hidden splendor.

As Bob proceeded, the distinct outline of a cabin with steep, sloping roof began to take shape. Over the next several hours, the cabin took on life. Windows carved in relief with shutters to each side were so realistic you could imagine the firelight flickering inside. The stone chimney broke through the rough exterior of the bark at just the right height with smoke curling up as on a cold winter's day.

Yes, Bob had a gift. In his experienced hands, wood came to life.

✝

I marvel at the intricacy of such delicate work. It is sharing God's gift with the world.

The One Who created us knows why He did so. In His hands, we become purposed. He alone sees the masterpiece hidden within, waiting to be revealed. And only by His hands can what He sees be revealed. He alone knows how to remove the things that mar the true beauty of what is hidden inside. Yet, He can only do this if we yield our lives to Him. And in the yielding, the Master Carver can create in us the likeness of His Son.

Prayer

"Lord, reveal in me the best I have to offer. Cut away anything that stands as a deterrent to that purpose. In Jesus' Name, amen."

Where Are We Leading?

December 4

An example, that you should follow...

1 Peter 2:21

As early as age three, Erica could be found trying to pull Daddy's tools from his work belt as it hung from a wall peg in the mudroom. She piled detergent boxes like steps to reach her goal. And several times she attained that goal only to be scolded for playing with Daddy's tools.

So Erica was beside herself with delight when on her fifth birthday she received her very own tool belt! Daddy explained to her that, like his own tools, her tools could be used to work on and repair broken things. Wanting to know the application of each tool, she asked Daddy to show her. As he removed each tool from his belt, Erica took its equivalent and did her best to imitate his actions. For weeks she went around the house *fixing* things.

One evening as Daddy was reading the paper, he noticed Erica playing with her hammer. He watched as she intentionally struck her thumb and hollered, "Stupid hammer!" then turned to seek her Daddy's approval.

What an eye-opener! She had apparently observed him earlier that day when he had done what she had just mimicked. With startling clarity, he understood the implications of his actions on his little girl. In that moment, he determined to be the best example he could.

✝

Every step we take is an invitation for someone to follow. And living an upright life is not always easy. But we are responsible for the impact our actions have on those who watch us. And make no mistake—someone is always watching.

Many of us live as if there are no consequences for our actions. We think that because God has not judged us swiftly, His judgment is not coming. If we are insensitive to the truth that no act, good or evil, will go unnoticed or unpunished, the fallout of an unrighteous life can have disastrous consequences, on us and those who look to us for guidance.

Jesus left us an example to follow, one that requires commitment and discipline, one that shows others the Way, the Truth, and the Life!

Prayer

"Help me remain aware of my influence on others. May my life lead people to You, Lord. In Jesus' Name, amen."

God's Word and the Water Softener

December 5

So then faith cometh by hearing, and hearing by the word of God.

Romans 10:17 (KJV)

One or two power flashes a month weren't unusual at the Parsons' family home. The electric company had explained that they were just *switching over*, a process that allowed them to do routine maintenance on transformers and outlying power grids.

The flash from two days ago had sent the water softener into error mode again, suspending the softening process. When this occurred, the water returned to its normally hard state within forty-eight hours.

They usually just reset the timing unit and digital clock and then initiated a regeneration cycle, resolving the hardness issue. It really wasn't much of an inconvenience. After all, they'd done without a softener for the first twenty-six years they'd lived here, filling jugs with drinking water from a spring two miles away. The softener had resolved that issue, relieving them of the constant transporting of eight one-gallon jugs every other day. So a short delay every once in a while didn't amount to much.

Mr. Parson headed for the basement, reset the unit, and tripped the regeneration button. Three hours later, the pH and iron levels had returned to their normal settings, and the water issues in the Parsons' household returned to normal.

✝

It's amazing how something so simple can have such a negative impact on our lives.

Like the Parsons' water, our spiritual condition can become hard without continual and proper treatment. And just like the need the water softener was created to resolve, God gave us His Word to condition our lives. It instructs us in daily living and shows us how to handle the issues we face each day.

We need a constant inflow of His life-giving Word. If we miss a single day, we might not notice any impact. But if we continually fail to nourish ourselves by reading God's Word and fellowshipping with other Christians, we will suffer setbacks and become susceptible and prone to making mistakes.

In order to assure ourselves the strength we need when we need it, we must constantly remain plugged in to the power supply.

Prayer

"Help me discipline myself to read Your Word and stay in constant contact with Your people, Lord. Keep me charged up and ready for action. In Jesus' Name, amen."

Class Is in Session!

December 6

How long shall I stay with you? How long shall I put up with you?

Matthew 17:17

"Do you remember the twelfth grade?" the comedian asked. "I'd finally arrived. I was a *senior!*" He said it with such reverence, with the knowing smile of one who had received *revelatory understanding.* "Man, I loved the twelfth grade! I especially loved the science experiments." He grinned. "Blew up the lab once! I accidentally knocked a bottle of chemicals into the sink. Smelled pretty bad, so I flushed it down with water! How was I to know that the chemicals and water created a toxic mixture? Man, you shoulda seen the girls faces when those sinks exploded!"

He paused as if reminiscing. "Of course, Mr. Fullen didn't think it was so funny. He glared at me from across the room and then slowly made his way over. With each step, my pulse beat harder and faster. When he got close enough, he put the *Fullen Clutch* on me!" Demonstrating the clutch, he made a claw with his right hand, reached across his chest, and latched onto his left shoulder, wincing as if he were experiencing tremendous pain. "We walked the whole way to the principal's office like that." He moved as if under Mr. Fullen's control. The audience was in stitches. Then he dropped the punch line. "Yep, I loved the twelfth grade. It was the best three years of my life!"

✝

How many of us continually fail the *spiritual* twelfth grade because of a non-chalant attitude toward learning?

In today's text, the disciples had been with Jesus for almost three years, yet had failed to grasp a complete understanding of Who He was, Who he represented, and what power and authority was available to them. They were failing their twelfth grade proficiency test, so to speak.

We, like the disciples, fail to learn certain spiritual lessons. Many times it's because we just don't pay attention. We fail to grasp the importance of our part in perpetuating the gospel. As Christians, it is our responsibility to pay attention when class is in session. Folks, class is always in session.

Prayer

"Place in my heart a great desire to learn kingdom lessons,
Lord. Help me grasp each concept as You present it
in ways I can understand. In Jesus' Name, amen."

When the Master Speaks

December 7

To call people … to the obedience that comes from faith.

Romans 1:5

Steve and Becky love their dog, Dakota. Steve is the disciplinarian; Becky is the softie. Steve demands Dakota's obedience; Becky spoils and dotes on him.

One day, Becky called Steve at work to tell him that Dakota refused to get into the bathtub for his weekly bath. He refused to move from his comfy pillow bed. Steve told Becky, "Put the dog on the phone."

"What?" Becky said incredulously.

"Put the dog on the phone," Steve reiterated. "I want to talk to him."

So Becky took the wireless phone to where Dakota was defiantly lounging, and holding his floppy ear out of the way, she held the receiver close enough for the dog to listen.

Steve gave one simple command, "Dakota, go get in the tub now!" And with that, he rose from his bed and went straight to the bathroom. He hopped into the tub and waited for Becky to bathe him.

Astonished, Becky asked, "How did you do that?"

"Simple," Steve answered. "Dakota knows who his master is. He knows I mean him no harm and would not tell him to do something unless it was important. When he heard me speak, he knew he could either obey and things would go well, or he could disobey, where there would be a consequence. He remembers the rewards he has received for his obedience and the consequences he's paid for disobeying. He simply made an informed choice."

✝

What a perfect example of unquestioning obedience! Steve, in his authority, asked Dakota for obedience. Dakota, wanting to please his master, chose to obey—a perfect metaphor of what God wants for His children.

But generally we are not as quick to respond. We demand explanations for why we should obey. We question God's motives instead of immediately submitting to His request.

Only through faith can we come to a place in our relationship with God where we trust Him enough to respond immediately, regardless of His command. And only through experience will we discover that He will never harm us or ask us to do anything without a divine purpose.

Prayer

"Show me the way to unquestioning obedience, Lord. Help me put my trust where it needs to be—in You. In Jesus' Name, amen."

Preparing to Fail

December 8

My sons, if sinners entice you, do not give in to them.

Proverbs 1:10

The drink took effect less than four minutes after he'd taken it. The rush was familiar, euphoric, and successful at numbing his pain.

As the familiar numbness flooded his brain, what he'd done became a reality. In one act of desperation, he'd thrown away his sobriety. The shame of his irresponsibility transcended those years as if he'd never quit! *Oh, God! What did I do?!*

An hour ago, he'd been facing a situation that threatened to overwhelm him. Instead of calling someone and fleeing from the temptation, he'd opted to *check out* emotionally. The holiday season brought unwanted memories and heartache, and in his weariness he just wanted some peace. Before he realized what he was doing, he found himself at the liquor store, purchasing the very brand of alcohol that had cost him his marriage and job twenty years ago.

In one act of weakness, he'd slammed back two shots, refusing to give himself time to process the imminent fallout. He knew what would happen but didn't care enough to stop himself from making such a huge mistake. Now, here he was, back where he swore he'd never return.

✝

When we attempt to fight the enemy on our own, we're asking for trouble. Alone and unprepared, we become an easier target. If we try to battle such a deceitful enemy alone in such a vulnerable state, we are committing a grievous mistake. We are actually preparing to fail.

In our strength alone we will fail against an enemy so powerful and cunning. Only God truly understands how easily we become ensnared. That we actually believe we can stand up to him and win shows how arrogant we are! We must admit our helplessness and ask for assistance.

God does not intend for us to fail, nor does He expect or want us to fight these battles on our own. He does, however, leave that choice up to us. He says, "My sons, if sinners entice you, run! God wants *us* to win and *our pride* to lose.

Prayer

"Thank You for the way of escape, Lord. Teach me to
set aside my foolish pride and ask for help before I get
beaten into submission. In Jesus' Name, amen."

Grace in Temptation

December 9

Because he himself suffered when he was tempted, he is able to help those who are being tempted.

Hebrews 2:18

Tanya and Joyce had been best friends since third grade. They shared similar interests and hobbies; they even read the same books. In truth, they were closer than most sisters. So it was a surprise when Joyce told Tanya she was pregnant. "How could you let that happen?" Tanya all but shouted. "I mean…I know *how* it happened, but what were you thinking?"

"I don't know, Tanya. We didn't mean for it to go that far; then it was over. What am I gonna do? Daddy will kill me when he finds out!"

"Well, he doesn't have to find out. Tell the school nurse you need an abortion. She'll hook you up, and nobody will ever know."

"I would know! I could never do that, Tanya! I can't believe you'd even consider abortion as an option. What I did was wrong, but I'm not going to make my baby pay for my indiscretions. Besides, Stewart and I talked about getting married."

"Okay, okay! I'm sorry. You just freaked me out for a second. And you know your dad won't kill you. He may be disappointed and ticked off for a while, but he loves you, J'cee. You could always give the baby up for adoption, you know. Look, whatever you decide, I'm here."

†

Jesus understands our temptation and forgives our iniquities when we turn from them and repent. His grace chases us until we stop running and patiently awaits our surrender. It's ready to embrace us if we turn back after just one mistake, but has the ability to cover them all.

We may think that because Jesus was a man He couldn't possibly understand the temptations women face. Scripture says He does understand; and He is waiting to help with a way of escape in the midst of the temptation, but will comfort and forgive us if we fail to accept that way of escape. He just wants us to know that He is prepared to meet us where we are.

Prayer

"Lord, I'm in need of Your grace more than ever. Please guide me to a place of safety and shelter. In Jesus' Name, amen."

Unresolved Pain

December 10

A quick-tempered man does foolish things.

Proverbs 14:17

In the blink of an eye, he'd grabbed Liam and slammed him up against the wall. Spittle flew from his mouth with each word. "You apologize right now...or so help me God..." His rage was so intense that he failed to hear his wife's first two pleas to stop. "Brandon! Stop! You're hurting him! Please! Stop!" Heather pulled at his arms, trying to get him to release the death grip he had on their sixteen-year-old son.

Her words finally registered, and Brandon was instantly gripped by a paralyzing fear. It had happened again! He'd lost control! And this time it had been with his son.

He released his grip. "Liam," he began, wanting to explain he hadn't meant for this to happen. He tried to say he was sorry, but the words wouldn't come. Sorry didn't begin to undo what he'd done or relieve the avalanche of shame he was experiencing.

The fear in his son's eyes told him all he needed to know. Liam was terrified! Brandon covered his face with his hands and began sobbing. He didn't see Heather tenderly embrace Liam or hear her explain that his father hadn't meant to hurt him.

This had gone too far. He had just violently attacked his son, and it needed to end right now!

Unbeknownst to Heather, Brandon had lost several thousand dollars through recent gambling. His deception had created unbearable stress, which in turn had begun to cause sudden fits of rage. He begged their forgiveness and vowed to take steps to get help.

✝

Anger, rage, fury—each word tries, yet does not completely capture the violent eruption that occurs when unresolved pain causes us to lose all perspective and constraint.

Driven by these unresolved issues, we vent our pain on those who we believe will forgive us. Behind it all lay deceptiveness and irrational thoughts. Without question, these are hidden issues awaiting resolution.

When we mistakenly try to resolve the issues on our own, it usually ends up like today's scenario. If you have anger issues, seek professional help and hold nothing back. Unresolved anger begins with our first secret.

Prayer

"Keep me from foolishness that leads to rashness,
Lord. Help peace to reign in my heart and
over my life. In Jesus' Name, amen. "

Measuring Success
December 11

He shall not fail nor be discouraged.

Isaiah 42:4 (KJV)

The bar was set pretty high concerning what constituted a *successful* college basketball season in Indiana. This one hadn't even approached the bar. The team finished with an overall record of 12 and 16 and a league record of 7 and 9. Many people in the community let them know how displeased they were. But they were a young team comprised of sophomores and freshman with only one junior. There was room for improvement.

As they hit the locker room after their final game, the lone junior spoke up. "I'm not going to tell you I'm completely satisfied with our season. But I'm also not going to let you leave this locker room for the final time without setting things straight." He had their attention. "As far as our record goes, we lost more than we won. But in those losses we fought hard; we never gave up! Our performance should never be measured by wins alone. We had a lot of huge victories this year. Look at our defense. Because of tremendous improvement, we beat three ranked teams that were expected to hand us our heads!" He went on to list improvements each teammate had made; he put the season in proper perspective. "Don't hang your heads in disappointment. Look people in the eye when you meet them on the street. Tell them what you learned from hard work!" He ended with, "Because of what we accomplished this year, I have hope for next season!"

✝

As toddlers, we don't jump up off the floor and start running. It takes scraping our hands and knees for an extended period of time before we learn to walk. If we only measure success by the number of wins we amass, many of our greatest victories will go unnoticed.

The world's take on what constitutes success is far removed from God's. He judges our efforts, not a record that includes perceived failures. His word to us is, "Learn from each setback. Do not become discouraged. Strive to live your life always doing your best." God, not the world, will judge our performance.

Prayer

"Help me measure success the way You do, Lord. Cause me to keep my head up and my eyes on You. In Jesus' Name, amen."

It Is Written

December 12

It is written …

Matthew 4:4

"I don't have much success memorizing Scripture," Gabi admitted. "You, on the other hand, seem to have a photographic memory!" She was referring to Clay's impressive ability to quote most of the Bible. He had committed long hours studying God's Word and wanted it available in case his Bible wasn't handy.

"How do you do it?" she asked.

"I use a page out of Hollywood." Clay grinned. "I pretend I'm learning a script. I'm the leading man reading lines with another actor for an upcoming movie. It's easier than simply reading and trying to remember."

"If I could learn to quote Scripture like you …" She let it hang, hoping her compliment would encourage Clay to give her some tips.

Instead, he cautioned her. "Quoting God's Word doesn't make you spiritual. And memorization is not the hallmark of spiritually. Frankly," Clay said seriously, "*knowing* the Word is vastly more important than quoting chapter and verse."

He shared what he felt was the perfect example. "When Jesus was tempted in the wilderness, He didn't say, 'Satan, in Exodus 20:2 it says, "Thou shall have no other gods before me."' He said 'It is written …' and quoted God's Word."

"Okay," Gabi said. "But isn't it important to know where it is so when I'm questioned about it I can show someone?"

"Yes, the ability to turn to the verse is important. But many people give up because they can't remember where to find it. I don't want *you* to do that."

✝

We place great importance on memorizing Scripture, and with good reason. God's Word is truth and life! The more we know, the better we understand God. His Word is useful for fending off the enemy or in resisting temptation. We should determine to know as much of it as possible.

Learning is best approached with longing instead of viewing it as some menial task to be accomplished. Remembering that the Holy Spirit is present will be infinitely helpful. If we begin by asking Him to make the connections necessary, we will find He is faithful. And until you learn where it is, do what Jesus did. Just say, "It is written."

Prayer

"Teach me to hide Your Word in my heart so it will
be readily available when I need it. Amen."

Divine Appointments
December 13

The LORD will keep you from all harm—he will watch over your life; the LORD will watch over your coming and going both now and forever more.

Psalm 121:7, 8

Two days following her initial ordeal in the trauma unit, her husband related the events that had led to her survival. In her hospital room, recovering from extensive, life-threatening injuries, she heard for the first time how critical things had been. She had been out with a group of friends on the way to a dinner party. Weather conditions were not the best, but they decided not to reschedule. On their way to the restaurant they had chosen, they were involved in a horrific crash. As it turned out, God was present in the details. The vehicle directly behind them was occupied by two nurses who began immediate first aid. In the vehicle following the truck that had collided with them was an EMT from a nearby fire station. He immediately called for a squad response. The home they wrecked in front of was owned by a pilot from the Life Flight rescue team. His phone call prompted the response of the last chopper allowed out that night. The rest of the teams were grounded due to the storm. Tears fell from their eyes as they felt God's embrace.

✝

God had arranged appointments in such a conspicuous way that this story lent itself to the witness of His involvement in each of our lives. Admittedly, not everyone has seen God move in such a miraculous way as this couple. But as the text says, God is always there, always watching us; and we may never know how often He moved mountains to keep us from harm. But you can be certain He has. These are not grand gestures on the part of God to sway our allegiance. They are acts of love toward His children. He expresses the same passion we do when we show our kids affection and love. There is nothing we wouldn't do to save our kids from death. He feels the same way.

Prayer

"I can't fathom the depth of Your love, Abba. My heart longs
to know that I really do mean that much to You. Speak
the truth of Your love to me. In Jesus' Name, amen."

Angry Blessings
December 14

Blessed are those who are persecuted because of righteousness, for theirs is the kingdom of heaven.

Matthew 5:10

Walking through the mall, the kids were passing out gospel literature, inviting everyone they encountered to join them for worship. Many took a moment to look at the material they had received, saying thank you. Some were noncommittal, and a few just snatched it from the youth, proceeding on, locked in their private worlds.

Then one man made a scene. After receiving the leaflet, he'd continued for a few strides when the message of the material hit him. Turning on his heel and hollering in a loud voice, he returned to the young man who'd given him the tract. He was clearly trying to make a scene. "Take this mindless propaganda back! I couldn't care less about your church and its services! You have no right to pass this religious junk out in a public place! Why, I'm gonna get security and have you thrown outta here!" With that, he spun around, looking anxiously for someone in authority.

The young man was undaunted. He'd heard this type of social speak before. "Don't infringe on my rights. There's supposed to be separation of church and state!"

You scream about your rights being violated, the young man thought, *but you don't seem to have any problem trying to violate mine,* he thought.

✝

We can be sincere and be sincerely wrong. Screaming the loudest doesn't automatically make someone right. As our Constitution dictates, living in a free world society gives us inherent rights. We may not agree with other people's choices, but we cannot attack them because we don't agree with them or share their ideologies.

We can, however, hold up and hold tight to our rights as children of God. Our God-given rights are immutable; no one can argue them away. They are ours to stand on for eternity. So when people holler or scream that we have offended them because of our beliefs, we have a right to stand our ground against intolerance.

Prayer

"Thank You, Lord, for rights that cannot be taken
away. Help me make a difference in this world for
You. Don't let me be beaten down or discouraged by
a world that chooses to deny Your existence. Help me
exhibit Your love and mercy. In Jesus Name, amen."

Does Hell Break Your Heart?

December 15

Freely you have received, freely give.

Matthew 10:8

The two young men seemed likely candidates for the associate pastor position the church was looking to fill, so the advisory committee scheduled them to preach. Fresh out of seminary, each was asked to bring a message on hell.

The first candidate preached passionately, trying to dissuade anyone who was listening to shun a life destined for eternal darkness. The second young man came the following week and also spoke of the horror awaiting those who rejected Jesus.

Later that day, the second young man received a call from the chairman of the committee offering him the pastorate.

The young man felt compelled to ask, "Why did you choose me?"

The chairman answered, "When the first young man spoke, he delivered a timely message about the horror of hell and why we should seek heaven instead. But when he talked about those condemned to hell, he sounded as if he was glad that they were getting their just reward. You also brought us a timely message expounding on heaven's attributes and hell's emptiness, focusing on the horror of eternity without God. When you spoke about those who are going to hell, it was evident that it broke your heart. Young man, we share your compassion for those who are perishing and want you to help us evangelize the people in our community so that none of them ends up in hell because we failed to reach out to them."

✝

It should break our hearts to know that people are perishing, separated from God for eternity. The moment they wake up in hell, they are faced with the knowledge that time and time again they rejected God's offer of salvation. That revelation will never end.

I question whether many of us give this much thought. If we do, we certainly don't allow it to grieve us too deeply; if the truth of this horror were ever to reach our hearts, we would be compelled to take action.

Like the disciples, we are commissioned to share Jesus with a lost and dying world.

Prayer

"Make this truth real in my heart, Lord. Cause me to have
a heart for those who are perishing. Help me share Your
plan of salvation with abandon. In Jesus' Name, amen."

It's a Short Trip Back*

December 16

Choose for yourselves this day whom you will serve.

Joshua 24:15

Jim and his family were privileged to spend a month on the island of St. Croix. Part of the U.S. Virgin Islands, St. Croix has retained a few British customs, one of which is driving on the left side of the road.

As they piled into their rental car, Jim, having driven his entire life in the United States, enlisted the help of his wife and two sons to keep him from driving on the "wrong" side of the road.

At the end of the first week, Jim noticed he wasn't giving as much thought to pulling into the left lane when leaving their villa. By the end of the second week, Jim was able to navigate without concentrating too much on not making mistakes.

By the end of their thirty days on the island, Jim found he could drive without thinking at all about overcoming old habits. So much so that he wondered whether he would have to undergo a similar period of adjustment once back in the States.

To his surprise, it was as if he had never learned to drive left of center. It amazed him that on his very first day home he didn't have to think about it at all. Driving on the right was as natural as taking his next breath, a seamless transition with no conscious thought required.

✝

It can be difficult changing the way we've always done things. This is also true in our walk with God. But once we've begun that walk, He calls us closer, inviting us to go deeper than we have previously ventured to risk. And each new step can feel awkward and uncomfortable.

It's not easy crucifying old habits. And many times, for various reasons, we give in only to find there was no transition at all; we simply reverted to sinful ways.

Choice is precious to God. He calls it free will. His desire is that in every choice we face, especially when discomfort threatens our walk, we would willingly lay down our will and choose His.

Prayer

"Father, I willingly give You each choice I'm faced with today. Help me overcome the desire to revert to my sinful nature as I meet each challenge. In Jesus' Name, amen."

* See Acknowledgements

It Takes More Grace

December 17

He leads me beside quiet waters.

Psalm 23:2

Jimmy was two body lengths above Karen as they ascended Martin's Peak, a virtually unknown outcropping of rock in Colorado. It was challenging enough to bring them back time and again. They loved the outdoors, and rock climbing had become an obsession for the young married couple.

They had climbed several routes and had successfully summited on three of their five attempts. Two of the ascensions proved dead ends.

Climbing this late in the season presented different risks. Ice formed on many of the handholds they normally used, causing them to be extra vigilant in choosing their route. This time they decided to take a route that added a measure of safety because it was on the south-facing wall.

Part way up, Karen glanced up to see Jimmy stationary, casting about for his next foothold. He seemed unsure of which direction to proceed so the next handhold would present itself.

Karen, seeing his plight, looked past him to an area that must have been a blind spot for Jimmy because of the steepness of the rock. "There's a handhold four meters above you to the right. The foothold you're looking at to your right will put you just under it," she offered.

"You sure?" he asked.

"I have to follow where you lead. What do you think?" Jimmy smiled and proceeded to the right, finding the handhold right where Karen said it would be.

✝

It takes more grace to step blindly in faith than it does to tell someone else to take that step while you observe. When we experience blind spots on the path with God, we have a tendency to look for an optional route. It's not easy stepping out in faith. But God would never bring us to harm.

The problem with believing this is that the faith required to do so comes only from experiencing His faithfulness. By trial and error, we find God at every turn.

In God's grace, we discover that a deeper relationship is possible. And if we listen, He will tell us where to step next.

Prayer

"I want to learn to trust You completely, Lord. Magnify
Your grace in me; give me courage to step into the
unknown and unseen as long as You are leading. Amen."

Only Seven Shopping Days Left!

December 18

The holy one born to you will be called the Son of God.

Luke 1:35

Jodie and Mattie were at the mall to find a present for their mother. Among some trinkets, Mattie noticed a small nativity. It was perfect! At the checkout counter, the cashier asked, "Did you find everything you were looking for? There's only seven shopping days left, you know!" Her bubbly attitude made the girls smile. Jodie looked at the young cashier and said, "Did you know that seven is God's perfect number?"

The girl looked uneasy. "I don't know much about that," she said. "I never spent much time in church." Shifting her focus back to the nativity, she scanned it and then curiously asked, "Why do Christians make such a big deal over a simple holiday?"

Recognizing the girl's question was sincere, Mattie said, "Because without that day, we would all be destined to spend eternity in hell."

Jodie asked, "Has anybody ever talked to you about Jesus and the meaning of Christmas?"

"My daddy didn't allow talk about Jesus in our house." She appeared embarrassed. "He said that Christianity was just a fairy tale, conjured up by weaklings who can't deal with life on its own terms."

Seeing they were holding up the line but not wanting to pass up an opportunity, Mattie asked the girl for her e-mail address. After trading contact info, the sisters left, promising to stay in touch and share the reason they celebrate Christmas.

†

Divine appointments like this are not uncommon. God will give us ample opportunities to witness His love if we look for them. Many Christians have the misguided notion that everyone they encounter has surely heard of Jesus. That's just not true. For with each generation, much of society slips a little further from God.

Part of our salvation experience is learning to share Jesus with those who have never met Him. Not knowing who they are, we must constantly be on the lookout.

Jesus came to set us free from sin and death. He has asked for our help in telling others the good news of the gospel.

Prayer

"Lord, give me a gentle boldness to tell others about
what Christmas means to me. Make me aware of each
opportunity You bring my way. In Jesus' Name, amen."

There Is Always Jesus!

December 19

The Counselor, the Holy Spirit, whom the Father will send in my name ... will remind *you* of everything I have said to you.

John 14:26

As Doris sat in on the Bible study of her daughter's home group, she frequently interrupted. "When are my children coming to get me?" Her daughter, Laura, would simply take her hand and say, "Mom, I'm right here. I'm your daughter, Laura." This had become commonplace due to Doris's battle with Alzheimer's. But on this night, an important lesson was taught by the one afflicted by this disease.

Part way through the study, Doris opened the Bible in her lap, turned to a specific text, and in a quiet, unassuming voice, asked, "May I read from God's Word? I believe it is relevant to your discussion."

Echoed by everyone else, the leader said, "By all means, Doris, please share what God has shown you."

In a strong voice, Doris read and then went on to explain the verse. "Our Jesus hides Himself in our heart at our conception. And when all other things fail or are lost to our mind, He surfaces, reigning supreme. There is always Jesus!"

Tears mingled with amens filled the room as a picture of Doris being cradled in the arms of her Savior emerged. She may not remember her name or her family, but she would never forget her Jesus!

†

Heart-wrenching to observe, Alzheimer's patients lose their own identity and the memory of those whom they have nurtured and loved. Such a cruel disease. And yet, God has not abandoned them.

To date, no one is able to sufficiently explain how or why memory loss becomes more than wondering where we left our car keys. This, for the most part, turns into role reversal; the parent, who for so long nurtured the child, now needs care. Babysitting takes on new meaning as they revert to a childlike existence. Yet, if we listen through the confusion, God assures us that all is not lost!

In one Spirit-filled moment, God shows us that when all else seems lost, there is always Jesus!

Prayer

"Lord of life, though we may not understand Your ways
and though we tire from the care giving, assure us today
that when all else is lost, there is always Jesus! Amen."

Going on with Jesus

December 20

You do not want to leave too, do you?

John 6:67

It was like watching an old black and white movie, and Kent was playing the role of a superhero, alone and against overwhelming odds. Standing before the crowd, he asked, "Will you stand against this evil that devours our children?" They shrunk from answering such a direct question. They wanted to save their children, but didn't want to be singled out by the conglomerate that wielded a form of power that seemed so unopposable. They wanted plausible deniability.

"Listen," Kent urged. "Our children hang in the balance! If we refuse to take action, *they* will pay the price. We cannot stand on the sidelines and expect nothing to happen!" He pleaded. But they would not be moved. They had suffered embarrassment and ridicule the last time they had stood against this foe. They would not do it again, regardless of the cost. Besides, they really didn't believe in an enemy so evil that it would sacrifice children for profit. Things would be okay as long as they didn't rock the boat.

"Friends," Kent appealed, "I know you're scared. But we must fight this battle!" Getting no response, he asked, "Are you really willing to sacrifice your children because of your fear?" The crowd dispersed as people turned and walked away.

✝

What a hard question! But necessary! Are we really willing to allow someone else to battle for our children's lives, their very souls, and not become personally involved because of fear?

We were born into a world at war. Satan is actively seeking recruits. Choosing not to fight doesn't stop his activities. And he won't stop recruiting our children just because we don't believe in inherent evil.

Listen as Jesus addresses the twelve. "You don't want to leave too, do you?" he asks. And Peter answers for them all. "Lord, to whom shall we go? *You* have the words of eternal life."

Our only chance is to not turn back. We must settle this matter in our hearts and go on with Jesus.

Prayer

"Lord, I confess there is fear in my heart. I hate
humiliation and pain, yet to not fight would be cowardly.
Show me how to follow You in confidence and walk
in Your strength each day. In Jesus' Name, amen."

Retirement Fund

December 21

Your heavenly Father knoweth that ye have need of all these things.
But seek ye first the kingdom of God, and his righteousness.

Matthew 6:32, 33 (KJV)

Sheldon had taken a job at his local Walmart. What made him different from other employees was that Sheldon was seventy-two.

A little over a year before, Lois, his wife, had become ill. Their insurance and savings had been depleted, and they were faced with mounting medical bills. Their providers didn't care that Medicare only paid usual and customary charges; they expected complete payment. So with no other options available, Sheldon was forced out of retirement and back into the workforce. God had led him to apply for this position, and his employer had seen the advantages of hiring someone with Sheldon's experience and disposition.

He never missed a day of work, ascribing to the theory that God had given him this assignment, and he intended to carry it out to the best of his ability. Day after day, Sheldon greeted shoppers with a smile and words of encouragement. He became so popular and well liked that people brought cards of thanks for his bright attitude and goodwill for Lois.

For six years, Sheldon worked and brightened lives, two full years after the medical bills were paid. He had always found fulfillment working for the Lord, and this assignment had provided so many lasting friendships and memories that he'd had a difficult time entering retirement once again.

✝

Sheldon's situation isn't all that uncommon. Many grandparents are raising their grandchildren while their children make a living. Many seniors work until they die, relishing their usefulness.

Retirement is a scheme Satan uses, keeping us busy building a nest egg large enough to *retire comfortably.* In the work, we can lose sight of God's will.

Scripture does not include the word or notion of retirement. Conversely, Jesus said not to worry about how we will be clothed or fed during our lifetime, our *entire* lifetime.

We are to seek the kingdom and God's righteousness; and in the seeking, we will learn to trust in His retirement fund.

Prayer

"Give me faith to live by and the knowledge of how
I am to serve You until I die, Lord. Then help me go
about doing the work You give me to do. Amen."

Ever Present

December 22

God is our refuge and strength, an ever-present help in trouble.

Psalm 46:1

Janet was frantic! She'd turned her back for only a moment, and when she turned around, Josh was nowhere in sight. "Josh!" she screamed again and again with no response. *Oh, dear God! What do I do?* her mind screamed. "Josh! Where are you? Joshua?" She ran in an ever-widening circle, hoping her screams would carry to wherever he was. Composing herself, Janet pulled out her cell phone and dialed 911.

"Deltona 911 operator. What is your emergency?" came the voice on the other end of the line.

Janet related events as calmly as she could. "My name is Janet Grady. I'm at Riverside Park on the west side of town. My son, Joshua, is missing. I turned around to get something out of my purse, and when I turned back, he was gone!"

"Janet," the woman said calmly, "how old is Josh and what is he wearing?"

Of course, she thought. "He's three and is wearing a gray tee shirt that says 'Daddy's Boy' on the front with blue jeans and white tennis shoes."

"All right, Janet," the woman said confidently. "Stay on the line with me. I have officers en route. They should be there momentarily."

"I hear sirens!" Janet said as their growing intensity confirmed the operator's statement.

In less than five minutes, officers found young Joshua. He'd wandered over the hill behind where they were picnicking and had found a shallow creek. He was fine other than being soaked from head to toe.

✝

Today's story parallels our spiritual journey. Many times, whether by impulse or ambition, we set off on our own and turn our backs on God, thinking His back then is turned on us. We take detours we were never intended to take, doing ourselves harm spiritually, emotionally, and sometimes physically.

We travel along until one day we discover we are miserable. Turning around, we look for God, expecting Him to be miles away. But unlike the scene in the park, God is ever present. He is always right behind us, waiting to reach down, pick us up, and dust us off. He never turns His back on us, ever!

Prayer

"Thank You for always being where I'm at, Lord. Help
me walk with instead of away from You. Amen."

Therefore...

December 23

Therefore we will not fear

Psalm 46:2

Reed was in a fix. That the fix was due to his own mistake did nothing to lessen his desire to be free of the mess he now found himself in. As a matter of fact, he had to fight the urge to blame the individual who had presented this grant opportunity that had gone awry.

But, being the one in charge, Reed realized that wasn't an option; he would assume responsibility and shoulder the blame instead of shifting it in order to exonerate himself. The company would probably lose the grant because of his oversight, but that couldn't be helped now.

He said a quick prayer and dialed his boss's extension.

His boss patiently listened as Reed explained his mistake; then he said, "It's okay, Reed. Just call the foundation and explain the oversight. We have a history with them. They have always dealt fairly with us, and I have no reason to believe they won't return the forms and allow you to make the necessary corrections."

It was then that Reed remembered this morning's devotional Scripture reference: "God is our refuge and strength, an ever-present help in trouble. Therefore we will not fear." *Even though it appears everything is falling apart,* he finished silently. God's promise was coming true even now! Peace flooded his soul as he said a silent prayer of thanks.

He was so excited he almost missed his boss add, "If they give you any grief, let me know. I'll call and speak with them."

✝

How often do we find ourselves panicking because we forget that we have the power of Almighty God at our disposal? He is anxious to add His strength to our problems. He genuinely wants us to walk in close relation with Him, listening for His guiding voice, knowing we can ask Him anything.

Not every problem will see quick resolution; but we can have peace, knowing that even in the midst of our struggles, we can rest in the understanding that He will cause us to be able to stand up under its weight.

Though the earth give way, *Almighty God* is our refuge, *therefore* we need not fear!

Prayer

"You are the Creator and Sustainer of all
things and my Almighty GOD; therefore, I
will not fear! In Jesus' Name, amen."

Beyond All Reason

December 24

For unto us a child is born, unto us a son is given.

Isaiah 9:6 (KJV)

It was Christmas Eve. Paul found himself staring at last year's gift from their son. He'd been unsettled about the wide-screen TV until Manny had his say. It went way beyond what they normally spent on each other. And even though Manny had a good job, Paul had been concerned. Being on the receiving end of such extravagance was uncomfortable.

Smiling, he remembered their conversation. He hadn't wanted to offend Manny by making him return it for a lesser item. On the other hand, he hadn't wanted him thinking he loved him for buying such a costly gift.

"Look, Dad," Manny had said. "I know we're not supposed to spend this much, and I know Christmas is not about presents. But it is about gifts, and your old TV is falling apart! I just wanted to be able to see what I'm watching whenever I'm here!" The mischief in his words bore witness to the fact he knew he wouldn't be denied.

Paul loved his children beyond words. And he knew they understood he would do anything for them. That's what made the gift so difficult to accept; parents were supposed to do for their children, not the other way around.

✝

At a time when the world was in its greatest need, God sent us His Son, a gift born out of a love so deep that we cannot fathom it. After all, how many of us would send our son into a dark world such as ours, knowing he would be persecuted, tortured, and killed by the very people we sent him to? All in the hopes they would understand that if they would follow him, he would lead them out of the darkness.

Jesus, in order that we might know the Father's heart, joined us on a cold morning in the form of a child. Being on the receiving end of such extravagance can be uncomfortable. But by laying our pride at the manger, we will discover a love beyond all reason.

Prayer

"Thank You, Father, for the costly gift of Your Son. Thank You, Jesus, for leaving heaven's safety to show us such love. May we never forget how precious a gift You are. Amen."

Before We Called

December 25

Before they call, I will answer.

Isaiah 65:24

"Sir," the voice on the other end of the phone said, "we need some of your son's blood. It is the rarest of all types; with it, we can save the lives of millions of people."

Was this some kind of sick joke? How could they possibly know that?

His son had been born just this morning and hadn't yet been named. Three months premature, weighing less than three pounds, his survival was still in question.

How could someone possibly know what his blood type is? Or for that matter, how could they know it had curative properties? And even if they did know, how could they ask such a question?!

"Sir, we need your decision now. If we don't give the children a serum from the antibodies your son's blood has, many of them will die. We need your son's blood."

This can't be happening! His mind was numb. His wife had died in childbirth, and now they were asking him to put his infant son's life in jeopardy by allowing them to remove much of the blood from his little body.

"Sir?" He dropped the receiver and returned to the hospital nursery. He looked at his tiny son in the basinet and wondered, *What am I supposed to do?*

✝

When God faced this situation, He never hesitated.

And before we called, God sent a baby, the symbol of the purest thing on earth. In an infant, there is no fault. Without a sacrifice pure enough to meet the demand of justice, we would be damned for eternity.

God sent a man who has the wisdom and strength to lead us through the murkiest waters and lift us from the greatest depths of despondency. God is a force Who will fight our battles with a love so fierce that He left His throne to live in our world.

God sent a Savior, the only One eligible to stand in our place, to take every punishment, every lash, every torment and be defiled because He could not stand that we would spend eternity without Him!

Before we called, God sent the answer.

Prayer

"Father of love, thank You for the life-giving blood
of Jesus! May we never fail to understand, as much as
humanly possible, what that sacrifice cost You. Amen."

Equipped with Pain

December 26

I consider that our present sufferings are not worth comparing with
the glory that will be revealed in us.

Romans 8:18

Burt wasn't as limber as he once was; his body took longer to recuperate. Cold
winter mornings made it even harder to rid himself of the stiffness. Today he
was hurting a bit more than usual because he had helped his son cut and split a
load of firewood two days before; the second day always seems the worst.

As he allowed the shower to massage his aching body, Burt complained
to God about additional physical suffering for what he considered a labor of
love. "I can't believe You'd allow me to experience added pain in this situation,
Lord. I mean, I was spending quality time with my son! Why should it hurt
so much?"

Strange conversation? Not really, Burt talked with God this way all the
time. When God spoke, which was frequently in Burt's case, it was always to
make a point.

This morning, God was quick to remind Burt that in his earlier years as a
student athlete he'd awakened on most Sunday mornings stiff and sore without
complaint. It was all part of playing sports. "So why, Burt, at fifty-five, do you
feel like I've betrayed you?" God asked.

"So You think I'm feeling sorry for myself?" Burt countered.

Burt wasn't positive, but he thought he heard God say, "Sorry, Burt. But
they chose to eat the fruit."

✝

Pain—physical, emotional, and spiritual—is the result of one act of disobedience. And each act of disobedience on our part will exacerbate the effect. It
may not seem fair because we didn't ask for it. But until this life is over, that's
the way it is.

Paul said that we have Jesus' promise that what we endure today is not to
be compared to what we are going to inherit. Jesus believed in us so profoundly
that he set aside his crown and endured a pain-filled life of His own. Though
this life is equipped with pain, hold on and look to your future glory!

Prayer

"Lord, when I'm out of strength, revive me. When I
feel like giving in, come to my rescue. Help me look
to eternity as I walk through today's pain. Amen."

Think Like Ants

December 27

Go to the ant, you sluggard, consider its ways and be wise!

Proverbs 6:6

Carrie was drawn to the way Solomon dealt with laziness by encouraging people to watch ants at work—not just their laboring, but how they orchestrated events by breaking them into smaller tasks.

Since New Mexico winters didn't drive all its insects into hibernation, Carrie decided to conduct her own experiment. Knowing the location of several anthills, Carrie took a sugar doughnut, lawn chair, and her camera equipment and set out for the woods.

Arriving at her destination, Carrie set the doughnut several feet from one particular anthill and then withdrew several more feet and set up her camera and tripod. Less than two minutes elapsed before the ants discovered the doughnut. *Amazing!* she thought, mesmerized by the fact that they were drawn to it so quickly. *There must be thousands of them!*

One by one, the ants climbed onto the doughnut, broke off a piece larger than their own body, and transported it back to the colony within the hill. In the span of two hours, the doughnut was gone! Not a single morsel of the sugary treat was left.

Returning home, Carrie took the digitally time-stamped pictures and arranged a PowerPoint slideshow for her laptop. She now had the perfect object lesson for next week's study!

✝

Sometimes we are overwhelmed by the big picture. We lack the ability to see it in doable pieces. And many times, because of its overwhelming nature, we procrastinate and put off doing the work at all.

We don't readily equate this action as being lazy; instead, we rationalize it as being over our head or out of our league and fail to consider ways in which we might approach it successfully. What a trap our fearful unwillingness to make mistakes becomes!

It is in the delay that doubt speaks to our heart. If by breaking the project down into smaller parts we could see the possibilities, we might not be so quick to delay.

Solomon says, "Think like ants!" Break events into smaller, easier-to-complete tasks. Then don't delay; get busy!

Prayer

"Sometimes I'm overwhelmed by the things that vie for my time, Lord. Help me learn to be like the ant, humbly enlisting help and eating the doughnut a piece at a time. Amen."

Ditches

December 28

Do not offer the parts of your body to sin ... rather offer yourselves to God.

Romans 6:13

The water poured into the ditch as fast as Darnell dug. He was trying to excavate around a broken water main so his crew could fix it, but it wasn't going very well. He ordered one of his men to dig a diversion ditch to reroute the water away from the broken pipe. He advised the man to begin the ditch at least fifty feet away and work his way back to the break. "It needs to be below the level of the main pipeline or it won't do us any good," Darnell added.

The man chose a low-lying area in an abandoned lot. It would hold a large volume of water if it was routed in that direction. Starting at the abandoned lot, he began the ditch. Twenty minutes later, the water broke through into the diversion ditch as the final bit of ground gave way. The water level around the broken pipe receded, and Darnell was able to excavate the area so his men could complete repairs.

Finished, they filled in the ditches using power tampers to pack the dirt and then laid new asphalt. Within hours, water was restored to residents' homes and traffic flowed normally through the neighborhood.

✝

Undeterred sin becomes like a broken water main in our lives. And many times, in true remorse, we attempt to dig ourselves out, yet fail, only to sink deeper into the sin-laden soil. We get so bogged down that we believe there's no way out. And for good reason: self-extrication never works. Eventually, sin floods our soul and drowns our spirit.

Fact: the more we dig, the deeper the ditch.

Truth: the only way out of our sin is to stop digging in the wrong ditch!

Answer: we must begin to dig a deeper ditch in God's direction. He can and wants to cover the sin in our lives, filling in the old ditch if we allow Him.

Only by constantly offering ourselves to God—digging toward Him instead of our sinful desires—can we rise from our ditches.

Prayer

"Lord, fill in the sinful areas of my heart. Cover them
with Your forgiveness and keep me from trying to
dig them up again. In Jesus' Name, amen."

Watchman

December 29

This is what the LORD says to me: "Go, post a watchman and have him report what he sees."

Isaiah 21:6

As he began the first fold in the flag, the SWAT commander reflected on his friend's life. Words like *duty* and *honor* immediately came to mind—never taken lightly, rarely spoken of, silently understood. The man being laid to rest was a husband, father, brother, son, and friend. He was a fifteen-year veteran who had laid down his life during the performance of his duties; a veteran whose thoughts were unlike the average civilian's. Upon entering any structure, business, or residence, he noted every door and surveillance camera. He formulated plans for every scenario. He determined how he would respond if someone entered with criminal intent, because he was *always* thinking about the safety of others.

Drawn from his thoughts by the twenty-one-gun salute, the commander was intensely aware that he would rather have been anywhere but here. But, doing what he would always do under difficult circumstances, he put aside his emotion, and performed his duties. He had come here today to honor and pay tribute to a fallen comrade; nothing would deter him. Then he'd get back on the wall; entrusted with the freedom of others.

✝

Jesus said, "Greater love has no one than this, that he lay down his life for his friends." His revelation to his disciples was about *duty* and *honor* in love. It was about loving others in a way that places their welfare ahead of our own, suffering temporarily, so that they might be safe.

Jesus was the *perfect* example. He suffered death on a cross so that we might be *saved*. The battleground was Gethsemane. Bent by anguish beyond our comprehension, wishing to be anywhere but there at that moment, He submitted to the Father's will. In that garden, Jesus showed us how to choose to defend the innocent over personal comfort. He rose up from praying and hung on the cross of Calvary—a wall no other could ever stand upon; offering a freedom no one else can provide.

Prayer

"Jesus, my Savior, thank You for choosing to die so that I might live. I ask Your protection over those who do as you did, to stand on the wall so that others might live. Amen."

Running in Rebellion

December 30

But Jonah ran away from the LORD.

Jonah 1:3

Pam quietly raised her bedroom window and climbed out on the roof. She laid the note she'd written on the windowsill and closed the window as quietly as possible. With as little noise as possible, she crept to the trellis and climbed to the ground. Pausing to take stock of her surroundings, Pam took one last look toward her parents' bedroom window and then slipped into the woods.

For two hours she followed the road to town, hiding in the bushes whenever she heard vehicles approaching. Reaching the rendezvous point, Pam took the flashlight from her backpack and, pointing it in a southerly direction, flashed it on and off three times in rapid succession. Moments later, her signal was returned. As Pam headed toward Gregory, she was beginning to have doubts about this. Hearing his approaching footsteps, Pam quelled the urge to turn around and run home. Instead, she cranked up her resolve and quietly called out, "Is that you, Greg?"

"It's me. You ready?" he asked.

"I guess," she said sullenly. "Do you really think this is the only way?"

He tried to put her doubt to rest. "Once they get your note, they'll realize they've been too hard on you. Then they'll be ready to listen," he said. "Just wait, you'll see."

"I hope you're right," she said but couldn't shake the sensation that what she was doing was wrong.

✝

Running from our problems doesn't bring resolution; it only delays the inevitable—facing our issues. We must meet our problems head on because no matter where we go, until they're dealt with, they remain.

Running away is a form of rebellion, born out of disappointment, anger, or resentment. In Jonah's case, it was all three. Jonah thought he knew what was best for Nineveh and made no effort to hide his displeasure with God.

God allowed Jonah the freedom to rebel. He even allowed Jonah to run away. But what He didn't do was break off His pursuit of Jonah. In the end, Jonah repented of his rebellion and delivered God's rebuke to Nineveh, which brought about their repentance and salvation—a lesson for us all.

Prayer

"Lord, keep my heart from rebellion. Draw me to Your
side and keep me there. In Jesus' Name, amen."

New Each Day

December 31

For his compassions never fail. They are new every morning.

Lamentations 3:22, 23

"So what's your New Year's resolution?" Regan asked.

"I'm not making one," Willie answered. "The last two resolutions I made, I had no intention of keeping. Why should I set goals I don't plan to keep?"

"Nothing ventured, nothing gained," Regan said in challenge.

"Why's it so important that I decide to do something positive for myself on New Year's Eve?" Willie countered. "I mean, I can make constructive changes to my life any day of the year. So why does it have to be right now, today?" he said with emphasis.

"Well..." Regan paused, pondering the truth in Willie's comment. It dawned on her that she might be doing something out of a misguided purpose. Whether he knew it or had just stumbled upon it by accident, there was validity in what Willie said. She finally answered, "Well, I guess I make a commitment each New Year's Eve because it's what I've always done." Struck by a deeper thought, she pondered aloud, "Does that make it wrong?"

"No, I don't think it's necessarily wrong," Willie responded; pausing a moment, he added, "But I've seen so many people set goals with good intentions, and when they didn't follow through, they wound up discouraged with a sense of defeat. I just think there's more to *why* we make lifestyle changes than *when* we decide to make them."

✝

Willie makes a valid point; *when* is not as important as *why* we do things. I'm not advocating that people stop making New Year's resolutions. If you purposefully commit to your goals, you can certainly attain life-changing experiences. The truth is that if we desire, we can commit to those experiences any day of the year. We need not wait until December 31 to change the way we live.

God wants us to understand that we can bring before Him anything, anytime. As His Word says, His compassions—His ability to forgive and offer us a fresh start—are new each day.

Prayer

"Father of forgiveness and life, help me live more for You
in this next year than I did in the past. And if I fail one
day, lift me up and help me make a new start. Amen."

Appendix

Acceptance/Encouragement/Hope/Inspiration

January 13
February 6, 18, 20, 23, 26, 27
March 2, 21
April 4, 17, 19, 20, 23, 28
May 6, 14, 20, 28
June 1, 7, 16
July 7, 12, 25
August 14
September 11, 15, 29
October 11, 13, 14
November 3, 7, 19, 22, 25, 30
December 12, 23, 24

Accountability/Christlikeness

January 16
March 3, 19
April 6
May 1
August 26
September 17, 21, 22, 23, 26
October 20, 23
November 9, 25, 30
December 16, 20, 29

Addiction/Alcohol–Substance Abuse

February 4
May 10
June 19, 26
August 7, 10, 30
September 7, 22
November 4, 22
December 8

Anger/Bitterness/Rebellion/Revenge

April 18
May 27
September 25
October 18
November 2
December 8, 10, 30

Compassion/Forgiveness/Grace/Mercy

January 6, 15, 16, 17
April 1, 7
May 8, 24, 25
July 22, 26
August 6
September 2, 14, 26
November 1, 22
December 9, 16, 29, 31

Death/Grief/Loss

January 2
March 14, 21
April 28
July 29
August 14
September 11
October 8
November 4
December 29

Depression/Disappointment/ Doubt/Fear

January 24
February 2, 19
May 21
June 7
July 5
August 19, 31
October 8, 10, 15, 25
November 15, 16, 18, 22
December 23, 29

Disobedience/Consequences

January 10, 18
February 28
March 25
April 6
May 10, 12, 15, 27
June 12, 28
August 4, 23

October 29
December 8, 22, 28, 30

Faith/Trust/Perseverance

January 3, 4, 14, 28
February 7, 17
March 9, 27, 29
April 1, 14, 19, 21
May 26
June 5, 10, 11, 15, 17, 22, 30
July 2, 10, 11, 27, 29
August 17, 20, 24
September 2, 9, 11, 16, 23
October 6, 10, 15, 18, 19, 22
November 6, 16
December 11, 12, 16, 17, 21, 23, 26, 28, 31

Free Will

January 7, 16, 21
March 5
May 30
August 13, 20, 28
September 11
November 2, 13
December 21

God's Will & Promises

January 16, 29
February 25, 29
April 3
May 3
August 20, 28
November 13, 23
December 3, 20, 21, 23, 25, 26, 29

January 26, 27
April 23, 24, 27
July 18, 30
August 22
October 21
November 12

Healing/Miracles (Spiritual & Physical)

January 1, 5
February 10
March 6, 12, 16, 21
April 11
June 1, 8, 17, 19
July 8
September 29
October 14
December 13, 25

Heartache/Shame/Suffering/Wounded Spirit

January 9, 19, 25
February 5
March 5, 14, 24
April 1
May 27
July 4, 12, 21
August 3, 14
September 11, 22
October 8, 25
November 4, 22
December 10, 26

Honesty/Humility/Integrity

February 16
March 7, 8
May 13
June 26
July 14, 22
August 23

September 8, 22, 24
October 1, 6, 21
November 3, 6, 21, 29

Love/Relationships/Marriage/Nurture

January 30
February 14
March 17, 18, 19
April 10, 24
May 2, 18, 20, 27
June 2, 5, 9, 23
July 14, 23, 25
September 1, 4, 6, 26, 29
October 3, 4, 5, 13
November 19, 28
December 3, 4, 20, 25

Lying/Deceit/Hypocrisy/Values/Ethics

January 16, 20
February 13
March 18
April 15, 25
May 8, 12
June 21, 26
July 14, 17, 22, 27, 31
August 13, 19, 23
September 3, 22, 25
October 1, 4, 21
November 3, 8, 20, 21
December 4

Obedience/Listening/Instruction

January 12
February 1, 15, 22
March 1, 28
April 14, 30
May 7, 11, 15, 22, 23
June 13, 16
July 1, 3, 21, 26, 27

August 5, 28, 29
September 14, 23, 27
October 5, 9, 11, 18
November 11, 13, 15, 23
December 3, 4, 6, 7, 16, 20, 22, 25, 31

Prayer/Praise/Thankfulness/Worship

May 23
June 18, 25, 29
July 2, 3, 28
August 16, 21
September 1, 13
October 8
November 7, 25, 27

Pride/Selfishness/Self-Control

January 8, 16
March 25
April 15
May 15
June 19, 21
July 6, 9, 13
August 8, 15
September 25, 28
October 1, 16, 27
November 28, 29
December 14, 22

Profanity/Gossip

January 16
March 10
June 28
October 26
November 20

Righteousness

January 16
June 4
July 31
September 27
October 3
December 16, 28

Sacrifice/Serving

January 23
February 8, 24
April 9, 14, 16, 23, 29
May 19, 29
June 24
July 19, 20
August 12, 22, 31
September 6, 26, 27
October 6, 30
November 11, 12, 23, 30
December 25, 29

Salvation/Sanctification/Reconciliation/Repentance

February 9, 11, 21
March 11, 29
April 5, 13, 20, 22, 26
May 4, 9, 14, 18, 28
June 3, 14, 19, 26
July 4, 5, 24, 29
August 1, 19, 27
September 7, 12, 15, 17, 18, 26
October 2, 3, 7
November 14, 24, 28
December 5, 6, 19, 24, 25, 29

Sexual Purity/Sexual Immorality

June 26
September 22
October 4, 17, 24
November 29

Spiritual Education & Growth

March 4, 29
May 16, 28, 30, 31
June 20, 27
July 12, 28
August 2, 9, 16, 29
September 1, 23, 30
October 9, 12, 29, 31
November 19, 23
December 2, 5, 6, 11, 12, 16, 23, 27, 31

Spiritual Warfare

March 15
April 12
June 22, 26
July 31
August 13, 21
September 19
November 29

Temptation/Testing/Worry

February 3
March 13
April 15
May 30
June 26
July 14
August 10
September 18
October 4
November 9
December 8, 9, 16, 28

Truth/Understanding

January 16, 31
March 18, 22
April 8, 12
May 29, 31
July 21, 31
August 11, 25
September 10, 11
October 3, 20, 28, 31
November 21, 24, 26
December 1, 2, 6, 14, 19, 20, 27, 28, 31

Wisdom

March 1, 19, 20
May 17, 31
July 16, 25
September 5, 10, 23
October 12, 22
November 17
December 1, 2, 27, 28

Witness/Testimony

March 23, 26
April 11, 14, 15
May 5
June 24
July 10, 15, 24
August 12, 18, 21
September 12, 20, 24, 27
October 2, 20
November 5, 7, 9, 10, 14, 18, 23, 24, 30
December 4, 13, 15, 18, 19

listen|imagine|view|experience

AUDIO BOOK DOWNLOAD INCLUDED WITH THIS BOOK!

In your hands you hold a complete digital entertainment package. Besides purchasing the paper version of this book, this book includes a free download of the audio version of this book. Simply use the code listed below when visiting our website. Once downloaded to your computer, you can listen to the book through your computer's speakers, burn it to an audio CD or save the file to your portable music device (such as Apple's popular iPod) and listen on the go!

How to get your free audio book digital download:

1. Visit www.tatepublishing.com and click on the e|LIVE logo on the home page.
2. Enter the following coupon code:
   2477-d585-c970-48a0-57e5-113b-e1f2-d4a3
3. Download the audio book from your e|LIVE digital locker and begin enjoying your new digital entertainment package today!